S0-BXD-838

N. Scott Momaday

American Indian Literature
and Critical Studies Series

N. Scott Momaday

Remembering Ancestors, Earth, and Traditions

An Annotated Bio-bibliography

By Phyllis S. Morgan

Introduction by Kenneth Lincoln

University of Oklahoma: Norman

FRONTISPIECE: *N. Scott Momaday, Oklahoma City, 2007.*
(Photograph by Yousef Khanfar)

LIBRARY OF CONGRESS CATALOGING-IN-PUBLICATION DATA

Morgan, Phyllis S., 1936–
N. Scott Momaday : remembering ancestors, earth, and traditions : an annotated bio-bibliography / by Phyllis S. Morgan ; introduction by Kenneth Lincoln. — 1st ed.
p. cm. — (American Indian literature and critical studies ; 55)
Includes bibliographical references and index.
ISBN 978-0-8061-4054-4 (hardcover : alk. paper)
1. Momaday, N. Scott, 1934– 2. Momaday, N. Scott, 1934—Bibliography.
3. Authors, American—20th century—Biography. 4. Kiowa Indians in literature.
5. Indians in literature. I. Title.
PS3563.O47Z78 2010
813'.54—dc22

2009030036

First edition

N. Scott Momaday: Remembering Ancestors, Earth, and Traditions: An Annotated Bio-bibliography is Volume 55 in the American Indian Literature and Critical Studies Series.

The paper in this book meets the guidelines for permanence and durability of the Committee on Production Guidelines for Book Longevity of the Council on Library Resources, Inc. ∞

1 2 3 4 5 6 7 8 9 10

Dedicated to

N. Scott Momaday,

the memory of Barbara Glenn Momaday,
November 17, 1942–September 20, 2008,

and

the memory of my parents

Contents

Illustrations

Figures

Map

The Delight Song of Tsoai-talee

I am a feather on the bright sky
I am the blue horse that runs in the plain
I am the fish that rolls, shining, in the water
I am the shadow that follows a child
I am the evening light, the luster of meadows
I am an eagle playing with the wind
I am a cluster of bright beads
I am the farthest star
I am the cold of the dawn
I am the roaring of the rain
I am the glitter on the crust of the snow
I am the long track of the moon in a lake
I am a flame of four colors
I am a deer standing away in the dusk
I am a field of sumac and the pomme blanche
I am an angle of geese in the winter sky
I am the hunger of a young wolf
I am the whole dream of these things
You see, I am alive, I am alive
I stand in good relation to the earth
I stand in good relation to the gods
I stand in good relation to all that is beautiful
I stand in good relation to the daughter of Tsen-tainte
You see, I am alive, I am alive.

N. Scott Momaday, *The Gourd Dancer* ©1976

Preface

It was the voice—a voice so commanding that it demanded my full attention. I could not recall ever hearing one quite like it. It was deep and resonant with perfect enunciation. I was compelled to drop what I was doing and walk close to the television set to get a better look at the person to whom this distinctive voice belonged. The program was the *Today Show*, hosted by anchors Hugh Downs and Barbara Walters, to which I listened every weekday to catch the morning news. That was early May 1969.

The voice, I discovered, belonged to a serious-looking young man who wore dark-rimmed eyeglasses. He was reading from his first novel (and third book), which had in the past few days been announced as the winner of the 1969 Pulitzer Prize for Fiction. His name was N. Scott Momaday. The announcement stated that he was the first American Indian to win a Pulitzer Prize, and his winning novel, *House Made of Dawn*, had been published in 1968 by Harper & Row in New York City. He was thirty-five, a young age to win this coveted prize. I made a mental note to remember his name and the title of his award-winning book.

His voice, referred to on occasion as "the voice that made Momaday famous," would not be forgotten through the ensuing years. I recognized it on the radio, particularly on National Public Radio, and on television in documentaries and series such as *The West*, an eight-part series produced by Ken Burns and Stephen Ives, that premiered on the Public Broadcasting System in 1996. It has always been a special occasion to see him in person and hear him deliver one of the hundreds of speeches and readings—counting classroom lectures the total would be thousands—he has given throughout the United States, in many European countries, and in far-flung places around the globe. As time passed, I realized I was not alone in being deeply and mysteriously awed by Momaday's voice and authoritative presence. He has the gift to transport one to other times and places, to make oral and written literature come alive, and to help others in understanding another worldview.

The young man I saw and heard that May morning in 1969 has become a leading figure of his time, a prominent writer in American and world literature. Today, Momaday is recognized as a novelist and nonfiction writer, and also as a consummate poet, essayist, autobiographer, educator, artist, playwright, editor, and humanist. He has earned an honored place for himself through accomplishments achieved in all these and other important roles. He has written and spoken over a long period of time about protection of the environment, the sacredness of the earth, and the critical need for a land ethic. His deep concern for the earth extends to traditional cultures that are also being threatened. The Buffalo Trust, a nonprofit foundation, was established by him to work with Native peoples in the United States and other parts of the world to preserve their cultural traditions and languages through the involvement of elders and youth.

This book is a tribute to N. Scott Momaday and a celebration of the works from his pen and paintbrush since one of his early poems became his first published writing. The poem, "Earth and I Gave You Turquoise," written while he was an undergraduate at the University of New Mexico, was published in the summer of 1959. When it appeared in print, he made the decision to call himself a professional writer. Since that first printing, a productive and eventful half century has passed. Fifty years as a published author with an impressive body of works is a significant milestone. Today, this poem and many of his other works continue to be read, studied, reprinted, and quoted.

It was ten years after the appearance of his first published work that Momaday would achieve literary success with the winning of the Pulitzer Prize. This was an historic event accompanied by accolades. celebrations, and publicity, and it would shape the course of his life. Momaday and his prize-winning novel have been given credit for sparking an astoundingly creative and productive period in the history of American Indian literature. This literary achievement acted like a catalyst, breaking down barriers and stimulating interest at home and abroad in creative works by Native Americans. In particular, it brought the attention of the American and international literary, academic, and publishing worlds to Native American writers and poets.

This period of literary activity was given the name "Native American Renaissance" by author, professor, and scholar Kenneth Lincoln, who contributed the Introduction to this book. Used by many to the present time, this term was defined by Lincoln in his book *Native American Renaissance*, published by the University of California Press in 1983, as "a written renewal of oral traditions translated into Western literary forms" (8). During the last forty years, an abundance of seminal and noteworthy works have been published by Native

Americans. This creative activity has infused American literature with new lifeblood.

In looking back over Momaday's long productive period, one cannot help but reflect on the journey he has made since he was born in Oklahoma in 1934. In *The Names: A Memoir*, published in 1976, he tells about being given the Kiowa name Tsoai-talee, which translates in English to Rock Tree Boy. Tsoai is the impressive, ancient monolith in northeastern Wyoming that was given the name Devils Tower by Euro-Americans. When he was six months old, his parents took him to Wyoming, where they spent time in the Black Hills and at Tsoai, a sacred place to the Kiowa and other tribes. After their return to Oklahoma, a Kiowa elder and storyteller named Pohd-lohk bestowed the name upon him. Years later, Momaday would write his own name poem, "The Delight Song of Tsoai-talee."

Momaday remarks about Pohd-lohk in *The Names*: "He believed that a man's life proceeds from his name, in the way that a river proceeds from its source" (xi). One may wonder whether Pohd-lohk had a vision of this little boy's future, full of promise and significant achievements. This wise elder must have had very good reasons for giving such an important name to him. He has achieved much, fulfilling the vision of the elder storyteller and the hopes and dreams of his loving parents and relatives. He has also brought understanding, wonder, and delight to millions close to home and around the world. I present this tribute to N. Scott Momaday on their and my behalf.

Phyllis S. Morgan
Albuquerque, New Mexico

Acknowledgments

My gratitude is extended to many who have assisted me in countless ways in carrying out the research that has gone into this bio-bibliography. I am grateful to N. Scott Momaday for his interest and assistance, especially during the early stage of this five-year project. His wife, the late Barbara Glenn Momaday, always expressed words of encouragement until her untimely death in September 2008. Special thanks are also extended to author-scholar-professor Kenneth Lincoln for his Introduction and to cartographer Ronald L. Stauber for the map designed for this book. Many thanks to editor Alessandra Jacobi Tamulevich, editorial assistant Ashley Eddy, managing editor Steven Baker, designer-typesetter Julie Rushing, and others at the University of Oklahoma Press for their assistance during the publishing of this work.

Without the concerted efforts of librarians and archivists, this type of work would be virtually impossible. I greatly appreciate the help of librarians and staffs of the following libraries and archives where I conducted research: The Center for Southwest Research and Zimmerman Library, University of New Mexico; the Main Library of the University of Arizona; the Stanford University Libraries; libraries of the University of California; the Albuquerque-Bernalillo County Library System; and the San Francisco Public Library.

Countless individuals have provided greatly appreciated assistance. I especially acknowledge the following individuals: Lillian Castillo-Speed, H. Thomas Cox; Dr. Donald C. Dickinson, John Drayton, Andrew Elder, Dr. Lawrence Evers, Philip Gaddis, Patricia Gargaro, Mary W. George, Daniel Gibson, Dana Gioia, Ellen Grantham, Helga Hoel, Dr. Ellen McCracken, Dr. Thomas M. Morales, Jocelyn Saidenberg, and Dr. Alan Velie.

Permissions

The author gratefully acknowledges permissions received to reprint copyrighted materials:

From N. Scott Momaday for permission to use his works and other materials under his copyright, including worldwide rights.

From *Ancestral Voice: Conversations with N. Scott Momaday* by Charles L. Woodward, by permission of the University of Nebraska Press. Copyright ©1989 by the University of Nebraska Press.

From *Earth Is My Mother, Sky Is My Father* by Trudy Griffin-Pierce. Copyright ©1992 by the University of New Mexico Press.

From *Master Class: Lessons from Leading Writers* by Nancy Bunge, by permission of the University of Iowa Press. Copyright ©2005 by the University of Iowa Press.

From *Homelands: A Geography of Culture and Place across America*, Richard L. Nostrand and Lawrence E. Estaville, eds. Excerpts from Steven M. Schnell's essay, "The Kiowa Homeland in Oklahoma," pp. 142–43. Copyright ©2002 by The Johns Hopkins University Press.

From *The Strength of Art: Poets and Poetry in the Lives of Yvor Winters and Janet Lewis*. Prepared by Brigitte Hoy Carnochan and with an introduction by N. Scott Momaday. Stanford: Stanford University Libraries, 1984. Courtesy of the Department of Special Collections and University Archives, Stanford University Libraries.

From *The Way to Rainy Mountain*, by N. Scott Momaday. Copyright ©1969 by the University of New Mexico Press.

About This Book

Part I of *N. Scott Momaday: Remembering Ancestors, Earth, and Traditions* contains a biography in the form of a long essay about this gentleman made of words who celebrated his seventy-fifth birthday in 2009, and about subjects of great importance to him. A chronology follows, focusing on his achievements and honors.

Part II, The Works of N. Scott Momaday, comprises as comprehensive a bibliography as possible, containing his broad range of published works. It also includes interviews and conversations with him, a listing of the anthologies containing his writings in this part, and other information of interest to a wide range of scholars and readers.

A significant number of Momaday's works have been reprinted, excerpted, and quoted. Such occurrences have been included in Part II for some of his most acclaimed works. A number of his poems, for instance, have been reprinted from their first publication date to the current time, and his famous passage, "The Remembered Earth," has been reprinted, quoted, and used in a variety of ways by others. Momaday has also repeated this passage and many of his other writings, poetry and prose, in his own works through the years. Readers and critics have noted and commented on this. He has explained that he is not concerned about changing his subject from writing to writing or book to book as much as he is concerned with telling one story and keeping the story going and carrying it farther. He has also remarked that this type of structure establishes continuity, which is very important to him. This is also a common pattern for the traditional storyteller when retelling a story.

Part III, Works about N. Scott Momaday and His Works, contains an extensive bibliography of published works by others, a wealth of essays, reviews, articles, and other publications. Generally not included in the bibliography are books and other writings that only mention Momaday's name in a listing of contemporary writers or that only make a very brief reference to him or one of his works. For example, some books examined for possible inclusion only mention his winning of the Pulitzer Prize without any further comment or discussion. Other types of sources of information have been included, such as Internet resources. At the end of Part III is a listing of unpublished dissertations and theses from universities across the United States and abroad.

The terms "American Indian" and "Native American" have been used interchangeably throughout this book because these two terms, in particular, are used frequently throughout the materials presented in this bio-bibliography, and many writers and others have a particular preference. Whichever term has been used by the authors, editors, and others included in this book, the aim has been to use the specific term or terms they have used in their works.

The following abbreviations are used throughout this work:

cm.	centimeters
comp(s).	compiler(s), compiled by
ed.	editor or edition
eds.	editors
gen.	general
illus.	illustrations
in.	inches
min.	minute(s)
mono.	monophonic
n.	note
no.	number
n.d.	no date
n.p.	no page or no pagination
n.s.	new series
pbk.	paperback
port(s).	portrait(s)
p. or pp.	page(s)
rev.	revised or review
sec.	section
ser.	series
trans.	translator(s), translated by
vol.	volume

Consulting the table of contents and index of this bio-bibliography will be helpful to readers and users of this resource.

Introduction

Kenneth Lincoln

From Forms of the Earth at Abiquiu

For Georgia O'Keeffe

. . . .

I made you the gift of a small, brown stone,
And you described it with the tips of your fingers
And knew at once that it was beautiful—
At once, accordingly you knew,
As you knew the forms of the earth at Abiquiu:
That time involves them and they bear away,
Beautiful, various, remote,
In failing light, and the coming of cold.

N. Scott Momaday

Drawing on traditions going back tens of thousands of years, a singular Kiowa writer, Navarre Scott Momaday, ignited the contemporary Native American Renaissance with the Pulitzer Prize for his novel *House Made of Dawn* (1968), no less than Langston Hughes fired the Harlem Renaissance. In our lifetime, hundreds of Native cultures have been reconfiguring on the fringes of urban density, and Momaday's international recognition is a literary vortex. Some 82 percent of Native Americans live off-reservation, over fifty thousand are enrolled in college today, a thousand-plus writers are in print. Crossing collective disciplines of multifaceted roots, Native American literatures trace back through ceremonial songs, festive dances, origin myths, trickster stories, morality tales, love lyrics, quieting lullabies, vision cries, death chants, and birth songs celebrated among two thousand tribal camps in the Western Hemisphere for some forty thousand years.

They are old men, or men
Who are old in their voices,
And they carry the wheel among the camps,
Saying: Come, come,
Let us tell the old stories,
Let us sing the sacred songs.

"Carriers of the Dream Wheel"

N. Scott Momaday is the literary voice of these communal wellsprings rising through the deep resources of American civilizations. His origins are the living roots of reborn oral literacy now known as the Native American Renaissance.

Scott is a large fellow with a stentorian voice and deeply set, lambent eyes. Since Stanford in the early 1960s, I've known this man as a mentor, model, and friend. "You know, Ken, I am a bear," he once said at a UCLA Indian Studies banquet thirty years ago. The man bears a sense of gravitas balanced with great good humor. He seems an old ursine soul transposed into an academic don who does not take his ancestry or learnings lightly. We would do well to measure the depth, vision, strength, and breadth of his accomplishments—and to consider why the works of this Native original are so pivotal to ancestral American culture and letters.

It is useful to begin at the beginning with Momaday's first published poem, "Earth and I Gave You Turquoise," written in 1958 on college break at a second-grader's desk in his mother's Jemez Day School classroom. This gifted Kiowa began, and continues to be, primarily a poet—a man made of singing words, to redact Wallace Stevens—or in the visionary language of Nicholas Black Elk upon seeing the "make-live" Ghost Dance *wanékia*, an "all-colors" grandfather who "spoke like singing" as everything everywhere danced to the song. What makes his 7/5 tonal-syllabic song-poem Native, beyond American, is the lyric depth and narrative breadth of speech fully human, familial, and therefore tribal, or Native American.

Earth and I gave you turquoise
    when you walked singing
We lived laughing in my house
    and told old stories
You grew ill when the owl cried
We will meet on Black Mountain

"Earth and I," the speaker begins, "gave you turquoise." This invocation turns on participant creativity, not a little solo god manqué making things up, as Coleridge posited. The earth is alive, sentient, active, partnering; stones and soil exist before, with, and after human—the earthen *humus* of life to which all life returns. Blue-green turquoise composites the earth's gift to humans, the cerulean depth of the liquid sky come to earth as healing stone, especially to restore eyesight. Pueblo infants wear turquoise earrings, Navajo lovers don turquoise necklaces and rings, Apache elders bedeck themselves with the medicinal stones of beauty.

The appeal of "Earth and I" is cooperative, not self-assertive—all at once spiritual and material and cognizant, even sacred in an earthly sense of the sky-water stone. The artist speaks in love as supplicant to his beloved, and he stands tribally in relationship to the significant other, a kinship rooted at the heart of all things. The stress falls on the collective, not the individual, reciprocal connection through an infinitely animate creation. There is no "making it up," but *working with* what is—as the Lakota medicine people tried to convey by explaining *Takuskanskan* to the Jesuits who wanted to know the name of the Lakota God. No single gendered deity like Yahweh or Allah runs high plains things. Theirs is more a multitude of spirits, a *Taku* or "power" that energetically "moves" (*skan*) through the "sky" (also *skan*) of all things, as the James R. Walker Lakota Papers, among the earliest intercultural Lakota documents, record over a century ago. The creation is alive, kinetic, animized, in a phrase, "What-moves-(all that)-moves." Anyone from Big Sky country knows of this motion, power, and energy that animates the heavens. The wind—or Lakota *Taté*—is one of four principal spirits along with sun, stone, and earth in a four-by-four pantheon. Interactive motion is all.

Speech as living wind moves human nature, and song rises up as breath from the danced earth through human beings. All art adds to and works with what is—the given reality before and beyond ego. Time is a collective gifting, ongoing, a giving back of beginning and ending, opening and closing. Space fills with collaborative sharing, and giving is sacredly, lovingly participant—what all related creatures do in common at their best.

I stress these points because readers want to know specifically what distinguishes Native American from generically Western art. The latter features creation as independent genius in making up things, from the Greek *poiein*, to make; the former remains communal, shared, collective, as in the much older Proto-Indo-European root *ar-*, to connect (art, arc, arm, architecture, articulate). To repeat, *co-kinship* lies at the common heart of tribal matters, and certainly it is the core of Momaday's writings.

Backtrack to a participant art of loving: each part, each "maker" or co-creator, exists only as *part of* a larger beloved continuum, without necessary or known origin or end. Native *making* means working with what is—arranging, presenting, fitting into the natural patterns. There is no heaven, hell, Big Bang, or Rapture, but an interdependent infinity warping around and between and within lover and beloved at the tribal center of the sacred hoop that halos the horizon of all life. The lovers themselves reenact creation, their humble giving and happy receiving. The anthropologist Barre Toelken calls this "sacred reciprocity"—the "re" and "pro," back and forth, of all things earthly in contiguous kinship. Consider earthen biomass from minerals (rocks give off nitrogen and hydrogen), to organic matter (plants secrete oxygen), to two-leggeds, four-leggeds, fins, skins, crawlers, and wings (animals emit carbon). With earthly wisdom of the ancients, there's no appreciable gap between Native knowledge and ecosciences.

I will bring corn for planting
    and we will make fire
Children will come to your breast
    You will heal my heart
I speak your name many times
The wild cane remembers you

In the beginning, Genesis says, "The whole *earth* was of one language" (11:1). Tribal creation myths tell of a time when humans, plants, animals, sun, moon, stars, and rocks spoke in common. And so indigenous stories speak of this life, earthen, earthly—not above in heaven, or below in hell, or beyond in eternity, but here and now—presently beloved, humanly sacred, patiently accepted, courageously honored. Consider the syntax of the collectively joined compound in "Earth *and* I gave you turquoise." Earth comes first (thou *and* I): pre-human, para-human, extra-human others are as honored relatives. The Cree say animals are "other-than-human-persons," and the Lakota speak to grandfathers in stones and address spirits in clouds and thunder. Earth forms the ground, base, or reality, as in grounded, that is, earthen or "clay," this earthly life. Land, soil, dirt, sand: *Oklahoma*, the Indian Territory where Momaday was born in 1934 and his ancestors long ago settled, comes from the Choctaw for "red-earth," as the Hebrew "Adam" comes from *Adama,* or "red-earth-person." Blood ties root earthen kin wherever people settle.

My young brother's house is filled
    I go there to sing
We have not spoken of you
    but our songs are sad
When Moon Woman goes to you
I will follow her white way

As with history, heritage, and etymology, Momaday's poem defers to a life force that precedes self, the extended horizon plane of this existence lived with others. Tribal context is all. Note the locally specific Diné details that narrate the poem's story: Black Mountain a sacred place; corn and wild cane as native grains; the young brother's house of mourning; Moon Woman casting the spirit "beauty-way" on lake water; Chinle an historic site of the deep temporal canyon; loom, mutton, and coffee providing daily Navajo staples; a black crow on one leg at Red Rock the sign of dyadic life to come. First-person "I" remains a culturally bounded participant, not a solitary self as loner or heroic individual out for personal gain. This is the art of partnering, a compounding, a co-joining of thou *and* I-other through conjunctive adding on. We exist as *us* all, a global human collecting.

> Tonight they dance near Chinle
>   by the seven elms
> There your loom whispered beauty
>   They will eat mutton
> and drink coffee till morning
> You and I will not be there

Lovers will walk singing and live laughing and connect through speaking. Collective relations as nouns become verbs in participles or gerunds ending *-ing.* It's a tribalizing, a familializing genealogy, a *be-loving.* A marriage of all tribal life forces transcends illness and death and the speaker's rich sense of loss. Genders cross and re-combine. At the end of the poem she will hear his horse's drumming hooves. They will meet on Black Mountain with sensual fire and children will come to her breasts. Futurity is the legacy of collective history, the tribal promise beyond personal loss without interruptive punctuation or end-stop.

> I saw a crow by Red Rock
>   standing on one leg
> It was the black of your hair
>   The years are heavy
> I will ride the swiftest horse
> You will hear the drumming hooves.

Yvor Winters, in *Forms of Discovery* (1967), laureled his doctoral student, the young Scott Momaday, among America's five best poets to the extent that Momaday had crafted one perfect poem, "Before an Old Painting of the Crucifixion," written at The Mission Carmel in June 1960. This is high praise from a literary lion of the American canon. Whether or not Momaday ranks with Dickinson and the modernists, whom he admired in his apprenticeship to the great tradition, this Kiowa native stands as godfather to a Native American Renaissance. For that, all readers of American literature and tribally activist writers interested in an indigenous heritage are thankful.

The Journey of Tai-me (1967) records Kiowa tribal legend without gloss in a hand-crafted volume limited to one hundred leather-bound copies. This rare book generated a public text that sold over 250,000 copies in forty years. Dedicated to his parents—Natachee Scott, the mixed-blood Cherokee teacher-writer, and Al Momaday, the Kiowa painter—*The Way to Rainy Mountain* (1969) carries his grandmother Aho's oral tradition forward through social sciences, personal witness, and his father's visual illustrations. The text is cross-disciplinary, multidimensional, and intercultural, framed by rhymed, metered lyric elegies to tribal legend. At the heart of the storytelling keen ancient women's voices emerging from a hollow log—the wondrous delight of Aho's interjective, "There were many people, and oh, it was beautiful"; Grandmother Spider raising the Sun Twins to people the nation; the unnamed dark beauty haunting the shadows just beyond the campfire; one-eyed centenarian Ko-sahn remembering a hundred-year-old woman carrying the Sun Dance sand on her back; and, ancient as they are, the women and men singing the sacred songs and telling the sovereign stories: "We have brought the earth. / Now it is time to play; / As old as I am, I still have the feeling of play." *The Way to Rainy Mountain* is a book of magical passages, a miracle document of tribal journey toward the dawn. Momaday has charted an ongoing cultural treasure of tale-telling and dance-singing and deep-rooting in the storied places of time and human imagining.

> East of my grandmother's house the sun rises out of the plain. Once in his life a man ought to concentrate his mind upon the remembered earth, I believe. He ought to give himself up to a particular landscape in his experience, to look at it from as many angles as he can, to wonder about it, to dwell upon it. He ought to imagine that he touches it with his hands at every season and listens to the sounds that are made upon it. He ought to imagine the creatures there and all the faintest motions of the wind. He ought to recollect the glare of noon and all the colors of the dawn and dusk.

The genesis of *House Made of Dawn* is the prose genius of place—Southwest desert and Jemez Pueblo in particular—and how the context of place gives distinctive character and voice to counter mainstream anonymity and loss. Abel is a figure running away in the dawn mist, a profile without surname. He stands allegorically for the postwar Indian, orphaned, shell-shocked, broken, and dislocated, indeed the biblical agrarian brother slain by his greedy brother Cain. Yet he is the heroic warrior twin of tribal myths bearing tragic wounds, and he brushes against the elusive shape-shifter of cautionary tales. Abel also represents Everyman as American Native isolato dispossessed of heritage, history, and human dignity, yet unvanquished and finally not to be silenced—Faulkner's southern nobility gone feral, Frost's hardscrabble New Englanders weeding stones, Hemingway's war-ravaged, big, two-hearted rivers shoaled, Prescott's Black Legend of the Hispanic-Indian Southwest deserts desiccated, Steinbeck's migrant West impoverished. Abel's journey from mating eagles over Jemez Pueblo, to war in Germany, to prison and Los Angeles relocation, and back home to New Mexico circles half the globe. His psyche moves through young suffering and soul trauma, to the healing touch of women and brotherly compassion, to rebirth in his grandfather's ceremonial steps and sacred song. Against all odds, the Native survivor keeps moving, running ceremonially and seasonally toward the ancestral dawn, and on his broken breath form the words of an ancient song, "*House made of pollen, house made of dawn. Qtsedaba.*" The incontrovertible Native heritage of forty thousand years movement, placement, and survival carry Abel forward into a renaissance of multicultural rebirth. After long night the sun also rises, as the ancients promised.

Published in 1974, *Angle of Geese* was followed within two years by the more inclusive gathering of poems, *The Gourd Dancer*, commercially vetted by Harper & Row, the publisher initiating the first series of contemporary Native American writing. Poetry does not stir big business in the United States, but it opens a door to Native American prose artists who begin as versifiers in an ancient tradition of song-poetry going back to Wordmaker and Orpheus, Samson Occom and Shakespeare.

Momaday etches free verse honorings of the magnificent eagle and lethal pit viper, the cautious deer and hard-natured crow, ancient women and life-long friends. He shapes syllabic tributes to the totemic bear, the companion canine, the mythic horse, and the marvelous angle of geese in the winter sky. There are prose poems on tribal shields and the colors of night, and everywhere flow communal gracings of the beauty and significance of austere desert and spare plains places. The Kiowa author gives us an epic name-chant: "I am a feather on the bright sky / I am the blue horse that runs in the plain / I am the fish that rolls, shining, in the water / I am the shadow that follows a child / I am the evening light, the luster of meadows." He notes the perishable recognition of human impermanence:

Desire will come of waiting
Here at this window—I bring
An old urgency to bear
Upon me, and anywhere
Is a street into the night,
Deliverance and delight—
And evenly it will pass
Like this image on the glass.

For those who treasure Native and American verse, *The Gourd Dancer* is precious, crafted stonework.

The Names, published like *The Gourd Dancer* in the nation's bicentennial year, contains a memoir and personal tribute to the extended ancestral family that raised the author a Native American. These are the named relatives four generations back: the incorrigible, blue-eyed Mexican captive Kau-au-ointy and her Kiowa husband Ah-kgoo-ahu and the pistol-toting Kentucky émigré I. J. Galyen marrying the Cherokee known only as Natachee; the great-grandparents, the stalwart Keahdinekeah wedded to Guipagho, the legendary warrior who died singing, then Pohd-lohk the arrow maker who gave infant Scott the name Tsoai-talee or Rock Tree Boy, and across the prairies toward the Ohio River, Mary and George Scott from Appalachia; grandfather Mammedaty, or "Walking Above," the peyote priest with an artist's long tapered hands, and grandmother Aho, whose name echoes the Kiowa for thanks, *a-hó,* and hill folk Theodore and Anne Ellis from Kentucky; and finally Huan-toa, Alfred Momaday, among the 1930s Oklahoma Native painters, and Natachee "Little Moon" Scott, his bride from Haskell Institute, the oldest surviving Indian college. By the time he writes *The Names* "in devotion / to those whose names I bear / and to those who bear my names," the artist is father of three daughters and a professor at Stanford, where he had earned his doctorate a decade earlier.

Animate place-names continue to make the man: Washita River, Anadarko, Rainy Mountain Creek, Mountain View, Wichita Mountains, Gallup, Shiprock, Chinle, Santa Fé, Valle Grande, Jemez Springs. And these places store memories of many things: Oklahoma arbors of willow and witch hazel; prairie grasshoppers and desert sidewinders; southwestern piñon pine and juniper; Pecos, his first hunting horse; and the Jemez Feasts of San Diego and Porcingula Our Lady of the Angels; ocotillo and mesquite; and Sefora Tosa, the beautiful Pueblo daughter who came daily to school for water. To add visual accuracy to this imaginative recounting of tribal places and names, there are family album photographs of everyone and assorted places. Their story names pool into one common headwater: "All the rivers ran down from that place, and many times I saw eagles in the air under me. And then there were meadows full of wildflowers, and a mist roiled upon them, the slow, rolling spill of the mountain clouds. And in one of these, in a pool of low light, I touched the fallen tree, the hollow log there in the thin crust of the ice."

The Ancient Child (1989), the author's second innovative novel, is a crosscut pastiche of Momaday's Native heritage, Western popular culture, and modernist Euro-American education, published by Doubleday twenty years after *House Made of Dawn.* The story lists its characters as in a play: primarily, the thirty-five-year-old, mixed-blood Locke Setman, or Set (Kiowa for bear), raised as an orphan in California, now a struggling artist in San Francisco; Grey, the singly named, multiracial, kitsch mythic, nineteen-year-old medicine charmer coming of age in Oklahoma; her dreamed lover, Billy the Kid, the romantic outlaw of border legend who notched his gun twenty-one times and was shot in the back at twenty-one by Sheriff Pat Garrett; grandmother Kope'mah, a granny Kiowa healer; Lola Bourne, a vexed urban siren; Bent Sandridge, Set's wise and kind stepfather; and Set-Angya, or Sitting Bear, an ancestral ancient who carries his son's bones around as tribal talismans. And then there is the Bear, mythic guardian spirit and the artist's totemic protector and loyal adversary.

This novel, a work of maverick fiction, mixes history and fable, dream and reminiscence, folk legend and chant, tribal myth and popular culture. Between old and young feminine beauty, animal freedom and human despair, in-law and outlaw, West Coast art and Oklahoma red-dirt reality, the story skips along in small bursts like a flat stone tossed across a pond of deep-currented dreams and memories.

Grey endures the unwanted lust of scurrilous men like the sullen Dwight Dicks, who molests her as she fantasizes intimacy with Billy the Kid. When Set's unknown Kiowa grandmother Kope'mah dies, the California artist inherits through Grey a medicine bundle of bear paw power that changes his painting career and sends him to Paris. Meanwhile, Grey daydreams a pop ballad chapbook of her outlaw fantasies with Billy the Kid, morphing between lifetimes and centuries, seeking teen destiny and true love. Bent, the good father figure, dies, and Set breaks down and through to his ursine guardian, Old Man Bear. He returns to Oklahoma, then to Lukachukai with Grey in her truck. Both go in search of beauty, or as the Navajo say, *hózhóni*, with twists—erotic, artistic, geologic, fantastic, familial, and mythic beauty. Grey lets on that she is a fusion of Diné and Kiowa, with Gaelic, French, and English blood tossed in. Her wounded lover grows whole again among Grey's Navajo relatives, and they conceive a multi-ethnic child.

Set ends the story on a landscape pilgrimage to the base of his namesake monolith, Tsoai the Rock Tree (Momaday's childhood sacred name), generally known as Devils Tower, near Sundance, Wyoming. Overhead, Ursa Major blesses him, as the Kiowa legend of the bear-brother and seven sisters clicks into place around Rock Tree, clawed by the mythological brother in pursuit of his seven sisters rising on the magical tree and becoming the Big Dipper. The star shadow of the bear rises against the Tower, a 1,267-foot volcanic monolith the Lakota call Mato Tipi, the House of the Bear. The tale recedes into the fictive night shadows of mythic time, as the text ends with the stars of Ursa Major painted on a Kiowa shield: *"And the last of his dreams was that of children moving to a wall of woods. They bobbed and skipped and tumbled away in the distance. He watched them for a time, and then he could no longer see them. They had already entered into the trees, into the darkness."*

In the Presence of the Sun (1992) gathers sketches and poems written between 1961 and 1991. Momaday showcases his fey fascination with the gunslinger of *corridos* and cowboy ballads in "The Strange and True Story of My Life with Billy the Kid." A visual and verbal section on Kiowa shields arcing back to illustrations in *The Way to Rainy Mountain* includes both the heraldic stories and black-and-white images of the plains shields themselves. These icons and tales exist separately as water color paintings opposite from prose gloss in a signed limited edition, *In the Presence of the Sun: A Gathering of Shields* (1991). The last section of the book includes new poems, among them "Mogollon Morning":

The long,
Long bands of rock,
Old as wonder, stand back.
I listen for my death song there
In rock.

Mortality and human fragility weigh on the artist's mind in these silver years. Three times in the collection Momaday invokes the haunting couplet: "These figures moving in my rhyme, / Who are they? Death and Death's dog, Time." The book opens and closes with a charcoal self-portrait of the artist in side view, declaring by the end, "He is a bear."

Natachee Scott Momaday taught and wrote children's stories. Her son wrote and illustrated an Indian Christmas story in 1994, *Circle of Wonder*, dedicated to his granddaughter Skye. The text is lavishly water colored around a Pueblo village's celebration of the birth of the Christ Child. The story is about Tolo, who believes he sees his deceased grandfather among the villagers who have lighted the festive bonfires. In his search for his grandfather, Tolo wanders toward the mountains where a circle of firelight draws him to a grand scarred Elk. A wounded predatory Wolf joins the firelight circle, then an Eagle seeking warmth and safety. All need compassion and comfort. Then Tolo understands the firelight circle of wonder that fits into all the visionary circles of the world, the seasonal gift of the Christ Child and wild animals, and the blessing of fire at dawn. Tolo wakes to a votive candle illuminating the Christmas crèche and knows that he is no longer poor or mute, but blessed with the strength of the Elk and song of the Wolf. *Qtsedaba,* the tale ends ceremonially and mysteriously, as with *House Made of Dawn.* The book is written, illustrated, and designed to evoke ceremonial wonder in a child's eyes.

Professor Momaday earned a Stanford doctorate in English literature and taught for over four decades at the University of California, Santa Barbara, the University of California, Berkeley, Stanford University, and the University of Arizona. He has lectured at many other universities in the United States and abroad. He wrote over one hundred pieces for *Viva*, weekly magazine of the *Santa Fe New Mexican*, in the early 1970s. He published political essays for *Ramparts*, eco-literary manifestos for the *Sierra Club Bulletin*, and travel pieces for the *New York Times Magazine*. Momaday has traveled the world lecturing, won the Academy of American Poets Prize, and received Italy's highest literary honor, the Premio Letterario Internazionale "Mondello."

Scott Momaday has written three full-length plays. His first, *The Indolent Boys*, has been performed across the country. He has crafted other theater pieces and screenplay narratives and worked with producer Richardson Morse in making *House Made of Dawn* into a feature-length film. He has overvoiced many a documentary for PBS, National Geographic, and the History Channel. His deeply resonant elocution and measured diction set a distinctive trademark of seasoned, cinematic narration. The living voice is his trademark.

In 1997, after thirty-four years of university posts, Momaday's *The Man Made of Words* was published by St. Martin's Press with illustrations by the author. Thirty-two collected essays, stories, and passages scan the primacy of language, the significance of place, and the centrality of storytelling in cultural definitions of tribal dignity, cultural wealth, and personal integrity. These are studies in Native ethnography, national etymology, and global philosophy. To read these essays and absorb their multidimensional grace, weight, and intelligence instills a sense of literary wonder, landscape beauty, and ethnic dignity. They are inspired by the creative originality and fresh vision of an artist-thinker seeing the world as though for the first time—seeing a reality made of sonorous and shaped language, a masculinity shaped by well chosen, ringing cadences, a man imaginatively and truly made of words to live by. Readers will long parse and ponder these writings, deep sources of Native thinking, speaking, and writing that represent the human evolution of eloquence and literacy in one man's Native work.

The dust jacket of *In the Bear's House* features a bear cub's elongated saffron face drawn by the author. The left eye is stretched diagonally upward and peers wistfully at the reader, a blue-shadowed brown eye dilated with darkness, contemplating time and eternity. Alert, muted, visually asymmetrical, dumbfounded with wonder, hunger, and interest in the world—the blue-visioned bear cub seems to gauge the viewer's curiosity. At the bottom of the jacket, the title is in Momaday's own hand.

In ancestral western Siberia, the artist learned of Native bear feasts at which the sacrificial bear presided in his own house. Those ceremonies traversed the Bering Strait and traveled down across the Canadian prairies with the Diné and others, into the intermountain plains and deserts of the Southwest, where the Kiowa artist lives out his life as an ursine grandfather: "Something in me hungers for wild mountains and rivers and plains. I love to be on Bear's ground, to listen for that old guttural music under his breath, to know only that he is near. And Bear is welcome in my dreams, for in that cave of sleep I am at home to Bear."

This miscellany of dramatic dialogues, new poems, and passages arrived in 1999, on the millennial eve. Another self-illustrated work, the collection underscores that the artist, like his father before, has been drawing and painting seriously for twenty-five years, since he turned fifty. His health at times precarious, Momaday is clearly looking at time, human creativity, and eternity through his spirit guardian's eyes. "To An Aged Bear" ends with an invocation of Old Man's temporal courage:

Mortality
Is your shadow and your shade.

Translate yourself to spirit;
Be present on your journey.

Keep to the trees and waters.
Be the singing of the soil.

The philosophic "Bear-God Dialogues" between Urset, the original Kiowa Grandfather Bear, and Yahweh, the Lord of Western history known to Native belief as The Great Mystery, foreground the collection with a deeply wizened sense of humor and play. Two old chiefs sit and talk of things temporal and time immortal, one earthbound, aged, and crotchety, heavy with living, the other all-knowing, compassionate, and sharp-tongued, lonely and unable to die. Imagine Orson Welles holding Socratic court with Sitting Bull. They talk of huckleberries and prayer, trout and time, dreams and freedom, wonder and thanksgiving, hunters and stories, silence and grace, dogs and speech, thought and the bones of the dead, time passing and the present moment. The eight dialogues end with Yahweh "out of time" and off to a meeting.

The poems that follow, old and new, constellate around old man bear, the embodied spirit of the wilderness, Momaday says, from Siberia and Moscow, to T'umen and Altamira, to Tucson and Jemez Springs. The collection ends with the prose outtake of the bear hunt from *House Made of Dawn* and the Kiowa legend of the bear-brother and seven sisters from *The Way to Rainy Mountain*. Finding a bear paw print near his family home in the mountains of Jemez Springs, New Mexico, the artist offers his earthly tribute to this intermediary of the immortal gods and mortal wilderness spirits: "And all who should lay eyes upon my work would know, beyond any shadow of a doubt, how much I love the bear whose print this is."

Mysterious, chiseled, and crafted, Momaday's fictions and prose memoirs appeal to broad audiences. The poetry and drama, more difficult, plumb the art of oral traditions, the poetics of the spoken voice, the aesthetics of the song-line, and the penetrance of the literary vision. Momaday's historical, political, literary, and ecological warnings lay largely unnoticed until collected in *The Man Made of Words*. Examine the cultural expanse and textural quality of this man's lifework. His words will be pondered and remembered for a long time. They reach back into the ancestral Native past, and forward into America's future with the resurgence of tribal cultures. Ours is a time of reconciliation, of new visions, of coming together, of rebirth and tribal continuation. N. Scott Momaday will long be regarded as the Grandfather Bear spirit of a Native American Renaissance in Western letters.

PART I

Biography and Chronology

A Life in a Rich and Exotic World

A Biography of N. Scott Momaday

"I grew up in a very rich and exotic world."

Momaday, Interview, 1981[1]

The Childhood Years

On a blustery Tuesday morning, February 27, 1934, at four o'clock, a healthy baby boy weighing over eight pounds greeted a new world at the Kiowa and Comanche Indian Hospital at Lawton, Oklahoma. The newborn's parents, Alfred Morris Momaday and Natachee Scott Momaday, welcomed their first, and only, child and named him Navarre Scott Momaday. They brought him home to his grandmother's house on the family's land in Kiowa County close to Mountain View, Oklahoma. Rainy Mountain, the sacred mountain of the Kiowas, is a short distance from his first home.

The birth certificate, signed by a doctor at the hospital, incorrectly recorded the boy's name as Novarro Scotte Mammedaty. The surname Momaday, which his father had begun to use in 1932 instead of the family surname, had been entered first, but was crossed out for reasons unknown. A notarized document was later issued by the U.S. government certifying his name, birth date, and other personal information. It also shows that his name was recorded on the official Kiowa Indian Census roll. This document ends with the following statement: "By Act of June 2, 1924 (43 Stat. 253), all Indians born within the territorial limits of the United States were declared to be citizens of the United States."[2] This law came into effect only ten years before his birth.

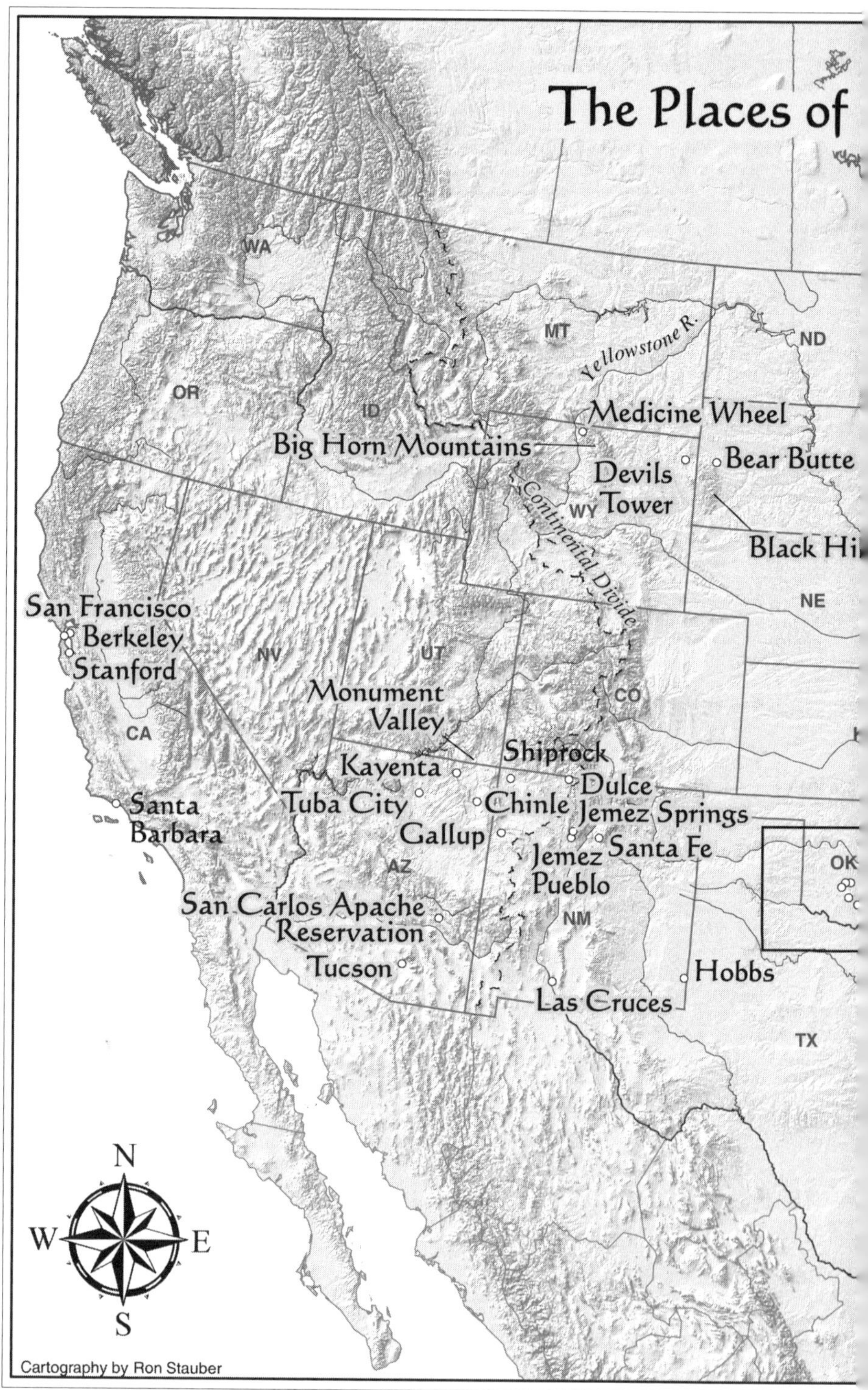
The Places of
WA
OR
ID
MT
ND
Yellowstone R.
Medicine Wheel
Big Horn Mountains
Devils Tower
Bear Butte
WY
Continental Divide
Black Hi
NE
San Francisco
Berkeley
Stanford
NV
UT
CO
Monument Valley
CA
Shiprock
Kayenta
Dulce
Tuba City
Chinle
Jemez Springs
Santa Barbara
Gallup
Santa Fe
Jemez Pueblo
OK
AZ
San Carlos Apache Reservation
NM
Tucson
Hobbs
Las Cruces
TX
N
W
E
S
Cartography by Ron Stauber

e events of one's life take
ace, *take place.*

The Names (1976)

When Momaday was six months old, his "first notable event" occurred. This was a long trip by automobile with his parents to the Black Hills and Devils Tower in the northeastern corner of Wyoming. A sacred place to the Kiowa and other Plains tribes, Devils Tower was named Tsoai (Rock Tree) by the Kiowas. Upon the family's return to Mountain View, Pohd-lohk, meaning Old Wolf and pronounced "Pole-haw," gave the little boy his Kiowa name, Tsoai-talee (Rock Tree Boy) during a ceremony held in the arbor at his grandmother's place.

In *The Names: A Memoir* (1976), Momaday's second autobiographical book, he remembers through his imagining that important event of receiving his Kiowa name from Pohd-lohk:

> He took up the child in his hands and held it high, and he cradled it in his arms, singing to it and rocking it to and fro. With the others he passed the time of day, exchanged customary talk, scattered small exclamations on the air: Yes, yes. Quite so. So it is with us. But with the child he was deliberate, intent. And after a time all the other voices fell away, and his own grew up in their wake. It became monotonous and incessant, like a long running of the wind. The whole of the afternoon was caught up in it and carried along. Pohd-lohk spoke, as if telling a story, of the coming-out people [the Kiowas], of their long journey. He spoke of how it was that everything began, of Tsoai, and of the stars falling or holding fast in strange patterns on the sky. And in this, at last, Pohd-lohk affirmed the whole life of the child in a name, saying: "Now you are Tsoai-talee."[3]

Momaday concludes his telling of this important event: "I am. It is when I am most conscious of being that wonder comes upon my blood, and I want to live forever, and it is no matter that I must die."[4]

When Momaday was still very young, he was given two other names. The second, a Kiowa name, Tso-Toh-Haw or Tsotohah, translates in English to "Red Bluff." This name seems fitting, since he grew up in red-earth places: Oklahoma, which means "red earth," from the Choctaw language; the Jemez area of New Mexico, where the mesas and other landforms are a deep, rich red; and the Navajo Reservation, with its monoliths of red sandstone towering above a crimson valley. His third name, Wanbli Wanji, is Sioux and means "Eagle Alone." Momaday does not know who gave him these names. It was a tribal custom for men to have three names, traditionally given at birth, adolescence, and adulthood.

Pohd-lohk was Momaday's step-great-grandfather, the second husband of Keahdinekeah, his father's grandmother. He was a Kiowa record keeper, a tribal historian and well respected by the Kiowas. For many years he faithfully recorded the most significant events in a ledgerbook, one of the calendar histories of the Kiowa people. One of the very first events recorded in it was the great Leonid meteor shower of 1833 that Momaday tells about in *The Way to Rainy Mountain* (1969), a most unforgettable time that marked the beginning of the historical period in the minds of the Kiowas. Pohd-lohk took the name George Poolaw in his later years and served as one of the informants of ethnologist Alice Lee Marriott (1910–92), who spent nearly ten years researching and recording the story of the Kiowas. Their past had always been continued and maintained in the people's oral tradition, which Momaday has reminded us is "but one generation removed from extinction."[5] The calendar kept by Pohd-lohk was included by Marriott with other Kiowa calendars in her book *The Ten Grandmothers*, first published in 1945. After his death in 1939, Pohd-lohk was buried in Rainy Mountain Cemetery.

Momaday's father, Alfred (Al) Morris Momaday (1913–81), was born on July 2, 1913, in a tipi on the homestead at Mountain View. He was given the Kiowa name Huan-toa (War Lance), and in 1932 changed his last name from Mammedaty to Momaday. His dream was to be an artist, which he pursued at Bacone College, located in Muskogee, Oklahoma, from 1931 to 1934. An exceptional art department was developing at the college, where he had the opportunity to study

Momaday's parents, Alfred Morris Momaday, 1913–1981, and Natachee Scott Momaday, 1913–1996, at home in New Mexico in the 1960s. (N. Scott Momaday Collection)

with the accomplished Cree artist Acee Blue Eagle. Al Momaday also studied at the University of New Mexico from 1936 to 1937 and later in 1956 at the University of California, Los Angeles. He made use of his drafting, drawing, and other skills in supporting his family during the hard times of the Great Depression in the 1930s. He served in the U.S. Army Corp of Engineers during World War II.

Al Momaday became a highly respected artist; his paintings have been shown in art exhibits and are held in museum and private collections across the United States and in European countries and Japan. The *St. James Guide to Native North American Artists* (1998) presents a selected list of over forty group exhibitions in twenty states where his work was shown from 1947 to 1990, including several exhibitions mounted after his death in 1981.[6] He and other Kiowa artists were significant participants during the period that made Oklahoma an important center of American Indian painting. He had grown up knowing the intricacies of Kiowa tribal ceremonies, legends, and history, and proudly identified with the Kiowa way. His images reflect his knowledge and pride. The illustrations in *The Way to Rainy Mountain* are excellent examples of Al Momaday's strikingly bold, two-dimensional paintings.

In positions of teacher, principal, and director of arts and crafts at the Jemez Day School of the Pueblo of Jemez in New Mexico, Al Momaday initiated a number of art programs and events to further young artists. Those events included the annual Jemez Pueblo Indian Arts Exposition and Powwow, which regularly drew thousands of visitors. He traveled extensively to promote American Indian painting, served as a judge at art shows, and became an art critic. His dream was fulfilled in many ways. Al Momaday passed away on November 11, 1981.

Mayme Natachee Scott Momaday was born in Fairview, Kentucky, on February 13, 1913, the third child of Theodore Scott and Anne Elizabeth Ellis Scott. Among her forebears, mostly English and French, was a Cherokee great-grandmother named Natachee. In 1918, when she was only five years old, Natachee Scott's mother died during the great influenza epidemic. She was, according to Momaday, "her father's darling," and she, in turn, worshipped him, remaining at home in Kentucky after her siblings had left.

As a young girl, Natachee Scott was aware of her distant female Cherokee relative, and as she grew up, her thoughts turned increasingly to her great-grandmother and her Native heritage. Momaday has remarked that she considered "Indian" more important in her life than the idea of being Cherokee: "She imagined who she was. This act of the imagination was, I believe, among the most important events of my mother's early life, as later the same essential act was to be among the most important of my own."[7]

Independent, strong-willed Natachee dreamed at an early age of becoming a writer, in particular a journalist. At age twelve she sold her first story for $1.75 to the local newspaper of Trenton, Kentucky, where her father was the sheriff for a period of time. Her first book, a small collection of poetry, was published when she was in her mid-teens. She traveled westward in 1929 to northeastern Kansas to begin her studies at Haskell Institute, the Indian school at Lawrence. She did not stay long at Haskell or other schools she attended, because she was very eager to seek her career as a writer and painter. She was intent on writing, and she especially wanted to write about Indians.

While at Haskell, Natachee became a close friend of her roommate, a Kiowa girl from Oklahoma named Lela Ware. They subsequently kept in touch and visited each other. As destiny or fate would have it, during a visit to Lela's home in Oklahoma, Lela introduced her cousin, a tall, handsome Kiowa man, to her friend Natachee. His name was Al Momaday. The couple married in 1933.

Momaday recalls that his mother always seemed to enjoy her life: "I remember her saying to me, when she talked about her life at the Jemez Day School, where she taught for twenty-five years, 'I loved every moment of that time.' That expression made a big impression upon me. I don't know how many people can say something like that. She meant it and that says something about her. . . . She was a woman of many parts—she could write, read, teach."[8] And she was also an accomplished painter. Her teaching career spanned from 1937 to 1972, the year she resigned from the Jemez Day School. Her most acclaimed book, *Owl in the Cedar Tree,* first published in 1965 and used in schools across the country, received awards. It was still in print in 2010. Natachee Scott Momaday passed away on September 26, 1996, and was buried next to her husband at Fairview Memorial Park in Albuquerque.

N. Scott Momaday's earliest memories are of being in Oklahoma with his parents, paternal grandmother, uncles, aunts, and other relatives on his father's side of the family. His grandfather, Mammedaty (1880–1932), died before Momaday's birth. Mammedaty was the son of Guipagho the Younger and grandson of Guipagho the Elder, a famous Kiowa chief known as Lone Wolf and for whom the town of Lone Wolf, located southwest of Mountain View, was named. Mammedaty, like his forebears, became a highly respected member of his tribe and a member of the Gourd Dance Society, one of the important soldier societies of the Kiowa tribe. The surname means "walking above," sometimes translated as "sky walker." When the Kiowas were given allotments of land after the reservation had been greatly reduced in size, he worked hard at farming. Although the Kiowas were buffalo hunters and never had an agricultural tradition, he prospered at growing cotton, wheat, and other crops. His portrait shows Mammedaty, standing tall at six feet, four inches and clothed in some of the regalia of the Gourd Dance Society.

Mammedaty built a house for his wife Aho, their children, and himself on the north side of Rainy Mountain Creek. The house was under construction in 1913 when Al, Momaday's father, was born in a tipi that had been set up near the construction site. Later, a large arbor was built in the place where the tipi had stood. Momaday wrote a four-part prose poem, "The Gourd Dancer: Mammedaty, 1880–1932," in honor of his grandfather, about whom he heard and imagined many good things:

> Mammedaty saw to the building of the house. Just
> there by the arbor, he made a camp in the old way.
> And in the evening when the hammers had fallen silent
> and there were frogs and crickets in the black grass—
> and a low, hectic wind upon the pale, slanting plane
> of the moon's light—he settled deep down in his
> mind to dream. He dreamed of dreaming, and of the
> summer breaking upon his spirit, as drums break upon
> the intervals of the dance, and of the gleaming gourds.[9]

Momaday's grandfather, Mammedaty, member of the Kiowa Gourd Dance Society, 1880–1932.
(N. Scott Momaday Collection)

In the last sequence of this prose poem, Momaday tells of a great honor paid to his grandfather at a traditional Kiowa giveaway ceremony. Mammedaty was summoned to the circle and watched as a beautiful black horse was led up to him. "Its mane and tail were fixed in braids and feathers, and a bright red chief's blanket was draped in a roll over its withers." The boy placed the reins in Mammedaty's hands. "And all of this was for Mammedaty, in his honor, as even now it is in the telling, and will be, as long as there are those who imagine him in his name."[10]

Mammedaty married Aho, Momaday's grandmother, after the turn of the twentieth century. The meaning of her name is not known; she used the English name Florence in later years. Momaday grew close to her in his early years, when he made trips back to Mountain View with his father, in particular during the summer months. He also became familiar with other family members and the Kiowa people.

Aho was born in July 1880, a time described by her grandson as one when "the Kiowas were living the last great moment of their history"[11] on the Southern

Momaday's grandmother, Aho, 1880–1965.
(N. Scott Momaday Collection)

Plains. At the age of seven, Aho took part in the last Kiowa Sun Dance. She attended the Rainy Mountain Boarding School and grew up an attractive, strong woman. Aho and Mammedaty had six children, two girls and four boys. She died in May 1965 with one of her daughters at her bedside, and was laid to rest in Rainy Mountain Cemetery.

Among Momaday's earliest memories are recollections of the arbor that had been constructed near his grandmother's house. He fondly recalls: "I loved the place, especially the arbor, because it was cool and had an earthen floor. It was very pleasant to be there, because Oklahoma can be very hot in the summer. Those first memories are very pleasant ones."[12]

Arbors were generally made of brush and long poles, although they could also be permanent structures. These were used by the Kiowa and other tribes of the Southern Plains to provide cooling shade and relief from the sweltering heat. Long before the arrival of refrigerated air or home air conditioners, these shelters served as welcome summer places for daily living, cooking, sleeping, and gatherings of family and friends. Arbors became "one of the material features that strengthen the Kiowas' attachment to place."[13] They are still seen in a few places in Oklahoma, built today by some Kiowas more as a statement of identity or to carry on an important tradition than for practical use. "It is a way for Kiowas to feel that they are living, at least in part, in the way their ancestors did."[14] The Mammedaty arbor, a square-frame building with a pitched roof supported by two large timbers, was the place of many family gatherings and social events.

Another early memory of life in Oklahoma was of times spent in "the little room in the ground," when the thunderstorms for which the Great Plains are notorious would sweep across the land, threatening destruction in their paths. Momaday remembers the smell of the damp earth, the sounds of pounding rain and hail on the well-secured door, and the deafening thunder and cracks of lightning.

Having often said that he has loved words since he was little, Momaday was asked whether he was ever told what his first word or words were, and he replied in the blink of an eye, "To be or not to be."[15] This response is an example of his humor and quick wit, which have always charmed those who have had discussions with or interviewed him. Continuing, he remarked: "I don't remember anyone ever telling me. However, my mother told me that when I was about eight or ten years old, I told her that I was going to win a Pulitzer Prize. I wanted to be a writer at a very early age, and I announced that to her one day and she reminded me of that many times. Lo and behold, it happened! I had ambition if nothing else in those days. I wanted to be a writer, but I didn't become one until 1959 with the publication of my first poem. But, you know, people who aspire to write think of themselves as writers before they really are writers."[16]

He remembers both parents telling and reading stories to him from the time he was very young. "I don't have any memories that are older than having heard stories from my father, particularly the Kiowa oral tradition stories, which became so very important in my life. My mother read and told stories to me, not from oral tradition so much as all kinds of things from English literature. They introduced me to words and language, and I fell in love with them. Hearing stories was very important to me when I was little. My parents, both of them in different ways, gave me a strong sense and love of language, and I have kept that through my life. Words have been extremely important to me."[17] Language and the power of words are among his most prominent subjects and themes.

His father told tales from the oral tradition that were full of wonder for a young boy, and he wanted to hear them retold again and again. His favorite was "The Story of the Arrowmaker," which Momaday, in turn, has introduced and retold to countless people through the ensuing years. He believes that this story may have been the first his father told him. "I fell in love with it. It is an adventure, an exciting story. My father was good at storytelling, and he made it unforgettable."[18] Many other stories were told to him, but he has consistently singled out this particular one. Years later, in 1970, Momaday recited this Kiowa story from oral tradition in his seminal address, "The Man Made of Words," given at the first Convocation of American Indian Scholars at Princeton University. He has retold it orally and in his writings numerous times, and many others have quoted and reprinted it.

Being an only child, Momaday and his parents became very close, forming their own cohesive, self-contained unit. A number of times they were outsiders to the particular cultures where they lived, their time at Jemez Pueblo being the prime example. "I took it all for granted as a child," he recalls, "but when I think back on it now, I wonder how it was possible to fit so easily into such situations. As a child I thought nothing of it. My parents may have had a very different idea of their position in relation to the cultural realities of Jemez Pueblo. They conducted themselves very well, and so their example was certainly affirmative."[19]

Momaday liked to watch as his father worked at his easel. He has recounted how much his father loved to paint, to teach painting, and to work in the company of other painters: "Some of my happiest memories are of painters coming to the house at Jemez. They would work with my father and have such a wonderful time together. I learned a lot about painting from him by osmosis. I wasn't interested in painting during my childhood. All I thought about was writing. But long after I had become an adult, I became interested in drawing and painting and sort of followed in my father's footsteps. That became an important part of my life and opened up another career for me."[20]

Momaday also remembers his father's "wonderful hand," his beautiful penmanship, and wishes he had inherited that from him. He has remarked with pride about his father: "He lived two lives and in two worlds; his Indian heritage was very strong in him, and I am sure he thought a lot about being Indian, about his childhood and growing up as a Kiowa. Then he moved away from the Kiowa people and entered into another world and found success in that. He lived in two worlds and did it with great skill. I admired him very much all through the years."[21]

Like most children, Momaday has many isolated memories of things that happened to him as a child: "My father, for instance, used to like telling the story of my doing something that deserved a reprimand or some punishment. I had gone away too far from the house or broken some rule, and he came home from work prepared to reprimand me. I was playing in a swing when he strode up to me. Unaware I was about to be reprimanded, I looked up at him and said with great enthusiasm and affection, 'Hi, Dad!' That completely disarmed him. He said later that he just couldn't punish me after that greeting. It was something he always remembered and loved telling that story to others."[22]

His mother was a literary person: "She was a writer, and a reader of course, and she introduced me to all kinds of literature as I was growing up. There were very few books for children in those days. From books, anthologies, and magazines, she read stories, tales, and poetry to me. She also told me about things that she had read, such as animals. I loved stories about animals. I had a big helping of that when I was very young."[23]

Momaday realized that his parents had high expectations for him, and he understood that they wanted him to realize himself, to excel, if possible. He recalls, "They were very gentle in the process. They did not put me under a lot of pressure, as so many children have placed upon them in today's world. I think I understood that their expectations were high—but, so were mine. From an early age, I wanted to achieve, and they were instrumental in that regard by allowing me to achieve in my own way with their unfailing support and encouragement. Of course, they were also strict in my growing up years, and I understood that they expected me to get along in the world and to treat others well."[24]

Since the family often lived where there were no playmates nearby, Momaday had to find ways to entertain himself and make use of his imagination. Reminiscing about that time in his life, he has remarked, "I think probably only children don't have a choice in that matter. They have to sustain themselves, and I think they probably develop an imagination before other children, who have playmates, do. They become self-sufficient in that way, and I think that's true of my experience. I lived in places when I was growing up where I didn't have any close friends, often because we were separated by a language barrier. So, I really did have to

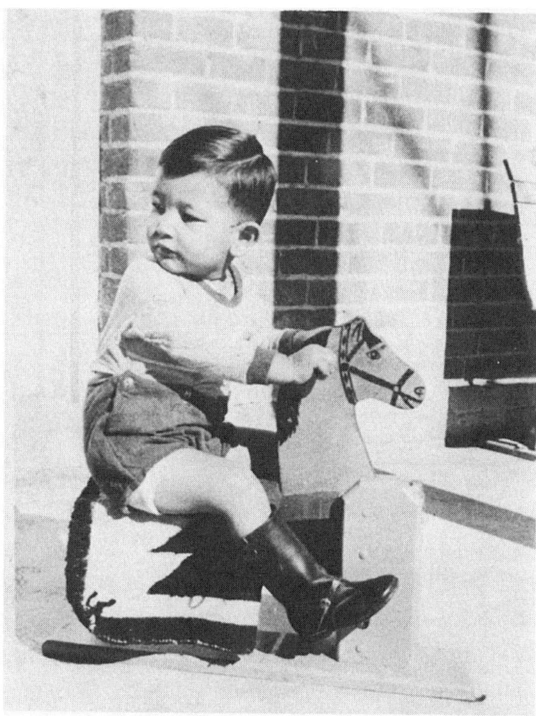

Momaday, two years old, riding his first horse, Tony, in 1936.
(N. Scott Momaday Collection)

entertain myself, and I think I probably became pretty good at it, developing my imagination and manufacturing all kinds of things like a child does."[25] Asked whether he was shy because of being an only child having little contact with other children, he commented: "Yes, I was shy. Less so as time went on, but certainly I was shy and may be still to a degree. But I used to be a lot more shy and that was a real part of my being."[26]

Concerning his favorite playthings, Momaday has often remarked about his early interest in and love of animals, horses and dogs in particular. Bears became much more important to him as he grew up and thought of himself as the bear in the Kiowa story of Tsoai, in which a boy turns into a bear. His first horse was a little rocking horse, which he named Tony, a trusty steed for adventuring and playing "Cowboys and Indians." He liked being both a cowboy and an Indian and would go back and forth, one day a cowboy, another day an Indian. He liked the idea of being a cowboy, because it seemed such an adventurous life.

After hearing stories of Billy the Kid, still considered New Mexico's most famous historical person, he sometimes pretended to be the notorious Kid. That was the beginning of a long and close relationship with Billy the Kid, who in later years became a subject of Momaday's poems, prose, essays, and paintings.

Billy came into his consciousness, Momaday thinks, when he was growing up in New Mexico during World War II. The family lived in the town of Hobbs, in the southeastern part of the state, from 1943 to 1946. "We were pretty close to Billy the Kid country, and I think I heard about him long before I read about him. He was a wonderfully colorful character, and so I began to imagine him and he became a companion in my imagination."[27]

Then, one day, Momaday discovered newspaperman-author Walter Noble Burns's *The Saga of Billy the Kid*, first published in 1926. It became a favorite book, one he has never forgotten the thrill of reading: "That book fortified my interest in Billy. It was a very good story. I think this book is seminal and an important book. Although it is largely fiction, it is nonetheless an important book, because it reveals the Kid as a rounded character, and it is well written and easy to read. In this book, he became a hero and a legendary figure."[28]

At about the same time, Momaday read the "Smoky" book, as it was known then, referring to *Smoky the Cow Horse*, by Will James (1892–1942), a very popular writer in his day. This book, published in 1926, became a favorite of young and older readers alike, and especially of boys. It impressed Momaday: "That was my first real experience of reading. Will James wrote a number of books about the life of cowboys, and his *Smoky the Cow Horse* was one of my first favorites. I fell in love with reading when I encountered that book."[29] Momaday believes this book gave him his first insight into the miracle of reading. It was a great literary experience, and he often tells about a later experience connected to the book and its author: "I used to tell people about my great affection for Will James's writing during my years at Stanford University. They would say, 'Oh, you mean William James,' referring to the American psychologist and philosopher, and I would reply, 'No, I mean Will James.'"[30] On a number of such occasions, he would have to explain exactly who Will James was.

"I imagined myself the whole time," recalls Momaday. "But Will James was important in that sense, and I may even have aspired to write because of his book. I wanted to write something like it and that is a common kind of experience. When I read something I admire particularly, I want to write like that. I say, 'How did this come to be, how can I write to that level?'"[31] When he was close to twelve years old and an independent reader, he began choosing books based on his own interests, favoring stories of adventure and about animals, which he believes helped to develop his love of poetry.

On numerous occasions, Momaday has said that he could not have wished for parents more supporting, encouraging, and giving of unconditional love. Remembering back to those childhood years, he has said that he learned a great deal from their examples. After their deaths, he spoke of his closeness to them:

> We were in contact regularly until they passed away. I called them frequently and that was something I depended upon, talking to them as long as they lived. Yes, I miss that very much. There are moments in my life now when I feel like picking up the phone and calling them. That moment passes, but it is very real—wanting to share things and wanting to tell them about things that have happened, this and that about what has come into my life. It's always a sad thing that I can't tell them—but maybe I can and do. Who knows?[32]

The Years on the Navajo Reservation (1936–1943)

"The vast and beautiful landscape of Diné bikeyah *was* my world."

Momaday, *The Names*[33]

Between 1936 and 1943, Momaday and his parents lived on the Navajo Reservation, first at Shiprock, located in the northwestern corner of New Mexico, and then at Tuba City and Chinle in Arizona. Chinle is situated at the westernmost end of the spectacular Canyon de Chelly. He and his mother also lived for a short period at the San Carlos Apache Reservation in southeastern Arizona while his father was in Oklahoma. During those years, a number of trips were made back and forth to Oklahoma, Kentucky, and other points east, primarily to visit his grandmother and other relatives on both sides of the family.

Momaday was a little over two years old in 1936, when his parents were invited by a Navajo friend to come to Gallup, New Mexico, where jobs were sometimes available with the Indian Service, later the Bureau of Indian Affairs. His father was able to find a job working for the Roads Department, and the family moved to Shiprock, named for the volcanic formation several miles southwest of the settlement. This imposing formation is regarded by the Navajos as a sacred place.

From time to time, Al Momaday drove a department pickup over the dirt roads to various places on the reservation. There were no cars on the reservation, except those that were government property or belonged to the Indian Service employees. When he was a few years older, Momaday would sometimes accompany his father: "I lived for those trips. I got a sense of the country then. It was wild and unending. We would come upon sheep camps in remote canyons and solitary family hogans. We saw a lot of people, but they were always off by themselves, it seemed, living a life of their own, each one having an individual existence in that huge landscape."[34]

The landscape is one of great beauty, variety, and color. Years later, when Momaday was learning to fly an airplane, he recalled the breathtaking landscapes of the Four Corners area: "I saw the land as a hawk or an eagle sees it, immense and wild and all of a piece." Once he flew with a friend to a trading post in the middle of the reservation, where he landed on a dirt road. It seemed as though they had flown backward in time, the place seemed so remote and undiscovered. "It was like Kayenta was in my earliest time on the reservation, so remote as to be almost legendary in the mind."[35] Today, Kayenta is a town of about five thousand people and an important stop on the reservation for travelers approaching or leaving Monument Valley.

Momaday's playmates were Navajo children and the children of Indian Service employees. There was often a language barrier, but that did not keep them from having fun whenever an opportunity arose for play. Those years on the Navajo Reservation led to a lifelong interest in Navajo history, culture, and language. His father learned to speak some of the Navajo language, and Momaday learned a little from him and others. He began developing "an ear" for the sounds of Navajo speech. Years later, in 1970, he returned to Navajo country to study the language formally, "in order to understand not only the meaning but the formation of it as well. It is a beautiful language, intricate and full of subtlety, and very difficult to learn."[36]

In his foreword to Trudy Griffin-Pierce's *Earth Is My Mother, Sky Is My Father* (1992), Momaday recalled his experience studying the Navajo language intensively for a summer at the Gallup branch of the University of New Mexico. His instructor, Alan Wilson, author of *Navajo Place Names* (1995), encouraged him to talk to Native speakers at every opportunity. On one occasion, Momaday stopped for a hitchhiker, a young man on his way to the Four Corners area. After running out of conversational expressions in Navajo, Momaday asked the man what the names were of the landmarks they passed. To his amazement there seemed to be a name for every object in sight:

> I had never encountered a more highly developed sense of place. I was left with the impression that this individual was exactly where he belonged: he could never be lost, for he knew precisely where he was in relation to this rock, that tree, the range of mountains in the distance, the sun and moon and stars. He stood at the very center of Creation. . . . The land, the earth is the foundation of all belief, all wonder, all meaning in the story of human existence.[37]

A Home-front Child at Hobbs (1943–1946)

"It seems to me that half the boys in Hobbs were named Billy."

Momaday, *The Names*[38]

After years of economic depression and hardship, jobs became more plentiful across the nation during World War II. In 1943 the Momadays said their farewells to *Diné bikeyah* and their Navajo friends and headed to southeastern New Mexico. They took up residence in Hobbs, a small town on the flat, dry, often hot plains, called the Staked Plains or *Llano Estacado,* a region very different from Navajo country.

It was wartime, and there were jobs in Hobbs. Momaday's father worked as a draftsman for an oil company and his mother worked in a personnel office and later in the Office of the Provost Marshal at the Hobbs Army Air Base. All minds were on the war effort; every age was affected by the war raging far away. Momaday was in the third grade when he arrived in Hobbs. He often played war games that were popular with all of the boys he knew: "Playing Army was in one way or another a big thing when I was little."[39] During World War II, he became one of the many called "the home-front children."

Billy Don Johnson was his best friend and a steadfast one, with whom Momaday spent much time. He also enjoyed Billy Don's big family, his down-to-earth parents, and all of the activity in their home. Momaday still savors thoughts of the mornings when he would wake up, after staying overnight with the family, to aromas of "bacon and chops, breads and gravy, coffee and cakes."[40] Moviegoing during the war years was a big thing, and Saturday afternoons would find the two buddies at the Reel Theatre.

The family moved closer to the Hobbs Army Air Base, several miles from the town. Momaday's parents gave him a new, shiny bicycle that he rode everywhere, including all around the base. It was a home of the B-17s, the famous Flying Fortresses. Those planes impressed him greatly, and he couldn't quite get over it when they gave way to the B-29s, "a kind of upstaging" in his mind. Getting around and seeing things gave him a sense of the war effort. He also sensed "a kind of patriotic sympathy to those days, the romantic integrity of a cause."[41]

The Teenage Years at Jemez in New Mexico (1946–1951)

"At Jemez I came to the end of my childhood."

Momaday, *The Names*[42]

MOMADAY'S PARENTS' HAD A DREAM. They dreamed of finding teaching positions in the same school. This finally occurred in 1946, when they were offered employment at the Jemez Day School, a two-teacher day school at the Pueblo of Jemez in New Mexico. Shortly before this opportunity arose, Natachee Momaday had taken a teaching position at the Cañoncito Day School, located between Albuquerque and Gallup on the Navajo Reservation. She had gone there on her own because there were no openings available at or close to Hobbs. Momaday and his father, who was still employed in Hobbs, remained behind with hopes of joining her in the coming months.

When his parents accepted positions at the Jemez Day School, Natachee Momaday left Cañoncito for Jemez, while he and his Dad packed their belongings and left Hobbs with a man who had agreed to take them in his truck. The trip was long and grueling; they also got lost and went some distance out of their way. The road to Jemez Pueblo, after leaving the main road at the village of San Ysidro, still five miles from the pueblo, turned into a horse-and-wagon path. Finally arriving at the pueblo late at night, Momaday was thoroughly exhausted and went straight to bed, falling asleep as soon as his head hit the pillow.

It was September 1946. Momaday was twelve years old, and he was embarking upon a most memorable part of his life. When he awoke the following morning he had what may be described as an epiphanic experience: "No expectation could possibly have been equal to the brilliance and exhilaration of that autumn New Mexican morning. Outside I caught my breath on the cold, delicious air of the Jemez Valley, lying out at six thousand feet. Around me were all the colors of the earth that I have ever seen. As I think back to that morning, there comes to my mind a sentence in Isak Dinesen's *Out of Africa*: 'In the highlands you woke up in the morning and thought: Here I am, where I ought to be.'"[43]

Built in 1929, the Jemez Day School was a large pueblo-style building with a stucco exterior and old *vigas* (wood beams). One wall of the building faced south and had large windows, making its two classrooms, each large enough to hold about thirty children, well lighted and inviting. His mother's classroom, the larger of the two, was for kindergarten and first through third grades; his father's was for fourth through sixth grades. Al Momaday also became the school's principal. He handled the administrative duties, organized parent groups, and initiated an arts program that brought widespread recognition to the school and its students. They were assisted by a woman from the pueblo who cleaned the classrooms, supervised the playground, prepared the pupils' noon meals, and sometimes served as an interpreter.

The Momadays' living quarters were on the opposite side of the building and equaled about the size of one classroom. Their quarters comprised a living room, kitchen, two bedrooms, and a bath. A door in the living room opened upon his mother's classroom, and beside the door was the only phone, a wall telephone with two bells and a crank. They shared a party line with the San Diego Mission at the pueblo and the Jemez Trading Post.

Resuming his seventh-grade studies in the mission school at the pueblo, he recalls, "I was in that position of great advantage again, that of being alone among my classmates at home in the English language. From another and more valid point of view, it was a position of disadvantage. I had no real benefit of instruction at the mission school, and consequently I remember very little."[44]

He vividly remembers, however, November 12, 1946, the Feast of San Diego, the patron saint of Jemez Pueblo, when he saw the dance for the first time at the age of twelve. It was a chilly, overcast autumn day filled with the most memorable sights and sounds. In the morning he watched from the windows of the Day School the arrival of people on the old wagon road. He saw a caravan of covered wagons that reached southward as far as the eye could see. After watching for some time, he could no longer contain himself and ventured outside, walking among the corrals and streets of the pueblo to the plaza. He stopped to watch the dancers, "in two long files of meticulous motion, determined as it was by the singing and the drums. It seemed to me that the singers—and especially the old men among them—bore everything up on the strength of their voices, the valley, the mountains, and the gray November sky; that if suddenly they should fall silent, the whole of Creation would collapse in a moment."[45]

On that wonderful day, Momaday had no idea that exactly twenty-six years later, on November 12, 1972, he would travel to Jemez Pueblo with three of his daughters to watch the dance and share the experience with them. It was a cold, cloudy day, like the one long ago. After watching the dance, they entered the house of their host, a boyhood friend of Momaday's, where a large table, laden with many delicious traditional foods, awaited the celebrants. They feasted on chili, posole, roasted venison, loaves of freshly baked bread, fruit pies, and an array of other foods.

When Momaday was thirteen, his parents gave him a horse, a quarter horse, a beautiful strawberry roan with light mane and tail. He named the energetic gelding Pecos. Together, they became as one, a centaur much like his Kiowa ancestors, great horse people called "the centaurs of the Southern Plains." Pecos secured a place for Momaday in his cultural history, a glorious period when the Kiowas belonged to the Horse Culture. They tell stories about horses, including one that has been retold by Momaday, "The Horse That Died of Shame." In this story, the horse died of shame because its owner committed an act of cowardice.

Riding Pecos gave Momaday a more expansive and thrilling view of the world around him:

> I could see more of it, how it reached away beyond all the horizons I had ever seen; and yet it was more concentrated in its appearance, too, and more accessible to my mind, my imagination. My mind loomed upon the farthest edges of the earth, where I could feel the full force of the planet whirling into space. There was nothing of the air and light that was not pure exhilaration, and nothing of time and eternity.

> I could feel my horse under me, rocking at my legs, the bobbing of the reins to my hand; I could feel the sun on my face and the stirring of a little wind at my hair. And through the hard hooves, the slender limbs, the supple shoulders, the fluent back of my horse I felt the earth under me. Everything was under me, buoying me up; I rode across the top of the world.[46]

At times, Billy the Kid would accompany Momaday on his long rides and adventures. He has remarked that they got along well together on those adventures, and it was good to have Billy's help in warding off desperados and other "glory-seeking punks."

Momaday attended a number of schools during his teenage years. After completing the seventh grade at the Jemez Pueblo mission school, he rode a school bus miles away to Santa Fe to attend school. From 1948 to 1951 he attended high schools in Albuquerque and Bernalillo, a small town north of Albuquerque. Because of the distance to Albuquerque, he stayed in a private home with a couple in the city. The woman's grandparents had known Billy the Kid, and she told him fascinating stories that had been told to her.

Commenting about those years, Momaday said: "I seemed to adjust pretty well to those experiences. I went to four different high schools. There were times when I knew that my peers were better prepared than I was, especially in graduate school, because I had such a helter-skelter kind of education growing up. I didn't have any college preparation really until my senior year in high school. I found that my classmates were better prepared than I was, but not so much better prepared that I couldn't catch up."[47]

In January 1973, over twenty-six years after the Momadays arrived at the pueblo and shortly after Momaday's parents resigned from their teaching positions, the Jemez Day School burned to the ground. At that time, Momaday was living in Santa Fe and writing a column in *Viva, Northern New Mexico's Sunday Magazine*, a weekly supplement of *The Santa Fe New Mexican*. In his column of January 14, titled "A Pyre of Moments, Peculiarly Mine," he tells of his visit to the pueblo to see what remained of the school. He found only a charred shell, an empty, forlorn space. The one thing remaining was a remnant of the old brick fireplace that had given so much warmth and cheer to him and to his parents, who had worked in that building for a quarter century. Gone was the second-grade pupil's desk in his mother's classroom where he wrote his first-published poem, "Earth and I Gave You Turquoise," during a break from the University of New Mexico. Gone was the hundred-year-old Seth Thomas clock that "chimed the hours of my growing up." He reminisced that "my most vivid and cherished boyhood memories are centered upon that place. I had wondered what would become of the Day School eventually. . . . It never occurred to me that it might be destroyed by fire. . . . In that place were invested many days of my life, and many of the very best, I believe."[48]

An Early Mentor at Jemez Pueblo—Fray Angélico Chávez

I weave a lariat of words
To catch the Winged Horse,
And with the cry of many birds
It whistles in its course.

But when my song is o'er, I fear
I caught no horse with wings:
For there's no Muse's lyre here—
It is the rope that sings.

"Cantares," a poem by Fray Angélico Chávez[49]

Among the people teenager Scott Momaday met and became friends with at Jemez Pueblo was the poet-priest Fray Angélico Chávez. Born Manuel Ezequiel Chávez (1910–96) in Wagon Mound, New Mexico, Fray Angélico, in addition to being a prolific poet and writer, priest and scholar, was an artist, historian, and archivist. He received his Franciscan habit in 1929 and became the first native New Mexican ordained by the Franciscan Order in 1937. His poetry drew praise from many people, including world-famous poet and critic T. S. Eliot (1888–1965). After reading a poem by Fray Angélico in the magazine *America,* Eliot sent complimentary remarks in a personal letter written in 1958. A special edition of one of his books of poetry, *The Virgin of Port Lligat* (1959), was published upon Eliot's recommendation.[50] Fray Angélico served as a missionary priest in several pueblo parishes and missions, including Jemez Pueblo, where he met a teenager who wanted to become a writer and poet when he grew up.

In addition to his religious duties, Fray Angélico served as the official postmaster at the pueblo, performing his duties in a little building that served as the post office. That was in the early 1950s, as Momaday recalls:

> Fray Angélico became a very important person in my life and the life of my mind. I knew of his work because my mother had some books written by him, and in my mind, he was a famous writer. . . . I became bold enough to go down to the post office and talk to him. I sought him out and asked him about writing. He was always very gracious and answered my questions. He gave me advice that was very important to me at that time. One of the things he said to me that I have always

> remembered was, "Don't be afraid to imitate a writer that you admire. There is nothing wrong with that and if you do it, you will develop your own voice. You will become original." I have always remembered that. He would say such things to me, and we would talk about some of his work. I think I may even have shown him some of my early scribblings, and we would talk about what a poem is. He gave me a lot of encouragement, as well as information and knowledge. I will always be very grateful to him for coming into my life at that point.[51]

Their friendship continued after Momaday went away to school, but as years passed their contact became less frequent. They would see each other again in 1959, when Fray Angélico officiated at the wedding of Scott Momaday and Gaye Mangold at the Church of Cristo Rey in Santa Fe.

A Year in Virginia at Augusta Military Academy (1951–1952)

> "[It] was a very practical decision. I had run out of schools."
>
> **Momaday to Charles Woodard,** *Ancestral Voice*[52]

THE TIME CAME WHEN Momaday's last year of high school was rapidly approaching. After considerable discussion and researching school brochures, he and his parents agreed that he spend his senior year at a school with a strong college preparatory program. They settled on Augusta Military Academy in Fort Defiance, Virginia, located west of Charlottesville and in the verdant Shenandoah Valley.

The day before he left for Virginia, Momaday went on a difficult climb by himself. In his descent from a high, rocky point, he discovered that he was in what seemed to be an impossible and extremely dangerous situation. "I believed then that I would die there. . . . I remember nothing else of that moment. I passed out of my mind, and the next thing I knew I was sitting down on the ground, very cold in the shadows, and looking up at the rock where I had been within an eyelash of eternity. That was a strange thing in my life, and I think of it as the end of an age. I should never again see the world as I saw it on the other side of that moment, in the bright reflection of time lost."[53]

Momaday's attendance at the boys-only military school began in the fall of 1951 on a scholarship. He worked hard throughout the ensuing months. Although he was under much pressure to compete, more than he had ever experienced until then, he recalls the time spent at the academy as a good experience. It brought some order and independence to his life, and he thoroughly enjoyed the strong sense of camaraderie that was also new to him. He later remarked: "The academy had a good educational program, but I think the real preparation had actually come from home. My parents were very creative people, and I got the best of my education from them. But in the superficial ways where one competes for grades and things like that, I wasn't as well prepared as my colleagues."[54]

Momaday received his diploma from the Academy in May 1952. His mother attended the commencement ceremonies. Years later he recalled that day: "I remember that I earned not only a diploma, but something called a 'white page,' as well—a certificate of good conduct. I suppose this is something like an honorable discharge, only rather more rare—like driving on the Hollywood Freeway for a year without suffering so much as a fender bender. It signified that I had no outstanding demerits at the end of the year. This sounds impressive, I know, but it means roughly that, for the sake of honor, I spent an inordinate amount of time policing the kitchen. Thus, within a military context, I graduated 'with honors.'"[55] Augusta Military Academy was one of a number of such academies that closed in later years, a trend during those times across the country.

Graduation at Augusta was Momaday's first formal commencement ceremony, the beginning of commencement exercises that would become an important part of his life in following years, as an undergraduate, a graduate student, and a professional academic. He has traveled countless miles to commencement ceremonies across the nation to address thousands of people. The ceremonies have never ceased to move him. "They seem monumental to me, among the really significant punctuation points in our daily lives. I am genuinely moved by the sight of young men and women, in academic regalia, stepping forward to take their diplomas and degrees. I can't help it; the way most women feel about weddings, I feel about commencements."[56]

In the spring of 1971, N. Scott Momaday and his father received honorary degrees together at Lawrence University in Appleton, Wisconsin. Four years later, in May 1975, two Momadays would appear together again in a commencement ceremony, this time at the University of New Mexico. The son gave the commencement address and his mother received an honorary Doctor of Humane Letters degree. Natachee Scott Momaday was recognized for her accomplishments as an award-winning writer, educator, and artist. At that time Momaday was a professor of English and comparative literature at Stanford University. Completing the circle, the University of New Mexico awarded him an honorary Doctor of Humane Letters degree in 2001.

Other commencements during which Momaday was awarded an honorary degree took place over the years at seventeen universities and colleges in the United States and at Université Blaise Pascal at Clermont-Ferrand in France.

Momaday's Undergraduate Years (1952–1958)

"I started writing seriously at the University of New Mexico."

Momaday, Interview[57]

IN THE FALL OF 1952 Momaday began his undergraduate studies at the University of New Mexico in Albuquerque uncertain about his career goals. After taking a variety of courses and changing majors, he decided to major in political science. He took speech courses because he had been shy about speaking during his earlier school experiences. He became active in debate and oratory, joined the debate team, and earned awards in oratory in his junior and senior years. He also acted in campus theatrical productions, appearing in roles in several plays, including *Death of a Salesman* and *Personal Appearance*.[58] Developing his oral communication skills would prove very useful in the years ahead. After many years of teaching and lecturing, he has remarked, "I am very much at home at the lectern and in all types of venues. Though I have become better at speaking, I am still better at writing my thoughts than speaking them. I can express myself very well if you give me a pad and pencil, but I am pretty good at talking off the cuff, too."[59] He also began writing in earnest and entered a few writing contests.

Political science influenced his thoughts about law. He became interested in a pre-law program and decided to return to Virginia, where he enrolled at the University of Virginia in Charlottesville in 1956. He enjoyed being on the campus and admired the beauty of the architecture, designed by President Thomas Jefferson. While a student there, he attended a lecture given by writer William Faulkner and questioned the author about the types of books he read. The author replied in a haughty manner that he didn't read, a response that was unexpected by Momaday. Still, he admires Faulkner's works, in particular *The Sound and the Fury.*

It soon became apparent to Momaday that the study of law was not for him. He headed home to Jemez Springs, where his parents were living at that time, and resumed his studies at the University of New Mexico. He received a bachelor's degree in political science with minors in English and speech at the 1958 spring commencement.

First Year of Teaching (1958–1959)

"Gladly wolde he lerne, and gladly teche."

Chaucer, *Canterbury Tales*[60]

AFTER HIS GRADUATION from the University of New Mexico, Momaday took a teaching position, his first professional appointment, for the 1958–59 school year, at the Dulce Independent School on the Jicarilla Apache Reservation. Located in northern New Mexico close to the Colorado line and about one hundred miles east of Farmington, Dulce was a remote place with wilderness country surrounding it. Dulce, meaning "sweet" in Spanish, took its name from a sweet-water spring located a few miles from the reservation headquarters and trading post. The area can be especially remote in winter, when large amounts of snow may fall and where the road in and out of the reservation, then unpaved, could be impassable for periods of time. It could also be a profoundly lonely place. The experience, however, helped Momaday learn how to sustain himself in his work. He came to depend upon his solitude in certain ways that he has continued to depend upon since that time.

The New Mexico State Department of Education had recently established a program for the teaching of speech in a number of New Mexico schools that had large American Indian enrollments. Every day of the school week, Momaday taught five classes to seventh, eighth, and ninth graders. He later recalled: "I had a fine rapport with my students, especially my seventh graders, and I became very fond of them, individually and collectively. I believe that they were exceptional as a group, very bright, very much alive to everything. Their sense of humor was truly remarkable. . . . We had some happy times."[61]

Momaday's annual salary was four thousand dollars. It seemed an enormous sum to him at the time. "I was a young bachelor in those days. . . . I reasoned that my expenses would amount to very little, and I believed in the adage that it isn't what you earn that matters; it's what you save. As it turned out, I saved nothing; but I lived well."[62] The well-stocked trading post may have ended up with most of those earnings.

He later wrote about his first year of teaching: "In a sense the year that I spent at Dulce was critical for me. The course of my future life was determined there. I wrote in my spare time, of which there was a good deal, full of peace and quiet; and on the basis of my writing I was admitted to graduate school in California."[63]

The Learning Years at Stanford University (1959–1963)

"Write little and write well."

Professor Yvor Winters's advice to Scott Momaday, graduate student[64]

IN LATE 1958, while teaching at Dulce, Momaday received a letter from Bobby Jack Nelson, a close friend from his undergraduate years who became a writer, published novelist, and adventurer. Nelson included information about a writing fellowship at Stanford University and told Momaday that he was going to apply for it and thought Momaday should apply, too. After thinking it over, he put together a portfolio, filled out the application form, and sent it to Stanford. A few months later, in early 1959, he received word in the mail of his selection from a group of applicants to receive a Wallace Stegner Creative Writing Fellowship, a fellowship in poetry; Momaday was the only one chosen that year. As he recalls, "Earth and I Gave You Turquoise" was among the examples of his poetry and prose that were included in his portfolio. This poem, his first to be published, appeared in the Summer 1959 issue of the *New Mexico Quarterly*, a literary journal published by the University of New Mexico from 1939 to 1969. Momaday's career as a published writer had begun.

In September 1959, Scott Momaday and Gaye Mangold were married in Santa Fe, with Fray Angélico Chávez officiating. They met at the University of New Mexico when both were undergraduate students. Formerly from the Midwest, Gaye graduated with a major in Spanish. They moved to California and quickly settled in. Momaday began his graduate studies with poet-critic Yvor Winters (1900–68), who was his major professor, advisor, and mentor during the graduate years at Stanford. Professor Winters taught the poetry writing course at the university and would become one of the most profound influences on Momaday's writing and professional career. He has frequently remarked that he owes much to Winters for what he knows about poetry.

Winters was considered by some to be a very difficult and cantankerous professor. Poet John Stevens Berry, a graduate fellow in Winters's small poetry-writing workshops at the same time as Momaday, later wrote, "One of three things could have happened: Scott could have broken and run (as some Stanford fellows did); or he could have become another 'Winters poet'; or he could have done what he did: master and gain Winters's fierce classical erudition and incorporate it into his talent."[65]

Momaday, Winters, and Winters's wife, writer-poet Janet Lewis (1899–1998), probably best known for her book *The Wife of Martin Guerre* (1941), became close friends. It was a friendship that continued until the deaths of Winters and Lewis. Momaday once commented that he felt he had known them before. A strong believer in destiny, he believes their meeting was meant to happen. The couple had lived in New Mexico in the Cerrillos and Madrid area south of Santa Fe. Like many others who moved to New Mexico in past decades, they arrived ill, both suffering from tuberculosis. And, like many others, their health was restored in the clear fresh air, comforting sunshine, and restful solitude.

Winters and his wife fell in love with the land and landscape of New Mexico. After spending a few years in a tuberculosis sanatorium, he taught school in Madrid, worked the soil, and planted peach trees, all of which brought him great joy. Both Winters and his wife wrote during their years in the Land of Enchantment. A mutual fondness for this special part of the world was something the couple and Momaday had in common, and it contributed to making their friendship a strong and lasting one.

When they were in California, Momaday visited the couple in their Los Altos home, where he and Winters held long conversations. They were at ease and in a comfortable place where, Momaday remembers, "pedantry had no place and never would, I learned something about English literature, and something about learning itself."[66] Winters gave Momaday loquats and artichokes, typical California produce, from his garden; Momaday, in turn, would bring from the pueblos oven-baked bread and *piki*, the paper-thin bread made with fine blue Indian cornmeal and sage ashes.

In 1984 Momaday wrote an introduction for the exhibition catalog of the collected papers of Yvor Winters and Janet Lewis that became part of the special collections of Stanford University. Recalling memories of his professor and friend, Momaday stated:

> Yvor Winters was a man of intense moral conviction. To this was added a native intelligence that was extraordinary, and a literary perception that was uncanny. He was a man who could hear a poem and visualize its structure simultaneously. And beside this, there was a quiet definitive confidence in him. He knew what he was about. When, as a student, I asked him a question concerning a poem, I did not dare to doubt that his answer was the final word. His knowledge of and sensitivity to poetry were unimpeachable, so it seemed to us who were his students. There were those who suspected tyranny in such an intelligence, who said that he was a dogmatist. They were mistaken. Yvor Winters was not an unreasonable man in any sense. Indeed, he stood in defense of reason the whole of his life.[67]

Winters presented his thoughts and beliefs about poetry in his book *Forms of Discovery* (1967): "Poetry is potentially (and actually, in certain poems) the most intellectual of the arts and the most difficult for the student. It is the finest medium that we have for the exploration and understanding of the complete human experience. . . . Unless we understand the history which produced us, we are determined by that history; we may be determined in any event, but the understanding gives us a chance."[68]

Letters were exchanged with the Winters over the years. Yvor Winters passed away in January 1968, leaving his wife of forty-two years. Sadly, he did not live to see Momaday become a Pulitzer Prize winner the following year. Winters would have been tremendously proud of his former graduate student and close friend.

It was remembered by many that in 1959 he had predicted N. Scott Momaday's success in the world of literature.

Momaday completed his thesis, "The Collected Poems of N. Scott Momaday," in June 1960 and received the Master of Arts degree in creative writing. He continued his graduate work at Stanford on two academic fellowships. In 1962 his poem "The Bear" was awarded the Academy of American Poets Prize, an important award and one of the early honors received for his writing. His doctoral study and research focused on the poetry of Frederick Goddard Tuckerman, a poet who was also a botanist and differed from the transcendentalists by bringing a scientific viewpoint to his writings. Momaday received the Doctor of Philosophy degree in English literature in 1963. His work on the collected poems of Tuckerman was published as *The Complete Poems of Frederick Goddard Tuckerman* by Oxford University Press in 1965. The book's foreword was written by Yvor Winters, who had suggested Tuckerman as the subject for Momaday's doctoral studies.

The UC Santa Barbara Years (1963–1969)

"I think *learning* is the word that should define the university."

Momaday to Charles Woodard[69]

MOMADAY'S FORTY-YEAR academic teaching career began in the fall of 1963 in the position of assistant professor of English at the University of California, Santa Barbara. The university is located in Goleta, rather than Santa Barbara proper, in close proximity to the Pacific Ocean. He taught creative writing and literature courses, and found the classroom at UC Santa Barbara to be "a highly charged and stimulating place."[70] There was also time for writing and other interests. He worked on a novel begun in New Mexico; it would become *House Made of Dawn*, published in 1968. It is a deeply moving story about an American Indian who returns after serving abroad during World War II. He finds that he is unable to resume his life on the reservation or to survive in a brutal urban environment to which he is relocated. His struggle is to recover his voice and cultural identity, and to be whole in being and spirit.

The first of Momaday's numerous published essays appeared in *Ramparts* in 1964, when he was an assistant professor at UC Santa Barbara. This essay is "The Morality of Indian Hating," which he later reprinted in *The Man Made of Words* (1997), adding an afterword because a considerable amount of time had passed since the essay's first printing.

Among the most beautiful locations in California, Santa Barbara was a pleasant place to raise a family. Two of his daughters were born there. Mission

Santa Barbara and the historic adobe buildings of the area were reminiscent of Santa Fe. Momaday later recalled that "Santa Barbara combines the best of both worlds, the mountains and the sea. It is a place of remarkable beauty and tranquil summer days. We had picnics in the back yard . . . or we went to the beach and had it to ourselves, watching the red sun sink into the dark Pacific. And from the headland we watched the migration of whales. I remember the hillsides of bougainvillea and ice plant, the citrus groves—and the day, November 22, 1963, John F. Kennedy was assassinated."[71]

Aho, Momaday's grandmother, passed away in May 1965 and was buried at Rainy Mountain Cemetery. Shortly before her death she took him to see Tai-me, the Sun Dance fetish of the Kiowas, his first viewing of this sacred medicine bundle. Memories of his grandmother working in the arbor and praying in her bedroom and of her deep regard for language filled his mind. Wanting to visit her grave, he headed to Oklahoma in July. It seemed fitting that he retrace "the way" of the Kiowas from the earliest place where they are known to have lived in the northern Rocky Mountains near the headwaters of the Yellowstone River. Their migration took place before 1700, when they headed east out of the mountains, subsequently arriving in sight of the great monolith Tsoai (Rock Tree) and the Black Hills. They had acquired horses and Tai-me along the way and were transforming themselves from forest hunter-gatherers to a Plains buffalo hunting and horse culture. From the Black Hills they continued their migration in a southerly direction, ending at Rainy Mountain, a knoll that rises out of the plains north of the Wichita Mountains.

The journey made by Momaday ended in Rainy Mountain Cemetery at Aho's

Early Spring at Rainy Mountain. *(Photograph by Phyllis S. Morgan)*

Aho's gravestone at Rainy Mountain Cemetery, near Mountain View, Oklahoma, where Momaday ended his journey in 1965 when he retraced the Kiowa migration route. Aho also used the name Florence. (Photograph by Phyllis S. Morgan)

gravestone. Soon after his return to California, he began working in earnest on *The Way to Rainy Mountain*, framing this unique, poetic autobiographical work with two poems, "Headwaters" and "Rainy Mountain Cemetery." It is told in three voices, the ancestral or legendary, the historical, and the personal. That journey, wrote Momaday, is "an evocation of three things in particular: a landscape that is incomparable, a time that is gone forever, and the human spirit, which endures."[72]

In early 1966, Momaday and two colleagues in the UC Santa Barbara Art Department began work on a limited edition containing the stories from the oral tradition of the Kiowas. The stories, told by his father, grandmother, and others, were collected on tape and transcribed by Momaday. The book, titled *The Journey of Tai-me*, was completed in 1967 and is the archetype of *The Way to Rainy Mountain*.

Momaday received a Guggenheim Fellowship for the 1966–67 academic year to study the "poetry of resistance" to American transcendentalism. Among the poets who departed from the Romantic poetry of the nineteenth century were Emily Dickinson (1830–86) and Frederick Goddard Tuckerman (1821–73). On leave from the university, Momaday and his family moved to Amherst, Massachusetts. He did his research there and at Harvard University, where Houghton Library served as his base. A considerable amount of his time was spent reading the poetry of Emily Dickinson, all 1,775 poems, in manuscript. He also read authors contemporary to her.

Upon his return to Santa Barbara in July 1967, Momaday was promoted to associate professor of English and resumed his teaching in the fall term. He completed his first novel, published by Harper & Row in 1968 with the title *House Made of Dawn*. Momaday had no inkling of the events the coming year held for him.

1969—An Eventful Year: The Winning of the Pulitzer Prize and Other Honors

"It is sort of hard to believe—but I am quite elated about it."

Momaday to newspaper writer[73]

MOMADAY'S EDITOR AT Harper & Row was Frances Monson McCullough, a graduate student at Stanford University at the same time as Momaday. She had been a student editor of *Sequoia*, the Stanford literary magazine, and was among the many impressed with his work and scholarship. After graduating, McCullough got her start in publishing in 1962 as a secretary to Blanche Knopf of the respected publishing house Alfred A. Knopf, Inc., in New York City. From Knopf, she moved to Harper & Row, where she became closely associated with poetry and edited a number of poets, including Sylvia Plath, Ted Hughes, and Robert Bly.

McCullough's interest in poets and poetry moved her to contact Momaday about putting together a collection of his poems. He responded that he did not have a collection readily available, but mentioned that he was working on a novel. He had decided to try fiction writing, because having concentrated so thoroughly on poetry at Stanford, he felt he needed some "elbow room," a break from a single, intense focus. Since McCullough was also involved in editing American fiction, she asked to see his novel. He mailed what he had in good form. After examining it, she told him that she was definitely interested and encouraged him to keep working on it. *House Made of Dawn* was the first book McCullough edited entirely on her own. Published in 1968, it won the Pulitzer Prize for Fiction in May 1969.

Momaday learned about his winning the Pulitzer Prize in a phone call received at his home in the early afternoon of May 5. When McCullough gave him the good news, he responded, "Are you kidding?"[74] The news came as a complete surprise; his first thought was that she was playing a joke. He had no idea that his book was even being considered. When an interviewer asked whether his mother was the first person he called, especially since he had told her when he was a young boy that he would win the Pulitzer Prize, Momaday replied that he couldn't remember. She was, however, among the first, and she was as surprised as he was over the unexpected news. Together, his proud parents made a congratulatory phone call to him that evening.

Almost immediately after receiving the news from his editor, Momaday began receiving calls from the *New York Times*, the *Los Angeles Times*, newspapers in New Mexico and across the country, news services, radio and television stations, magazines, and other news organizations. There were calls asking him for interviews and speaking engagements. There were also receptions, dinners, readings, book signings, and a variety of other events. He virtually ceased working for a time.

The first news item in the "Current" section of the May 19, 1969, issue of *Publishers Weekly* announced: "'Momaday' is a name derived from a Kiowa Indian word that means 'sky walker.' That's not a bad description these days for the thirty-five-year-old Indian author who with his first novel, 'House Made of Dawn' (*Harper & Row*) just won the Pulitzer Prize in fiction."[75] The novel had been favorably reviewed by *Publishers Weekly* a year earlier in its April 1, 1968, issue.

Momaday was named Outstanding Indian of the Year at the American Indian Exposition in Oklahoma and inducted into the Kiowa Gourd Dance Society, an honor of great significance, since his father and grandfather were members of this society. He also received the Zimmerman Award, the highest award given to alumni by the University of New Mexico.

Two days after the announcement about the winning of the Pulitzer Prize, a news release was distributed by the Office of Public Information of the University of California at Berkeley: "N. Scott Momaday, the American Indian novelist who this week was awarded the Pulitzer Prize for fiction, will join the faculty at the Berkeley campus this fall. . . . He will hold the title of associate professor of English and comparative literature."[76]

The UC Berkeley Years (1969–1972)

"Momaday will begin a new course on American Indian mythology this spring."[77]

From "Man of Two Worlds," *California Monthly*

In September 1969 Momaday transferred to UC Berkeley, one of the nation's leading public universities, known for its strong academic programs. The 1960s had been a time of ferment at UC Berkeley, a campus where movements of a political, social, artistic, or philosophical nature were common. Momaday felt that constructive things would result from the activities of those years and was glad to be on the campus as a new decade approached. The family moved to Kensington, a residential area near the campus. His teaching schedule included creative writing courses in the Department of English and courses in American literature in the Department of Comparative Literature.

In the spring of 1970, a new course, "American Indian Mythology, Legend, and Lore: An Idea of Oral Tradition and Literature," was introduced by Momaday. He considered this course to be "the basis of a unique center for collecting and studying Indian lore in comparative literature."[78] The program, sometimes referred to as the Berkeley Project, would encompass courses in American Indian languages and the study and preservation of indigenous languages. Students and research assistants would be recruited from various locations, including the American Southwest, to do the fieldwork, travel to reservations, and record oral traditions. The experience he had gained in this type of fieldwork led to his interest in establishing such a program. It would be incorporated into the Department of Comparative Literature rather than an ethnic studies program that was also being planned at the university. Another new course in 1970 was "Navajo Language and Literature," developed and taught by Momaday, in which he introduced the structure and elements of the language.

Momaday was promoted to a full professorship at UC Berkeley in the 1970–71 academic year. At the end of June 1972, he resigned from his tenured position after accepting an appointment as professor of English and comparative literature at Stanford University. According to an article in the *San Francisco Examiner*, Momaday had been hired away from UC Berkeley.

It was during this period of time that Scott and Gaye Momaday separated. Their marriage ended in divorce in 1973. His daughters resided in Santa Fe with their mother.

A Visiting Professor at New Mexico State University (1972–1973)

"[The class] is large, expectant, intent upon the quality of its own attention."

Momaday on the first day of class at NMSU.[79]

Momaday's new appointment at Stanford was scheduled to begin in the fall quarter of 1973. This left the 1972–73 academic year open for him. An invitation was received and accepted to be the first Visiting Distinguished Professor of Humanities at New Mexico State University (NMSU), located in southern New Mexico at Las Cruces. He was not as familiar with the southern part of the state as he was with the northern and central parts and looked forward to his association with the university.

Assigned to the English Department at NMSU for the academic year, Momaday taught, among other courses, one titled "Oral Tradition and American Literature." This course, with varying names, became what he referred to as his "standard," and he taught it every year throughout his academic career. In a newspaper article announcing his new appointment, Momaday explained the course: "I try to focus upon the relationship between oral and written traditions and to indicate respective attitudes toward language and the function of story telling."[80]

During this period, Momaday also concentrated on his writing projects, including weekly essays for his column in *Viva: Northern New Mexico's Sunday Magazine*, a supplement of the *Santa Fe New Mexican*, the American West's oldest continuously published newspaper. In one of his columns written while he was at NMSU, he told about heading out early one weekend morning on his bicycle with the first light of dawn showing behind the fluted peaks of the Organ Mountains to the east.[81] He relished the clear, cool autumn air as he pedaled through Las Cruces and the lush agricultural area of Mesilla Valley, ending at the plaza of old Mesilla, an historic town southwest of Las Cruces. As he reached the plaza, the bells of the church began to ring. He parked his bike outside the church and attended Mass. Afterwards, he walked around the old town and stopped on the corner of the plaza where Billy the Kid had been incarcerated, tried, and sentenced. That was in April 1881. Billy was shot and killed by Sheriff Pat Garrett three months later. Momaday's thoughts turned to his "strange and true life with Billy the Kid" and their adventures on horseback at Jemez.

Academic Years at Stanford University and Abroad (1973–1981)

"It feels like coming home. I sort of identify with Stanford."

Momaday to campus reporter.[82]

TEN EVENTFUL YEARS had passed since Momaday's graduation from Stanford. He was returning to his alma mater as a professor. A news release announced that he would be teaching courses in American literature, American Indian literature, and creative writing. Once the fall quarter was underway, he told a campus reporter: "I like the physical place and I like the department; though it was a different department when I was a student."[83]

A Stanford University news release appeared in early October 1973 with the headline, "Scott Momaday's Course Attracts 200." It stated: "Stanford's newest professor of English, Scott Momaday, gives his scholarly field new meaning when he talks about 'American literature.' In addition to teaching and enjoying such stalwarts of the tradition as poets Emily Dickinson and Wallace Stevens, Momaday is involved in studying and teaching the oral literature of Native Americans."[84]

His course was "American Indian Mythology, Legend, and Lore." In the early 1970s, an enrollment of over two hundred students in one course was a large class, particularly at a private university such as Stanford, as compared to some class numbers today. That number of students impressed those who initially thought such a course would not receive much interest because it seemed "esoteric." The events of the 1960s, however, had created significant interest in Native American subjects, particularly among younger people. They were also aware that the course would be taught by a Pulitzer Prize winner who was becoming a prominent figure in American literature.

One of the texts used in this course was Momaday's *The Way to Rainy Mountain*. He explained to the campus reporter that "the tales told in it reflect an attitude about the importance of language, an extraordinary belief in the efficacy of language."[85] Another course developed by him, "The Landscape in American Literature," also became very popular. In addition to his teaching, he continued his writing, including working on an autobiographical narrative that would be published three years later, in 1976, with the title, *The Names: A Memoir.* Two books were published in 1974; these were his first poetry collection, *Angle of Geese and Other Poems*, and a beautiful collaborative volume, *Colorado: Summer, Fall, Winter, Spring*, with famous photographer David Muench.

In the spring of 1974, Momaday took a leave from Stanford to travel to Russia and teach as a visiting professor of twentieth-century American literature at the State University of Moscow, also referred to as the University of Moscow. The university has long been considered a prestige institution, equivalent to Harvard or Stanford in the United States. Russia was part of the Soviet Union at that time. U.S.-USSR exchange programs were most unusual during the era of the Cold War. Momaday and another professor were selected by a committee of scholars and the U.S. Department of State. This program became part of the Fulbright-Hays exchange programs.

Momaday did not know what to expect upon his arrival, but soon learned that about one hundred graduate students, many of whom were writing graduate papers and theses about American literature, had signed up for his course. He also discovered that they spoke English well and found them "very bright and industrious and tense."[86] They were highly competitive because they were vying for a very small number of university teaching positions. He told a writer for the *Washington Post* that his students had "a degree of sophistication equal to [his] American students" and that they were "almost as familiar" with the authors he was teaching, among them John Steinbeck, William Faulkner, and Ernest

Hemingway. In terms of their knowledge about post–World War II poets, such as Sylvia Plath, Allen Ginsberg, and Robert Lowell, Momaday stated: "They were aware of the names, at least. I don't think any of this [literature] was completely strange to them. They asked intelligent questions about these writers, usually questions which indicated a certain knowledge of the work."[87]

Momaday lectured once a week and consulted with his students on an individual basis throughout the term, answering a broad range of questions about American literature specifically and America in general. During this experience, he made several lasting friendships. A Russian student working on a thesis about American Indian literature met Momaday at the Moscow airport. The greeter was Alexander Vaschenko, who wrote the first dissertation on American Indian literature at the University of Moscow and became a respected scholar and author of works about American literature, American Indian and Chicano literatures in particular. They have kept in touch since that first meeting.

Having a great deal of time to himself, Momaday filled it with writing poetry and prose—and drawing. This was the beginning of his serious interest in visual expression. In the preface to *In the Presence of the Sun: Stories and Poems, 1961–1991* (1992), he remarked about this time of intense activity: "Something about this time and place made for a surge in me, a kind of creative explosion. I wrote numerous poems, some on the landscapes of my native Southwest, urged, I believe, by an acute homesickness. And I began to sketch."[88] After he returned to the Stanford campus, he audited a course in drawing and studied with a professional artist. The urge to become a visual artist was real.

An excellent example of this "creative explosion" is "The Colors of Night," a sequence of eight poetic stories, or prose poems, which he described as "quintessential novels, concentrated stories of time, place, and presence."[89] He wanted to bring together all of the colors of the night to present the mythical world view of the Native American. This prose poem was printed in a limited edition in 1976. Another poem, "Abstract: Old Woman in a Room," was dedicated to Olga Sergeevna Akhmanova, a respected poet and head of the English Department at the University of Moscow. Akhmanova and Momaday had many conversations about Russia and its people, their academic subjects, and their writing. A number of poems written in Russia were published in 1976 in his second poetry collection, *The Gourd Dancer.*

In 1977 Momaday made a lecture tour of Europe for the U.S. Department of State, speaking in France, Germany (West Germany at this time), Ireland, Finland, and the Black Sea region. He lectured as a visiting professor at the University of Regensburg in Germany. It was at that university where he first met Regina Heitzer. They were married in Regensburg in July 1978. One daughter, named Lore, was born in 1980. Their marriage ended in divorce.

In early 1981, in an interview in Santa Fe for the *Navajo Times*, Momaday confided to the reporter: "My parents still live at Jemez and I would like to live near them. I've been teaching at Stanford a long time. . . . I'd like a job closer to home."[90] Shortly after making that statement, Momaday resigned from his tenured professorship at Stanford and accepted an academic appointment as professor of English at the University of Arizona in Tucson.

The Academic Years in Arizona (1981–2005)

"It took longer to drive to the airport in Albuquerque than it did to fly to Tucson."

Momaday on commuting to teach at the University of Arizona.[91]

AFTER MOMADAY'S APPOINTMENT to the University of Arizona was announced, an article appeared in the *Navajo Times* in which Vine Deloria, Jr., scholar and author, made the following statement: "His [Momaday's] addition completes the greatest concentration of top American Indian scholars assembled at a single university."[92] At that time, Deloria was a professor in the political science department and was also serving as the director of the American Indian Studies program, which did not have its own director until 1991.

The head of the English Department, Dr. Edgar A. Dryden, told the *Navajo Times* that "Momaday's hiring placed the University of Arizona into the nation's forefront of American Indian Studies and American literature."[93] It was announced that Momaday would teach a graduate course in American Indian oral literature and an undergraduate course in the literature of the West. In August 1981 he joined the Literature Program of the Department of English, which remained his home program and department throughout his tenure to the time of his retirement as Regents Professor of English in 2005. He held a joint appointment with the American Indian Studies program and almost all of the courses he taught were cross-listed with that program.[94]

The change from the lush green environment and Mediterranean climate of the Stanford area to the hot, dry, Sonoran Desert environment of Tucson and the University of Arizona, the "Great Desert University," signaled that he was returning to the Southwest. Although Momaday has lived in a number of different places in the United States and abroad, he has always thought of himself as being a native of the Southwest, especially since it is where he spent most of his formative years. His residence on aptly named Roller Coaster Road, north and west of the university, had views of mountains, spectacular sunsets, and a myriad of wildlife visitors from coyotes to roadrunners and quail—and the occasional rattlesnake. It was a pleasant place for writing and imagining.

During the summers of 1986 and 1987, twenty years after he retraced the Kiowa migration route to Oklahoma, Momaday traveled over parts of the route again. This time he was accompanied by Charles L. Woodard, an English professor at South Dakota State University who wrote his doctoral dissertation on Momaday's writings. They met for lengthy conversations in several cities in 1986 and took a leisurely journey over parts of the ancestral migration route in 1987, with a stop at the sacred Bighorn Medicine Wheel in northern Wyoming. Their six conversations were published in Woodard's *Ancestral Voice: Conversations with N. Scott Momaday* by the University of Nebraska Press in 1989. This book helps one to gain a deeper understanding of the importance for Momaday of remembering ancestors, earth, and traditions.

Momaday believes there is great value in looking into the past. Individuals can understand themselves much more completely, he believes, if they have a sense of their heritage. He also believes that people today are not sufficiently concerned with the past: "We live in a world in which the immediate emphasis is placed upon the immediate present and so much concentration is placed upon the present, while the past and future are ignored. When we lose sight of the past, the loss is significant."[95] That loss is even more acute for those whose cultures and languages are in danger of being lost. It is true that there are many people who take their own backgrounds for granted. To Momaday, that is a sad, unfortunate situation.

Momaday accepted an invitation in 1989 to be a visiting scholar at the School of American Research (SAR), described by him as an anthropological think tank. His experience at SAR, located in a quiet residential area of Santa Fe, was a pleasant one. During his time there, he commuted to Tucson to teach one day a week, while at SAR he participated in dialogue with other scholars and provided input in group discussions. His second novel, *The Ancient Child: A Novel*, had been released by the publisher earlier in 1989. At SAR he worked on compiling a collection of new poems and previously published writings, issued in 1992 with the title *In the Presence of the Sun: Stories and Poems, 1961–1991*, and entirely illustrated by him. In 2007 the School of American Research became the School for Advanced Research on the Human Experience. Momaday has served on the SAR board of trustees and continues to serve as one of its Senior Scholars.

The 1990s were full of activity: teaching; speaking; attending conferences and symposiums; traveling; and writing books, essays, stories, poems, plays, reviews, and more. His playwriting received increasing attention, in particular his stage play *The Indolent Boys*, first presented in a staged reading in 1992 and in its world premiere in 1994. Books published during this period were *In the Presence of the Sun: A Gathering of Shields* (1991), a limited edition of stories and drawings of

Plains Indian shields, which are among his most important subjects to write about and paint; *In the Presence of the Sun: Stories and Poems, 1961–1991* (1992); *Circle of Wonder: A Native American Christmas Story* (1993), his first children's book with full-color illustrations by him; a collection of his writings, *The Man Made of Words: Essays, Stories, Passages* (1997); and writings about bears and Bear (always with a capital B) in a colorful book, *In the Bear's House* (1999).

In 1998 Momaday came home to New Mexico, continuing to commute to the University of Arizona to teach one day a week. He came home to live in Stonehenge, the 130-year-old house in Jemez Springs purchased by his parents in 1959 and inherited by him after his mother's death. He described this old house, called the Benevides house in *House Made of Dawn*, in a letter written in 1959 to longtime friend Barbara Glenn, as "large, old and rickety, just the thing for my writing."[96] With thick adobe walls and impressive lava-rock fireplaces, it exudes a personality all its own, a strong, solid, silent witness to passing history. Some restoration has been carried out as time permitted; and outside, an open, kiva-like structure was constructed with native rock and aligned to the sun and moon.

In June 2002 Scott Momaday married Barbara Gregg Glenn, a friend since before his days at Stanford. A poet and writer, she was a graduate student in English and held a Wallace Stegner Fellowship in poetry at Stanford in the mid-1970s. She also became an attorney and was her husband's literary representative. Dividing their time between homes in Jemez Springs and Santa Fe, they considered themselves residents of New Mexico, although much of their time was spent in traveling far from home. Like his Kiowa ancestors, Momaday has always enjoyed being in motion, traveling here and there, and recalling the journeys made. He has traveled and lectured extensively in the United States, having been to all of the fifty states and spoken at least once in each, many times in others. His travels have taken him across North America and the Arctic region, throughout Europe, across Russia to Siberia, to Tibet and other parts of Asia, and to places in Australia and Latin America. A frequent destination is France, where Momaday's works are part of a required national graduate degree curricula.

A National Medal of Arts Recipient Leads an Eventful Post-Academic Life (2005–)

Momaday officially retired from the University of Arizona in the spring of 2005 with the title of Regents Professor Emeritus. Numerous activities and projects have kept Momaday very occupied. Among those is the advancement of the goals of The Buffalo Trust, a nonprofit foundation established by him in

1998 to work with indigenous peoples in the United States and around the world to preserve their cultures, oral history, and archival records. He serves as the Trust's director and chairman. Also, he was named Artist for Peace by UNESCO in 2003 and has been engaged in collaborative projects benefiting indigenous communities around the world.

Since his retirement from the University of Arizona, Momaday has had two books published, both in Oklahoma. The first, *Four Arrows & Magpie,* a children's book, was published in 2006 by the HAWK Publishing Group of Tulsa. It was one of three books published commemorating Oklahoma's one hundredth birthday. The second, his first book of plays, is *Three Plays: The Indolent Boys, Children of the Sun, and The Moon in Two Windows,* published by the University of Oklahoma Press in 2007.

Illness caused Scott and Barbara Momaday to move to Oklahoma City in mid-2006 in order to be close to medical specialists. Following heart surgery and recuperation, Momaday has kept a nearly full schedule of work and activities that includes being inducted into the Oklahoma Writers Hall of Fame in 2007, serving in his appointment as the Oklahoma Centennial Poet Laureate during 2007 and 2008, and being named the Poet Laureate of the Kiowa in 2008. He received honorary degrees from the University of Minnesota and the University of Illinois, Chicago, in 2009.

Barbara Glenn Momaday passed away in Oklahoma City on September 20, 2008, after a courageous battle with cancer. In November 2007 Barbara and Scott traveled to Washington, D.C., for a joyous event. Scott received the National Medal of Arts, the nation's highest honor for artistic excellence, in a ceremony presided over by President George W. Bush and First Lady Laura Bush in the East Room of the White House. The award citation reads:

> To N. Scott Momaday for his writings and his work that celebrate and preserve Native American art and oral tradition. He has introduced millions worldwide to the essence of Native American culture.

N. Scott Momaday's legacy reaches far beyond regional and national boundaries. His works, in all their many forms, and his other endeavors have had, and will continue to have, universal significance. His voice is for all peoples, all places, and all times.

Notes

1. N. Scott Momaday, Interview, February 25, 1981, in *Master Class: Lessons from Leading Writers*, by Nancy Bunge (Iowa City: University of Iowa Press, 2005), 52.

2. Momaday, *The Names: A Memoir* (New York: Harper & Row, 1976), 42.

3. Ibid., 56–57.

4. Ibid., 57.

5. Momaday, "The Man Made of Words" (address), *Indian Voices: The First Convocation of American Indian Scholars*, ed. Rupert Castro (San Francisco: Indian Historian Press, 1970), 60.

6. Roger Matuz, ed., *St. James Guide to Native North American Artists* (Detroit: St. James Press, 1998), 384–85.

7. Momaday, *The Names*, 25.

8. Interview with N. Scott Momaday, January 24, 2006.

9. Momaday, *The Gourd Dancer* (New York: Harper & Row, 1976), 35.

10. Ibid., 37.

11. Momaday, *The Way to Rainy Mountain* (Albuquerque: University of New Mexico Press, 1969), 6.

12. Interview with N. Scott Momaday, January 24, 2006.

13. Steven M. Schnell, "The Kiowa Homeland in Oklahoma," *Homelands: A Geography of Culture and Place across America*, eds. Richard L. Nostrand and Lawrence Estaville (Baltimore: John Hopkins University Press, 2001), 142.

14. Ibid., 143.

15. Interview with N. Scott Momaday, January 24, 2006.

16–32. Ibid.

33. Momaday, *The Names*, 61.

34. Momaday, "Going into Navajo Land," *Viva: Northern New Mexico's Sunday Magazine, Santa Fe New Mexican*, October 22, 1972, 2.

35. Ibid.

36. Ibid.

37. Trudy Griffin-Pierce, *Earth Is My Mother, Sky Is My Father* (Albuquerque: University of New Mexico Press, 1995), xvi.

38. Momaday, *The Names*, 85.

39. Interview with N. Scott Momaday, January 24, 2006.

40. Momaday, *The Names*, 87.

41. Ibid., 83.

42. Ibid., 160.

43. Ibid., 121.

44. Ibid., 127.

45. Momaday, *Viva, Santa Fe New Mexican*, November 19, 1972, 2.

46. Momaday, *The Names*, 155–56.

47. Interview with N. Scott Momaday, January 24, 2006.

48. Momaday, *Viva, Santa Fe New Mexican*, January 14, 1973, 2.

49. Fray Angélico Chávez, "Cantares," *Cantares: Canticles and Poems of Youth, 1925–1932*, edited by Nasario García (Houston: Arte Público Press, 2000), 3.

50. Phyllis S. Morgan, *Fray Angelico Chavez: A Bibliography of His Published Writings, 1925–1978* (Santa Fe, New Mexico: The Lightning Tree, 1980), 15.

51. Interview with N. Scott Momaday, January 24, 2006.

52. Charles L. Woodard, *Ancestral Voice: Conversations with N. Scott Momaday* (Lincoln: University of Nebraska Press, 1989), 9.

53. Momaday, *The Names*, 161.

54. Interview with N. Scott Momaday, January 24, 2006.

55. Momaday, *Viva, Santa Fe New Mexican*, June 10, 1973, 2.

56. Ibid., 57.

57. Woodard, *Ancestral Voice*, 200.

58. "Momaday Wins Poetry Fellowship," *Albuquerque Journal*, May 17, 1959, 10.

59. Interview with N. Scott Momaday, January 24, 2006.

60. Geoffrey Chaucer, *The Canterbury Tales*, in *Bartlett's Familiar Quotations*, 17th ed. (Boston: Little, Brown, 2002), 308.

61. Momaday, "A Crucial Year in Dulce. . . ." *Viva, Santa Fe New Mexican*, February 18, 1973, 3.

62. Ibid.

63. Ibid.

64. Chris Tucker, "Scott Momaday, Writing Little But Writing Well," *Dallas Morning News*, November 8, 1981.

65. John Stevens Berry, "Brilliant Son of the Kiowas: N. Scott Momaday," *Lincoln* (Nebraska) *Sunday Journal-Star*, March 16, 1986, H15.

66. Momaday, "The Man Who Took Literature Seriously," *Viva, Santa Fe New Mexican*, September 2, 1973, 8.
67. Momaday, "Introduction," *The Strength of Art: Poets and Poetry in the Lives of Yvor Winters and Janet Lewis*, by Brigitte Hoy Carnochan (Stanford, California: Stanford University Libraries, 1984), 7.
68. Ibid.
69. Woodard, *Ancestral Voice*, 200.
70. Interview with N. Scott Momaday, January 24, 2006.
71. Momaday, "Life in Three Wonderful Cities," *Viva, Santa Fe New Mexican*, March 25, 1973, 2.
72. Momaday, "Prologue," *The Way to Rainy Mountain*, 4.
73. Howard Bryan, "'Hard to Believe' Says Momaday after Winning a Pulitzer Prize," *Albuquerque Tribune*, May 6, 1969, A7.
74. Eloise Dungan, "It's a Year of 'Firsts' for Author Scott Momaday," *California Living, San Francisco Sunday Examiner and Chronicle*, Week of September 21, 1969, 6–7, 9.
75. "Currents," *Publishers Weekly*, May 19, 1969, 25.
76. News Release, Office of Public Information, University of California, Berkeley, May 7, 1969.
77. "Man of Two Worlds: A Profile of N. Scott Momaday," *California Monthly*, February 1970, 23.
78. Ibid.
79. Momaday, "Reflections on the First Day of Class," *Viva, Santa Fe New Mexican*, September 10, 1972, 2.
80. "Dr. N. Scott Momaday Named Visiting Professor for NMSU," *Albuquerque Journal*, April 27, 1972, B12.
81. Momaday, "So Crisply Autumn," *Viva, Santa Fe New Mexican*, October 8, 1972, 2.
82. *Campus Report*, Stanford University, October 10, 1973.
83. Ibid.
84. News Release, Stanford University News Service, October 9, 1973.
85. Ibid.
86. Woodard, *Ancestral Voice*, 43.
87. Robert Joffee, "American Lit, Soviet Style," *Washington Post*, December 7, 1974.
88. Momaday, *In the Presence of the Sun: Stories and Poems, 1961–1991* (New York: St. Martin's Press, 1992), xx.

89. Matthias Schubnell, *N. Scott Momaday: The Cultural and Literary Background* (Norman: University of Oklahoma Press, 1985), 233.

90. Trisha Stanton Clayton, “Momaday on Art and Philosophy,” *Navajo Times*, February 12, 1981.

91. Interview with N. Scott Momaday, January 24, 2006.

92. “Momaday Joins U of A Faculty,” *Navajo Times*, March 26, 1981.

93. Ibid.

94. Lawrence Evers, e-mail to Phyllis S. Morgan, March 6, 2008.

95. Momaday, “A Vision Beyond Time and Place,” *Life*, July 2, 1971, 67.

96. Ruth Lopez, “Write of Springs,” *Pasatiempo, Santa Fe New Mexican*, February 26–March 4, 1999, 32.

N. Scott Momaday Chronology

Compiled by Phyllis S. Morgan

1934

Navarre Scott Momaday is born on Tuesday, February 27, to Alfred Morris (Al) Momaday (February 13, 1913–November 11, 1981) and Mayme Natachee Scott Momaday (February 13, 1913–September 26, 1996) at the Kiowa-Comanche Indian Hospital in Lawton, Oklahoma. During the summer, at the age of six months, Scott is taken by his parents to Devils Tower in eastern Wyoming and is given the Kiowa name Tsoai-talee (Rock Tree Boy) by Kiowa storyteller Pohd-lohk.

1935

The family lives at Momaday's paternal grandmother's farm near Mountain View, Oklahoma, on the Kiowa Reservation.

1936–43

The family moves from Oklahoma to Gallup, New Mexico, in 1936. Scott lives with his parents, who worked for the Indian Service. They also live at Shiprock, New Mexico, and at Tuba City and Chinle in Arizona, all located on the Navajo Reservation. For a short period, his mother and he stay at the San Carlos Apache Reservation in Arizona.

1943

The family moves to Hobbs in eastern New Mexico, where his parents are employed in wartime jobs.

1946

The family moves to Jemez Pueblo, New Mexico, where his parents taught at the Jemez Day School for twenty-five years. Scott attends the Franciscan Mission School at Jemez.

1947

Attends Leah Harvey Junior High School in Santa Fe, New Mexico.

1948–51

Attends Our Lady of Sorrow School in Bernalillo, New Mexico; St. Mary's in Albuquerque; and Bernalillo Public High School.

1951–52

Completes his senior year and graduates with honors from the Augusta Military Academy at Fort Defiance, Virginia, where he received an Alden J. Blethan Memorial Scholarship.

1952–56

Enters undergraduate studies at the University of New Mexico in Albuquerque, majoring in political science with minors in English and speech. Leaves in 1956 to enter the pre-law program of the University of Virginia at Charlottesville, but returns to UNM in 1957.

1957–58

Completes undergraduate work and graduates from the University of New Mexico with a Bachelor of Arts degree in political science.

1958–59

Teaches English, writing, and speech to junior and senior high students at the Dulce, New Mexico, Independent School on the Jicarilla Apache Reservation.

1959

Momaday's first published poem, "Earth and I Gave You Turquoise," is published in the Summer 1959 issue of the *New Mexico Quarterly.*

Receives word that he is the recipient of the Wallace Stegner Creative Writing Fellowship in poetry at Stanford University in California.

Marries Gaye Mangold in September. His early mentor and friend, Fray Angélico Chávez, officiated. The couple moves to California. They have three daughters, Cael, Jill, and Brit. The marriage ends in divorce in 1973.

1959–60

Works on graduate studies in English at Stanford University. His major advisor is poet-critic Yvor Winters.

Receives the Master of Arts degree in creative writing at Stanford in June 1960. His thesis title is "The Collected Poems of N. Scott Momaday."

1961

Continues graduate studies toward a doctoral degree at Stanford. Presents an original poem, "Cocoon," written for the annual Phi Beta Kappa Dinner held on campus.

1962

Receives a John Hay Whitney Foundation Opportunity Fellowship for the 1962–63 academic year and a Stanford Wilson Dissertation Fellowship.

Receives the Academy of American Poets Prize for his poem "The Bear."

1963

A short story titled "The Well" is published in the May issue of *Ramparts*.

Earns the Doctor of Philosophy degree in English literature from Stanford University. The title of his dissertation is "An Edition of the Collected Poems of Frederick Goddard Tuckerman."

Begins his forty-year distinguished academic teaching career in the position of assistant professor of English at the University of California, Santa Barbara, in the fall term.

1964

Essay "The Morality of Indian Hating" is published. Writes poetry and fiction in addition to teaching at UC Santa Barbara.

1965

Momaday's paternal grandmother, Aho, passes away in Oklahoma in May. In July he retraces the Kiowa migration route, ending at her gravestone in Rainy Mountain Cemetery. Works on taping and transcribing Kiowa legends and stories from the oral tradition.

The Complete Poems of Frederick Goddard Tuckerman, his first book, edited by him and based on his research and writing at Stanford, is published by Oxford University Press. Yvor Winters contributes the foreword.

Receives a Guggenheim Fellowship for the 1966–67 academic year. Takes a leave of absence from UC Santa Barbara and moves to Amherst, Massachusetts.

1966–1967

Studies Emily Dickinson's poetry and transcendental literature at Amherst and at Harvard University in Cambridge. Devotes the major part of his time to reading Dickinson in manuscript. Returns to Santa Barbara in 1967 to resume teaching.

Receives an appointment for the academic year to the Humanities Institute from the Regents of the University of California, which provides financial support for research.

1967

The Journey of Tai-me, a fine hand-printed, limited edition, is privately printed at UC Santa Barbara in collaboration with Bruce S. McCurdy, printmaker, and D. E. Carlsen, typographer.

Promoted to associate professor of English at UC Santa Barbara.

1968

House Made of Dawn, his first novel, is published by Harper & Row in New York City.

Receives the Helene Wurlitzer Foundation of New Mexico fiction award for "Two Sketches from *House Made of Dawn*," published in the Summer 1967 issue of the *New Mexico Quarterly.*

1969

House Made of Dawn wins the Pulitzer Prize for Fiction. Momaday becomes the first American Indian awarded a Pulitzer Prize since its inception in 1917.

The Way to Rainy Mountain is published by the University of New Mexico Press.

Named Outstanding Indian of the Year at the American Indian Exposition held at Anadarko, Oklahoma.

Inducted into the Gourd Dance Society (Taimpe Society), one of the oldest Kiowa societies, which meets annually at Carnegie, Oklahoma.

Receives the Zimmerman Award, the highest award presented to alumni by the University of New Mexico.

Transfers from UC Santa Barbara in mid-1969 to assume the position of associate professor of English and comparative literature at the University of California, Berkeley.

1970

Presents his most acclaimed address, "The Man Made of Words," at the First Convocation of American Indian Scholars, convened by the American Indian Historical Society of Princeton University. It was published later that year by the Indian Historian Press.

Introduces a new course, "American Indian Mythology, Legend, and Lore: An Idea of Oral Tradition and Literature," in the winter 1970 term at UC Berkeley. This course about Native American oral tradition is taught by Momaday every year throughout his academic teaching career.

Promoted to full professor of English and comparative literature effective at the beginning of the 1970–71 academic year and receives another appointment to the Humanities Institute from the Regents of the University of California.

Studies the Navajo language in an intensive summer program at University of New Mexico, Gallup.

Writes a movie script based on the classic novel, *The Man Who Killed the Deer*, by Frank Waters.

Collaborates with composer Louis W. Ballard on an opera with contemporary American Indian themes that is partly based on *The Way to Rainy Mountain*.

Receives an honorary Doctor of Humane Letters degree from Central Michigan University, Mount Pleasant.

1971

Introduces and teaches a new course, "Navajo Language and Literature," in the comparative literature program at UC Berkeley with a primary goal of conserving legends and folklore.

Writes essay, "The American Land Ethic," which draws attention to the tradition of respect for nature practiced by Native Americans and the importance of this tradition to modern American society.

Receives a National Institute of Arts and Letters grant.

Begins a thirty-year role as a consultant to the National Endowment for the Arts and the National Endowment for the Humanities.

Momaday and his father receive honorary degrees from Lawrence University, Appleton, Wisconsin.

1972

Resigns from the University of California and leaves UC Berkeley in June. Accepts an academic professorship at Stanford University to begin in 1973.

Accepts an invitation to lecture during the 1972–73 academic year as the first Visiting Distinguished Professor of the Humanities at New Mexico State University in Las Cruces.

Co-writes with Richardson Morse the screenplay for a film version of *House Made of Dawn*, directed and produced by Morse and Firebird Films.

Begins a weekly column appearing under his name in the April 16, 1972, issue of *Viva, Northern New Mexico's Sunday Magazine*, a weekly supplement of the *Santa Fe New Mexican*. The column runs through the December 9, 1973, issue.

Addresses the International Congress of Learned Societies in the Field of Religion, held in Los Angeles, drawing upon his 1970 speech "The Man Made of Words."

1973

Colorado: Summer, Fall, Winter, Spring, a book collaboration with photography by David Muench and text by Momaday, is published by Rand McNally, Chicago. It receives the Geographic Society of Chicago Publications Award.

Joins the Stanford University faculty as professor of English and comparative literature in the fall quarter, having been officially appointed to the professorship in 1972.

1974

Angle of Geese and Other Poems, Momaday's first collection of poetry, is published by David Godine of Boston.

Momaday and Muench share the Western Heritage "Wrangler" Award, established by the Cowboy Hall of Fame and Western Heritage Center (later changed to National Cowboy and Western Heritage Museum), for *Colorado: Summer, Fall, Winter, Spring.*

Accepts an invitation to become one of the first exchange professors of American literature in the Soviet Union. Takes a leave from Stanford University to lecture on twentieth-century American literature at the University of Moscow during the spring session.

Begins to develop his artistic skills in earnest in the early 1970s. During the time spent in Russia, Momaday works on sketching and drawing, as well as writing poetry. Audits a drawing course upon his return to Stanford.

1975

Before an Old Painting of the Crucifixion, The Mission Carmel, June 1960 (poem) is privately printed in one hundred copies by Valenti Angelo of San Francisco.

Opens the American Issues Forum series of Bicentennial lectures at the Palace of Fine Arts in San Francisco.

Receives an honorary Doctor of Humane Letters degree from the University of Massachusetts at Amherst.

1976

The Gourd Dancer, Momaday's second book of poetry, is published by Harper & Row in New York City. Three of his sketches are used in this book.

The Names: A Memoir, an autobiographical book, is published by Harper & Row in New York City.

The Colors of Night, a prose poem, is published by Arion Press of San Francisco.

Studies art with artist Leonard Baskin.

1977

Makes a lecture tour of Europe for the U.S. Department of State, speaking in Germany (West Germany at that time), France, Ireland, Finland, and the Black Sea area. During this tour, he lectures at the University of Regensburg in Germany.

Receives an honorary Doctor of Humane Letters degree from the University of Wisconsin at Milwaukee.

Nominated for a Nobel Prize.

1978

Lectures as a visiting professor at the University of Regensburg in Germany and travels in several European countries, including Russia, to meet with writers and poets.

Marries Regina Heitzer, a native of Bavaria, on July 21 in Kelheim, near Regensburg, where they met at the university the year before. One daughter, Lore, is born in California in 1980. Their marriage ends in divorce.

Presents lecture, "Kiowa Oral Tradition," at the annual Modern Language Association of America convention in New York City.

Becomes a trustee of the Museum of the American Indian, Heye Foundation, New York City.

1979

Receives the Premio Letterario Internazionale Mondello, the Mondello Prize, Italy's highest literary award.

Returns to Germany to lecture and travel. Also travels to Greenland, on assignment from *National Geographic*, where he researches circumpolar peoples. This experience builds upon his interest and study of Eskimos and their culture, having researched the Eskimo villages in Alaska and the Northwest Territories of Canada.

Is a visiting professor and lecturer in the Council of Humanities and Creative Writing Program of Princeton University at Princeton, New Jersey, from February to June. He also lectures at Columbia University in New York City.

Momaday's first one-man show of drawings and paintings is held at the University of North Dakota Art Galleries in Grand Forks. This show was subsequently exhibited at galleries in Minneapolis, Minnesota, and Norman, Oklahoma.

Receives an honorary Doctor of Fine Arts degree from the College of Ganado in Arizona.

1980

Named Author of the Year by the California Association of Teachers of English.

Momaday and his parents show their work together for the first time at the R. C. Gorman Navajo Gallery in Albuquerque.

Receives honorary Doctor of Humane Letters degrees from Yale University, New Haven, Connecticut, and from Hobart and William Smith Colleges, Geneva, New York. He also receives an honorary Doctor of Fine Arts degree from Morningside College, Sioux City, Iowa.

1981

Momaday's father, Al Momaday, an award-winning painter and respected educator, passes away in New Mexico on November 11.

Accepts an appointment to the University of Arizona faculty as full professor in the Department of English and begins teaching on campus in the fall session. Resigns from his tenured academic position at Stanford University and moves to Tucson.

Serves as a juror in the selection of the winner of the Pulitzer Prize for Fiction.

1982

Joins with his mother in exhibiting their art work at a memorial art show held in honor of the late Al Momaday at the Lovena Ohl Gallery in Scottsdale, Arizona.

Receives a first-place juried exhibit award at the annual Oklahoma for Indian Opportunities art exhibit held in Norman.

Receives an honorary Doctor of Humane Letters degree from the College of Santa Fe, Santa Fe, New Mexico.

1983

Receives the Western Literature Association's Distinguished Service Award and life membership.

1984

Serves as a juror in the selection of the recipient of the Neustadt Prize for International Literature.

1985

Lectures as a visiting professor at the University of Regensburg in Germany during the summer months.

Accepts invitation as a writer-in-residence at Southeast University in Washington, D.C.

Serves on the executive board of PEN American Center from 1985–86.

1986

Speaks at the Aspen Writers Conference in Aspen, Colorado.

Begins extensive conversations about his life and work with Charles L. Woodard, professor of English at South Dakota State University. They meet in Tucson, Santa Fe, and Aspen.

Travels in Europe and exhibits paintings and drawings at Basel, Switzerland, and Heidelberg, Germany (West Germany at this time).

Serves as the chair of the Pulitzer Prize for Fiction jury.

1987

Returns to the University of Regensburg to lecture and travels in West Germany and other European countries.

Inducted into the Oklahoma Hall of Fame by the Oklahoma Heritage Association.

Receives the New Mexico Endowment for the Humanities Service Award.

Continues conversations with Charles L. Woodard as they travel together along parts of the migration route of the Kiowas. Their conversations are published in 1989 by the University of Nebraska Press in Woodard's *Ancestral Voice: Conversations with N. Scott Momaday.*

1988

Selected for membership on the Distinguished Board of Scholars of the Library of Congress, Washington, D.C.

1989

The Ancient Child, Momaday's second novel, is published by Doubleday in New York City.

Receives the first annual Native American Prize for Literature at the University of California, Santa Cruz.

Exhibits paintings and other art at the Lovena Ohl Gallery in Scottsdale, Arizona.

1989–90

Takes a sabbatical from the University of Arizona to become the Katrin H. Lamon Resident Scholar at the School of American Research in Santa Fe.

1990

Addresses the Global Forum on Environment and Development for Survival, held in Moscow, USSR, a conference devoted to critical environmental issues.

Receives the 1989 Jay Silverheels Achievement Award from the National Center for American Indian Enterprise Development in Los Angeles. He is selected for achieving personal and professional success while contributing to his community.

Named a trustee of the new National Museum of the American Indian to be constructed in Washington, D.C. He was one of the Heye Foundation's nominees.

Becomes a trustee of the Grand Canyon Trust, headquartered at Flagstaff, Arizona.

1991

In the Presence of the Sun: A Gathering of Shields, a limited, signed edition written and drawn by Momaday, is published by the Rydal Press, Santa Fe.

Receives the Wallace Stegner Award from the Center of the American West at the University of Colorado at Boulder.

LewAllen Gallery and the Rydal Press exhibit in Santa Fe Momaday's drawings and paintings from *A Gathering of Shields.*

Serves on the Award Committee to select the 1991 winner of the North American Indian Prose Award.

Selected as poster artist by the Southwestern Association on Indian Affairs.

Receives an honorary Doctor of Laws degree from the University of Vermont, Burlington.

1992

In the Presence of the Sun: Stories and Poems, 1961–1991, is published by St. Martin's Press, New York.

The Indolent Boys, Momaday's first full-length play, is presented in a staged reading at Harvard University's Agassiz Theatre.

Participates in the Poetics and Politics reading series at the University of Arizona in Tucson. This series, founded by the English Department, brought together thirteen of the nation's most accomplished American Indian writers.

Receives the Returning the Gift Lifetime Achievement Award, the first lifetime award presented by the Native Writers Circle of the Americas, at the first North American Native Writers' Returning the Gift Festival held at Norman, Oklahoma.

Named a Fellow of the Gihon Foundation Council on Ideas.

Receives an honorary degree from Ohio University, Athens, and a special commendation from the Harvard Foundation, Harvard University.

A twenty-year retrospective exhibit of Momaday's drawings and paintings is shown at the Wheelwright Museum of the American Indian in Santa Fe. The exhibit began in the latter part of 1992 and extended into 1993.

1993

Circle of Wonder: A Native American Christmas Story, Momaday's first children's book, is published by Clear Light Publishing, Santa Fe.

The Indolent Boys is presented in staged readings to full houses at Harvard University's Agassiz Theatre.

Inducted as an Achiever by the American Academy of Achievement, a Museum of Living History, Washington, D.C., and presented the Academy's Golden Plate Award.

Receives the UCSD Medal from the University of California, San Diego.

Receives an honorary Doctor of Education degree from Wheelock College, Boston, Massachusetts.

1994

The Indolent Boys has its world premiere at the Syracuse Stage in Syracuse, New York, in February. The play is directed by Tazewell Thompson.

Delivers the Charter Lecture at the University of Georgia, Athens. His speech is titled "The Mystery of Language: Native American Oral Tradition."

Receives the Gibson Lifetime Achievement Award from the Oklahoma Center for the Book at the 1994 Oklahoma Book Awards.

"A Gathering of Shields" is the chosen theme of the annual Institute of American Indian Arts Foundation dinner and auction held in Santa Fe.

1995

A gallery showing of paintings and monoprints by Momaday is held at the Horwitch-LewAllen Gallery in Santa Fe.

1996

Natachee Scott Momaday, mother of Scott and an award-winning author and educator, passes away on September 26. She is buried next to her husband at Fairview Memorial Park in Albuquerque.

Serves as the main commentator providing on-screen context for *The West,* an eight-part documentary series premiered on the Public Broadcasting System.

Receives the New Mexico Governor's Award for Excellence in the Arts.

1997

A Man Made of Words: Essays, Stories, Passages is published by St. Martin's Press, New York City.

Children of the Sun, a play for children created by Momaday and his daughter Cael, opens in March in its world premiere at the John F. Kennedy Center Theater Lab in New York City. This play was commissioned by the J. F. K. Center for the Performing Arts.

Works on a screenplay for director Chris Eyre (*Smoke Signals*) about the Carlisle Indian Industrial School (1879–1918). This screenplay, *The Moon in Two Windows*, is published in 2007 by the University of Oklahoma Press.

1998

Founds The Buffalo Trust, a nonprofit foundation established to work with indigenous peoples in the United States and other parts of the world in preserving their cultures, oral history, and archival records. Momaday is the Trust's director and chairman.

1999

In the Bear's House is published by St. Martin's Press, New York City.

Named "An Oklahoma Treasure" in a proclamation by Oklahoma Governor Frank Keating.

Receives the New Mexico Governor's Award for Literature.

Begins serving on the board of First Nations Development Institute, headquartered in Longmont, Colorado, and continues as a board member to 2007.

Lectures at the Haskell Indian Nations University and the University of Kansas at Lawrence.

Travels to Siberia in April, his third trip to this part of the world.

National Public Radio's *Weekend Edition* interviews Momaday about his Christmas story *A Circle of Wonder* and about his childhood memories of Native American Christmas celebrations in New Mexico.

Returns to New Mexico to live in his Jemez Springs home, commuting to Tucson to continue his teaching at the University of Arizona.

2000

Children of the Sun is staged with choreographed dance at the Barter Theatre, the State Theatre of Virginia, located at Abingdon. The play is directed by Katy Brown and runs two months.

Named Regents Professor of English at the University of Arizona, Tucson.

Receives The Saint Louis Literary Award in a ceremony held at Busch Memorial Center in St. Louis.

Nominated as a candidate for the 2000 Neustadt International Prize for Literature.

2001

Named the inaugural University of Alaska, Fairbanks, Northern Momentum Teacher-Scholar.

Serves as keynote speaker for UNESCO's International Symposium on Indigenous Identities held at the Kennedy Center in New York City.

Participates in Brainstorm 2001, an annual conference sponsored by the editors of *Fortune* magazine and the Aspen Institute. This is Momaday's first appearance at this invitational conference.

Receives an honorary Doctor of Humane Letters degree from the University of New Mexico, Albuquerque.

2002

Marries long-time friend and literary representative Barbara Glenn, like him a graduate of Stanford University and a Wallace Stegner Creative Writing Fellow in poetry.

The Indolent Boys is performed by the Southwest Repertory at the Museum of Indian Arts and Culture in Santa Fe and in Albuquerque at the University of New Mexico's Rodey Theater. A reading was also presented at the Heard Museum in Phoenix.

Speaks at Poetics and Politics II: Lectures by Eminent Native Scholars and Writers, held at the University of Arizona to commemorate the twentieth anniversary (1982–2002) of its American Indian Studies Program.

In a first public appearance together with renowned New Mexico authors Rudolfo Anaya and Tony Hillerman, Momaday discusses the writing process and other wide-ranging topics before an overflow audience at the Jemez Valley High School.

Attends *Fortune*'s Brainstorm 2002.

2003

Les enfants du soleil, a French translation of *Children of the Sun*, is published by Le Seuil, Paris, France. At this time, the play had not yet been published in English.

Receives the Humanities Prize of the Autry National Center for the American West. He is a founding member of the Stewardship Council of the Center, which was formerly called the Autry Museum of Western Heritage.

Named Artist for Peace by UNESCO, the first American awarded this honor since the United States rejoined UNESCO, and is involved in partnership projects with indigenous peoples around the world.

Receives the Premio Fronterizo, the highest award presented by the Border Book Festival, at the festival held in Las Cruces and Old Mesilla, New Mexico.

Receives an honorary doctoral degree from Université Blaise Pascal at Clermont-Ferrand in France. This is the first honorary degree awarded to Momaday in Europe.

Accepts an appointment to the board of St. John's College, Santa Fe.

Participates in *Fortune*'s Brainstorm 2003.

2004
Delivers a welcoming address at the inauguration of the National Museum of the American Indian in Washington, D.C., in his role as a founding trustee and as the "voice" of the museum.

Formally recognized as UNESCO Artist for Peace in a special ceremony in Paris.

The Tucson Symphony performs "Beyond the Silence of Sorrow," a song cycle by award-winning composer Roberto Sierra based on six poems by Momaday. Heidi Grant Murphy is the featured soprano.

Selected as a nominee for the Nobel Prize for Literature for 2005.

Participates in a panel discussion at the Tenth Circuit Judicial Conference held at Park City, Utah.

Receives an honorary Doctor of Humane Letters degree at the University of Oklahoma, Norman.

2005
Retires from the University of Arizona as Regents Professor Emeritus after twenty-three years of academic service.

The Indolent Boys is presented in a radio adaptation written by Lori Tubert. This production is broadcast on the American Indian Radio on Satellite (AIROS) network through the cooperation of the Autry Museum of Western Heritage and the Wells Fargo Radio Theatre Program.

Joins the School of American Research at Santa Fe as a Senior Scholar and continues as a board member.

Becomes an honorary trustee of the Grand Canyon Trust, headquartered at Flagstaff, Arizona.

Receives an honorary Doctor of Humane Letters degree from the University of Tulsa at Tulsa, Oklahoma.

Speaks at the Short Story Festival held in Santa Fe, New Mexico.

2006
Four Arrows & Magpie: A Kiowa Story, a book for children, is published by HAWK Publishing Group of Tulsa, Oklahoma, in commemoration of Oklahoma's one hundredth birthday.

Receives the Aspen Prize for Literature from the Aspen Writers Foundation during its Summer Literary Festival.

Joins the faculty of the Institute of American Indian Arts College and Museum, Santa Fe.

Provides interpretations of land ethics in voiceovers and on screen in the Public Broadcasting System's presentation, "Remembered Earth," which premiered on PBS channels in February. The program, written, filmed, and produced by John Grabowska, begins with Momaday's recitation of his frequently quoted passage "The Remembered Earth."

Speaks as a special guest at the gala dinner of the fifth annual Native American Film Festival and Cultural Weekend in Palm Springs, California.

Named honoree of the 2006 Pony Moon Gala held in Oklahoma City. An exhibition of his paintings, "The Visual Voice of Kiowa Author N. Scott Momaday," is shown at the Jacobson House Native Art Center on the University of Oklahoma campus.

2007

Three Plays: The Indolent Boys, Children of the Sun, and The Moon in Two Windows, Momaday's first collection of plays, is published by the University of Oklahoma Press, Norman.

Receives the National Medal of Arts, the nation's highest honor for artistic excellence, in a ceremony presided over by President George W. Bush and First Lady Laura Bush at the White House in November.

Appointed the Oklahoma Centennial Poet Laureate by Governor Brad Henry and inducted into the Oklahoma Writers Hall of Fame at an event held at Philbrook Museum of Art and presented by the Oklahoma Center for Poets and Writers and Oklahoma State University, Tulsa.

Speaks at a keynote event during the Alaska Forum on the Environment held at Anchorage.

Lectures in the Honors College of the University of Oklahoma.

Participates in a panel discussion with two other authors, all of whom had authored a book selected by Stanford University to be read by all incoming students before the new student orientation. *The Way to Rainy Mountain* was one of the three selected.

Addresses the Class of 2007 at the St. John's College commencement in Santa Fe.

Signs his books as an invited author at the National Book Festival, presented by the Library of Congress and hosted by First Lady Laura Bush in Washington, D.C.

The School of American Research changes its name to The School for Advanced Research on the Human Experience. Momaday continues as a Senior Scholar.

2008

Named the Poet Laureate of the Kiowa.

Receives the 2008 Oklahoma Humanities Award from the Oklahoma Humanities Council.

Speaks at the Rasmuson Theater of the National Museum of the American Indian, Washington, D.C.

Delivers the closing keynote address, "The Spiritual Aspects of Landscape and Water," at the 13th Annual Water Conservation & Xeriscape Conference held at Albuquerque.

Speaks at the 36th annual Symposium of the American Indian held at Northeastern State University's Center for Tribal Studies in Tahlequah, Oklahoma.

Gives the keynote lecture at the annual Mayborn Literary Conference held in Dallas, Texas.

Speaks on the oral tradition at the annual Guy Stanton Ford Memorial Lectureship at the University of Minnesota, Minneapolis.

Barbara Glenn Momaday, wife of N. Scott Momaday, passed away on September 20 in Oklahoma City, where private services were held. Her ashes were scattered at Rainy Mountain and Jemez Springs.

2009

The Journey of Tai-me, originally available only in a hand-printed limited edition, is published in a hardcover edition by the University of New Mexico Press.

In the Presence of the Sun: Stories and Poems, 1961–1991, originally published by St. Martin's Press in 1992, is reprinted in a paperback edition by the University of New Mexico Press.

Receives an honorary Doctor of Humane Letters degree from the University of Minnesota, Minneapolis.

Receives an honorary Doctor of Humane Letters degree from the University of Illinois, Chicago, his seventeenth honorary degree.

Part II

The Works of N. Scott Momaday

A Bibliography

Published Books and Private Printings

A Chronological Listing of First Editions and First Printings

1965 *The Complete Poems of Frederick Goddard Tuckerman* (a collection edited by N. Scott Momaday)

1967 *The Journey of Tai-me* (a collection of Kiowa tales)

1968 *House Made of Dawn* (fiction)

1969 *The Way to Rainy Mountain* (mixed-genre autobiography)

1974 *Colorado: Summer, Fall, Winter, Spring* (nonfiction; text by N. Scott Momaday with photography by David Muench)

1974 *Angle of Geese and Other Poems* (poetry)

1975 *Before an Old Painting of the Crucifixion, The Mission Carmel, June 1960* (privately printed poem)

1976 *The Colors of Night* (a prose poem printed in a limited edition)

1976 *The Gourd Dancer* (poetry)

1976 *The Names: A Memoir* (autobiography)

1980 *We Have Been Lovers, You and I* (privately printed poem)

1989 *The Ancient Child: A Novel* (fiction)

1991 *In the Presence of the Sun: A Gathering of Shields* (a collection of stories and drawings of Plains Indian shields)

1992 *In the Presence of the Sun: Stories and Poems, 1961–1991* (a literary collection)

1993 *Circle of Wonder: A Native American Christmas Story* (children's book)

1997 *The Man Made of Words: Essays, Stories, Passages* (a literary collection)

1999 *In the Bear's House* (a literary collection)

2003 *Les enfants du soleil* (children's book in French)

2006 *Four Arrows and Magpie: A Kiowa Story* (children's book)

2007 *Three Plays: The Indolent Boys, Children of the Sun, and The Moon in Two Windows* (a collection of plays)

Books and Private Printings

1. ***The Complete Poems of Frederick Goddard Tuckerman***, edited with an introduction by N. Scott Momaday. Critical foreword by Yvor Winters. New York: Oxford University Press, 1965. xxviii, 217 pp.

   This book is based on the scholarly research done by Momaday for his doctoral dissertation, "An Edition of the Complete Poems of Frederick Goddard Tuckerman," completed at Stanford University in 1963. Tuckerman (1821–73), a lifelong resident of Massachusetts, was among the most outstanding poets of the nineteenth century. He was a graduate of Harvard University and a contemporary of Emily Dickinson (1830–86).

2. ***The Journey of Tai-me***. Santa Barbara, California: Privately printed, 1967. Unpaged. Illus., 25 × 28 cm. Printed in a fine limited edition of one hundred hand-printed, numbered copies at the College of Creative Studies of the University of California, Santa Barbara. Printed on handmade paper and bound in calfskin binding with slipcase.

   Each book was signed by Momaday on the half-title page. Art prints in this collaborative project were done by Bruce S. McCurdy. A lithograph print, signed by McCurdy, was placed loose inside the front cover of each book. Typographer D. E. Carlsen also signed each copy.

   Momaday described this special edition as the archetype of *The Way to Rainy Mountain* (1969). It contains his translations of legends and tales from Kiowa oral tradition, arranged to indicate the chronological and geographical progression of the Kiowa migration that took place over many generations and many hundreds of miles. During their migration, the Kiowas acquired

Tai-me, the Sun Dance fetish of the tribe. It could be viewed only during Sun Dance ceremonies and was kept safe by an official caretaker.

The book was printed after Momaday retraced the route of the Kiowa migration and after interviewing Kiowa elders, from whom he received a wealth of history and wisdom. There are thirty-three Kiowa tales in *The Journey of Tai-me*. Twenty-three of these were carried over to *The Way to Rainy Mountain*.

New printing of hand-printed limited ed. Albuquerque: University of New Mexico Press, 2009. First UNM Press printing. 106 pp. Illus. (six black-and-white drawings by N. Scott Momaday), 7 × 8 in. (20.5 cm.). In hardcover.

3. ***House Made of Dawn***. First edition. New York: Harper & Row, 1968. Winner of the Pulitzer Prize for Fiction for 1969. viii, 212 pp. No illus., 5½ × 8½ in. (21 cm.). Printed in hardcover with dust jacket designed by David McIntosh. A black-and-white portrait of Momaday, taken in Santa Barbara, California, is on the back of the dust jacket. The first printing consisted of 7,500 copies.

Reprints:

New York: Signet Books, New American Library, 1969, ©1968. 191 pp., 18 cm. This first paperback printing, November 1969, is a reprint of the 1968 Harper & Row hardcover edition.

London: Victor Gollancz Ltd., 1969. 212 pp.

New York: Penguin Books, 1973. (pbk.)

New York: Perennial Library, Harper & Row, 1977, ©1968. 191 pp., 18 cm. (pbk.)

Franklin Center, Pennsylvania: Franklin Library, 1977. Limited edition in hardcover with illustrations by artist Bart Forbes. 249 pp., 22 cm.

New York: Harper & Row, 1989, ©1968. First Perennial Library edition. (pbk.)

Tucson: University of Arizona Press, 1996, ©1968. Reprint of the original edition published by Harper & Row in 1968. 212 pp., 21 cm. (The N. Scott Momaday Collection)

New York: HarperPerennial, division of HarperCollins, 1999, ©1968. First Perennial Classics edition. viii, 198 pp., no illus., 5¼ × 8 in. (20 cm.). Two essays are included at the end of this edition: “N. Scott Momaday,” a biography by Hal Hager, pp. 187–93, with portrait; and “House Made of Dawn, 1968,” by anonymous writer, pp. 195–98. The portrait of Momaday, taken by daughter Lore, also appears on the back cover. This paperback edition does not have the same page numbering as the hardcover edition published in 1968.

New York: McGraw-Hill Higher Education, 2001, ©1968. Reprint of 1st ed. (pbk.)

New York: HarperPerennial (HarperCollins), 2008. Twenty-sixth printing of the First Perennial Classics edition (1999).

Translations of *House Made of Dawn*:

Finnish translation. *Alkuperäiset Amerikkalaiset.* Translated by Markku Henrikson. Helsinki: Gaudeamus, 1985.

French translation. *La maison de l'aube.* Translated by Daniel Bismuth and edited by Jean-Paul Bertrand. Preface by Yves Berger. Collection Nuage Rouge. Monaco: Éditions du Rocher, 1993. 278 pp. A second edition was published by Éditions du Rocher, 1995. Reprinted, Paris: Gallimard, 1996. 304 pp.

German translations:

Haus aus Dämmerung. Translated by Jeannie Ebner. Berlin: Frankfurt am Main: Verlag Ullstein, 1978. 246 pp. (hardcover)

Haus aus Morgen Dämmerung. Translated by Jochen Eggert. Munich: Eugen Diederichs, 1988.

Italian translations:

Casa fatta d'alba. Translated by Franco Meli and edited by Loraine Willis. First edition. Milan: Guanda, 1979. Momaday was awarded Italy's highest literary honor following the publishing of this translation. Reprinted in a second edition by Guanda, 1988, ©1979.

Casa fatta di alba. Translated by Franco Meli and edited by Loraine Willis. Third edition. Parma: Ugo Guanda Editore, 1995, ©1979. Cover illustration, *Red and Yellow Cliffs*, by Georgia O'Keeffe, 1940. Includes an essay, "Dove stoi andando?" by Franco Meli at the end of this book, pp. 187–200.

Norwegian translation. *Hus av Demring.* Oslo: J. W. Cappelens Forlaga·s, 1975.

Polish translation. *Dom UTKany Ze Switu.* Warsaw: Ksiqzkai Wiedza, 1976.

In addition to the translations cited above, a Danish translation was published in 1986, a Russian translation was published in Moscow in 1993, and a Turkish translation has also been published.

House Made of Dawn has received a great amount of critical attention and in-depth study since it was first published and announced a Pulitzer Prize–winning novel. Its many levels have been dissected and examined by numerous scholars.

It tells the story of Abel, who has returned from World War II to his home, Walatowa (the name the Jemez gave their pueblo), and discovers that he cannot recover his tribal identity. He is relocated to Los Angeles and finds that he cannot survive as a whole being in an urban environment. Abel is faced with a dilemma, and his inarticulateness reveals that his dilemma is very deep. After going through heartbreaking struggles, he returns home. The story has a circular structure, with Abel running at its beginning and end. After returning to the pueblo, there is a glimmer of hope for his recovery. He has begun a process of healing and transformation as he runs toward the House Made of Dawn.

4. ***The Way to Rainy Mountain***. First edition. Albuquerque: University of New Mexico Press, 1969. viii, 88 pp., 2 unpaged. Illus., 6¼ × 9½ in. (24 cm.). This clothbound book has eleven black-and-white illustrations by Al Momaday and was designed by Bruce Gentry.

   Reprints:

   New York: Ballantine, 1970, ©1969 UNM Press. First Ballatine Books printing. Ballantine Walden ed., March 1970. 119 pp., 18 cm. (pbk.)

   New York: Ballantine, 1972, ©1969 UNM Press. Second Ballantine Books printing. Ballantine Walden ed., January 1972. 119 pp. (pbk.)

   Albuquerque: University of New Mexico Press, 1976, ©1969. First UNM Press paperback ed. Illustrations, including cover illustration, by Al Momaday. x, 89 pp. Illus., 6 × 9¼ in. (23.5 cm.).

   New York: Ballantine, 1976, ©1969 UNM Press. 88 pp. Illus., 24 cm. (pbk.)

   Tucson: University of Arizona Press, 1996, ©1969 UNM Press. 88 pp. Illus., 6¼ × 9½ in. (24 cm.) (The N. Scott Momaday Collection)

   Albuquerque: University of New Mexico Press, 2001, ©1969. ix, 89 pp. Illus., 6 × 9¼ in. (23.5 cm.). This is the twenty-fifth anniversary edition and the sixteenth printing of the 1976 UNM Press paperback edition, with a new preface by Momaday.

   The full text of the book, from the beginning poem "Headwaters" to "Rainy Mountain Cemetery" at the end, pp. 2–89, was reprinted in *American Literature: A Prentice Hall Anthology, Concise Edition*. Emory Elliott, gen. ed. Englewood Cliffs, New Jersey: Prentice Hall, 1991. 2089–2113.

   In 2002 the full text was published in a hardbound edition: *The Way to Rainy Mountain: With Related Readings*. Glencoe Literature Library. New York: Glencoe/McGraw-Hill. 113 pp. No illus., 6¼ × 9¼ (24 cm.).

Translations of *The Way to Rainy Mountain*:

Chinese translation (Mandarin). *Tong xiang yin yu shan di dao lu.* Shanghai: Shanghai yi wen chu ban she, April 1994. 94 pp. Illus. (black-and-white), 19 cm. Translated by Zhuwan Yi and published with the permission of the University of New Mexico Press. Twenty thousand copies were published.

French translation. *Le chemin de la montagne de pluie.* Translated by Philippe Gaillard. Illustrations by Al Momaday. Monaco: Éditions du Rocher, 1995. This book is also included in a boxed set of three translations in paperback, including *House Made of Dawn* and *The Ancient Child*; distributed by Collection Folio (no. 2935). Reprint, Paris: Gallimard, 1997. 120 pp. Illus. (pbk.)

German translation. *Der Weg zum Regenberg.* Translated by Peter Baume. Idstein, Germany: Baum Publications, 1991.

Italian translation. *La via al monte della pioggia.* Translated by Gaetano Prampolini. Milan: La Salamandra, 1989. Reprinted with title *Il viaggio a Rainy Mountain*, translated and edited by Gaetano Prampolini. Collona Indianoamericana. Milan: La Salamandra, ©1989. 166 pp. Illus., 20 cm.

Japanese translation. *Reini mauten e no ruchi.* Tokyo: Shobun-sha, ©1976, arranged with the University of New Mexico Press through Charles E. Tuttle Co. 166 pp. 20 cm. (pbk.)

Turkish translation. *Yagmur Dagina Giden Yol.* Translated by Arif Kizilay. Istanbul: AkisKitap, 2005. 96 pp. 21 cm. (pbk.)

Momaday has described the unique format and the principle of narration used in *The Way to Rainy Mountain* as being "in a sense experimental." He refers to the use of three distinct narrative voices: the ancestral voice; the voice of historical commentary; and the personal voice, which is his own. The first of these voices, the ancestral, or legendary, is his translation of the Kiowa stories from the oral tradition. Each translation is situated by itself on a left-hand page, while the second and third voices are on the right-hand, or odd-numbered, page of the book. These three voices are differentiated through the use of three different typefaces.

The Kiowa stories or legends in *The Journey of Tai-me* are not numbered. Twenty-three of the thirty-three stories in *The Journey of Tai-me* were carried over to *The Way to Rainy Mountain* and were numbered with Roman numerals. The following table lists the stories and matches those in *The Way to Rainy Mountain* with those that appeared in *The Journey of Tai-me*.

Number of Story in *WRM*	Beginning Words of the Story	Number of Story in *Tai-me*
I	"You know everything had to begin. . . ."	1st
II	"They were going along, and some were hunting."	Not in *Tai-me*
III	"Before there were horses the Kiowas had dogs."	10th
IV	"They lived at first in the mountains."	2nd
V	"After that the woman grew lonely."	3rd
VI	"The Sun's Child was big enough to walk. . . ."	4th
VII	"The years went by and the boy still had the ring. . . ."	5th
VIII	"Now each of the twins had a ring. . . ."	6th
IX	"The next thing that happened to the twins. . . ."	7th
X	"Long ago there were bad times."	8th
Introduction on page 8	"Eight children were at play. . . ." ("The Kiowa Story of Tsoai")	9th
XI	"A long time ago there were two brothers."	11th
XII	"An old man there was who lived with his wife and child."	15th
XIII	"If an arrow is well made, it will have tooth marks upon it." ("The Story of the Arrowmaker")	12th
XIV	"The Kiowa language is hard to understand. . . ."	Not in *Tai-me*
XV	"Quoetotai was a good-looking young man. . . ."	19th
XVI	"There was a strange thing, a buffalo with horns of steel."	17th
XVII	"Bad women are thrown away."	13th
XVIII	"You know, the Kiowas are a summer people."	Not in *Tai-me*
XIX	"On a raid against the Utes, one of two brothers was captured."	14th
XX	"Once there was a man who owned a fine hunting horse." ("The Horse That Died of Shame")	16th
XXI	"Mammedaty was the grandson of Guipagho. . . ."	25th
XXII	"Mammedaty was the grandson of Guipagho and he got on well most of the time."	26th
XXIII	"Aho remembered something, a strange thing."	23rd
XXIV	"East of my grandmother's house, south of the pecan grove, there is buried a woman in a beautiful dress."	24th

One other story, the last of the thirty-three stories in *The Journey of Tai-me*, was used in the Epilogue of *The Way to Rainy Mountain*. This story, beginning on p. 86, was told by Ko-sahn, the hundred-year-old woman who came to the house of Momaday's grandmother in Oklahoma.

The Way to Rainy Mountain has been Momaday's most popular book. It is among the best-selling books published by the University of New Mexico Press. Today it is considered a classic. A great deal of attention has been given to it by reviewers and critics. It has proved over the years to be a very effective book for teaching and learning about American Indian literature. Kenneth M. Roemer has described it as "a mixed-genre life narrative" in *Approaches to Teaching Momaday's "The Way to Rainy Mountain"* (1988), Lawana Trout called it "a cultural memoir" in *Native American Literature: An Anthology* (1998), and Andrew Wiget designated it "an extended prose poem" in *Native American Literature* (1985). It has been described in numerous ways because of its unique departure from traditional literary forms.

5. ***Colorado: Summer, Fall, Winter, Spring.*** Photography by David Muench; text by N. Scott Momaday. Chicago: Rand McNally, 1973. 120 pp. First paperback printing: Chicago: Rand McNally, 1976.

   Momaday collaborated with David Muench, world-famous landscape and nature photographer, in creating a remarkable book extolling Colorado's natural beauty throughout the four seasons of the year. Momaday contributed his lyrical, poetic writing to accompany Muench's photography. The book received an award from the Geographic Society of Chicago and the Western Heritage "Wrangler" Award from the Cowboy Hall of Fame and Western Heritage Center, now called the National Cowboy and Western Heritage Museum, in Oklahoma City.

6. ***Angle of Geese and Other Poems.*** First Godine Poetry Chapbook Series, no. 5. Boston: David R. Godine, Publisher, 1974, ©1974 N. Scott Momaday. Jan Schreiber, gen. ed. Designed by Carol Shloss. 28 pp., 3 unpaged leaves at end of book, 5½ × 8½ in. (21.5 cm.). Bound in hardcover with a red-and-white leaf design. There are no illustrations in this book. It is dedicated to Cael, Momaday's oldest daughter.

   Momaday's first published poetry collection comprises eighteen poems and prose poems. Among previously published poems are "The Bear," which won the Academy of American Poets Prize in 1962, and "Earth and I Gave You Turquoise," his first published poem. Prose poem, "The Story of a Well-Made Shield" and a cycle of poems, "Plainview: 1–4," are representative of the variety of poetry in this book. The title poem, "Angle of Geese," was placed at the end.

7. ***Before an Old Painting of the Crucifixion, The Mission Carmel, June 1960.*** San Francisco: Valenti Angelo, 1975, ©1975 N. Scott Momaday. 14 pp. 16 cm. One hundred copies of this poem were printed on fine paper with hand-colored embellishments for the Friends of Valenti Angelo. Each copy, bound in blue paper, was signed by Angelo and Momaday on facing pages.

8. ***The Colors of Night.*** Arion Press Broadsides, no. 3. San Francisco: Arion Press, 1976. Five hundred copies of this limited edition broadside were printed. The illustrations are by Momaday and consist of six drawings in a terracotta color on a sheet of cream-colored paper, folded and placed in a gray paper cover. The full sheet measures 14 × 22 inches. When folded, it measures 7½ × 11¼ inches. *The Colors of Night* is a sequence of eight prose poems, each one telling about a different color.

9. ***The Gourd Dancer.*** Drawings by Momaday. New York: Harper & Row, 1976. 64 pp. Illus., 6 × 8¼ in. (21 cm.). This second collection of poetry was issued in both hardcover and paperbound editions. The hardcover book is cloth bound with a dust jacket, on the back of which is a black-and-white portrait of the poet. A note on the jacket announces that a recording of Momaday reading from his work was produced by Pathways of Sound.

   The forty-three poems in Momaday's second book of poetry, a tribute to his grandfather Mammedaty, are presented in three parts: Part I, "Angle of Geese," with twenty poems, the last of these being "Angle of Geese"; Part II, "The Gourd Dancer," with eleven poems and prose poems; and Part III, "Anywhere Is a Street into the Night," with twelve poems. Each part, beginning with a masterful line drawing by Momaday, is dedicated to daughters Cael, Jill, and Brit.

   Most of the poems in Part I were previously published in *Angle of Geese* (1974). Several of the poems in Part III were written in Russia in 1974, when Momaday was a visiting professor teaching American literature at the University of Moscow. This collection begins with his award-winning "The Bear," one of his most frequently reprinted and studied poems.

10. ***The Names: A Memoir.*** First ed. New York: Harper & Row, 1976. xii, 170 pp. Illus., ports., 6¾ × 8¾ in. (23 cm.). Cloth-bound hardcover with dust jacket. Includes a glossary of Indian names and words from the book.

    Reprints:

    First Harper Colophon ed. New York: Harper & Row, 1977. 170 pp. (pbk.) The cover is a photo montage of Al, Natachee, and Scott Momaday.

    Tucson: Sun Tracks and University of Arizona Press, 1987, ©1976. Sun Tracks, An American Indian Literary Series, vol. 16. Larry Evers, ser. ed. x, 170 pp. Illus., ports., 5½ × 8½ in. (21.5 cm.). The cover illustration, "Dragonfly," is by Momaday.

    Tucson: University of Arizona Press, 1999, ©1976. 170 pp. Illus., 22 cm. (pbk.)

Translations of *The Names: A Memoir*:

French translation. *Les noms, mémoires.* Translated by Danièle Laruelle. Collection Nuage Rouge. Monaco: Éditions du Rocher, 2001. 180 pp.

Italian translation. *I nomi.* Translated and edited by Laura Coltelli. Collana Indianoamericana. Milan: La Salamandra. This book includes an afterword by Coltelli titled "Linguaggio, immaginazione e memoria."

Polish translation. *IMIONA.* Translation by Robotnicza Spóldzielnia Wydawnicza. Warsaw: Ksiażka_i_ Wiedza, 1982, ©1976 N. Scott Momaday. 201 pp. This includes the glossary from the first edition of *The Names.*

Momaday's autobiographical memoir about his childhood and his parents, grandparents, and other relatives is written in an imaginative, lyrical, and loving way. It presents his life from his birth in Oklahoma through his growing up years in Oklahoma, New Mexico, and Arizona, ending with the year he leaves home to complete his high school education at a military academy in Virginia. This memoir becomes all the more precious and memorable through the old portraits and photographs kept and cherished.

11. ***We Have Been Lovers, You and I*** (poem) [Madison, Wisconsin]: Crepuscular Press, ©1980. Printed on one sheet, measuring 36 × 26 cm., and folded to 17 × 26 cm. One hundred and thirty copies of this poem were printed in Palatine italic and signed by Momaday. Thirty-five of these copies have parfleche wrappers. The title is from the first line of the poem. There is only one illustration, which is by Momaday.

12. ***The Ancient Child: A Novel.*** New York: Doubleday, 1989. 313 pp., 3 unpaged at end of book, 5½ × 8½ in. (21.5 cm.). Hardcover issued October 1989.

Reprint:

First HarperPerennial ed. New York: HarperCollins Publishers, 1990, ©1989. xvi, 313 pp., 2 unpaged, 5¼ × 8 in. (20.5 cm.). This paperback was reprinted by arrangement with Bantam Doubleday Dell Publishing Group. There are no illustrations, except for the cover illustration of a bear by Laurie Dolphin.

Translation of *The Ancient Child: A Novel*:

French translation. *L'enfant des temps oubliés.* Translated by Danièle Laruelle. Collection Nuage Rouge. Monaco: Éditions du Rocher, 1996, 1997. This translation in paperback is also available in a boxed set with paperback printings of *House Made of Dawn* and *The Way to Rainy Mountain.* Reprint, Paris: Gallimard, 1998.

Momaday's second novel appeared two decades after his first, *House Made of Dawn* (1968). It shapes the Kiowa myth of the boy who turns into a bear into a story set in contemporary times. The story has autobiographical elements. For instance, the young man who becomes a bear is an artist living in California, and he returns to his grandmother's house after her death. He is aided in his transformation by a young medicine woman, Grey. Billy the Kid also plays a role in this story, which has been described as a book-length prose poem. Its artistic elements and qualities include the titles of its four major parts: Planes, Lines, Shapes, and Shadows.

13. ***In the Presence of the Sun: A Gathering of Shields***, written and drawn by N. Scott Momaday. Santa Fe, New Mexico: The Rydal Press, 1992, ©1991. 24 unpaged leaves (48 unnumbered pages). Illus., 12 × 10 in. (23 cm.). The publisher of this limited edition was Clark Kimball.

    One hundred and forty copies were printed by letterpress on fine Mohawk papers at Eric Johnson's Okeanos Press in Oakland, California. Twenty-six of those copies were signed, lettered, and placed in slipcases. These copies have sixteen original pen-and-ink drawings engraved on zinc plates, individually printed and colored in as many as eight colors by Momaday. One hundred and fourteen copies, signed and numbered, have sixteen uncolored plates of the original drawings. The story of each shield is on the right-hand page of the book, with the drawing of the shield on the opposite, or left-hand, page. A three-page introduction, "A Word on the Plains Shield," precedes the stories. Momaday signed all copies on the colophon at the back of the book, which is dedicated to Lore, his youngest daughter.

    This beautiful book is a work of art and of language, bound in a yellow cloth binding as brilliant as the sun and placed in a linen-covered slipcase of the same color. Momaday emphasizes that the stories of the shields are meant to be told aloud and in the presence of the sun. He states: "The stories ought to be told in the early morning or late afternoon, when the sun is close to the horizon, and always in the presence of the sun." The publisher's brochure announcing the book states that the shields and their stories are "imagined in his mind's eye and offered by his heart's mind."

    Forty-eight complete, unbound suites, numbered and signed, with the sixteen shield drawings in color, were also printed. Each shield drawing is covered by a guard sheet and preceded by a letterpress printing of its story. At the beginning of the suite is a loose title page with the title "Sixteen Plains Indian Shield Drawings by N. Scott Momaday." Eighteen of these suites were reserved for sale as complete sets.

14. ***In the Presence of the Sun: Stories and Poems, 1961–1991***. New York: St. Martin's Press, 1992. Issued October 1992. Illustrated by Momaday. xxiv, 143 pp. Illus., 6 × 9½ in. (24 cm.). Published in hardcover in a trade edition and a limited edition. The sixty black-and-white illustrations, all by Momaday, comprise a variety of media, including watercolor, acrylic, ink, etching, and pencil. Endpaper and book jacket art are also by him.

    Reprint:

    New York: St. Martin's Press, 1993. xx, 143 pp. Illus., 6 × 9½ in. (24 cm.) (pbk.)

    Albuquerque: University of New Mexico Press, 2009. 184 pp. Illus., 6 × 9 in. (23 cm.). First UNM Press paperback printing. This printing contains Momaday's drawings.

    This literary collection comprises four parts: "Selected Poems," containing twenty-nine previously published poems; "The Strange and True Story of My Life with Billy the Kid"; "In the Presence of the Sun: A Gathering of Shields," with the sixteen shields and stories first published in Momaday's book with the same main title; and "New Poems," presenting twenty-seven poems.

    Momaday explains in the book's preface that the poems in this collection were written over a period of thirty years and the drawings were made over nearly twenty.

15. ***Circle of Wonder: A Native American Christmas Story***. Santa Fe: Clear Light Publishers, 1993. 40 pp. Illus., port., 8½ × 10 in. (26 cm.). Hardcover. All illustrations, including those on the dust jacket, are in color and by Momaday. An audio recording of Momaday telling the story is also available.

    Reprint:

    Albuquerque: University of New Mexico Press, 1999. 40 pp. Illus., 26 cm. Paperbound trade ed.

    This children's book had its beginning as a bedtime story told by Momaday to his daughters when they were very young. The story was first published with the title, "The Circle: A Fable of Christmas," in *Viva*, a weekly supplement of the *Santa Fe New Mexican*, in December 1972. It was published in a different and longer form in Part Four of *The Names* (1976), 137–42. He did not think of publishing it as a separate book until after his first granddaughter was born.

    This story of a mute boy named Tolo takes place at Jemez Pueblo during the pueblo's Christmas ceremonies. It tells about Tolo spending summers with his elderly grandfather in his little dwelling set in a beautiful meadow at the foot of a mountain. When his grandfather passes away, Tolo becomes very lonely. During the Christmas procession, he believes he sees his grandfather and tries to follow him. After running a long way, Tolo comes to a large bonfire on the rim of the meadow and is joined by an elk, a wolf, and an eagle. Believing his grandfather is also nearby, Tolo and the animals form a circle of wonder and good will that encompasses them, the mountain, and the whole world.

16. ***The Man Made of Words: Essays, Stories, Passages***. First ed. New York: St. Martin's Press, 1997. x, 211 pp. Illus., 6¼ × 9½ in. (24 cm.). Hardcover with dust jacket. Illustrations on the book jacket, title page, and at the beginning of each part of the book are by Momaday. He also did the self-portrait opposite the title page. A color illustration on the back of the dust jacket is from *Circle of Wonder*. This book is dedicated to his late professor and friend, Yvor Winters, and to Janet Lewis, Winters's wife.

Reprint:

New York: St. Martin's Griffin, 1997. x, 211 pp. Illus., 6 × 9¼ in. (23.5 cm.). Trade paperbound first ed. Illustrations on the book jacket, title page, and at the beginning of each part of the book are by Momaday. Cover design is by Christine Von Bree.

Translation of *The Man Made of Words*:

French translation. *L'Homme fait de mots*. Translated by Danièle Laruelle. Collection Nuage Rouge. Paris: Éditions du Rocher, 1998.

The Man Made of Words has three parts, each introduced by Momaday, containing thirty-eight of his writings from a period spanning thirty years. Part One, "The Man Made of Words," comprises ten essays that have become well-known and reprinted or quoted. Part Two, "Essays in Place," consists of nine essays about places where he has traveled and are of particular significance to him. Several of these essays were published in the *New York Times Magazine*, to which he has contributed a number of writings about his extensive travels. Part Three, "The Storyteller and His Art," with nineteen stories, reflects his multifaceted life and wide-ranging interests. A number were first published in his weekly column in *Viva: Northern New Mexico's Sunday Magazine*, a supplement of the *Santa Fe New Mexican*, in 1972 and 1973.

Momaday remarks about these writings in the book's Preface: "I perceive the writings herein as the pieces of a whole, each one the element of an intricate but unified design. They are the facets of a verbal prism, if you will, patterns like the constellations. The design, in this instance, is the very information of language, that miracle of symbols and sounds that enable us to think, and therefore to define ourselves as human beings" (1).

17. ***In the Bear's House***. First ed. New York: St. Martin's Press, 1999. 96 pp. Illus., 7½ × 9 in. (24 cm.). Hardcover with dust jacket. Drawings, paintings, cover and jacket art, and calligraphy are by N. Scott Momaday.

    Reprint:

    New York: St. Martin's Press, 2000. Trade paperbound ed.

    This book about Bear (Urset, the original Bear) and bears has been described as a mixed-genre literary collection. The bear has fascinated and inspired Momaday for a long time, particularly since his Kiowa name, Tsoai-talee, connects him to the Kiowa story of the boy who turned into a bear. The bear holds great significance in his creative vision and expressions, both written and oral, in many forms that encompass the novel, poetry, painting and drawing, playwriting, storytelling, and teaching.

    Momaday declares in his Introduction: "Let me say at the outset that this is not a book about Bear (he would be spoken of in the singular and masculine, capitalized and without an article), or it is only incidentally about him. I am less interested in defining the being of Bear than in trying to understand something about the spirit of wilderness, of which Bear is a very particular expression. Even Urset, who is the original Bear and comes directly from the hand of God, is symbolic and transparent, more transparent than real, if you will. He is an imitation of himself, a mask. If you look at him very closely and long enough, you will see the mountains on the other side. Bear is a template of the wilderness" (9).

    In the Bear's House begins with "The Bear-God Dialogues," eight in all in which Yahweh, the Creator, and Urset, the original Bear, have splendid discussions of a worldly and otherworldly nature. The second part begins with Momaday's award-winning poem, "The Bear," and presents a variety of poetry, prose poems, and stories that treat the bear in all of his marvelous aspects. The last part, "Passages," presents two stories: "The Bear Hunt" and "The Transformation," the latter telling the "Kiowa Story of Tsoai," accompanied by Momaday's commentary.

18. ***Les enfants du soleil (The Children of the Sun)***. Text by N. Scott Momaday; translated into French by Danièle Laruelle. Illustrated by Federica Matta. Paris: Éditions du Seuil, 2003.

This paperbound book for children has been published only in French. The story is based upon a traditional Kiowa narrative about twin heroes, children born of an earthly mother and the god who is The Sun. Through the Twins, the Kiowas are related to the deity of the Sun Dance. There is a story within the story that tells about Aila, the young woman who marries The Sun and brings color to the world. This book was adapted from Momaday's play for the stage, *Children of the Sun*, published in *Three Plays* in 2007 (see below). His daughter Cael recorded the story for her first child, and together Momaday and Cael collaborated on the book for children.

19. ***Four Arrows and Magpie: A Kiowa Story.*** Text and illustrations by N. Scott Momaday. Tulsa, Oklahoma: HAWK Publishing Group, 2006. 35 pp. Illus. in color, 9 × 9 in. (23 cm.). Paperbound ed. only. A color portrait of Momaday is on the back cover.

    This book is one of three published in a joint endeavor of the Oklahoma Arts Institute, the Oklahoma Centennial Commission, and ONEOK to commemorate and celebrate the State of Oklahoma's Centennial in 2007. This Kiowa story from oral tradition is about courage and bravery. Twins, the boy Four Arrows and his sister Magpie, save the shield and dog of Charging Bear, a great warrior.

20. ***Three Plays.*** First ed. Oklahoma Stories and Storytellers, vol. 3, ser. ed. Teresa Miller. Norman: University of Oklahoma Press, 2007. x, 177 pp. Illus., 5½ × 9¼ in. (23.5 cm.). Clothbound with dust jacket. Includes an illustration by Momaday.

    This is Momaday's first collection of published plays, consisting of two stage plays, *The Indolent Boys* and *Children of the Sun*, and a screenplay, *The Moon in Two Windows*. *The Indolent Boys*, which has been performed in several states, recounts a tragedy that happened in 1891 when three Kiowa boys ran away from the boarding school in Anadarko, Oklahoma, and froze to death. The incident is preserved in tribal memory and recorded in Kiowa calendars. The story of *Children of the Sun* is briefly described above. The screenplay, *The Moon in Two Windows*, is set in Pennsylvania, where children of various tribes were forced to go, traveling far from their homes to live and work at the Carlisle Indian Industrial School, founded in 1879 by Richard Henry Pratt. It tells the stories of those children.

Published Essays, Stories, and Passages with Reprintings, Excerpts, and Quotes Used in Works by Others

1963

21. **"The Well"** (story). *Ramparts* (Layman's Press, Menlo Park, California) 2, no. 1 (May 1963): 49–52.

    This story has been reprinted in the following books:

    A Nation of Nations, edited by Theodore L. Gross. New York: Macmillan, 1971. 420–25.

    Earth Song, Sky Spirit: Short Stories of the Contemporary Native American Experience, edited and with an introduction by Clifford E. Trafzer. New York: Anchor Books, Doubleday, 1993. 97–103.

1964

22. **"The Morality of Indian Hating"** (essay). *Ramparts* 3, no. 1 (Summer 1964): 29–40. Reprinted in *The Man Made of Words: Essays, Stories, Passages*. New York: St. Martin's Press, 1997. 57–76. Momaday added an "Afterword" (76).

    Reprinted or quoted in the following works:

    An excerpt was included in Lawrence J. Evers, "Words and Place: A Reading of *House Made of Dawn*." *Western American Literature* 11, no. 4 (Winter 1977): 297–320. Reprinted in *Critical Essays on Native American Literature*, edited by Andrew Wiget. Boston: G. K. Hall, 1985. 227. The excerpt is from p. 40 of *Ramparts*.

    Quoted in "Introduction" to "Word Senders: Special Issue on American Indian Translation," edited by Kenneth Lincoln. *American Indian Culture and Research Journal* 4, nos. 1–2 (1980): 12. Lincoln used the quote in an essay published in *Three American Literatures*, edited by Houston A. Baker, Jr. New York: Modern Language Association of America, 1982. It appeared again in Lincoln's essay in *Smoothing the Ground: Essays on Native American Oral Literature*, edited by Brian Swann. Berkeley: University of California Press, 1983. 19. It is also in Lincoln's *Native American Renaissance*. Berkeley: University of California Press, 1983. 39.

    An excerpt appeared in *The People and the Word: Reading Native Nonfiction*, by Robert Warrior. Minneapolis: University of Minnesota Press, 2005. 178–79.

Quoted in essay, "More than One Way to Tell a Story," by Tish Eshelle Twomey. *Studies in American Indian Literatures* 19, no. 2 (Summer 2007): 37.

Quoted in essay, "Native American Literary Responses to the Old World," by Lee Schweninger. *American Indian Culture and Research Journal* 27, no. 2 (2003): 75, n.31.

Excerpt in essay, "The Mystery of Language: N. Scott Momaday, An Appreciation," by Jace Weaver. *Studies in American Indian Literatures* 20, no. 4 (Winter 2008): 76.

1966

23. **"Three Sketches from *House Made of Dawn*"** (excerpts). *Southern Review*, n.s., 2, no. 4 (October 1966): 933–45. The first two sketches, "The Sparrow and the Reed," 933–37, and "Homecoming," 937–41, are from chapters "July 20" and "July 21" in Part 1, "The Longhair," *House Made of Dawn* (1968). The third sketch is "The Albino," 941–45, from chapter "July 25" in Part 1, "The Longhair."

1967

24. **"The Story of the Arrowmaker."** This is a Kiowa story of profound importance to Momaday. He has remarked in his writing and speaking that the arrowmaker is "the man made of words." The publishing history of this story began with *The Journey of Tai-me*, privately printed in Santa Barbara in 1967. It is the twelfth story in this collection of stories from the Kiowa oral tradition. It was published the following year in "Two Tales from *The Journey of Tai-me*" in "American Indian Issue," edited by John Ridland. *Little Square Review*, nos. 5–6 (Spring–Summer 1968): 31.

    "The Story of the Arrowmaker" became the first part, the ancestral or legendary voice of Story XIII in *The Way to Rainy Mountain* (1969), 46. It was also published in 1969 in an essay, "The Story of the Arrowmaker," by Momaday, in the *New York Times Book Review*, May 4, 1969, p. 2.

    The story is an important part of Momaday's 1970 seminal address, "The Man Made of Words," published in *Indian Voices: The First Convocation of American Indian Scholars*, edited by Rupert Costo. San Francisco: Indian Historian Press, 1970. 59–60. It appeared in Momaday's essay, "The Native Voice," published in the *Columbia Literary History of the United States*, Emory Elliott, gen. ed. New York: Columbia University Press, 1988. 11–12. Also reprinted in the essay, "The Arrowmaker," in *The Man Made of Words: Essays, Stories, Passages*. New York: St. Martin's Press, 1997. 9–10.

This story has been reprinted numerous times in published works written or edited by others:

The Portable North American Indian Reader, edited by Frederick W. Turner III. New York: Viking, 1974. 586.

"Landscapes: An Interview with N. Scott Momaday," by William T. Morgan, Jr. *Sequoia* 19, no. 2 (Winter 1975): 39. Reprinted in *Sequoia* 23, no. 1 (Autumn–Winter 1978): 21. Reprint in *Conversations with N. Scott Momaday,* edited by Matthias Schubnell. Jackson: University Press of Mississippi, 1997. 45.

Literature of the American Indians: Views and Interpretations, edited by Abraham Chapman. New York: New American Library, 1975. 107–108.

The Remembered Earth: An Anthology of Contemporary Native American Literature, edited by Geary Hobson. Albuquerque, New Mexico: Red Earth, 1979. 171. Reprinted by University of New Mexico Press, 1981. 171.

Growing Old at Willie Nelson's Picnic and Other Sketches of Life in the Southwest, edited by Ronald B. Querry. College Station: Texas A&M University, 1983. 18.

Paraphrased in *Native American Renaissance,* by Kenneth Lincoln. Berkeley: University of California Press, 1983. 44. Reprinted in Lincoln's essay, "Native American Literatures." *Smoothing the Ground: Essays on Native American Oral Literature,* edited by Brian Swann. Berkeley: University of California Press, 1983. 21.

Symposium of the Whole: A Range of Discourse toward an Ethnopoetics, edited by Jerome Rothenberg and Diane Rothenberg. Berkeley: University of California Press, 1983. 414–16.

N. Scott Momaday: The Cultural and Literary Background, by Matthias Schubnell. Norman: University of Oklahoma Press, 1985. 58.

Ancestral Voice: Conversations with N. Scott Momaday, by Charles L. Woodard. Lincoln: University of Nebraska, 1989. 116.

Narrative Chance: Postmodern Discourse on Native American Indian Literatures, edited by Gerald Vizenor. Albuquerque: University of New Mexico Press, 1989. 55. Reprint, Norman: University of Oklahoma Press, 1993. 55.

Paraphrased in *Forked Tongues: Speech, Writing, and Representation in North American Indian Texts,* by David Murray. Bloomington: Indiana University Press, 1991. 14.

America in 1492: The World of the Indian Peoples before the Arrival of Columbus, edited by Alvin M. Josephy, Jr. New York: Alfred A. Knopf, 1992. 18.

Parabola 20, no. 3 (Fall 1995): 21–23.

Smoke Rising: The Native North American Literary Companion, edited by Janet Witalec. Detroit: Visible Ink Press, 1995. 333–34.

Essay by Sally L. Joyce in *American Writers*, A. Walton Litz, editor in chief. Supplement IV, Part 2. New York: Macmillan, 1996. 487.

Introduction to *Defending Mother Earth: Native American Perspectives on Environmental Justice*, edited by Jace Weaver. Maryknoll, New York: Orbis Books, 1996. 2.

Earth's Mind: Essays in Native Literature, by Roger Dunsmore. Albuquerque: University of New Mexico Press, 1997. 123–24.

Making Literature Matter: An Anthology, by John Schilb and John Clifford. Boston: Bedford/St. Martin's, 2000. 215.

The Native American Oral Tradition: Voices of the Spirit and Soul, by Lois J. Einhorn. Westport, Connecticut: Praeger, 2000. 28–29.

Introduction to *Wordarrows: Native States of Literary Sovereignity*, by Gerald Vizenor. Lincoln: University of Nebraska Press, 2003. vii–viii.

Writing Home: Indigenous Narratives of Resistance, by Michael D. Wilson. East Lansing: Michigan State University Press, 2008. 14–15. The story is paraphrased and discussed in the book.

25. **"The Way to Rainy Mountain"** (essay). *The Reporter*, January 26, 1967, 41–43. After its first printing in *The Reporter*, Momaday used this essay in a slightly different form in *House Made of Dawn* (1968), in the chapter titled "January 27," in Part 2, "The Priest of the Sun," 127–36. It is the story told by Tosamah, orator and Priest of the Sun.

In 1969 this writing, again with some changes, became the "Introduction" of *The Way to Rainy Mountain*, published by the University of New Mexico Press. The introduction begins: "A single knoll rises out of the plain in Oklahoma, north and west of the Wichita Range. For my people, the Kiowas, it is an old landmark, and they gave it the name Rainy Mountain." It ends: "Looking back once, I saw the mountain and came away." This introduction has appeared on pages 5 to 12 of the first edition of *The Way to Rainy Mountain*, the paperbound edition published in 1976, and all subsequent reprintings by the University of New Mexico Press.

"The Way to Rainy Mountain" was selected for inclusion in *Best American Essays of the Century*, edited by Joyce Carol Oates and co-edited by Robert Atwan. Boston: Houghton Mifflin, 2000. 313–18.

The "Introduction" to *The Way to Rainy Mountain* has been reprinted in a broad range of other published works:

Forgotten Pages of American Literature, by Gerald W. Haslam. Boston: Houghton Mifflin, 1970. 51–56.

American Indian Authors, by Natachee S. Momaday. Boston: Houghton Mifflin, 1971, ©1972. 125–31.

Touch the Earth: A Self-Portrait of Indian Existence, by T. C. McLuhan. New York: Promontory Press, 1971. 21.

The Portable North American Indian Reader, edited by F. W. Turner III. New York: Viking, 1974, ©1973. 580–86.

American Indian Literature: An Anthology, edited and with an introduction by Alan R. Velie. Norman: University of Oklahoma Press, 1979. 246–51.

This Song Remembers: Self-Portraits of Native Americans in the Arts, edited by Jane B. Katz. Boston: Houghton Mifflin, 1980. 196–201.

Growing Old at Willie Nelson's Picnic and Other Sketches of Life in the Southwest, edited by Ronald B. Querry. College Station: Texas A&M University Press, 1983. 11–17.

Essay: Reading with the Writer's Eye, by Hans P. Guth and Renée V. Hausmann. Belmont, California: Wadsworth, 1984. 30–35.

Writers of the Purple Sage, edited by Russell Martin and Marc Barasch. New York: Viking, 1984. 1–7.

The Norton Book of Nature Writing, edited by Robert Finch and John Elder. New York: W. W. Norton, 1990. 774–79.

American Indian Literature: An Anthology, edited and with an introduction by Alan R. Velie. Rev. ed. Norman: University of Oklahoma Press, 1991. 205–210.

American Literature: A Prentice Hall Anthology. Concise ed. Emory Elliott, gen. ed. Englewood Cliffs, New Jersey: Prentice Hall, 1991. 2091–2095. This edition includes the body of *The Way to Rainy Mountain* through the Epilogue, 2088–2113.

Tapestry: A Multicultural Anthology, Alan C. Purves, gen. ed. Paramus, New Jersey: Simon & Schuster, 1993. 76–81.

The Heath Anthology of American Literature, edited by Paul Lauter. 2nd ed., vol. 2. Lexington, Massachusetts: Heath, 1994. 2724–25 (excerpt).

Native American Literature: A Brief Introduction and Anthology, edited by

Gerald Vizenor. New York: HarperCollins, 1995. 60–64.

Smoke Rising: The Native North American Literary Companion, edited by Janet Witalec. Detroit: Visible Ink, 1995. 327–33.

Constructing Nature: Readings from the American Experience, edited by Richard Jenseth and Edward E. Lotto. A Blair Press Book. Upper Saddle River, New Jersey: Prentice Hall, 1996. 231–36.

75 Readings: An Anthology, edited by Santi Buscemi and Charlotte Smith. 6th ed. New York: McGraw-Hill, 1997. 68–72.

Native American Literature: An Anthology, compiled and edited by Lawana Trout. Lincolnwood, Illinois: NTC/Contemporary Publishing Group, 1998, ©1999. 367–73.

The Literary West: An Anthology of Western American Literature, edited by Thomas J. Lyon. New York: Oxford University Press, 1999. 208–13.

Nature Writing: The Tradition in English, edited by Robert Finch and John Elder. New York: W. W. Norton, 2002. 737–42.

Norton Anthology of American Literature. 6th ed. Nina Baym, gen. ed. New York: W. W. Norton, 2003. 2322–26.

The Portable Sixties Reader, edited by Ann Charters. New York: Penguin Books, 2003. 581–86.

50 Essays: A Portable Anthology, edited by Samuel Cohen. Boston: Bedford/St. Martin's, 2004. 265–71.

The New World Reader, edited by Gilbert H. Muller. Boston: Houghton Mifflin, 2005. 31–37.

One Hundred Great Essays, edited by Robert DiYanni. 2nd ed. Penguin Classics. New York: Pearson Longman, 2005. 555–61.

Speak Like Singing, by Kenneth Lincoln. Albuquerque: University of New Mexico Press, 2007. 132–33. Under heading "Plains Origins."

In addition to the "Introduction," many parts of *The Way to Rainy Mountain* have been reprinted and quoted in anthologies, essays, and other publications. For example, the "Prologue" on pp. 3–4 of *The Way to Rainy Mountain* has appeared in other published works since its original publication. It begins: "The journey began one day long ago on the edge of the northern Plains" (3). Some of those reprintings appear in the following works:

Sun Tracks: An American Indian Literary Quarterly 1, no. 3 (Winter 1971–72): 1. Cover illus. by Al Momaday.

The Portable North American Indian Reader, edited and with an introduction by F. W. Turner III. New York: Viking, 1974, ©1973, 578–80.

American Literature: A Prentice Hall Anthology. Concise ed. Emory Elliott, gen. ed. Englewood Cliffs, New Jersey: Prentice Hall, 1991. 2090–91.

The Heath Anthology of American Literature. 2nd ed., vol. 2. Paul Lauter, gen. ed. Lexington, Mass.: Heath, 1994. 2723–24.

Native American Autobiography: An Anthology, edited by Arnold Krupat. Madison: University of Wisconsin Press, 1994. 402–403. The Prologue is accompanied by Stories III–VI, X–XI, and XXI–XXIV, pp. 403–14. These are complete, each with the three voices that are unique to *The Way to Rainy Mountain.*

Constructing Nature: Readings from the American Experience, edited by Richard Jenseth and Edward E. Lotto. Upper Saddle River, New Jersey: Prentice Hall, 1996. 230–31.

Native American Literatures: An Introduction, by Suzanne Evertsen Lundquist. New York: Continuum, 2004. 60.

The Heath Anthology of American Literature, edited by Paul Lauter. Vol. E. Boston: Houghton Mifflin, 2006. 2481–82.

26. **"The Bear and the Colt"** (excerpt). In "Two Sketches from *House Made of Dawn.*" *New Mexico Quarterly* 37, no. 2 (Summer 1967): 101–105. This sketch appeared before the novel was published. It is from chapter "February 27" in Part 4, "The Dawn Runner," *House Made of Dawn* (1968), 198–204. Momaday also included it under the title, "The Bear Hunt," in *In the Bear's House* (1999), 83–89.

Other appearances of "The Bear and the Colt" include the following:

Speaking for Ourselves: American Ethnic Writing, edited by Lillian Faderman and Barbara Bradshaw. Glenview, Illinois: Scott Foresman, 1969. 472–76.

American Indian Authors, written and edited by Natachee Scott Momaday. Boston: Houghton Mifflin, 1971, ©1972. 119–24.

With the title "Francisco's Bear Hunt" in *American Indian Literature: An Anthology,* edited by Alan R. Velie. Norman: University of Oklahoma Press, 1979. 336–42. Also in Velie's revised edition, published by the University of Oklahoma Press, 1991. 315–19.

27. **"The Eagles of the Valle Grande"** (excerpt). In "Two Sketches from *House Made of Dawn.*" *New Mexico Quarterly* 37, no. 2 (Summer 1967): 105–111.

The story of the eagles appears in chapter "July 21" in Part 1, "The Long Hair," *House Made of Dawn* (1968), 14–22.

Reprinted in the following books:

Speaking for Ourselves: American Ethnic Writing, edited by Lillian Faderman and Barbara Bradshaw. Glenview, Illinois: Scott Foresman: 1969. 476–81.

Literature of the American Indian, edited by Thomas E. Sanders and Walter W. Peek. Beverly Hills, California: Glencoe Press, 1973. 492–97.

Braided Lives: An Anthology of Multicultural Writing. St. Paul: Minnesota Humanities Commission, 1991. 43–48.

Red Land, Red Power: Grounding Knowledge in the American Indian Novel, by Sean Kicummah Teuton. Durham, North Carolina: Duke University Press, 2008. 62–63.

28. **"The Heretical Cricket"** (essay). *Southern Review*, n.s., 3, no. 1 (January 1967): 43–50. This essay focuses on "The Cricket," a poem written by Frederick Goddard Tuckerman. Momaday, editor of *The Complete Poems of Frederick Goddard Tuckerman* (1965), discusses the poem in the context of the literature of resistance to American transcendentalism. Tuckerman's poem was published nearly one hundred years after he wrote it.

29. **"The Kiowa Story of Tsoai."** This story first appeared as "The Seven Sisters" in *The Reporter*, January 26, 1967, 41–43.

From the oral tradition of the Kiowas, this story is the legend of Rock Tree (Devils Tower). Momaday has stated that this story exemplifies the sacred for him. It tells about eight children, seven sisters and their brother, at play. The boy turns into a bear and begins chasing his sisters. They run and jump onto a tree trunk that rises high into the sky. The bear is close behind and claws the trunk as it rises. The seven sisters become the stars of the Big Dipper.

Following the story's appearance in *The Reporter*, it appeared later in 1967 in *The Journey of Tai-me*, a privately printed book in one hundred copies. It is the ninth story in this book. Momaday also used the story in chapter "January 27" in Part 2, "The Priest of the Sun," *House Made of Dawn* (1968), 131.

"The Kiowa Story of Tsoai" was used by Momaday in his "Introduction" to *The Way to Rainy Mountain*, on p. 8 of the hardcover edition (1969) and paperback edition (1976), published by the University of New Mexico Press. This introduction appeared again in *The Names: A Memoir*, originally published in 1976 by Harper & Row, on p. 55, and reprinted on the same page of the Sun

Tracks series, vol. 16, published by the University of Arizona Press in 1996. The story was also included in Momaday's essay, "Ancient Vision," published in *Revue Française D'Études Américaines*, no. 38 (November 1988): 375–76.

In addition to its appearances in his earlier books, Momaday used this story as the "Prologue" to *The Ancient Child*, first published by Doubleday in 1989 on p. 1, and reprinted in 1990 in the First HarperPerennial paperback edition, also on p. 1. It later appeared in Momaday's essay "Revisiting Sacred Ground," *The Man Made of Words: Essays, Stories, Passages* (1997), 122, and in "The Transformation: Kiowa Story of Tsoai," *In the Bear's House* (1999), 91–92. It has also been used in a number of his speeches and lectures.

"The Kiowa Story of Tsoai" has appeared in a number of published works, including those in which the "Introduction" of *The Way to Rainy Mountain* has been reprinted. This story, sometimes appearing with a different title, has been reprinted by itself in the following works written or edited by others:

With the title, "The Story of Devils Tower," in *Ancestral Voice: Conversations with N. Scott Momaday*, by Charles L. Woodard. Lincoln: University of Nebraska Press, 1989. 14.

Interview with Momaday conducted by Suzanne Wise and published in the *Poetry Society of America Newsletter*, no. 34 (Fall 1990): 29.

With the title, "The Legend of the Eight Children," in *The Lightning Within*, edited by Alan R. Velie. Lincoln: University of Nebraska Press, 1991. 14–15. Reprint (pbk.), Lincoln: University of Nebraska Press, 1993. 14–15.

Family of Earth and Sky: Indigenous Tales of Nature from around the World, edited by John Elder and Hertha D. Wong. Boston: Beacon Press, 1994. 78.

Essay about Momaday by Sally Joyce in *American Writers*, edited by A. Walton Litz. Supplement IV, Part 2. New York: Macmillan, 1996. 486.

With the title "Eight Children" in essay by Susan Roberson in *American Indian Quarterly* 22, nos. 1–2 (Winter–Spring 1998): 36.

Paraphrased in *Looking West*, by John D. Dorst. Contemporary Ethnography. Philadelphia: University of Pennsylvania Press, 1999. 193.

Literary Masters, vol. 12, *N. Scott Momaday*, by Lee Schweninger. Detroit: Gale, 2001. 13.

A Great Plains Reader, edited by Diane D. Quantic and P. Jane Hafen. Lincoln: University of Nebraska Press, 2003. 55.

With the title, "The Seven Sisters," in *Archaeoastronomy* 12–13 (2005): 32.

With the title, "Eight Sisters," in *Reading, Learning, Teaching: N. Scott Momaday,* by Jim Charles. New York: Peter Lang, 2007. 24.

Poet Maxine Kumin credited "The Story of Tsoai" from the "Prologue" of *The Ancient Child* for her inspiration in writing a poem titled "Credo," published in one of her poetry collections: *Looking for Luck: Poems,* edited by Maxine Kumin. New York: W. W. Norton, 1992. 15–16.

1968

30. **"Two Tales from *The Journey of Tai-me*"** (stories). "American Indian Issue," edited by John Ridland. *Little Square Review,* nos. 5–6 (Spring–Summer 1968): 30–31. The tales are "The Beginning," p. 30, and "The Arrow" ("The Story of the Arrowmaker"), p. 31. These are the first and twelfth stories in *The Journey of Tai-me.* Both also appear in *The Way to Rainy Mountain.*

1969

31. **"First Novelists: Thirty-eight New Writers Discuss Their First Published Novel; N. Scott Momaday, Harper-1969"** (brief essay). *Library Journal* 93, no. 11 (June 1, 1968): 2271. (port.) Momaday contributed a short piece about his recently published first novel, *House Made of Dawn.*

32. **"The Remembered Earth"** (passage). This is Momaday's most frequently repeated passage. It first appeared as the third, or personal, voice of Story XXIV in *The Way to Rainy Mountain,* on p. 83 of the hardcover edition (1969) and paperback edition (1976) published by the University of New Mexico Press.

    Momaday included this passage in his landmark address, "The Man Made of Words," presented in 1970 to the assembly attending the First Convocation of American Indian Scholars held at Princeton University. It was published later that year in *Indian Voices,* edited by Rupert Costo. San Francisco: Indian Historian Press, 1970. 52. It was also included in his essays, "The Native Voice" (1988) and "An American Land Ethic" (1970).

    Momaday has recited this passage on numerous occasions. The full passage, as it was published in *The Way to Rainy Mountain,* begins with the sentence, "East of my grandmother's house the sun rises out of the plain." This sentence is generally omitted, and the passage appears in print or is heard as follows:

    > Once in his life a man ought to concentrate his mind upon the remembered earth, I believe. He ought to give himself up to a particular landscape in his experience, to look at it from as many angles as he can, to wonder about it, to dwell upon it. He ought to imagine that he touches it with his hands at every season and listens to the sounds that are made

upon it. He ought to imagine the creatures there and all the faintest motions of the wind. He ought to recollect the glare of noon and all the colors of the dawn and dusk.

"The Remembered Earth" has been reprinted or quoted in the following works:

Review essay, "More Than Language Means," by Kenneth Fields. *Southern Review*, n.s., 6, no. 1 (Winter 1970): 202.

Review essay, "The Remembered Earth: Momaday's *House Made of Dawn*," by Carole Oleson. *South Dakota Review* 11, no. 1 (Spring 1973): 59. This review also appeared in *Contemporary Literary Criticism*, vol. 95 (1997), 218.

Literature of the American Indians: Views and Interpretations, edited by Abraham Chapman. New York: New American Library, 1975. 99.

Essay, "N. Scott Momaday, Racial Memory, and Individual Imagination," by Barbara Strelke. *Literature of the American Indians*, edited by Abraham Chapman. New York: New American Library, 1975. 356.

Interview, "Landscapes: N. Scott Momaday," conducted by William T. Morgan, Jr., and published in *Sequoia* 19, no. 2 (Winter 1975): 39, and *Sequoia* 23, no. 1 (Autumn–Winter 1978): 21. Reprint in *Conversations with N. Scott Momaday*, edited by Matthias Schubnell. Jackson: University Press of Mississippi, 1997. 45.

Review by Dudley Wynn of *The Way to Rainy Mountain*. *New Mexico Historical Review* 51, no. 3 (July 1976): 260.

Circle without End, edited by Frances G. and Gerald Scott Lombardus. Happy Camp, California: Naturegraph, 1982. 17.

Essay, "Native American Literatures: 'old like hills, like stars,'" by Kenneth Lincoln. In *Three American Literatures*, edited by Houston A. Baker, Jr. New York: Modern Language Association of America, 1982. 118.

Review essay by Kenneth Lincoln in *American Indian Culture and Research Journal* 6, no. 1 (1982): 95.

Native American Renaissance, by Kenneth Lincoln. Berkeley: University of California Press, 1983. 106.

Essay, "Tai-me to Rainy Mountain," by Kenneth Lincoln. *American Indian Quarterly* 10, no. 2 (Spring 1986): 103.

The Good Red Road: Passages into Native America, by Kenneth Lincoln, with Al Logan Slagle. San Francisco: Harper & Row, 1987. 14–15. Reprint, Bison Books ed. Lincoln: University of Nebraska Press, 1997. 14–15.

N. Scott Momaday: The Cultural and Literary Background, by Matthias Schubnell. Norman: University of Oklahoma Press, 1985. 150.

Artic Dreams, by Barry Lopez. London: Picador; New York: Charles Scribner's Sons, 1986. ix.

Dictionary of Literary Themes and Motifs, edited by Jean-Charles Seigneuret. Vol. 2. Westport, Connecticut: Greenwood Press, 1988. 1007.

Essay, "The Way to Rainy Mountain: Momaday's Work in Motion," by Kimberly Blaeser. *Narrative Chance: Postmodern Discourse on Native American Indian Literatures,* edited by Gerald Vizenor. Albuquerque: University of New Mexico Press, 1989. 53. Reprint, Norman: University of Oklahoma Press, 1993. 53.

American Indian Literatures, by A. LaVonne Brown Ruoff. New York: Modern Language Association of America, 1990. 9.

Literatures of the American Indian, by A. LaVonne Brown Ruoff. New York: Chelsea House, 1991. 20.

Extraordinary American Indians, by Susan Avery and Linda Skinner. Chicago: Childrens Press, 1992. 188.

In the Spirit of the Earth: Rethinking History and Time, by Calvin Martin. Baltimore: Johns Hopkins University Press, 1992. 94.

Being in the World: An Environmental Reader for Writers, edited by Scott H. Slovic and Terrell F. Dixon. New York: Macmillan, 1993. 608.

Paraphrased by Kenneth M. Roemer in his essay, "Ancient Children at Play." *Critical Perspectives on Native American Fiction,* edited by Richard F. Fleck. Washington, D.C.: Three Continents Press, 1993. 100.

Tapestry: A Multicultural Anthology, Alan C. Purves, gen. ed. Paramus, New Jersey: Globe, 1993. 82.

Native American Autobiography: An Anthology, edited by Arnold Krupat. Madison: University of Wisconsin Press, 1994. 414.

American Indian Quotations, edited by Howard Langer. Westport, Connecticut: Greenwood Press, 1996. 162 (entry no. 596).

Essay about Momaday by Sally L. Joyce in *American Writers,* A.Walton Litz, editor in chief. Supplement IV, Part 2. New York: Macmillan, 1996. 486.

Essay, "N. Scott Momaday," by Matthias Schubnell in *American Nature Writers,* edited by John Elder. Vol. 2. New York: Simon & Schuster, 1996. 642.

"Introduction: Notes from a Miner's Canary," by Jace Weaver. *Defending*

Mother Earth: Native American Perspectives on Environmental Justice, edited by Jace Weaver. Maryknoll, New York: Orbis, 1996. 2.

Writing and America, edited by Gavin Cologne-Brookes et al. New York: Longman, 1996. 228.

Essay, "N. Scott Momaday: *House Made of Dawn,*" by Bernadette Rigal-Cellard. Paris: Didier Érudition, CNED, 1997. 67.

Voices of Native America, edited by Hap Gilliland. Dubuque, Iowa: Kendall Hunt, 1997. 37.

Essay, "Fusion," by Katharine Beebe. *Mirage* (University of New Mexico Alumni Association) 15, no. 2 (Winter 1998): 17.

Native American Literature: An Anthology, compiled and edited by Lawana Trout. Lincolnwood (Chicago), Illinois: NTC/Contemporary Publishing Group, 1998, ©1999. 283–84.

A Short Season: Story of a Montana Childhood, by Don Morehead and Ann Morehead. Lincoln: University of Nebraska Press, 1998. 1.

American Indian Portraits. Macmillan Profiles Series. New York: Macmillan Reference USA, 2000. 160.

Sing with the Heart of a Bear, by Kenneth Lincoln. Berkeley: University of California Press, 2000. 278.

Essay, "Ceremonial Healing," by Roberta Rosenberg. *MELUS* 27, no. 3 (Fall 2002): 118.

Of Earth and Elders: Visions and Voices from Native America, by Serle L. Chapman. 2nd ed. Missoula, Montana: Mountain Press Publishing, 2002. 68.

The People and the Word: Reading Native Nonfiction, by Robert Warrior. Minneapolis: University of Minnesota Press, 2005. 176.

The Heath Anthology of American Literature. Vol. E, *Contemporary Period: 1945 to the Present,* edited by Paul Lauter. Boston: Houghton Mifflin, 2006. 2487.

Reading, Learning, Teaching: N. Scott Momaday, by Jim Charles. New York: Peter Lang, 2007. 58.

Speak Like Singing, by Kenneth Lincoln. Albuquerque: University of New Mexico Press, 2007. 36.

Listening to the Land: Native American Literary Responses to the Landscape, by Lee Schweninger. Athens: University of Georgia Press, 2008. 136.

Red Land, Red Power: Grounding Knowledge in the American Indian Novel, by Sean Kicummah Teuton. Durham, North Carolina: Duke University Press, 2008. 246, n.2.

Geary Hobson used the title of this passage as the main title of his anthology, *The Remembered Earth: An Anthology of Contemporary Native American Literature*, which was published in 1979 by Red Earth Press and reprinted by the University of New Mexico Press in 1981. The passage is on the book's dedication page (p. vii) and pp. 64–65.

In 2006, John Grabowska and Momaday collaborated on an Idaho Public Television special titled "Remembered Earth: New Mexico's High Desert." John Grabowska wrote and produced the program, and Momaday provided commentary on land ethics. See also the section "Nonprint Media: Video Recordings."

Also in 2006, the Public Broadcasting System (PBS) featured this familiar passage on its website under "Circle of Stories: Share Your Story," inviting readers to share their own stories about a landscape that inspired them.

33. **"Things That Were Truly Remarkable"** (passage). This is the third, or personal, voice of Story XXI in *The Way to Rainy Mountain* (1969), 73. It begins: "Mammedaty saw four things that were truly remarkable."

Reprinted:

Essay by Barbara Strelke in *Literature of the American Indians*, edited by Abraham Chapman. New York: New American Library, 1975. 355–56.

Shaking the Pumpkin: Traditional Poetry of the North American Indian, compiled and edited by Jerome Rothenberg. Rev. ed. Albuquerque: University of New Mexico Press, 1991. 228.

Nature Writing: The Tradition in English, edited by Robert Finch and John Elder. New York: W. W. Norton, 2000. 740.

34. **"A Word Has Power"** (passage). This is the sixth story in *The Journey of Tai-me* (1967), and the second, or historical, voice of Story VIII in *The Way to Rainy Mountain* (1969), 33. The passage reads:

> A word has power in and of itself. It comes from nothing into sound and meaning; it gives origin to all things. By means of words can a man deal with the world on equal terms. And the word is sacred.

Reprinted or quoted in the following works:

Essay, "More Than Language Means," by Kenneth Fields. *Southern Review*, n.s., 6, no. 1 (January 1970): 197.

The Way: An Anthology of American Indian Literature, edited by Shirley Hill Witt and Stan Steiner. New York: Alfred A. Knopf; Vintage Books, 1972. 38–39.

Essay, "N. Scott Momaday: Racial Memory and Individual Imagination," by Barbara Strelke. *Literature of the American Indians,* edited by Abraham Chapman. New York: New American Library, 1975. 354.

William T. Morgan, Jr., interview, "Landscapes: N. Scott Momaday." *Sequoia* 19, no. 2 (Winter 1975): 40, and *Sequoia* 23, no. 1 (Autumn–Winter 1978): 22. Reprint in Schubnell, *Conversations* (1997), 4.

Seeing with a Native Eye: Essays on Native American Religion, edited by Walter Holden Capps. New York: Harper & Row, 1976. 61.

Essay, "New Interpretations of Native American Literature," by Galen Buller. *American Indian Culture and Research Journal* 4, nos. 1–2 (1980): 167–68.

Essay, "Tai-me to Rainy Mountain," by Kenneth Lincoln. *American Indian Quarterly* 10, no. 2 (Spring 1986): 115.

Ancestral Voice: Conversations with N. Scott Momaday, edited by Charles L. Woodard. Lincoln: University of Nebraska Press, 1989. 77.

Essay, "Monologue and Dialogue in Native American Autobiography," by Arnold Krupat. *The Voice in the Margin: Native American Literature and the Canon.* Berkeley: University of California Press, 1989. 186.

In the Spirit of the Earth: Rethinking History and Time, by Calvin Martin. Baltimore: Johns Hopkins University Press, 1992. 92.

Defending Mother Earth: Native American Perspectives on Environmental Justice, edited by Jace Weaver. Maryknoll, New York: Orbis, 1996. xi-xii.

"Introduction," *In a Sacred Manner I Live,* edited by Neil Philip. New York: Clarion Books, 1997. 11.

The Native American Oral Tradition, by Lois J. Einhorn. Westport, Connecticut: Praeger, 2000. 103.

Essay, "Native American Literatures," by P. Jane Hafen. *A Companion to American Indian History,* edited by Philip J. Deloria and Neal Salisbury. Malden, Massachusetts: Blackwell, 2002. 240.

"Introduction," *Speak to Me Words: Essays on Contemporary American Indian Poetry,* edited by Dean Rader and Janice Gould. Tucson: University of Arizona Press, 2003. 7–8.

A Seat at the Table: Huston Smith in Conversations with Native Americans on Religious Freedom, edited by Phil Cousineau. Berkeley: University of California Press, 2006. 81.

1970

35. **"An American Land Ethic"** (essay). *Sierra Club Bulletin* 55, no. 2 (February 1970): 8–11. Momaday included this essay in *The Man Made of Words: Essays, Stories, Passages* (1997), 42–49.

    Reprinted or quoted in the following publications:

    Ecotactics: The Sierra Club Handbook for Environmental Activists, edited by John G. Mitchell and Constance L. Stallings. New York: Trident Press, 1970. 97–105. (full essay)

    Essay by Raphael Rothstein in *New York Times Book Review*, August 9, 1970, 4–5.

    Native American Renaissance, by Kenneth Lincoln. Berkeley: University of California Press, 1983. 103.

    Excerpt in "Readings," *Sierra* 77, no. 3 (May–June 1992): 151–52.

    Being in the World: An Environmental Reader for Writers, edited by Scott H. Slovic and Terrell Dixon. New York: Macmillan, 1993. 605–11. (full essay)

    Essay by Lee Schweninger in *MELUS* 18, no. 2 (Summer 1993): 53.

    Coyote at Large: Humor in American Nature Writing, by Katrina Schimmoeller Peiffer. Salt Lake City: University of Utah Press, 2000. 172.

36. **"The Man Made of Words"** (address). *Indian Voices: The First Convocation of American Indian Scholars*, edited by Rupert Costo. San Francisco: Indian Historian Press, 1970. 49–62. This reference is to the full address delivered by Momaday during this convocation held at Princeton University. It is one of his most renowned, reprinted, and referred to works. Momaday used the title for his book of collected essays, stories, and passages, *The Man Made of Words* (St. Martin's Press, 1997).

    Reprinted in full or part in the following works by others:

    Literature of the American Indians: Views and Interpretations, edited by Abraham Chapman. New York: New American Library, 1975. 96–110. (full essay)

    The Remembered Earth: An Anthology of Contemporary Native American Literature, edited by Geary Hobson. Albuquerque, New Mexico: Red Earth Press, 1979. Reissued by University of New Mexico Press, 1981. 162–73. (full essay)

Symposium of the Whole: A Range of Discourse toward an Ethnopoetics, edited by Jerome Rothenberg and Diane Rothenberg. Berkeley: University of California Press, 1983. 414–16.

Quoted in *The Way of the Human Being*, by Calvin Martin. New Haven, Connecticut: Yale University Press, 1999. 32.

Family of Earth and Sky: Indigenous Tales of Nature from around the World, edited by John Elder and Hertha D. Wong. Boston: Beacon Press, 1994. 293–307. (full essay)

Native American Literature, An Anthology, compiled and edited by Lawana Trout. Lincolnwood (Chicago), Illinois: NTC/Contemporary Publishing Group, 1998, ©1999. 635–49. (full essay)

Nothing but the Truth: An Anthology of Native Amercian Literature, edited by Lloyd Purdy and James Ruppert. Upper Saddle River, New Jersey: Prentice Hall, 2001. 82–93. (full essay)

Quoted in "Introduction," *Wordarrows*, edited by Gerald Vizenor. Lincoln: University of Nebraska Press, 2003. vii–viii.

A statement made by Momaday in his address, "The Man Made of Words," that has created considerable discussion is "an Indian is an idea which a given man has of himself." It appears in the full address first published in *Indian Voices: The First Convocation of American Indian Scholars*, edited by Rupert Costo (Indian Historian Press, 1970), 49. This statement was made by Momaday in response to the question, "What is an American Indian?" He stated, "The answer of course is that an Indian is an idea which a given man has of himself. And it is a moral idea, for it accounts for the way in which he reacts to other men and to the world in general. And that idea, in order to be realized completely, has to be expressed" (49).

Momaday's statement is quoted and discussed in a number of essays and writings by others. It has been reprinted or quoted in the following published works:

Literature of the American Indians: Views and Interpretations, edited by Abraham Chapman. New York: New American Library, 1975. 97.

Paraphrased in "Introduction" to "Special Issue No. 2 on American Indian Translation," edited by Kenneth Lincoln. *American Indian Culture and Research Journal* 4, no. 4, (1980): 2.

Essay by Galen Buller in *American Indian Culture and Research Journal* 4, nos. 1–2 (1980): 166.

Essay by Kenneth Lincoln, "A Contemporary Tribe of Poets." *American Indian Culture and Research Journal* 6, no. 1 (1982): 95.

"Introduction," *Studies in American Indian Literature: Critical Essays and Course Designs*, edited by Paula Gunn Allen. New York: Modern Language Association of America, 1983. ix.

Native American Renaissance, by Kenneth Lincoln. Berkeley: University of California Press, 1983. 77, 206.

"Introduction," *Indian Lives: Essays on Nineteenth- and Twentieth-Century Native American Leaders*, edited by L. G. Moser and Raymond Wilson. Albuquerque: University of New Mexico Press, 1985. 10.

N. Scott Momaday: The Cultural and Literary Background, by Matthias Schubnell. Norman: University of Oklahoma Press, 1985. 41.

Essay by Paula Gunn Allen in *Recovering the Word: Essays on Native American Literature*, edited by Brian Swann and Arnold Krupat. Berkeley: University of California Press, 1987. 563.

Essay by Elaine Jahner in *Narrative Chance: Postmodern Discourse on Native American Literatures*, edited by Gerald Vizenor. Albuquerque: University of New Mexico Press, 1989. 164. Reprint (pbk.), Norman: University of Oklahoma Press, 1993. 164.

American Indian Literatures: An Introduction, Bibliographic Review, and Selected Bibliography, by A. LaVonne Brown Ruoff. New York: Modern Language Association of America, 1990. vi.

Interview with Momaday conducted by Gabrielle Tayac in "Views from the Shore: Toward an Indian Voice in 1992," edited by José Barreiro. Special issue. *Northeast Indian Quarterly* 7, no. 3 (Fall 1990): 7.

Interview, "N. Scott Momaday," by Louis Owens. In *This Is about Vision*, edited by William Balassi et al. Albuquerque: University of New Mexico Press, 1990. 62.

Conversations with N. Scott Momaday, edited by Matthias Schubnell. Jackson: University of Mississippi Press, 1997. 185.

Forked Tongues: Speech, Writing, and Representation in North American Indian Texts, by David Murray. Bloomington: Indiana University Press, 1991. 14.

Essay by Rodney Simard in *World Literature Today* 66, no. 2 (Spring 1992): 244.

"Introduction," *Other Destinies: Understanding the American Indian Novel*, by Louis Owens. Norman: University of Oklahoma Press, 1992. 5.

Essay by Wolfgang Hochbruck in *New Voices in Native American Literary Criticism,* edited by Arnold Krupat. Washington, D.C.: Smithsonian Institution Press, 1993. 206.

Introductory essay by Julie LaMay Abner to "Teaching American Indian Literatures Issue," edited by Abner. *Studies in American Indian Literatures,* ser. 2, 8, no. 2 (Summer 1996): 2.

Killing the White Man's Indian: Reinventing Native Americans at the End of the Twentieth Century, by Fergus M. Bordewich. New York: Doubleday, 1996. 67.

Post-Tribal Epics: The Native American Novel between Tradition and Modernity, by Giorgio Mariani. Lewiston, New York: Edwin Mellen Press, 1996. 67.

Essay by Darrell J. Peters in *American Indian Quarterly* 21, no. 3 (Summer 1997): 472.

Essay by Linda Krumholz in *Leslie Marmon Silko: A Collection of Critical Essays,* edited by Louise K. Barnett and James L. Thorson. Albuquerque: University of New Mexico Press, 1999. 78.

Essay by Jana Sequoya Magdaleno in *Postcolonial Theory and the United States,* edited by Amritjit Singh and Peter Schmidt. Jackson: University Press of Mississippi, 2000. 283.

Blood Narrative, by Chadwick Allen. Durham, North Carolina: Duke University Press, 2002. 179.

Indian Country: Essays on Contemporary Native Culture, by Gail Guthrie Valaskakis. Waterloo, Ontario, Canada: Wilfrid Laurier University Press, 2005. 240.

Essay by Helmbrecht Breinig in *Transatlantic Voices: Interpretations of Native North American Literatures,* edited by Elvira Pulitano. Lincoln: University of Nebraska Press, 2007. 57.

Essay by Gaetano Prampolini in *Transatlantic Voices: Interpretations of Native North American Literatures,* edited by Elvira Pulitano. University of Nebraska Press, 2007. 68.

Writing Home: Indigenous Narratives of Resistance, by Michael D. Wilson. East Lansing: Michigan State University Press, 2008. 14.

A. LaVonne Brown Ruoff stated in her preface to *American Indian Literatures* (1990): "This volume uses as its basic definition of *American Indian identity* that given by N. Scott Momaday in 'The Man Made of Words': 'an idea which a given man has of himself'" (vi).

Another statement, or passage, from "The Man Made of Words" that has been quoted and discussed in the works of other writers appears on p. 55 of *Indian Voices* (1970):

> We are what we imagine. Our very existence consists in our imagination of ourselves. Our best destiny is to imagine, at least, completely, who and what, and *that* we are. The greatest tragedy that can befall us is to go unimagined.

Reprinted or quoted in the following:

Literature of the American Indians: Views and Interpretations, edited by Abraham Chapman. New York: New American Library, 1975. 103.

The Remembered Earth, edited by Geary Hobson. Albuquerque: University of New Mexico Press, 1980. 167.

Epigraph of essay by Tom Pew in *American West* 23, no. 5 (September–October 1986): 6.

Essay by Paula Gunn Allen in *Recovering the Word*, edited by Brian Swann and Arnold Krupat. Berkeley: University of California Press, 1987. 566.

Essay by Bernard A. Hirsch in *American Indian Quarterly* 12, no. 1 (Winter 1988): 4.

Essay by Judith Mountain Leaf Volborth in *Native American Literatures*, edited by Laura Coltelli. Forum, no. 1. Pisa, Italy: SEU (Servizio Editoriale Universitaria), 1989. 67.

Essay by Kimberly M. Blaeser in *Narrative Chance: Postmodern Discourse on Native American Indian Literatures*, edited by Gerald Vizenor. Albuquerque: University of New Mexico Press, 1989. 39. Reprint, Norman: University of Oklahoma Press, 1993. 39.

Interview, "N. Scott Momaday," by Louis Owens. In *This Is about Vision*, edited by William Balassi et al. Albuquerque: University of New Mexico Press, 1990. 64. Reprinted in *Conversations with N. Scott Momaday*, edited by Matthias Schubnell. Jackson: University of Mississippi Press, 1997. 185.

Essay by Kimberly M. Blaeser in *World Literature Today* 66, no. 2 (Spring 1992): 233.

Other Destinies: Understanding the American Indian Novel, by Louis Owens. Norman: University of Oklahoma Press, 1992. 93. Reprint (pbk.), University of Oklahoma Press, 1994. 93.

"Introduction" to "Contemporary Native Art: A Bibliography," by Lawrence Abbott. *American Indian Quarterly* 18, no. 3 (Summer 1994): 384.

Mediation in Contemporary Native American Fiction, by James Ruppert. Norman: University of Oklahoma Press, 1995. 154, n.5.

American Indian Quotations, edited by Howard J. Langer. Westport, Connecticut: Greenwood Press, 1996. 63.

Essay by Karen L. Wallace in *American Indian Culture and Research Journal* 20, no. 4 (Fall 1996): 94.

Essay by Kathleen Blake Yancey in *Writing Portfolios in the Classroom,* edited by Robert C. Calfee and Pamela Perfumo. Mahwah, New Jersey: Lawrence Erlbaum Associates, 1996. 83 (epigraph), 101.

The Heart as a Drum: Continuance and Resistance in American Indian Poetry, by Robin Riley Fast. Ann Arbor: University of Michigan Press, 2000. 37.

"Introduction" to "Imagining a New Indian," by Malea Powell, in issue "Native American Literature: Boundaries and Sovereignties," edited by Kathryn W. Shanley. *Paradoxa,* no. 15 (2001): 211.

Toward a Native American Critical Theory, by Elvira Pulitano. Lincoln: University of Nebraska Press, 2003. 133.

A History of American Literature, by Richard Gray. Malden, Massachusetts: Blackwell, 2004. 804.

Native American Literatures: An Introduction, by Suzanne Evertsen Lundquist. New York: Continuum, 2004. 67–68, 204.

Essay by Elvira Pulitano in *Louis Owens: Literary Reflections on His Life and Work,* edited by Jacquelyn Kilpatrick. Norman: University of Oklahoma Press, 2004. 91.

Indian Country: Essays on Contemporary Native Culture, by Gail G. Valaskakis. Waterloo, Ontario, Canada: Wilfred Laurier University Press, 2005. 3.

Paraphrased in *Listening to the Land: Native American Literary Responses to the Landscape,* by Lee Schweninger. Athens: University of Georgia Press, 2008. 134.

1971

37. **"The American Indian: A Contemporary Acknowledgement"** (review essay). *Intellectual Digest* 2, no. 1 (1971): 12, 14. Momaday writes about the increasing attention devoted to books by and about American Indians and reviews several.

38. **"Bringing on the Indians"** (review essay). *New York Review of Books* 16, no. 6 (April 8, 1971): 39–42. See also the section "Reviews of Published Works by Other Authors."

39. **"A Vision beyond Time and Place"** (essay). *Life* (magazine), July 2, 1971, 66–67.

1972

40. **"The Circle: A Fable of Christmas"** (story). *Viva, Northern New Mexico's Sunday Magazine,* supplement of the *Santa Fe New Mexican,* December 24, 1972, 4. This is a separate story published in *Viva;* it is not from Momaday's column published in this issue. The story was published in Part Four of *The Names: A Memoir* (1976), 137–42. In a different form, it became Momaday's first children's book, *Circle of Wonder: A Native American Christmas Story.* The story is based on his memories of Christmas at the Pueblo of Jemez in New Mexico.

    An excerpt from *Circle of Wonder* was reprinted in *The Serpent's Tongue: Prose, Poetry, and Art of the New Mexico Pueblos,* edited by Nancy Wood. New York: Dutton Books, 1997. 52.

41. **"The Man Made of Words"** (speech). In *Religion and the Humanizing of Man,* edited by James M. Robinson. Plenary Addresses from the International Congress of Learned Societies in the Field of Religion, September 1–5, 1972, Los Angeles, California. 2nd rev. ed. Waterloo, Ontario, Canada: Waterloo Lutheran University, 1973. 191–203.

    Momaday used the title, "The Man Made of Words," for this address, which is not the same as his 1970 address, although parts of it were included. His remarks were adapted for presentation to theologians and other scholars of religion. This address did not appear in the first edition of *Religion and the Humanizing of Man* because it was not available when that edition was published for distribution at the conference.

1973

42. **"Flight on the Wind"** (excerpt). In *Literature of the American Indian*, edited by Thomas E. Sanders and Walter W. Peek. Pasadena, California: Glencoe Press, 1973. 492–97. This is the story of the eagles told in Part 1, "The Longhair," *House Made of Dawn* (1968). See also entry no. 27.

1974

43. **"I Am Alive"** (essay). *The World of the American Indian*, edited by Jules B. Billard. Vine Deloria, Jr., and William C. Sturtevant, consultants. Story of Man Library. Washington, D.C.: National Geographic Society, 1974. 11–14, 23–26. This essay is from a lecture given by Momaday at UCLA in May 1970.

    Excerpts from this essay appear in the following works:

    Indian Ecology, by J. Donald Hughes. El Paso: Texas Western Press, University of Texas at El Paso, 1983. 59.

    Ancestral Voice: Conversations with N. Scott Momaday, by Charles L. Woodard. Lincoln: University of Nebraska Press, 1989. 154–55, 192.

    North American Indian Ecology, by J. Donald Hughes, with a new foreword. 2nd ed. El Paso: Texas Western Press, University of Texas at El Paso, 1996. 59.

    Essay section, "'Blood Memory' and 'Crossblood Survivors': Refigurations and Critiques of Essentialized Identities," by Pauline Turner Strong and Barrik Van Winkle. *Cultural Anthropology* 11, no. 4 (November 1996): 560.

44. **"The Writing of Nonfiction Prose"** (essay). *Teaching Creative Writing.* Washington, D.C.: Government Printing Office, 1974. 94–131. This essay and the one that follows were published in conjunction with the Conference on Teaching Creative Writing held at the Library of Congress in January 1974.

    A statement about the act of imagination included by Momaday in this essay was quoted by Kimberly M. Blaeser in "The New 'Frontier' of Native American Literature: Disarming History with Tribal Humor," in "Native American Perspectives on Literature and History," edited by Alan R. Velie and Gerald Vizenor. *Genre: Forms of Discourse and Culture* 25, no. 4 (Winter 1992): 362.

45. **"The Writing of Poetry"** (essay). *Teaching Creative Writing.* Washington, D.C.: Government Printing Office, 1974. 26–64.

1975

46. **"A Note on Contemporary Native American Poetry"** (introduction). *Carriers of the Dream Wheel: Contemporary Native American Poetry*, edited

by Duane Niatum. New York: Harper & Row, 1975. xix–xx. Reprint (pbk.), San Francisco: Harper & Row, 1981. xix–xx.

Excerpted or quoted in the following works:

Essay, "History in the Colors of Song," by Duane Natium. In *Coyote Was Here,* edited by Bo Schöler. The Dolphin, no. 9. Aarhus, Denmark: SEKLOS, 1984. 30–31.

"Introduction," by Duane Niatum in *Durable Breath: Contemporary Native American Poetry,* edited by John E. Smelcer and D. L. Birchfield. Anchorage, Alaska: Salmon Run Press, 1994. vii–viii.

Essay, "The Transformational Tracks of the Marginalized Life," by Duane Niatum, in issue "Native American Literature: Boundaries and Sovereignties," edited by Kathryn W. Shanley. *Paradoxa: Studies in World Literary Genres,* no. 15 (2001): 78.

47. **"The Pear-Shaped Legend: A Figment of the American Imagination"** (prose and poetry). With drawings by Momaday. *Stanford Magazine* 3, no. 1 (Spring–Summer 1975): 46–48. As Momaday walks across the Stanford campus, the strange and true story of his life with Billy the Kid comes to his mind. Included are several poems and prose poems that became part of "The Strange and True Story of My Life with Billy the Kid" in *American West* (1985) and *In the Presence of the Sun* (1992).

48. **"Praise So Dear"** (essay). *Imprint of the Stanford Libraries Associates* 1, no. 2 (October 1975): 3–9. This is a commemorative writing by Momaday about Yvor Winters.

49. **"The Priest of the Sun"** (excerpt from *House Made of Dawn*). In chapter 6 of *The Writer and the Worlds of Words,* edited by Robert Bain and Dennis G. Donovan. Englewood Cliffs, New Jersey: Prentice Hall, 1975. 352–57.

50. **"To the Singing, to the Drums"** (essay). *Natural History* 84, no. 2 (February 1975): 38–45. (port.) Momaday describes his thoughts and feelings associated with the celebration of the Kiowa Gourd Dance, performed annually on the Fourth of July at Carnegie, Oklahoma.

Reprinted as follows:

Ants, Indians, and Little Dinosaurs. Selected from *Natural History* and edited by Alan Ternes. New York: Charles Scribner's Sons, 1975; © 1975 American Museum of Natural History. 250–56. (full essay)

Excerpts were reprinted in "Kiowa Powwows: Continuity in Ritual Practice," by Benjamin R. Kracht. *American Indian Quarterly* 18, no. 3 (Summer 1994): 321.

1976

51. **"The End of Childhood"** (excerpt). This writing first appeared in *The Names: A Memoir* (1976) and is from chapter 4, Part Four, p. 160. It begins: "At Jemez I came to the end of my childhood." It has been recited by Momaday and others.

    Reprinted in *Native American Literature: An Anthology*, compiled and edited by Lawana Trout. Lincolnwood (Chicago), Illinois: NTC/Contemporary Publishing Group, 1998, ©1999. 488–91.

52. **"The events of one's life take place, *take place*."** This statement first appeared in *The Names: A Memoir* (1976), p. 142. It also appears in his essay, "I Wonder What Will Happen to the Land," *The Man Made of Words* (1997), 187. It is an excellent example of statements made by Momaday in his writings and speeches that have caught the attention and imagination of others.

    Quoted from *The Names* in the following works:

    Ancestral Voice: Conversations with N. Scott Momaday, by Charles L. Woodard. Lincoln: University of Nebraska Press, 1989. 49.

    Epigraph of chapter 2 in *Place and Vision: The Function of Landscape in Native American Fiction*, by Robert M. Nelson. New York: Peter Lang, 1993. 41.

    Epigraph of essay by Susan L. Roberson in *American Indian Quarterly* 22, nos. 1–2 (Winter–Spring 1998): 31.

    "Fusion: Pulitzer Prize Winning Author . . . Conveys the Oneness of Life," by Katharine Beebe. *Mirage* (University of New Mexico Alumni Association magazine) 15, no. 2 (Winter 1998): 18.

    "Introduction" to "Special Issue on Western Autobiography," edited by Kathleen Boardman and Gioia Woods. *Western American Literature* 37, no. 2, (Summer 2002): 147.

    Epigraph of "Introduction: What's Western about Western Autobiography?" In *Western Subjects: Autobiographical Writing in the North American West*, edited by Kathleen Boardman and Gioia Woods. Salt Lake City: University of Utah Press, 2004. 1.

    Essay by Melody Graulich in *Western Subjects: Autobiographical Writing in the North American West*, edited by Boardman and Woods. University of Utah Press, 2004. 388.

Native American Literatures: An Introduction, by Suzanne Evertsen Lundquist. New York: Continuum, 2004. 70, 213.

Indian Country: Essays on Contemporary Native Culture, by Gail G. Valaskakis. Waterloo, Ontario, Canada: Wilfrid Laurier University Press, 2005. 113.

Listening to the Land: Native American Literary Responses to the Landscape, by Lee Schweninger. Athens: University of Georgia Press, 2008. 145.

53. **"A First American Views His Land"** (essay). *National Geographic* 150, no. 1, Bicentennial Issue (July 1976): 13–18. Reprinted in *The Man Made of Words* (1997), 30–41, accompanied by the four parts of Momaday's poem, "New World."

Reprinted or quoted as follows:

Dreamtime: Concerning the Boundary between Wilderness and Civilization, by Hans Peter Duerr. Oxford: Basil Blackwell, 1987. 241–42.

Earth's Insights: A Survey of Ecological Ethics from the Mediterranean Basin to the Australian Outback, by J. Baird Callicott. Berkeley: University of California Press, 1994. 124.

"Contemporary Native Art," by Lawrence Abbott. *American Indian Quarterly* 18, no. 3 (Summer 1994): 383.

At Home on the Earth: Becoming Native to Our Place: A Multicultural Anthology, edited by David Landis Barnhill. Berkeley: University of California Press, 1999. 19–29.

Literature and Nature: Four Centuries of Nature Writing, Part IV: *1900–1999*, edited by Bridget Keegan and James C. McKusick. Upper Saddle River, New Jersey: Prentice Hall, 2001. 1037–44.

American Earth: Environmental Writing since Thoreau, edited by Bill McKibben and Al Gore. A Special Publication of The Library of America. New York: Literary Classics, 2008. 570–81. (port., plate 53)

Listening to the Land: Native American Literary Responses to the Landscape, by Lee Schweninger. Athens: University of Georgia Press, 2008. 131 (epigraph), 137.

54. **"Kiowa Legends from *The Journey of Tai-me*"** (stories). *Sun Tracks: An American Indian Literary Magazine* 3, no. 1 (Fall 1976): 6–8. There are six legends published in this issue. These were not carried over from *The Journey of Tai-me* to *The Way to Rainy Mountain*.

55. **"The Names"** (passage). This first appeared in Part One of *The Names*. It begins the first paragraph of Part One on p. 3 as follows:

> The names at first are those of animals and of birds, of objects that have one definition in the eye, another in the hand, of forms and features on the rim of the world, or of sounds that carry on the bright wind and in the void.

Reprinted in the following works by others:

Review, "The 'Autobiography of an Imagination,'" by Lawrence Rothfield. *Stanford Daily*, May 6, 1977.

Essay by Susan L. Roberson in *American Indian Quarterly* 22, nos. 1–2 (Winter–Spring, 1998): 31.

"Literary Animals" in *Fugitive Poses: Native American Indian Scenes of Absence and Presence*, by Gerald Vizenor. Lincoln. University of Nebraska Press, 1998. 132.

Indian Country: Essays on Contemporary Native Culture, by Gail G. Valaskakis. Waterloo, Ontario, Canada: Wilfred Laurier University Press, 2005. 118.

Circle of Life: Traditional Teaching of Native American Elders, by James David Audlin (Distant Eagle). Santa Fe, N.M.: Clear Light Publishing, 2006. 129.

56. **"Native American Attitudes to the Environment"** (essay). In *Seeing with a Native Eye: Essays on Native American Religion*, edited by Walter Holden Capps. New York: Harper & Row, 1976. 79–85. This essay was adapted from transcriptions of remarks made by Momaday during a faculty-student discussion. Momaday writes about the fundamental Native American ethic in respect to nature and the physical world.

Reprinted or quoted in the following published works:

Essay, "Writing Nature: Silko and Native Americans as Nature Writers," by Lee Schweninger. *MELUS* 18, no. 2 (Summer 1993): 48.

Wisdom Sits in Places: Landscape and Language among the Western Apache, by Keith H. Basso. Albuquerque: University of New Mexico Press, 1996. 34–35, 64–65.

Essay, "Anthropological Studies of Native American Place Naming," by Thomas F. Thornton. *American Indian Quarterly* 21, no. 2 (Spring 1997): 222.

Reprinted as chapter 1, "Introduction," in *Stars Above, Earth Below: American Indians and Nature*, edited by Marsha C. Bol. Niwot, Colorado: Roberts Rinehart Publishers for the Carnegie Museum of Natural History, 1998. 3–11.

Quoted in "'Everywhere There Was Life': How Native Americans Can Save the World." *Mixedblood Messages: Literature, Film, Family, Place,* by Louis Owens. Norman: University of Oklahoma Press, 1998. 226.

Listening to the Land: Native American Literary Responses to the Landscape, by Lee Schweninger. Athens: University of Georgia Press, 2008. 137.

57. **"Oral Tradition and the American Indian"** (speech). In *Contemporary Native American Address,* edited by John R. Maestas. Provo, Utah: Brigham Young University, 1976. 294–306. This speech was given at the university in 1975.

1979

58. **"Francisco's Bear Hunt"** (excerpt). In *American Indian Literature: An Anthology,* edited and with an introduction by Alan R. Velie. Norman: University of Oklahoma Press, 1979. 336–42. Reprinted in Velie's revised edition published by the University of Oklahoma Press in 1991. 315–19. This excerpt is from chapter "February 27" in Part 4, "The Dawn Runner," *House Made of Dawn* (1968), 198–204. It has also appeared with the title "The Bear and the Colt." See entry no. 26.

59. **"The Language of the Tribes"** (review essay). *Washington Post Book World,* January 28, 1979, L1. For other reviews, see also the section "Reviews of Published Works by Other Authors" in this part of the bio-bibliography.

1980

60. **"The Meadows of Uelen"** (story). In *Wonders: Writings and Drawings for the Child in Us All,* edited by Jonathan Cott and Mary Gimbel. New York: Rolling Stone Press, Summit Books, 1980. 428–29. This story is accompanied by a line drawing of a unicorn by Momaday.

61. **"N. Scott Momaday: 'February 27' from *House Made of Dawn* (1968)"** (excerpt). In *Mirrors and Mirage: Fiction by Nineteen,* edited by Albert J. Guerard. Portable Stanford Series. Stanford, California: Stanford Alumni Association, 1980. 125–31. This excerpt is from Part 4, "The Dawn Runner," 193–208.

62. **"N. Scott Momaday, Kiowa Poet and Novelist"** (excerpts). In *This Song Remembers: Self-Portraits of Native Americans in the Arts,* edited by Jane B. Katz. Boston: Houghton Mifflin, 1980. 195–201. Excerpts are from "The Man Made of Words," *House Made of Dawn,* and *The Way to Rainy Mountain.*

63. **"Tsoai and the Shield Maker"** (story). *Four Winds: The International Forum for Native American Art, Literature, and History* 1, no. 3 (Summer 1980): 38–43.

1983

64. **"From *The Way to Rainy Mountain*"** (excerpts). In *Growing Old at Willie Nelson's Picnic and Other Sketches of Life in the Southwest*, edited by Ronald B. Querry. College Station: Texas A&M University Press, 1983. 11–20. (port.) The excerpts include the book's introduction and Stories III, XIII, and XXII.

65. **"His name was Cheney, and he was an arrowmaker . . . ."** (excerpt). In *Native American Renaissance*, by Kenneth Lincoln. Berkeley: University of California Press, 1983. vi. This is the third, or personal, voice of Story XIII in *The Way to Rainy Mountain*, 47.

1984

66. **"From *The Names*"** (excerpts). In *Words in the Blood: Contemporary Indian Writers of North and South America*, edited and with an introduction and notes by Jamake Highwater. New York: New American Library, 1984. 42–46. Excerpts comprise Momaday's brief foreword (xi), "Prologue" (1), and chapter 1, Part One, 3–6.

67. **"Joseph Brant, 1743–1807: Man of Two Worlds"** (review essay). *New York Times Book Review* 89 (May 13, 1984): 7.

68. **"To Save a Great Vision"** (essay). In *A Sender of Words: Essays in Memory of John G. Neihardt*, edited by Vine Deloria, Jr. Salt Lake City, Utah: Howe Brothers, 1984. 30–38. Reprinted in *The Man Made of Words: Essays, Stories, Passages*. New York: St. Martin's Press, 1997. 21–29. Black Elk had a great vision to pass on to humankind, and poet John Neihardt used his gifts to preserve it.

1985

69. **"First Encounters—Discovering the Land of Light"** (travel essay). In "The Sophisticated Traveler," Part 2, *New York Times Magazine*, March 17, 1985, 40–41, 62–64, 73, 76–77. This travel piece is about northern New Mexico throughout the seasons. Reprinted under the title "Discovering the Land of Light," in *Enchanting Places and How to Find Them*, edited by A. M. Rosenthal and Arthur Gelb. London: Ebury Press, 1986; New York: Villard Books, ©1986. 231–37.

70. **"The Strange and True Story of My Life with Billy the Kid"** (poetry and prose poems). *American West* 22, no. 5 (September–October 1985): 54–65. Momaday used the full "story" as Part II of *In the Presence of the Sun: Stories and Poems, 1961–1991* (1992). 41–69. Color illustrations are from Momaday's *Billy the Kid Suite*. See also the section "Paintings and Drawings."

1986

71. **"On Bavarian Byways"** (travel essay). In "The Sophisticated Traveler," Part 2, *New York Times Magazine,* October 5, 1986, 28–29, 78–81. This travel essay is about the cities and landscape of the southeast corner of Germany. Reprinted in *The Man Made of Words* (1997), 139–47.

72. **"Set"** (excerpt). In *The New Native American Novel: Works in Progress,* edited by Mary Dougherty Bartlett. Albuquerque: University of New Mexico Press, 1986. 41–49. Momaday contributed a piece from *The Ancient Child: A Novel,* published by Doubleday in 1989.

1987

73. **"Everett Ruess: The Dark Trail into Myth"** (essay). *American West* 24, no. 2 (April 1987): 66–70. Momaday described Ruess as a "lonely heroic figure who bravely confronts his destiny because he must." Momaday was quoted in the essay "Wandering Soul," by Leo W. Banks. *Tucson Weekly,* May 8–14, 1997, 18–20.

74. **"Landscape with Words in the Foreground"** (essay). In *Old Southwest/New Southwest: Essays on a Region and Its Literature,* edited by Judy Nolte Lensink. Tucson, Arizona: Tucson Public Library, 1987. 1–5. Passages from *The Names* and *The Ancient Child* are included in this essay, which was cited in "The Deserts and Literature II," *Arid Lands Newsletter* (University of Arizona, Tucson), no. 50 (November–December 2001): 1. Readers can access this essay at http://cals.arizona.edu/OALS/ALN/aln50/momaday.html.

75. **"Personal Reflections"** (essay). Chapter 16 of *The American Indian and the Problem of History,* edited by Calvin Martin. New York: Oxford University Press, 1987. 156–61. Momaday responds to a question posed by Martin regarding the most crucial issues existing over the past five hundred years connected to Indian and white relations.

    Reprinted or quoted in the following works:

    Excerpt with title, "The Power and Beauty of Language," reprinted in *Native Heritage: Personal Accounts by American Indians, 1790 to the Present,* edited by Arlene Hirschfelder. New York: Macmillan, 1995. 73–74. This excerpt is from pp. 160–61 of the essay.

    Storied Voices in Native American Texts, by Blanca Schorcht. Indigenous Peoples and Politics. New York: Routledge, 2003. 93.

    Listening to the Land: Native American Literary Responses to the Landscape, by Lee Schweninger. Athens: University of Georgia Press, 2008. 138.

1988

76. **"Ancient Vision"** (essay). *Revue française d'études américaines* [Paris, France] 13, no. 38 (November 1988): 369–76.

77. **"Native American Literary History"** (letter to editor). Book Review Desk, *New York Times*, February 21, 1988, 37. Momaday wrote a letter about a comment made by a *New York Times* reviewer regarding his essay, "The Native Voice," published in *The Columbia Literary History of the United States* (1988). The reviewer noted that Momaday covered Native American literature in "only" eleven pages. Momaday states in his letter that he did not take the comment as an insult, but rather as an honor, because he was asked to write the essay about the subject and to make it that precise length. He added that his essay is "a concise and intelligible statement concerning the integrity of American literature from its origins through 2,000 years of native oral and written tradition to contemporary American prose and poetry." See also the following citation.

78. **"The Native Voice"** (essay). *The Columbia Literary History of the United States*. Emory Elliott, gen. ed. New York: Columbia University Press, 1988. 5–15. Reprinted in a shortened form and titled "The Native Voice in American Literature" in *The Man Made of Words* (1997), 13–20. This reprinting consists of pp. 5–10 of the essay in *The Columbia Literary History of the United States.*

    Reprinted, excerpted, or quoted in the following:

    Epigraph at the beginning of the "Preface" of *Narrative Chance: Postmodern Discourse on Native American Indian Literatures*, edited by Gerald Vizenor. Albuquerque: University of New Mexico Press, 1989. ix. Reprint (pbk.), Norman: University of Oklahoma Press, 1993. ix. The quote is from p. 7 of "The Native Voice" (1988).

    Epigraph of chapter 1, "The First American Literature." *Literatures of the American Indian*, by A. LaVonne Brown Ruoff. New York: Chelsea House, 1991. 13.

    Quoted in *The Text and the Voice: Writing, Speaking, and Democracy in American Literature*, by Alessandro Portelli. New York: Columbia University Press, 1994. 210.

    Excerpt in *Stories and Stone: Writing the Anasazi Homeland*, edited by Reuben Ellis. Boulder, Colorado: Pruett, 1997. 19–20.

    Quoted in *The Heart as a Drum*, by Robin Riley Fast. Ann Arbor: University of Michigan Press, 2000. 31.

Cited in "An Ensemble Performance of Indians in the Act: Native Theater Past and Present." *Studies in American Indian Literatures* 16, no. 1 (2004): 34–35.

Native American Literatures: An Introduction, by Suzanne Evertsen Lundquist. New York: Continuum, 2004. 60.

Excerpt titled "Man-Made Passages" in chapter 7, "Plains Ways: N. Scott Momaday." *Speak Like Singing: Classics of Native American Literature*, by Kenneth Lincoln. Albuquerque: University of New Mexico, 2007. 127–28.

Quoted in chapter 1, "'They Have Stories, Don't They?'" by Hartwig Isernhagen. In *Transatlantic Voices: Interpretations of Native North American Literatures*, edited by Elvira Pulitano. Lincoln: University of Nebraska Press, 2007. 4. The quotes are from pp. 5, 6, 10, and 13 of "The Native Voice" (1988).

79. **"Sacred and Ancestral Ground"** (travel essay). In "The Sophisticated Traveler," Part 2, *New York Times Magazine*, March 13, 1988, 28–30, 81. Reprinted with the title, "Revisiting Sacred Ground," in *The Man Made of Words* (1997), 118–23. Momaday writes about the Great Plains and the American Indian and about the trip he made in 1986 and 1987 with Charles L. Woodard over the migration route of the Kiowas.

Reprinted or quoted as follows:

Epigraph of essay, "There's Great Good in Returning: A Testimonio," by Yolanda Chávez Leyva. *Frontiers* 24, nos. 2–3 (2003): 1.

New York Times website: www.nytimes.com/ref/travel/sophisticated/16ST-MOMADAY.html.

80. **"N. Scott Momaday"** (statement). In *Literature and Landscape: Writers of the Southwest*, by Cynthia Farrah. El Paso: Texas Western Press, University of Texas at El Paso, 1988. 57. (port. on p. 56) Momaday responded to a question posed by Farrah concerning the role that the landscape has played in compelling him to write. Forty-nine other southwestern authors presented in this book answered the same question.

1989

81. **"Only an Appearance"** (essay). In *Native American Literatures*, edited by Laura Coltelli. Forum, no. 1. Pisa, Italy: SEU (Servizio Editoriale Universitaria), 1989. 1–3. Momaday tells why he became a writer and a painter. His artwork follows on pp. 4–8.

82. **"The Seven Sisters: American Indian Mythology and the Landscape"** (lecture). *Halcyon: A Journal of the Humanities* 11 (1989): 1–17. (port.) This

lecture, titled "The Kiowa Story of Tsoai," was given at the Annual Humanities Committee Fall Lecture at the University of Nevada in 1989.

1990

83. **"Native Voices"** (testimony from interview). In "View from the Shore: American Indian Perspectives on the Quincentenary," edited by José Barreiro. Special issue. *Northeast Indian Quarterly* 7, no. 3 (Fall 1990): 6–7. Momaday's testimony, in essay form, is from a July 1989 interview conducted by Gabrielle Tayac.

    Reprinted in *Native American Testimony: A Chronicle of Indian-White Relations from Prophecy to the Present, 1492–1992*, edited by Peter Nabokov, with a foreword by Vine Deloria, Jr. 2nd ed. New York: Viking, 1991. 436–39. Reprinted in rev. ed., Penguin Books, 1999, 437–40.

1991

84. **"She Is Beautiful in Her Whole Being"** (excerpt). In *Talking Leaves: Contemporary Native American Short Stories*, introduced and edited by Craig Lesley, with Katheryn Stavrakis. New York: Dell Publishing, 1991. 200–207. This is chapter 3 in Book Three, "Shapes," of *The Ancient Child: A Novel* (1989), 290–99.
85. **"Tosamah's Story"** (excerpts). In *The Lightning Within: An Anthology of Contemporary American Indian Fiction*, edited and with an introduction by Alan R. Velie. Lincoln: University of Nebraska Press, 1991. 4–18. Reprint (pbk.), Norman: University of Nebraska Press, 1993. 4–18. Excerpts are from chapter "January 26," 89–98, and the full chapter "January 27," 127–36, in Part 2, "The Priest of the Sun," *House Made of Dawn* (1968). Tosamah is The Right Reverend John Big Bluff Tosamah, pastor and Priest of the Sun, and an important character in the novel. The excerpts are preceded by an introduction, "N. Scott Momaday," by Velie, pp. 1–3.
86. **"A Word on the Plains Shield"** (introduction). *In the Presence of the Sun: A Gathering of Shields*. Santa Fe, New Mexico: Rydal Press, 1992, ©1991. unpaged. Reprinted in Part III of *In the Presence of the Sun: Stories and Poems, 1961–1991*. New York: St. Martin's Press, 1992. 73–75. This piece introduces the shields and their stories.

1992

87. **"The Becoming of the Native: Man in America before Columbus"** (essay). Chapter 1 in *America in 1492: The World of the Indian Peoples before the*

Arrival of Columbus, edited and with an introduction by Alvin M. Josephy, Jr.; developed by Frederick E. Hoxie. New York: Alfred A. Knopf, 1992. 13–19.

A quote from this essay was used by Colin G. Calloway in his introduction to *The World Turned Upside Down: Indian Voices from Early America,* edited by Calloway. Boston: Bedford Books of St. Martin's Press, 1994. 12. The quote, from p. 18 of Momaday's essay, concerns the oral tradition of his ancestors.

88. **"A Gathering of Shields"** (essay). *Native Peoples* 5, no 3 (Spring 1992): 28–33. Written and illustrated by N. Scott Momaday. Four shield drawings from the limited letterpress edition of *In the Presence of the Sun: A Gathering of Shields.* Reprinted in *Native Peoples* 11, no. 1, Special Tenth Anniversary Issue (Fall–Winter 1997): 56–61.

89. **"New Mexico: Passage into Legend: Billy the Kid and the Kid's Country"** (travel essay). In "The Sophisticated Traveler," Part 2, *New York Times Magazine,* October 18, 1992, 22–23, 36, 38–40. Momaday writes about the land and the short life of Henry McCarty, better known as Billy the Kid. Reprinted as "New Mexico Passage into Legend," *The Man Made of Words* (1997), 154–62.

90. **"La nouvelle littérature indienne: Premiers contacts des Indiens avec le roman"** (essay). Translated into French by Simone Pellerin. In *Destins croisés: cinq siècles de rencontres avec les Amérindiens.* Paris: UNESCO/Albin Michel, 1992. 313–21. The new fiction of contemporary American Indian writers is the focus of this essay.

91. **"Remote as the Stars Are His Sentiments Just Now"** (excerpt). In *New Writers of the Purple Sage: An Anthology of Contemporary Western Writers,* collected and with an introduction by Russell Martin. New York: Penguin, 1992. 49–59. This is chapter 17 in Book One, "Planes," of *The Ancient Child* (1989), 76–89.

92. **"A Word on Billy the Kid"** (introduction). This biographical sketch of Billy introduces Momaday's "The Strange and True Story of My Life with Billy the Kid." *In the Presence of the Sun: Stories and Poems, 1961–1991* (New York: St. Martin's Press, 1992), 43. This writing appeared earlier without a title as the introduction to "The Strange and True Story of My Life with Billy the Kid," published in *American West* 22, no. 5 (September–October 1985): 56–65.

1993

93. **"From *House Made of Dawn*"** (excerpt). In *Plains Native American Literature.* Multicultural Literature Collection. Upper Saddle River, New

Jersey: Globe Fearon, 1993. This excerpt is chapter "January 27" in Part 2, "The Priest of the Sun," *House Made of Dawn* (1968), 127–36.

94. **"From *The Names*"** (excerpt). In *Visions of America: Personal Narratives from the Promised Land*, edited by Wesley Brown and Amy Ling. New York: Persea Books, 1993. 116–21. The editors note that this excerpt is from *The Names*, published by Sun Tracks and the University of Arizona Press, ©1976, 119–28.

95. **"From *The Names: A Memoir*"** (excerpts). In *Growing Up Native American: An Anthology*, edited and with an introduction by Patricia Riley. New York: William Morrow, 1993. 215–35. The excerpts are from chapter 3, pp. 92–114, and chapter 4, pp. 114–15, of Part Three.

96. **"Names and Being"** (essay). In *American Invention*, by Lothar Baumgarten. New York: Guggenheim Museum, 1993. 4–5. This book is about the function and philosophy of museums. It is a photographic study that explores the relationship between a museum and the objects it possesses.

97. **"Sacred Places"** (essay). In *Sacred Places: Native American Sites* (Sierra Club Special Edition Calendar). San Francisco: Sierra Club, 1993. Reprinted in *The Man Made of Words* (1997), 113–17. Momaday believes that sacred places are the truest definitions of the earth and that sacred ground is earned through acts of sacrifice.

    Reprinted or quoted in the following works:

    Aboriginal Voices 2, no. 1 (1995): 28–29.

    Cited in Chadwick Allen's essay "Engaging the Politics and Pleasures of Indigenous Aesthetics." *Western American Literature* 41, no. 2 (Summer 2006): 170.

    ACCESS: English; Building Literacy through Learning, by Elva Durán et al. Wilmington, Massachusetts: Great Source Education Group, Houghton Mifflin, 2005. 139.

    Listening to the Land: Native American Literary Responses to the Landscape, by Lee Schweninger. Athens: University of Georgia Press, 2008. 148.

98. Untitled excerpts from *The Names* appeared*"Daddy's Gone to War": The Second World War in the Lives of America's Children*, by William M. Tuttle, Jr. New York: Oxford University Press, 1993. These are from the following chapters: chapter 8, "Children Play War Games," 136–37; chapter 9, "Children's Entertainment: Radio, Movies, Comics," 156; chapter 10, "The Fractured Homefront: Racial and Cultural Hostility," 178–79; and chapter 15, "The

Homefront Children at Middle Age," 262. Momaday reflects on his experiences growing up during World War II.

Another appeared in *Named in Stone and Sky: An Arizona Anthology,* edited by Gregory McNamee. Tucson: University of Arizona Press, 1993. 117. A description of Monument Valley is from Part Two, 68–69.

1994

99. An untitled article written by Momaday appeared under the headline, "World Premiere: The Indolent Boys by N. Scott Momaday," in *StageView: News and Views from the Syracuse Stage* (Syracuse, New York), February–March 1994, p. 1.

100. **"From *House Made of Dawn*"** (excerpt). In chapter 13, "Tribal Restoration Phase One Continued: 1944–53." *Indian Country: A History of Native People in America,* by Karen D. Harvey and Lisa D. Harjo. Golden, Colorado: North American Press, 1994. 189–90. The excerpt is from chapter "February 20" in Part 3, "The Night Chanter," *House Made of Dawn* (1968), 157–59.

101. **"Feast Day (1968)"** (excerpts). In *Voice of the Turtle: American Indian Literature, 1900–1970,* edited and with an introduction by Paula Gunn Allen. New York: A One World Book, Ballantine Books, 1994. 257–77. These excerpts are from chapters "July 25," 38–84, and "August 2," 85–86, in Part 1, "The Longhair," *House Made of Dawn* (1968).

102. **"Values"** (quotation). In Part One, "Values," of *Words of Power: Voices from Indian America,* edited by Norbert S. Hill, Jr. Golden, Colorado: Fulcrum, 1994. 1. An excerpt from the quotation was reprinted in *Wisdom Sits in Places: Landscape and Language among the Western Apache,* by Keith Basso. Albuquerque: University of New Mexico Press, 1996. 34–35.

1995

103. **"From My Home of Jemez"** (excerpt). In *Home Places: Contemporary Native American Writing from Sun Tracks,* edited by Larry Evers and Ofelia Zepeda. Sun Tracks, vol. 31. Tucson: University of Arizona Press, 1995. 51–53. This excerpt is from Part Four, *The Names* (1976), 120–22.

104. **"House Made of Dawn"** (excerpt). In *American Indian Voices,* edited and with introduction and notes by Karen D. Harvey, with consultant Lisa D. Harjo. Writers of America. Brookfield, Connecticut: Millbrook Press, 1995. 79–80, 82. This excerpt is from chapter "February 20," in Part 3, "The Night Chanter," *House Made of Dawn* (1968), 157–59.

105. **"The Names"** (excerpt). In *Native American Literature: A Brief Introduction and Anthology,* edited by Gerald Vizenor. New York: HarperCollins Publishers, 1995. 65–67. This excerpt is from Part Four, *The Names,* 152–54 and 160–61.

106. **"The Photography of Horace Poolaw"** (essay). *Aperture,* no. 139 (Summer 1995): 14–19. Poolaw (1906–84) is remembered for his outstanding images of Kiowa life. Seven of his photographs are included. This essay also appeared in *Strong Hearts: Native American Visions and Voices,* edited by Peggy Roalf. New York: Aperture, 1995.

107. **"The Power and Beauty of Language"** (excerpt). In *Native Heritage: Personal Accounts by American Indians, 1790 to the Present,* edited by Arlene Hirschfelder. New York: Macmillan, 1995. 73–74. This is from Momaday's "Personal Reflections," in *The American Indian and the Problem of History,* edited by Calvin Martin. New York: Oxford University Press, 1987, 160–61. A quote from this essay is in *The Native American Oral Tradition,* by Lois J. Einhorn. Westport, Connecticut: Praeger, 2000. 72–73.

108. **"The Rise of the Song"** (excerpts). In *Native American Literature: A Brief Introduction and Anthology,* edited by Gerald Vizenor. New York: HarperCollins, 1995. 130–41. These excerpts are chapters "February 27," 193–208, and "February 28," 209–12, in Part 4, "The Dawn Runner," *House Made of Dawn* (1968).

1996

109. **"The American West and the Burden of Belief"** (essay). In chapter 7, "The Great Die-up: 1877–1887." *The West: An Illustrated History.* Narrative by Geoffrey C. Ward. Based on a documentary film script by Geoffrey C. Ward and Dayton Duncan. Preface by Stephen Ives and Ken Burns, with contributions by N. Scott Momaday. Boston: Little, Brown & Co., 1996. 377–83. Reprinted in *The Man Made of Words* (1997), 89–107.

An excerpt from this essay was reprinted in "Fusion: Pulitzer Prize Winning Author N. Scott Momaday Conveys the Oneness of Life," by Katharine Beebe. *Mirage* (University of New Mexico Alumni Association), Winter 1998, 18.

110. **"The Athlete in a State of Grace"** (essay). In *Super Bowl XXX Official Game Program, 1996,* 213. In this program, published by the National Football League, Momaday recalls witnessing performances of athletes in "a state of grace." Super Bowl XXX was played in Sun Devil Stadium, Tempe, Arizona, on January 28, 1996.

111. **"At Home in the World"** (essay). In *Testimony: Writers of the West Speak on Behalf of Utah Wilderness*, compiled by Stephen Trimble and Terry Tempest Williams. Minneapolis, Minnesota: Milkweed Editions, 1996. 64–65. This book was printed in a larger format in 1995 by West Wind Lithograph, Salt Lake City.

112. **"A Divine Blindness: The Place of Words in a State of Grace"** (essay). *Georgia Review* 50, no. 2 (Summer 1996): 301–10. Reprinted in *The Man Made of Words* (1997), 80–88. This essay connects Native American mythology and the physical blindness of writer Jorge Luis Borges in exploring imagination and oral tradition in storytelling. It also discusses the creation of *The Way to Rainy Mountain.*

    Reprinted in "Selected Essays, 1947–1997." Special Double Issue. *Georgia Review* 55–56, nos. 4–1 (Winter 2001–Spring 2002): 350–59.

113. **"Disturbing the Spirits: Indian Bones Must Stay in the Ground"** (op-ed piece). In "News Summary," *New York Times*, November 2, 1996, sec. 1, p. 2. This writing relates to the claiming of prehistoric remains by Native Americans and the 1990 federal law (Native American Graves Protection and Reparation Act) on reparation of those remains.

    Reprinted or quoted in the following works:

    RED INK 5, no. 2 (Spring 1997): 10. This reprint is followed by a rebuttal titled "OK Scott, Where's the Beef?" by Vine Deloria, Jr., 11.

    Reference to in "Indian Presence with No Indians Present: NAGPRA and Its Discontents." *Native American Religious Identity: Unforgotten Gods*, edited by Jace Weaver. Maryknoll, New York: Orbis Books, 1998. 106.

    "An Archaeology without Alienation." *Skull Wars*, by David Hurst Thomas. Phoenix, Arizona: Oryx Press, 2000. 256–57.

114. **"From *The Names*"** (excerpts). In "Memory, Culture, and Identity." Chapter 4 of *The Anatomy of Memory: An Anthology*, edited by James McConkey. New York: Oxford University Press, 1996. 236–42. These excerpts, used to define Momaday's views about memory, language, and naming, are from the following parts of *The Names* (1976): Preface, xi; Part Two, 61–63; Part Three, 92–93; and Part Four, 145–47 and 160–61.

115. **"Granada, Andalusia's Heart and Soul"** (travel essay). In "Sophisticated Traveler Magazine," *New York Times Magazine*, May 12, 1996, 28–30, 32–34. Momaday presents observations and insights about this Andalusian city, the

last bastion of Moorish Spain. Reprinted with some changes and a different title, "Granada: A Vision of the Unforeseen," *The Man Made of Words* (1997), 148–53.

116. **"Tsoai** (1989)**"** (excerpt). In *Song of the Turtle: American Indian Literature, 1974–1994,* edited and with an introduction by Paula Gunn Allen. New York: A One World Book, Ballantine Books, 1996. 165–76. This is chapter 16, "It Shines like a Vague, Powdered Mask, like a Skull," in Book One, "Planes," *The Ancient Child* (1989), 51–73.

1997

117. "Afterword" to essay "The Morality of Indian Hating." *The Man Made of Words: Essays, Stories, Passages* (1997), 76. This is Momaday's earliest essay in this book. He added an afterword because the essay was written in the early 1960s, when he was a university student and it was "no longer timely in all of its parts" (76).

    A quote from the "Afterword" was included in *Listening to the Land: Native American Responses to the Landscape*, by Lee Schweninger. Athens: University of Georgia Press, 2008. 148.

118. **"The Centaur Complex"** (essay). *The Man Made of Words* (1997), 77–79. Momaday writes about man and horse as one.

119. **"An Encounter in Greenland"** (essay). *The Man Made of Words* (1997), 176–77. Tells about a visit to the Eskimo village of Siorpaluk and an encounter with a hunter and an iceberg. This essay was reprinted in *Seattle Review* 27, no. 1 (2005): 44–45.

120. **"For the Storyteller, Language Does Indeed Represent the Only Chance for Survival"** (essay). *Chronicle of Higher Education* 43, no. 42 (June 27, 1997): B11.

121. **"From *The Names: A Memoir*"** (excerpts). In *The Portable Western Reader*, edited and with an introduction by William Kittridge. New York: Penguin, 1997. 449–59. Two excerpts are from Part One, chapter 7, pp. 41–42, and chapter 8, pp. 42–57.

122. **"The Homestead on Rainy Mountain Creek"** (essay). *The Man Made of Words* (1997), 163–66. Parts of this essay are from Part One of *The Names* (1976).

123. **"Jay Silverheels"** (essay). *The Man Made of Words* (1997), 183–84. This is about the life and death (1980) of Harold J. Smith (Mohawk), the man who played Tonto and rode with, but in the shadow of, the Lone Ranger on radio and television.

124. **"On Common Ground in Siberia: A Meeting of Native Peoples from New Mexico and Russia"** (essay). *New York Times Magazine*, September 14, 1997, 48–52. Momaday recounts a long train ride to Siberia and meetings with Siberian natives.

125. **"On Tradition"** (quotation). Epigraph at the beginning of "Tradition," chapter 2 of *Voices of Native America*, edited by Hap Gilliland. Dubuque, Iowa: Kendall-Hunt, 1997. 9.

126. **"Pecos Warriors at Jemez"** (excerpt). In *The Serpent's Tongue: Prose, Poetry, and Art of the New Mexico Pueblos*, edited by Nancy Wood. New York: Dutton Books, 1997. 194–95. This is about the Eagle Watchers Society from chapter "July 21," in Part 1, "The Longhair," *House Made of Dawn* (1968), 15–16.

127. **"Sacred Images"** (essay). *The Man Made of Words* (1997), 127–31. Momaday writes about the ancient rock paintings and engravings of prehistoric times, in particular those in Spain, France, and the American Southwest.

128. **"Zagorsk: To the Spiritual Center of Russia"** (essay). *The Man Made of Words* (1997), 132–38.

1998

129. **"The End of Childhood"** (excerpt). In *Native American Literature*, compiled and edited by Lawana Trout. Lincolnwood, Illinois: NTC/Contemporary Publishing Group, 1998, ©1999. 488–90. This excerpt is from Part Four of *The Names* (1976), 160–61. It begins, "At Jemez I came to the end of my childhood" (160).

1999

130. **"The Transformation"** (passages). *In the Bear's House* (1999), 91–95. Momaday tells the Kiowa story of Tsoai and continues with a telling of what happened after the children in the story disappeared.

Reprinted as "Transformation" in *The Year's Best Fantasy and Horror, Thirteenth Annual Collection*, edited by Ellen Datlow and Terri Windling. New York: St. Martin's Griffin Press, 2000. 55–57.

2000

131. **"Keahdinekeah"** (excerpt). In *Native American Literature*. Prentice Hall Literature Library. Upper Saddle River, New Jersey: Prentice Hall, 2000. 76–77. This is from Part Two of *The Names* (1976), 64–65. When he was very young, Momaday and his father visited his great-grandmother in Oklahoma.

2001

132. **"11 Takes on Terror: We Asked Our Cover Subjects for Their Reactions to the World Trade Center Disaster"** (statement). *Fortune* (magazine) 144, no. 11 (November 26, 2001), 123. In this cover story, Momaday, as an author and the founder of The Buffalo Trust, gives his personal impressions of the September 11, 2001, terrorist attack.

133. **"The Buffalo Trust"** (pamphlet). Santa Fe: The Buffalo Trust, 2001. n.p. This publication provides information about the nonprofit foundation established by Momaday and its activities.

134. **"Last Words"** (quotation). *Sierra* 86, no. 3 (May 2001): 100. A quotation from Momaday's address to the assembly attending the First Convocation of American Indian Scholars in 1970 is printed in *Sierra* on a full-page illustration of an outdoor scene under the stars: "We may be perfectly sure of where we are in relation to the supermarket and the next coffee break, but I doubt that any of us knows where he is in relation to the stars and to the solstices." This is from p. 54 of *Indian Voices* (1970), edited by Rupert Costo. Momaday also included it in his essay "An American Land Ethic," *The Man Made of Words* (1997), 47–48.

    Reprinted in the following books:

    This Song Remembers: Self-Portraits of Native Americans in the Arts, edited by Jane B. Katz. Boston: Houghton Mifflin, 1980. 196.

    The Native American Oral Tradition, by Lois J. Einhorn. Westport, Connecticut: Praeger, 2000. 61.

135. **"On Columbus's Quincentennial"** (essay). In *Native American Perspectives: A Historical Reader*. Evanston, Illinois: McDougal Littell, 2001. 210–13.

136. A statement made by Momaday in *The Names* (1976), "The most brilliant colors are there, I believe, . . ." is the epigraph on page one of Part One, "Lighting Out: The American West as Mythic Province," *Mythmakers of the West: Shaping America's Imagination*, by John A. Murray. Flagstaff, Arizona: Northland, 2001. The full statement about the Four Corners area is from p. 69 of *The Names*.

137. An untitled essay about "the sacred," signed by Momaday, appeared in the section "Voices from Native America" of *We, the People of Earth and Elders*, photographed, edited, and compiled by Serle L. Chapman. Missoula, Montana: Mountain Press, 2001. 257–62. A full-page photograph of Momaday is on p. 255, with a biographical sketch on p. 256.

138. An untitled statement made by Momaday about three things that distinguish American Indians within the human family was published in *Indian Country,* by Gwendolen Cates. New York: Grove Press, 2001. n.p. A full-page portrait is opposite his statement. The three distinguishing things are a sense of language, an extraordinary aesthetic sense, and a strong sense of spirituality.

2003

139. **"The Christmas Orange"** (story). *Native Peoples* 17, no. 1 (November–December 2003): 44. The gift of an orange was once a precious thing.

140. **"Excerpt from *The Names*** (1976)**."** In *A Great Plains Reader,* edited by Diane D. Quantic and P. Jane Hafen. Lincoln: University of Nebraska Press, 2003. 4–14. This excerpt is from Part One, chapter 8, pp. 42–57.

141. **"From *House Made of Dawn*"** (excerpts). These are from chapter "January 26," in Part 2, "The Priest of the Sun," and appeared in two books: *The Portable Sixties Reader,* edited by Ann Charters. New York: Penguin, 2003. 362–66; and *Literature of the American West: A Cultural Approach,* by Greg Lyons. New York: Longman, 2003. 383–88.

2004

142. **"Special Prayer by N. Scott Momaday."** *The Heard Museum 75th Anniversary Proclamation Day Program, June 18, 2004,* edited by Dana McGuinness, with Mary Hudak. Phoenix, Arizona: Heard Museum, 2004. n.p.

143. **"Science, Tradition, and the Future"** (dialogue). In *The Epic of Evolution: Science and Religion in Dialogue,* edited by James B. Miller. Advances in Human Evolution Series. Upper Saddle River, New Jersey: Pearson Prentice Hall, 2004. 206–208. This is the Bear-God Dialogue titled "Evolution," first published by St. Martin's Press in *In the Bear's House* (1999), 39–41.

144. **"The stories were old and dear . . ."** (excerpt). In "Our Universes." Chapter 1 of *Native Universe: Voices of Indian America,* edited by Gerald McMaster and Clifford E. Trafzer. Washington, D.C.: National Museum of the American Indian, Smithsonian Institution, in association with National Geographic, 2004. 23. This is the inaugural book of the National Museum of the American Indian. The excerpt is from Part 2, "The Priest of the Sun," *House Made of Dawn* (1968), 94–95.

145. **"The Testament of Allan Houser"** (essay). In *Native Modernism: The Art of George Morrison and Allan Houser,* edited by Truman T. Lowe. Washington, D.C.: National Museum of the American Indian, in association with the

University of Washington Press, Seattle, 2004. 66–77. This book was published in conjunction with an exhibition held at the National Museum of the American Indian from September 2004 to Summer 2005.

146. **"A Triumph of Human Spirit"** (address). In *American Indian, A Special Commemorative Issue.* Washington, D.C.: National Museum of the American Indian, 2004. 13. (port.) This publication commemorates the museum's inauguration. Momaday, a founding trustee, gave this welcoming address during the inaugural program.

2005

147. **"Community"** (prose piece). *Seattle Review* 27, no. 1 (2005): 46. Momaday writes about the sense of community in an Indian village set in a deep canyon. This writing and the three reprintings that follow appeared in this issue in a special section, "N. Scott Momaday: Fiction, Poetry, and Essays," 36–47.

148. **"An Encounter in Greenland"** (essay). *Seattle Review* 27, no. 1 (2005): 44–45. This appeared earlier in *The Man Made of Words* (1997), 176–77.

149. **"February 28"** (excerpt from Part 4, "The Dawn Runner," *House Made of Dawn*). *Seattle Review* 27, no. 1 (2005): 37–38.

150. **"The Indian Dog"** (essay). *Seattle Review* 27, no. 1 (2005) 42–43. This piece first appeared under the title, "Caveat Emptor," in Momaday's column in *Viva*, October 21, 1973, 6. Reprinted with a few changes as "The Indian Dog" in *The Man Made of Words* (1997), 172–73. Reprinted in *In Brief: Short Takes on the Personal*, edited by Judith Kitchen and Mary Paumier Jones. New York: W. W. Norton, 1999. 169–70.

151. **"Fritz Scholder, Luiseño, October 6, 1937–February 10, 2005."** *Native Peoples* 18, no. 3 (May–June 2005): 34. Momaday eulogizes the renowned painter in remarks made during a memorial held at the Institute of American Indian Arts in Santa Fe.

152. **"The Seven Sisters"** (conference paper). In Part III, "Native Astronomical Traditions of the Americas." *Songs from the Sky: Indigenous Astronomical and Cosmological Traditions of the World.* West Sussex, United Kingdom: The Center for Archaeoastronomy and Ocarina Books, 2005. 32–37. From the selected proceedings of the First International Conference on Ethnoastronomy, Smithsonian Institution, Washington, D.C., September 1983. First published in *Archaeoastronomy* (1996), 12–13. Momaday drew from several parts of *The Way to Rainy Mountain* for this presentation.

2006

153. **"The Kiva in My Yard"** (essay). In *Su Casa* (Hacienda Press, Albuquerque, New Mexico), Winter 2006, 148. Momaday's open-air kiva is aligned to the sun and the moon.

154. Quotes from *The Way to Rainy Mountain* are used in *Home Ground: Language for an American Landscape*, edited by Barry Lopez and Debra Gwartney. San Antonio, Texas: Trinity University Press, 2006. 288, 365. Momaday's quotes are used to define the landscape terms "rain shadow" and "tower."

155. **"The Priest of the Sun: Los Angeles, 1952, January 26"** (excerpt). In *Writing the Cross Culture: Native Fiction on the White Man's Religion*, edited by James Treat. Golden, Colorado: Fulcrum, 2006. 94–106. This excerpt is from Part 2, "The Priest of the Sun," *House Made of Dawn* (1968), 89–98, 109–14.

156. **"The Voices of Encounter"** (essay/prose poem). In *Lewis and Clark through Indian Eyes*, edited by Alvin M. Josephy, Jr., with Marc Jaffe. New York: Alfred A. Knopf, 2006. 183–92. (port.) Three voices, one being Sacagawea's, tell of their encounters with the white man during this epic odyssey, a vision quest with great consequences for all.

2007

157. **"One Who Brings the Light"** (excerpt). In "An Oklahoma Centennial Tribute," by David Draper Clark. *World Literature Today* 81, no. 6 (November–December 2007): 37–38. The excerpt is from *Children of the Sun*, published in Momaday's *Three Plays* (2007). Momaday also wrote an introduction, "Author's Note about the Play." This special section presents writings from "three of Oklahoma's finest authors, N. Scott Momaday, Joy Harjo, and Jim Thompson" (32).

158. **"When Dogs Could Talk: Among Words in a State of Grace"** (essay). *World Literature Today* 81, no. 5 (September–October 2007): 15–17. (port.) This writing is part of the issue's cover story, "Endangered Languages: Voices on the Brink of Extinction," edited by Binion Sydney and David Shook.

2008

159. **"Remembrance"** (short essay). In *Fritz Scholder: An Intimate Look*, by Joseph M. Sanchez. Santa Fe: Institute of American Indian Arts Museum, 2008. Published on the occasion of an exhibition of paintings by Fritz Scholder, held at the IAIA Museum from July 2008 to February 2009.

Stories of Plains Shields

Momaday's stories and drawings of the great tribal shields were originally published in the limited signed edition of *In the Presence of the Sun: A Gathering of Shields,* published by Rydal Press, 1991, ©1992. Its contents were reprinted in Part 3 of *In the Presence of the Sun: Stories and Poems, 1961–1991,* published by St. Martin's Press in 1992. 71–107.

The contents in both books begin with the prose poem, "The Story of a Well-Made Shield," followed by a short introduction, "A Word on the Plains Shield." The sixteen stories of shields are presented below in the order in which they appear in both books. Pages are not numbered in *In the Presence of the Sun: A Gathering of Shields.* The page numbers shown below are those in Part 3 of *In the Presence of the Sun: Stories and Poems, 1961–1991*:

160. "The Story of a Well-Made Shield," 73

161. Introduction, "A Word on the Plains Shield," 73–75

162. "The Shattered Sky Shield," 77

163. "The Shield That Came Back," 79. Reprinted in *Anthology of Modern American Poetry,* edited by Cary Nelson (2000), 1006.

164. "The Floating Feathers Shield," 81

165. "Bote-talee's Shield," 83

166. "The Sun Dance Shield," 85

167. "The Plainest of Shields," 87

168. "The Shield of the Time of the Bluebonnets," 89

169. "The Shield of Which the Less Said the Better," 91

170. "The Shield That Died," 93

171. "Walking Bear's Shield," 95

172. "The Shield of Pai-matone's Brothers," 97

173. "The Shield That Was Touched by Pretty Mouth," 99

174. "The Shield That Was Looked After by Dogs," 101

175. "The Muddy Horses Shield," 103

176. "The Shield That Was Brought Down from Tsoai," 105

177. "The Shield of Two Dreams," 107

Each of these sixteen stories is accompanied by its image painted by Momaday. The drawings appear on the left-hand, or even-numbered, pages facing their stories. Drawings of shields are in color in *In the Presence of the Sun: A Gathering of Shields.* All drawings in Part 3 of *In the Presence of the Sun: Stories and Poems, 1961–1991,* are in black and white. See also the section "Paintings and Drawings in Works by Momaday and Others."

Anthologies and Literary Collections Containing Momaday's Writings

Many of the works by Momaday presented in the preceding section, as well as his poems, prose poems, and other works in the following sections of this part of the bio-bibliography, are found in the following anthologies and literary collections. Full citations are provided for these books.

1960

178. *Poetry for Pleasure: The Hallmark Book of Poetry.* Selected and arranged by the editors of Hallmark Cards, Inc. Garden City, New York: Doubleday, 1960. 60–61. "Earth and I Gave You Turquoise" was selected for this anthology.

1969

179. *The American Indian Speaks in Poetry, Fiction, Art, Music, Commentary.* Edited by John R. Milton. Vermillion: University of South Dakota, 1969. 194 pp. The text of this anthology is identical to the contents of the Summer 1969 issue of *South Dakota Review,* vol. 7, no. 2. The two publications were issued simultaneously. Andrew Wiget describes this volume as "the first real anthology of contemporary Native American writing." Although Momaday is not included among the forty writers and artists, Milton does include him in the introduction, "Indians Speak for Themselves," as "one of the contemporary writers who possess, in one way or another, an extraordinary understanding of the Indian" (4).

180. *Quest for Reality: An Anthology of Short Poems in English.* Selected by Yvor Winters and Kenneth Fields. Chicago: Swallow Press, 1969. 199 pp. This is the companion volume to Winters's *Forms of Discovery* (1967), in which he discusses and critiques many of the poems that appear in this anthology.

181. *Speaking for Ourselves: American Ethnic Writing.* Edited by Lillian Faderman and Barbara Bradshaw. New York: Foresman, 1969.

1970

182. *Forgotten Pages of American Literature.* Edited by Gerald W. Haslam. Boston: Houghton, 1970.

1971

183. *The American Indian Speaks II.* Edited by John R. Milton. Vermillion: University of South Dakota, 1971, and *South Dakota Review* 9, no. 2 (Summer 1971). 199 pp. The latter is the second special issue devoted entirely to contemporary

art and writing of the American Indian. The two publications were issued simultaneously. There is no contribution by Momaday in this collection, although Milton included *House Made of Dawn* and *The Way to Rainy Mountain* in his "Selected Bibliography of American Indian Writing," p. 198.

184. *Literature of the American West.* Edited by J. Golden Taylor. Boston: Houghton Mifflin, 1971.

185. *Touch the Earth: A Self-Portrait of Indian Existence.* Edited by T. C. McLuhan. New York: Simon & Schuster, 1971.

186. *American Indian Anthology.* Compiled by Benet Tvedten. Marvin, South Dakota: Blue Cloud Abbey, 1971. Includes contemporaries of Momaday.

1972

187. *American Indian Authors.* Compiled and written by Natachee Scott Momaday. Boston: Houghton Mifflin, 1971, ©1972. (port.)

188. *Shaking the Pumpkin: Traditional Poetry of the Indian North Americas.* Compiled by Jerome Rothenberg. Vintage Books ed. Garden City, New York: Doubleday, 1972. See also Anthologies—1991.

189. *The Way: An Anthology of American Indian Literature.* Edited by Shirley H. Witt, with Stan Steiner. Vintage Books ed. New York: Alfred A. Knopf; Vintage, 1972.

1973

190. *From the Belly of the Shark: A New Anthology of Native Americans.* Edited by Walter Lowenfels. Vintage Books ed. New York: Random House-Vintage, 1973.

191. *Literature of the American Indian.* Edited by Thomas E. Sanders and Walter W. Peek. Beverly Hills, California: Glencoe Press, 1973.

192. *Poetry of the Desert Southwest.* Edited by James E. Quick. Phoenix, Arizona: Baleen Press, 1973.

1974

193. *The Man to Send Rain Clouds: Contemporary Stories by American Indians.* Edited by Kenneth Rosen. New York: Vintage Books, Random House, 1974.

194. *The Portable North American Indian Reader.* Edited and with an introduction by Frederick W. Turner III. New York: Viking, 1974. See also Anthologies—1977.

195. *Voices from Wah'Kon-Tah.* Edited by Robert K. Dodge and Joseph B. McCullough. New York: International Publishers, 1974. See also Anthologies—1985.

1975

196. *Carriers of the Dream Wheel: Contemporary Native American Poetry.* Edited by Duane Niatum. New York: Harper & Row, 1975. See also Anthologies—1981.

197. *Literature of the American Indians: Views and Interpretations; A Gathering of Indian Memories, Symbolic Contexts, and Literary Criticism.* Edited and with an introduction and notes by Abraham Chapman. New York: New American Library, 1975.

1976

198. *Contemporary Native American Address.* Edited by John R. Maestas. Provo, Utah: Brigham Young University, 1976.

199. *Seeing with a Native Eye: Essays on Native American Religion.* Edited by Walter H. Capps. New York: Harper & Row, 1976.

200. *Understanding Poetry.* Edited by Cleanth Brooks and Robert Penn Warren. 4th ed. New York: Holt, Rinehart & Winston, 1976.

1977

201. *The Portable North American Indian Reader.* Edited and with an introduction by Frederick W. Turner III. Harmondsworth, United Kingdom; New York: Penguin, 1977, ©1974. See also Anthologies—1986.

1978

202. *Native American Perspectives.* Edited by Larry Evers et al. Sun Tracks series, vol. 4. Tucson, Arizona: Sun Tracks, 1978.

1979

203. *American Indian Literature: An Anthology.* Edited and with an introduction by Alan R. Velie. Illustrated by Danny Timmons. Norman: University of Oklahoma Press, 1979. See also Anthologies—1991.

204. *The Remembered Earth: An Anthology of Contemporary Native American Literature.* Edited by Geary Hobson. Albuquerque, New Mexico: Red Earth Press, 1979. Over seventy American Indian writers are anthologized in this book. See also Anthologies—1981.

1980

205. *Mirrors and Mirage: Fiction by Nineteen.* Edited by Albert J. Guerard. Portable Stanford Series. Stanford, California: Stanford Alumni Association, 1980.

206. *This Song Remembers: Self-Portraits of Native Americans in the Arts.* Edited by Jane B. Katz. Boston: Houghton Mifflin, 1980. (port.)

207. *Wonders: Writings and Drawings for the Child in Us All.* Edited by Jonathan Cott and Mary Gimbel. New York: Rolling Stone Press, Summit Books, 1980.

1981

208. *Carriers of the Dream Wheel: Contemporary Native American Poetry.* Edited by Duane Niatum. San Francisco: Harper & Row, 1981, ©1975. Momaday introduces this volume with "A Note on Contemporary Native American Poetry," pp. xix–xx. The title of this anthology is from Momaday's poem with the same title.

209. *The Remembered Earth: An Anthology of Contemporary Native American Literature.* Edited by Geary Hobson. First University of New Mexico Press printing. Albuquerque: UNM Press, 1981, ©1979. This acclaimed anthology was originally published in 1979 by Red Earth Press, Albuquerque. Hobson borrowed the main title from Momaday's famous passage, "The Remembered Earth."

210. *Southwest Fiction.* Edited by Max Apple. New York: Bantam Books, 1981, ©1980.

1982

211. *Circle without End: A Sourcebook of American Indian Ethics.* Edited by Frances G. Lombardus and Gerald Scott Lombardus. Happy Camp, California: Naturegraph Publishers, 1982.

212. *A Green Place: Modern Poems.* Compiled by William Jay Smith. New York: Delacorte Press/Seymour Lawrence, 1982.

1983

213. *The Clouds Threw This Light: Contemporary Native American Poetry.* Edited by Phillip Foss. Santa Fe, New Mexico: Institute of American Indian Arts Press, 1983.

214. *Growing Old at Willie Nelson's Picnic and Other Sketches of Life in the Southwest.* Edited by Ronald B. Querry. College Station: Texas A&M University Press, 1983. (port.)

215. *Songs from This Earth on Turtle's Back: Contemporary American Indian*

Poetry. Edited by Joseph Bruchac. Greenfield Center, New York: Greenfield Review Press, 1983.

216. *Symposium of the Whole: A Range of Discourse toward an Ethnopoetics.* Edited and with commentaries by Jerome Rothenberg and Diane Rothenberg. Berkeley: University of California Press, 1983.

1984

217. *A Sender of Words: Essays in Memory of John G. Neihardt.* Edited by Vine Deloria, Jr. Salt Lake City, Utah: Howe Brothers, 1984.

218. *Words in the Blood: Contemporary Indian Writers of North and South America.* Edited and with an introduction and notes by Jamake Highwater. New York: New American Library, 1984.

219. *Writers of the Purple Sage: An Anthology of Recent Western Writing.* Edited and with an introduction by Russell Martin and Marc Barasch. New York: Viking, 1984.

1985

220. *Die weiten Horizonte* (*The Vast Horizons*). Edited and compiled by Roswith von Freydorf and Teut Andreas Riese. [Stuttgart, Germany]: Guido Pressler Verlag, 1985. This anthology presents American poetry from 1638 to 1980. The poems are printed in English on left-hand pages and in German on right-hand, or odd-numbered, pages.

221. *New and Old Voices of Wah'Kon-Tah: Contemporary Native American Poetry.* Edited by Robert K. Dodge and Joseph B. McCullough. Foreword by Vine Deloria, Jr. New York: International Publishers, 1985.

222. *Through Native Eyes.* Edited by Cynthia Flood. Richmond, British Columbia, Canada: Open Learning Institute, 1985.

1986

223. *The New Native American Novel: Works in Progress.* Edited by Mary Dougherty Bartlett. New America, vol. 6. Albuquerque: University of New Mexico Press, 1986.

224. *The Portable North American Indian Reader.* Edited by Frederick W. Turner III. Harmondsworth, United Kingdom; New York, Penguin Books, 1986.

225. *Strong Measures: Contemporary American Poetry in Traditional Forms.* Edited by Philip Dacey and David Jauss. New York: Harper & Row, 1986.

226. *Survey of American Poetry.* Vol. 10, *Mid-century to 1984.* Great Neck, New York: Poetry Anthology Press, 1986. Prepared by Editorial Board, Roth Publishing.

1987

227. *Contemporary Religious Poetry.* Edited by Paul Ramsey. Mahwah, New Jersey: Paulist Press, 1987.

228. *I Tell You Now: Autobiographical Essays by Native American Writers.* Edited by Brian Swann and Arnold Krupat. Lincoln: University of Nebraska Press, 1987. Although Momaday does not have an essay in this anthology, there are pertinent comments about his "literary autobiographies" in the "Introduction" by Swann, p. xi, and about *House Made of Dawn* in the essay by Jim Barnes, pp. 93–94, 97.

229. *Recovering the Word: Essays on Native American Literature.* Edited by Brian Swann and Arnold Krupat. Berkeley: University of California Press, 1987.

1988

230. *Harper's Anthology of 20th Century Native American Poetry.* Edited by Duane Niatum. Introduction by Brian Swann. New York: HarperCollins, 1988.

1989

231. *Anthologie de la poésie Amérindienne contemporaine.* Translated, edited, and with an introduction by Manuel Van Thienen. Les cahiers de poésie-rencontres, no. 25. Saint-Symphorien d'Ozou, France: Poésie-rencontres, 1989.

232. *Narrative Chance: Postmodern Discourse on Native American Indian Literatures.* Edited by Gerald Vizenor. American Indian Literature and Critical Studies, vol. 8. Albuquerque: University of New Mexico Press, 1989. Transferred to Vizenor in 1992. Reprinted, Norman: University of Oklahoma Press, 1993.

233. *Poetes Indiens d'Amérique.* Translated into French by Louis Olivier and Charles Juliet. Mortemart, France: Rougerie, 1989. This is a French anthology of poems written by American Indian poets.

1990

234. *The Heath Anthology of American Literature.* Edited by Paul Lauter et al. Lexington, Massachusetts: Heath; Boston: Houghton Mifflin, 1990.

235. *The Norton Book of Nature Writing.* Edited by Robert Finch and John Elder. New York: W. W. Norton, 1990.

1991

236. *American Indian Literature: An Anthology.* Edited and with an introduction by Alan R. Velie. Rev. ed. Norman: University of Oklahoma Press, 1991.

237. *American Literature: A Prentice Hall Anthology.* Concise ed. Emory Elliott, gen. ed. Englewood Cliffs, New Jersey: Prentice Hall, 1991.

238. *The Best of the West: An Anthology of Classic Writing from the American West.* Edited by Tony Hillerman. New York: HarperCollins, 1991.

239. *Braided Lives: An Anthology of Multicultural American Writing.* St. Paul: Minnesota Humanities Commission, 1991.

240. *The Lightning Within: An Anthology of Contemporary American Indian Fiction.* Edited and with an introduction by Alan R. Velie. Lincoln: University of Nebraska Press, 1991. Reprinted in Bison Book ed., Lincoln: University of Nebraska Press, 1993, ©1991.

241. *Shaking the Pumpkin: Traditional Poetry of the Indian North Americas.* Compiled by Jerome Rothenberg. Rev. ed. Albuquerque: University of New Mexico Press, 1991.

242. *Talking Leaves: Contemporary Native American Short Stories, An Anthology.* Introduced and edited by Craig Lesley, with Katheryn Stavrakis. New York: Laurel, 1991.

1992

243. *America in 1492: The World of the Indian Peoples before the Arrival of Columbus.* Edited and with an introduction by Alvin M. Josephy, Jr.; developed by Frederick E. Hoxie. New York: Alfred A. Knopf, 1992.

244. *Der Gesang des Schwarzen Bären: Lieder und Gedichte der Indianer.* Edited by von Werner Arens and Hans-Martin Braun. Münich, Germany: Verlag C. H. Beck, 1992.

245. *Looking for Luck: Poems.* Edited by Maxine Kumin. New York: W. W. Norton, 1992.

246. *New Writers of the Purple Sage: An Anthology of Contemporary Western Writers.* Collected and with an introduction by Russell Martin. New York: Penguin, 1992.

1993

247. *Being in the World: An Environmental Reader for Writers*. Edited by Scott H. Slovic and Terrell F. Dixon. New York: Macmillan, 1993.

248. *Critical Perspectives on Native American Fiction*. Edited by Richard F. Fleck. Critical Perspectives Series. Washington, D.C.: Three Continents Press, 1993.

249. *Earth Song, Sky Spirit: Short Stories of the Contemporary Native American Experience*. Edited and with an introduction by Clifford E. Trafzer. New York: Anchor Books, Doubleday, 1993.

250. *Growing Up Native American: An Anthology*. Edited and with an introduction by Patricia Riley. Foreword by Inés Hernandez. New York: William Morrow, 1993. Reprint (pbk.), New York: Quill/HarperCollins, 2002.

251. *An Introduction to Literature: Fiction, Poetry, Drama*. Edited by Sylvan Barnet et al. 10th ed. New York: HarperCollins, 1993.

252. *Kaleidoscope: Stories of the American Experience*. Edited by Barbara Perkins and George Perkins. New York: Oxford University Press, 1993.

253. *Named in Stone and Sky: An Arizona Anthology*. Edited by Gregory McNamee. Tucson: University of Arizona Press, 1993.

254. *Narrative Chance: Postmodern Discourse on Native American Indian Literatures*. Edited by Gerald Vizenor. Reprint, Norman: University of Oklahoma Press, 1993.

255. *Plains Native American Literature*. Multicultural Literature Collection. Upper Saddle River, New Jersey: Globe Fearon, 1993.

256. *Tapestry: A Multicultural Anthology*. Alan C. Purves, gen. ed. Paramus, New Jersey: Simon & Schuster, 1993.

257. *Visions of America: Personal Narratives from the Promised Land*. Edited by Wesley Brown and Amy Ling. New York: Persea Books, 1993.

1994

258. *American Lives: An Anthology of Autobiographical Writing*. Edited by Robert F. Sayre. Wisconsin Studies in American Autobiography. Madison, Wisconsin: University of Wisconsin, 1994.

259. *Durable Breath: Contemporary Native American Poetry*. Edited by John E. Smelcer and D. L. Birchfield. Introduction by Duane Niatum. Anchorage,

Alaska: Salmon Run Press, 1994. Although none of Momaday's poems are included in this anthology, an excerpt from his introduction to *Carriers of the Dream Wheel* (1975) is included in Niatum's introduction.

260. *Family of Earth and Sky: Indigenous Tales of Nature from around the World.* Edited by John Elder and Hertha D. Wong. The Concord Library. Boston: Beacon Press, 1994.

261. *Harper American Literature.* 2nd ed. Donald McQuade, gen. ed. Vol. 2. New York: HarperCollins College Publishers, 1994, ©1993.

262. *The Heath Anthology of American Literature.* 2nd ed. Paul Lauter, gen. ed. Vol. 2. Lexington, Massachusetts: Heath, 1994. Includes biographical sketch of Momaday by Kenneth M. Roemer.

263. *Les Indiens d'Amérique.* Edited by David Hurst Thomas, Jay Miller, Richard White, Peter Nabokov, and Philip J. Deloria. Collection Nuage Rouge. Paris: Éditions du Rocher, 1994.

264. *Native American Autobiography: An Anthology.* Edited by Arnold Krupat. Wisconsin Studies in American Autobiography. Madison: University of Wisconsin Press, 1994.

265. *Voice of the Turtle: American Indian Literature, 1900–1970.* Edited and with an introduction by Paula Gunn Allen. New York: A One World Book, Ballantine Books, 1994.

266. *Words of Power: Voices from Indian America.* Edited by Norbert S. Hill, Jr. Golden, Colorado: Fulcrum; published in association with American Indian Science and Engineering Society, 1994.

1995

267. *American Indian Voices.* Edited by Karen D. Harvey. Writers of America Series. Brookfield, Connecticut: Millbrook Press, 1995.

268. *The Columbia Anthology of American Poetry.* Edited by Jay Parini. New York: Columbia University Press, 1995.

269. *Models of the Universe: An Anthology of the Prose Poem.* Edited by Stuart Friebert and David Young. Oberlin, Ohio: Oberlin College Press, 1995.

270. *Native American Literature: A Brief Introduction and Anthology.* Edited by Gerald Vizenor. HarperCollins Literary Mosaic Series. New York: HarperCollins College Publishers, 1995.

271. *Native Heritage: Personal Accounts by American Indians, 1790 to the Present.* Edited by Arlene Hirschfelder. New York: Macmillan, 1995.

272. *The Norton Anthology of American Literature.* Edited by Nina Baym. 4th ed. New York: W. W. Norton, 1995.

273. *Smoke Rising: The Native North American Literary Companion.* By Joseph Bruchac, managing ed., and Janet Witalec, ed., with Sharon Malinowski. Detroit: Visible Ink Press, 1995.

1996

274. *The Anatomy of Memory: An Anthology.* Edited by James McConkey. New York: Oxford University Press, 1996.

275. *Constructing Nature: Readings from the American Experience.* Edited by Richard Jenseth and Edward E. Lotto. A Blair Press Book. Upper Saddle River, New Jersey: Prentice Hall, 1996.

276. *The Norton Anthology of Poetry.* Edited by Margaret Ferguson, Mary Jo Salter, and Jon Stallworthy. 4th ed. New York: W. W. Norton, 1996.

277. *Poetry of the American West: A Columbia Anthology.* By Alison Hawthorne Deming. New York: Columbia University Press, 1996. 204–206.

278. *Song of the Turtle: American Indian Literature, 1974–1994.* Edited and with an introduction by Paula Gunn Allen. New York: A One World Book, Ballantine Books, 1996.

1997

279. *75 Readings: An Anthology.* Edited by Santi Buscemi and Charlotte Smith. 6th ed. New York: McGraw-Hill, 1997.

280. *The Portable Western Reader.* Edited and with an introduction by William Kittredge. New York: Penguin Books, 1997.

281. *The Serpent's Tongue: Prose, Poetry, and Art of the New Mexico Pueblos.* Edited by Nancy Wood. New York: Dutton, 1997.

282. *Stories and Stone: Writing the Anasazi Homeland.* Edited and with an introduction by Reuben Ellis. Boulder, Colorado: Pruett Publishing, 1997.

283. *Voices of Native America.* Collected, selected, and edited by Hap Gilliland. Dubuque, Iowa: Kendall/Hunt Publishing, 1997.

1998

284. *The Heath Anthology of American Literature.* Edited by Paul Lauter. Vol. 2. Boston: Houghton Mifflin, 1998.

285. *An Introduction to Poetry.* By X. J. Kennedy and Dana Gioia. 9th ed. New York: Longman, 1998.

286. *Literature: An Introduction to Fiction, Poetry, and Drama.* Edited by X. J. Kennedy and Dana Gioia. 7th ed. New York: Longman, 1998.

287. *Native American Literature: An Anthology.* Compiled and edited by Lawana Trout. Lincolnwood (Chicago), Illinois: National Textbook Co./Contemporary Publishing Group, 1998, ©1999.

288. *Stars Above, Earth Below: American Indians and Nature.* Edited by Marsha C. Bol. Niwot, Colorado: Roberts Rinehart Publishers for the Carnegie Museum of Natural History, 1998.

1999

289. *At Home on the Earth: Becoming Native to Our Place: A Multicultural Anthology.* Edited by David Landis Barnhill. Berkeley: University of California Press, 1999.

290. *In Brief: Short Takes on the Personal.* Edited by Judith Kitchen and Mary Paumier Jones. New York: W. W. Norton, 1999.

291. *The Literary West: An Anthology of Western American Literature.* Edited by Thomas J. Lyon. New York: Oxford University Press, 1999.

2000

292. *Anthology of Modern American Poetry.* Edited by Cary Nelson. New York: Oxford University Press, 2000.

293. *The Best American Essays of the Century.* Edited by Joyce Carol Oates; co-edited by Robert Atwan. Boston: Houghton Mifflin, 2000. The Introduction to *The Way to Rainy Mountain* (1969) was selected for this collection of outstanding essays.

294. *Making Literature Matter: An Anthology for Readers and Writers.* By John Schilb and John Clifford. Boston: Bedford/St. Martin's, 2000.

295. *Native American Literature.* Prentice Hall Literature Library. Upper Saddle River, New Jersey: Prentice Hall, 2000.

296. *Sing with the Heart of a Bear: Fusions of Native and American Poetry, 1890–1999*. By Kenneth Lincoln. Berkeley: University of California Press, 2000.

297. *The Year's Best Fantasy and Horror, Thirteenth Annual Collection*. By Ellen Datlow and Terri Windling. New York: St. Martin's Press, 2000.

2001

298. *Defining Travel: Diverse Visions*. Edited by Susan L. Roberson. Jackson: University Press of Mississippi, 2001.

299. *Essays in Context*. Edited by Sandra Fehl Tropp and Ann Pierson D'Angelo. New York: Oxford University Press, 2001.

300. *Literature and Nature: Four Centuries of Nature Writing*. Edited by Bridget Keegan and James C. McKusick. Upper Saddle River, New Jersey: Prentice Hall, 2001.

301. *The Nature of Native American Poetry*. Edited by Norma C. Wilson. Albuquerque: University of New Mexico Press, 2001.

302. *Nothing but the Truth: An Anthology of Native American Literatures*. Edited by John Lloyd Purdy and James Ruppert. Upper Saddle River, New Jersey: Prentice Hall, 2001.

303. *Poetry: An Introduction*. Edited by Michael Meyer. 3rd ed. Boston: Bedford/St. Martin's Press, 2001.

2002

304. *The Heath Anthology of American Literature*. Edited by Paul Lauter. 4th ed. Boston: Houghton Mifflin, 2002.

305. *Nature Writing: The Tradition in English*. Edited by Robert Finch and John Elder. New York: W. W. Norton, 2002. This edition was previously published as *The Norton Book of Nature Writing* (1990).

306. *Poetry in Motion from Coast to Coast: 120 Poems from the Subways and the Buses*. Edited by Elise Paschen and Brett F. Lauer. New York: W. W. Norton, 2002.

307. *Whisper and Shout: Poems to Memorize*. Edited by Patrice Vecchione. Chicago: Cricket Books, 2002.

2003

308. *A Great Plains Reader*. Edited by Diane D. Quantic and P. Jane Hafen. Lincoln: University of Nebraska Press, 2003.

309. *The Norton Anthology of American Literature: Literature since 1945*. 6th ed. Nina Baym, gen. ed. Vol. E. New York: W. W. Norton, 2003.

310. *The Portable Sixties Reader*. Edited by Ann Charters. New York: Penguin, 2003.

2004

311. *50 Essays: A Portable Anthology*. Edited by Samuel Cohen. Boston: Bedford/St. Martin's Press, 2004.

312. *In Company: An Anthology of New Mexico Poets after 1960*. Edited by Lee Bartlett, V. B. Price, and Dianne Edenfield Edwards. Mary Burritt Christiansen Poetry Series. Albuquerque: University of New Mexico Press, 2004.

313. *Native Universe: Voices of Indian America*. Edited by Gerald McMaster and Clifford E. Trafzer, with a foreword by W. Richard West. Washington, D.C.: National Geographic Society, 2004.

314. *Twentieth-Century American Poetry*. Edited by Dana Gioia, David Mason, and Meg Schoerke. Boston: McGraw-Hill, 2004.

2005

315. *The Anthology: Poems for Poetry Out Loud: National Recitation Contest*. Edited by Dan Stone and Stephen Young. Washington, D.C.: National Endowment for the Arts and Poetry Foundation, 2005. Momaday reads poetry aloud in this collection. See also the section "Internet and Online Resources."

316. *Fifty Great Essays*. Edited by Robert DiYanni. 2nd ed. Penguin Classics. New York: Pearson Longman, 2005.

317. *Lasting: Poems on Aging*. Edited by Meg Files. Tucson, Arizona: Pima Press, Pima Community College, 2005.

318. *Literature: An Introduction to Fiction, Poetry, and Drama*. Edited by X. J. Kennedy and Dana Gioia. New York: Pearson Longman, 2005.

319. *Master Class: Lessons from Leading Masters*. Edited by Nancy Bunge. Iowa City: University of Iowa Press, 2005.

320. *The New World Reader: Thinking and Writing about the Global Community*. Edited by Gilbert H. Muller. Boston: Houghton Mifflin, 2005.

321. *The Norton Anthology of Poetry*. Edited by Margaret Ferguson, Mary Jo Salter, and Jon Stallworthy. 5th ed. New York: W. W. Norton, 2005.

322. *One Hundred Great Essays*. Edited by Robert DiYanni. New York: Pearson Longman, 2005.

323. *On the Wing: American Poems of Air and Space Flight*. Edited by Karen Yelena Olsen. Iowa City: University of Iowa Press, 2005.

2006

324. *American Religious Poems: An Anthology by Harold Bloom*. Edited by Harold Bloom and Jesse Zuba. New York: The Library of America, 2006.

325. *The Heath Anthology of American Literature*. Vol. E, *Contemporary Period: 1945 to the Present*. Edited by Paul Lauter. Boston: Houghton Mifflin, 2006.

326. *Literature: An Introduction to Reading and Writing*. Edited by Edgar V. Roberts and Henry E. Jacobs. 3rd compact ed. Upper Saddle River, New Jersey: Pearson Prentice Hall, 2006.

327. *Page to Page: Retrospectives of Writers from "The Seattle Review."* Edited by Colleen J. McElroy. Seattle: University of Washington Press, 2006.

328. *The Wadsworth Anthology of Poetry, Shorter Edition*. Edited by Jay Parini. Boston: Thomson Wadsworth, 2006. A compact disc is available containing poetry read by Momaday and others.

329. *Writing the Cross Culture: Native Fiction on the White Man's Religion*. Edited by James Treat. Golden, Colorado: Fulcrum, 2006.

2007

330. *Literature: An Introduction to Fiction, Poetry, Drama, and Writing*. By X. J. Kennedy, Dorothy M. Kennedy, and Dana Gioia. 5th compact ed. New York: Pearson Longman, 2007.

331. *Speak Like Singing: Classics of Native American Literature*. By Kenneth Lincoln. Albuquerque: University of New Mexico Press, 2007.

2008

332. *American Earth: Environmental Writing since Thoreau*. Edited by Bill McKibben; foreword by Al Gore. A Special Publication of The Library of America. New York: Literary Classics of the United States, 2008.

2009

333. *Inner Journey: Views from Native Traditions; Black Elk, Leslie Marmon Silko, and N. Scott Momaday*. Parabola Anthology Series. Sandpoint, Idaho: Morning Light Press, 2009.

Newspaper Column in *Viva: Northern New Mexico's Sunday Magazine*

Momaday's column appeared weekly from April 16, 1972 through December 9, 1973 in the supplement *Viva: Northern New Mexico's Sunday Magazine* of the *Santa Fe New Mexican*, the oldest continuously published newspaper in the American West.

334. (Untitled) *Viva*, April 16, 1972, 2.

Momaday relates an incident reported in the *Santa Fe New Mexican* on February 27, 1872, involving Colonel Otto Firpo, son of explorer Viktor Maximilian Firpo, and an ancient sling shot, or dullimer, which Momaday received on his tenth birthday. This essay appears under the title "Chopetl" in *The Man Made of Words* (1997), 196–97.

335. "Can a Dog Be Pious?" *Viva*, April 23, 1972, 2.

Momaday's black Labrador retriever, Cacique, attends the Blessing of the Animals held at Cristo Rey Church in Santa Fe on the Feast Day of Saint Anthony, Abbot. This essay, with some changes, appears under the title "An Element of Piety" in *The Man Made of Words* (1997), 193–95.

336. (Untitled) *Viva*, April 30, 1972, 2.

Luis Atencio, proprietor of El Paragua Restaurant at Espanola, New Mexico, and a good friend, is described by Momaday as "one of those people who by the sheer force of their presence seem to determine the reality of a given place." One paragraph from this column was included in Momaday's essay "Dreaming in Place" in *The Man Made of Words* (1997), 209–11.

337. "A Special Sense of Place." *Viva*, May 7, 1972, 2.

The author confesses that for him "a sense of place" is "a thing of moments." Whether he has been at Monument Valley, the beach at Santa Barbara, or the Valle Grande, "at that moment it was simply the place I like best in the world." This essay, with revisions, appears as "The Octopus" in *The Man Made of Words* (1997), 207–208.

338. "The Night the Stars Fell." *Viva*, May 14, 1972, 2.

The great Leonid meteor shower of 1833, a phenomenon that occurred on November 13, 1833, was recorded in a ledger book by the Kiowa elder, Pohd-lohk, who gave Momaday his Kiowa name, Tsoai-talee (Rock Tree Boy). This essay appears, with revisions, under the title "When the Stars Fell" in *The Man Made of Words* (1997), 170–71.

339. "An Incident on a Road in Spain." *Viva*, May 21, 1972, 2.

The moral of this mini-tragedy is that age does bring wisdom to some people. This essay, with revisions, appears under the title "A Turning Point" in *The Man Made of Words* (1997), 178–79.

340. "A Bridge, a Ghost, a Cowboy." *Viva*, May 28, 1972, 2.

Three vignettes on the nature of man involve the Golden Gate Bridge, a ghost that dwells in Santa Fe, and a cowboy who recognizes another cowboy when he sees one. A vignette from this column was included in his essay "Dreaming in Place" in *The Man Made of Words* (1997), 209–11.

341. "Singing about the Beauty of the Earth." *Viva*, June 4, 1972, 2.

Momaday offers his heartfelt belief that "as a nation, we have failed to articulate the beauty of the world, because we have not perceived that the world is beautiful." An excerpt from this essay appears in Charles L. Woodard's *Conversations with N. Scott Momaday* (1989), 189.

342. "Going to the Movies." *Viva*, June 11, 1972, 2.

After viewing a number of classic films back to back, Momaday comments on three: *The Little Tramp* with Charlie Chaplin, *Gone with the Wind*, and *To Have and Have Not.*

343. "The Woman Who Knew Africa." *Viva*, June 18, 1972, 2.

Isak Dinesen (pseudonym of Karen Blixen) wrote the classic *Out of Africa*, acclaimed by Momaday as "one of the great books of our time." A shortened version of this essay appears under the title "Graceful and At Ease" in *The Man Made of Words* (1997), 191–92.

344. "Growing Up at Jemez Pueblo." *Viva*, June 25, 1972, 2.

In the autumn of 1946 at the age of twelve, Momaday arrived at Jemez Pueblo for the first time. It was a wonderful place for him to live, learn, and grow up in a multitude of ways. This essay appears with the title "Riding Is an Exercise of the Mind" in *In the Presence of the Sun: Stories and Poems, 1961–1991* (1992), 45–47.

345. "The Influence of Edmund Wilson." *Viva*, July 2, 1972, 2.

The passing of poet, playwright, novelist, and critic Edmund Wilson is lamented by Momaday. He considers Wilson one of the foremost literary personages of his time. Wilson was instrumental in the early stages of Momaday's literary career. A shortened version of this essay appears under the title "Teresita" in *The Man Made of Words* (1997), 198–99.

346. "Learning from the Indian." *Viva*, July 9, 1972, 2.

Among the numerous things one can learn from the Indian is an ethical approach to the natural world, which Momaday believes must "inform all of our efforts to preserve life on this planet."

347. "Revisiting the Family Home." *Viva*, July 16, 1972, 2.

Stonehenge is the name of his home, which originally belonged to his parents. An old structure of oak timbers, stone, and adobe, it has for Momaday "a kind of Druidic mystery" about it.

348. "Driving East for Kiowa Dancing." *Viva*, July 23, 1972, 2.

Momaday begins by telling the story of how the Gourd Dance of the Kiowa came to be. Every year on the Fourth of July, the Gourd Dance, or Taimpe, Society holds the dance and other ceremonies. He has been a member of this society since 1969.

349. "What Will Happen to the Land?" *Viva*, July 30, 1972, 2.

Momaday ponders this question. He also wonders what will happen to his existence on it, because each person exists as part of his environment. This essay appears as "I Wonder What Will Happen to the Land" in *The Man Made of Words* (1997), 186–88.

350. "A Love Affair with Emily Dickinson." *Viva*, August 6, 1972, 2.

Momaday reveals his long-standing love affair with one of America's greatest poets. He learned much about language from her, having had the good fortune to read all of her poems, most in manuscript, over the period of a year at Amherst, her home town in Massachusetts. References to and quotes from this essay are found on pp. 25 and 244 of Kenneth Lincoln's *Sing with the Heart of a Bear* (2000) and in his essay "Native Poetics," published in *Modern Fiction Studies*, Spring 1999.

351. "Visiting the Big City." *Viva*, August 13, 1972, 2.

Upon the occasion of his eldest daughter's eighth birthday, Momaday treats Cael to her first visit to New York City. He reminisces about their adventures.

352. "The Isolation of Quincy Tahoma." *Viva*, August 20, 1972, 2.

Momaday remembers Tahoma, who grew up on the Navajo Reservation and attended the Santa Fe Indian School, which became the Institute of American Indian Arts. He recalls with delight the visits made by Tahoma to Jemez

Pueblo to visit and paint with his father, artist and teacher Al Momaday. This essay appears as "Quincy Tahoma" in *The Man Made of Words* (1997), 180–82.

353. "Going to the Opera in the Rain." *Viva*, August 27, 1972, 16.

A spectacular thunderstorm with crashing thunder and brilliant lightning magnifies the drama of a performance of "La Grande Duchesse" at the Santa Fe Opera.

354. "Does One Write by Necessity . . . or by Choice?" *Viva*, September 3, 1972, 6.

Momaday opines that a person becomes a writer because he or she must write, rather than by making a decision or consciously choosing to write.

355. "Reflections on the First Day of Class." *Viva*, September 10, 1972, 2.

This first day of class occurred at New Mexico State University in Las Cruces. Momaday was starting the fall term as Visiting Distinguished Professor.

356. "Looking at Life with Journal and Lens." *Viva*, September 17, 1972, 2.

Keeping a journal, according to Momaday, is "a good thing." Having kept a journal for many years, he find it serves, much like a camera, as "a lens through which one might see in a precise and extraordinary way."

357. "Bewitched." *Viva*, September 24, 1972, 2.

Momaday admits that his daughters' fascination with stories about witches may be caused, at least in part, by his own fascination with such tales. An excerpt from this essay appeared in Marc Simmons's introduction to his book *Witchcraft in the Southwest: Spanish and Indian Supernaturalism on the Rio Grande*. Flagstaff, Arizona: Northland Press, 1974. 2–3. Reprint, Lincoln: University of Nebraska Press, 1980, ©1974. 2–3.

358. "Listening to Sorrow." *Viva*, October 1, 1972, 20.

Momaday tells about the life and death of Bessie Smith, considered the greatest blues singer who ever lived.

359. "So Crisply Autumn." *Viva*, October 8, 1972, 2.

Written while teaching at New Mexico State University, Momaday relates rising before dawn on a Sunday morning and riding his bike in the growing light. He recalls: "There is something like Genesis, like Creation at that hour of the day; and outside, breathing deeply of it, you feel intensely alive."

360. "Conscious Questioning." *Viva*, October 15, 1972, 2.

Beginning this essay with a passage from the Spanish philosopher Unamuno asserting that people are unable to think of themselves as not existing, Momaday proceeds to tell about a most frightening experience he had while climbing down a mountain.

361. “Going into Navajo Land.” *Viva*, October 22, 1972, 2.

Momaday reminisces about the time he lived on the Navajo Reservation with his parents. It was during trips made with his father crisscrossing the reservation on dirt roads that he got a sense of the land. This essay appears under the title “The Photograph” in *The Man Made of Words* (1997), 174–75.

362. “Cherish the Legend of Billy the Kid.” *Viva*, October 29, 1972, 2.

The point made by Momaday is that the legend should be cherished, not the man named Henry McCarty, William Bonney, or some other alias. It is the legend that has become a folk phenomenon.

363. “The Indians and the Dodgers.” *Viva*, November 5, 1972, 2.

While the title may cause one to think that the subject is baseball, this essay is about national politics. He remarks that the Indian is possibly more “worldly wise” about politics than most other Americans.

364. “The Persistent Life Force of Mexico.” *Viva*, November 12, 1972, 2.

On a trip with a friend across the U.S.-Mexican border to have dinner and visit in Juarez, Momaday perceives “a life force that is indistinguishable from one generation to another.”

365. “Twenty-six Years Ago, on This Day.” *Viva*, November 19, 1972, 2.

Momaday returns to Jemez Pueblo on November 12 for the Feast of San Diego. His daughters accompany him to see the dance and visit the pueblo that he first saw at the age of twelve. Matthias Schubnell quoted from this essay in his *N. Scott Momaday: The Cultural and Literary Background* (1985), 5. Also quoted in *The Text and the Voice: Writing, Speaking, and Democracy in American Literature*, by Alessandro Portelli (1994), 12.

366. “Reflections on the Uncertainty of Winter.” *Viva*, November 26, 1972, 2.

Momaday offers his sonnet “Plainview: 1” and a few personal vignettes. Parts of this column were used in his essay “The Head of a Man” in *The Man Made of Words* (1997), 200–201.

367. “Hurrah for Sir Francis Drake—and Thanks.” *Viva*, December 3, 1972, 2.

After reading a book about the life of Sir Francis Drake, Momaday asserts that

Drake's voyage across the Pacific Ocean served as a catalyst in the Spaniards' exploration northward from Mexico.

368. "Three Personalities, One Landscape." *Viva*, December 10, 1972, 2.

In explaining the meaning of "a sense of place," Momaday tells how three friends, Joe Tosa of Jemez Pueblo, Fray Angélico Chávez, and Georgia O'Keeffe, personified the New Mexican landscape and reflected a special connection to the land.

369. "Way Down Yonder in the Pawpaw Patch." *Viva*, December 17, 1972, 2.

Momaday ruminates about driving through the countryside with his daughter Brit, the writing of a poem, the gracious lady who cleans his house, and a great fire in San Francisco. One passage from this column was included in his essay "Dreaming in Place" in *The Man Made of Words* (1997), 209–11.

370. "Approaching the Intricate Topic Obliquely." *Viva*, December 24, 1972, 2.

Momaday presents three anecdotes and an extraordinary tale.

371. "Figments of Sancho Panza's Imagination." *Viva*, December 31, 1972, 2.

This essay offers a charming quartet of musings about Sancho Panza and the Knight Errant, Don Quixote.

372. "The Great Wisdom of Elephant Jokes." *Viva*, January 7, 1973, 2.

Momaday charms the reader with a kite-flying story, two innocuous elephant jokes, and a dog tale.

373. "A Pyre of Moments, Peculiarly Mine . . ." *Viva*, January 14, 1973, 2.

Visiting the charred ruin of the Jemez Day School after a devastating fire, Momaday recalls the happiness of living there with his parents during his adolescence.

374. "'I Love You, and I Love Your Furry Nose.'" *Viva*, January 21, 1973, 2.

Momaday shares two love letters—not his own, but those of Prudence Mather and Juvenal Moskowitz (could they be real people?) and a lunch at The Compound in Santa Fe.

375. "Coolidge, N.M.: A State of Mind, a Point of View." *Viva*, January 28, 1973, 2.

Recalling the summer he lived at this small settlement located east of Gallup and near the Continental Divide, Momaday marvels at the beauty of the landscape he saw from dawn to dusk.

376. "A Time to Hold All Day Long in Your Lungs." *Viva*, February 4, 1973, 2.

The spell and wonder of winter are presented in a collection of vignettes.

377. "A Typically Miserable Flight to an Unusually Fine Reward." *Viva*, February 11, 1973, 3.

A frequent flyer, Momaday is accustomed to holding patterns and missing connecting flights. He finally arrived in Washington, D.C., and attended a conference on teaching creative writing that, unlike his flight, uplifted his mind and spirit.

378. "A Crucial Year in Dulce, and a Boy I Shall Call David." *Viva*, February 18, 1973, 3.

Momaday reflects on his first professional teaching appointment following his graduation from college in 1958.

379. "Indignation, Young and Old." *Viva*, February 25, 1973, 3.

Momaday declares: "Youth—the best of it—and the prime of life are surely periods of supreme indignation." He provides two examples: an indignant college student and a feisty nonagenarian who knew Billy the Kid.

380. "Laughter through Tears." *Viva*, March 4, 1973, 7.

François Villon (real name François de Montcorbier) was born in Paris in 1431 and became one of France's greatest poets. He was also a notorious figure in the Paris underworld. He received a death sentence that was commuted to banishment from France.

381. "A Columnist Recalls . . ." *Viva*, March 11, 1973, 15.

Celebrating the first anniversary of this column in *Viva*, Momaday says that writing a column has been a good thing for him in various ways. In particular, he finds that it demands a different kind of energy and imagination.

382. "A Few Thoughts about Buffalo." *Viva*, March 18, 1973, 2.

Momaday confides his deep ethnic respect for this amazing creature. He believes that the most criminal act committed against the wilderness was the senseless slaughter of the great herds. The first three paragraphs of this essay appear with a few changes as "One Morning in Oklahoma" in *The Man Made of Words* (1997), 185.

383. "Life in Three Wonderful Cities." *Viva*, March 25, 1973, 2.

Charlottesville, Virginia, Santa Barbara, California, and San Francisco are three American cities that Momaday holds close to his heart.

384. "Cryptic Tale from Past." *Viva*, April 1, 1973, 7.

While going through old papers, Momaday came across several pages of a story's rough draft and admits he has not given the story a thought since composing it.

385. "In Praise of Books since 868." *Viva*, April 8, 1973, 2.

To Momaday, the book is "a thing of infinite possibility." He discusses the development of alphabetic writing and the first printed books.

386. "Letters: A Window to the Past." *Viva*, April 15, 1973, 2.

After reading a passage from a letter he had written fifteen years earlier when teaching in Dulce, New Mexico, Momaday confides that to him, it was like "a returning, a doubling back in time."

387. "About the Is-ness of It All." *Viva*, April 22, 1973, 2.

There is an "is-ness" to the summer season, declares Momaday. Everything he sees, from the games children play to the towering clouds over the mountains, tells him that this is so.

388. "A Brief Look at Three Kids." *Viva*, April 29, 1973, 2.

Momaday describes the varied activities of three of his daughters when they were five, eight, and ten years old.

389. "At Best—A Minor Tragedy?" *Viva*, May 6, 1973, 24.

Momaday presents a mini-drama in which there are two actors, author Isak Dinesen and Billy the Kid. It is Billy's turn to tell a tale, this one being about a man with no name.

390. "Finding a Need for Nature." *Viva*, May 13, 1973, 2.

One spring day after a long, wet winter, Momaday and a friend take a hike into the blooming desert of the Doña Ana Mountains. After they return and have dinner, the two make a sudden decision. They grab their sleeping bags and head back for a night under the stars in that beautiful place.

391. "Some Positive Signs of Spring." *Viva*, May 20, 1973, 11.

Rejoicing over the welcome signs of spring in Santa Fe, Momaday also expresses his joy over the recent return of La Conquistadora, the holy statue whose "autobiography" was written by Fray Angélico Chávez.

392. "A Highly Seasoned Column." *Viva*, May 27, 1973, 2.

Momaday enjoys cooking and the culinary arts, and admires anyone who can cook very well. He believes that such skill requires a special kind of intelligence.

393. "An Opportunity to Speak Out." *Viva*, June 3, 1973, 2.

Preparing to leave for Alaska, where he will speak about man's relationship to the land, Momaday draws from his essay "An American Land Ethic," in which he states: "In order truly to realize ourselves in relation to the earth, we must conceive of the earth as sacred."

394. "Graduation Brings Memories." *Viva*, June 10, 1973, 2.

Writing after giving the commencement address at the Institute of American Indian Arts in Santa Fe, Momaday remarks that he is always genuinely moved by such ceremonies.

395. "Day Tripping over Alaska." *Viva*, June 17, 1973, 8.

Taking a day trip by air to the North Slope of Alaska confirms for Momaday that a day does not begin to do justice to this vast, fascinating land.

396. "That Which Glistens." *Viva*, June 24, 1973, 2.

Reporting that he has seen more Anglo-American men on both coasts wearing silver and turquoise, Momaday applauds the movement, a style that he believes expresses the wearer's spirit.

397. "Procession of Glad People." *Viva*, July 1, 1973, 2.

"Santa Fe," writes Momaday, "is a city of processions." He describes a procession from the Church of Cristo Rey and a much smaller one comprising his daughters and himself to view a marvelous sunset.

398. The column did not appear in the July 8, 1973, issue.

399. "In the Mind's Eye." *Viva*, July 15, 1973, 2.

In a charming vignette, Momaday receives a phone call from a former student and imagines that she is actress Claire Bloom.

400. "A Memory that Persists in the Blood." *Viva*, July 22, 1973, 9.

An important event remembered by Momaday in his mind is the Kiowa dance at which his grandfather Mammedaty, who lived before Momaday was born, was given a beautiful horse.

401. "A Garment of Brightness." *Viva*, July 29, 1973, 2.

Momaday writes about a remarkable aesthetic perception in the Indian world. An excerpt from this essay is in *Ancestral Voice: Conversations with N. Scott Momaday*, by Charles L. Woodard (1989), 151–52.

402. "Sister of Charity and Desperado." *Viva*, August 5, 1973, 2.

Sister Blandina Segale came from Ohio to New Mexico and the Colorado Territory in 1872 and first met Billy the Kid at Trinidad, Colorado, where he did her a favor. This essay, in shortened and revised form, appears under the title "The Physicians of Trinidad" in *The Man Made of Words* (1997), 202–204.

403. "Thoughts on Life." *Viva*, August 12, 1973, 8.

Momaday presents his thoughts through a selection of his poetry and prose poems that include "The Delight Song of Tsoai-talee" and "Four Notions of Love and Marriage."

404. "The Dark Priest of Taos." *Viva*, August 19, 1973, 19.

Padre Antonio José Martínez of Taos is considered by Momaday to be among "the most provocative and fascinating" personages in the history of northern New Mexico. This essay appears with a few revisions in *The Man Made of Words* (1997), 205–206.

405. "A Dialogue on the Opera." *Viva*, August 26, 1973, 4.

While chatting about the Santa Fe Opera, a friend remarks to Momaday that it is unique in a variety of ways, including the landscape, the architecture, and the "costumes" of the operagoers.

406. "The Man Who Took Literature Seriously." *Viva*, September 2, 1973, 8.

Yvor Winters, poet and critic, was Momaday's professor and advisor at Stanford University. They remained close friends after Momaday left the university. He praises Winters for having been steadfast to his principles.

407. "Unholy Sights." *Viva*, September 9, 1973, 7.

Two stories tell about encounters that took place during Momaday's childhood: one with a harmless snake, and the other with an eccentric old man who lived at Jemez Pueblo.

408. "The Toll Road." *Viva*, September 16, 1973, 9.

People who run seem to Momaday to be an imaginative bunch. He tells a story told to him by a friend who is a serious runner; it is a marvelous parable about acknowledging another's place in the world. A shortened version of this essay appears in *The Man Made of Words* (1997), 189–90.

409. "One of the Wild, Beautiful Creatures." *Viva*, September 23, 1973, 13.

Momaday recounts a hunt in which he took part at about the age of thirteen, when he had a different view of hunting. He carried a mortally wounded goose for a long distance, watching its life slowly ebb away. This essay was reprinted in "Post-Symbolism and Prose Poems: Momaday's Poetry," chapter 3 of *Four American Indian Literary Masters: N. Scott Momaday, James Welch, Leslie Marmon Silko, and Gerald Vizenor*, edited by Alan R. Velie. Norman: University of Oklahoma Press, 1982. 38–40.

410. "A Delicate Matter This Equation." *Viva*, September 30, 1973, 12.

Momaday speaks with solemnity and great compassion of the trials and agonies of adolescence. Having been there himself, he has not forgotten how it was to be on "the edge of despair."

411. (Untitled.) *Viva*, October 14, 1973, 2.

An old man living in Portland, Oregon, tells Momaday about the wonderful summers he spent during his boyhood with the family of Chief Joseph, the leader of the Nez Perce. He also confesses regretting something he did not do because he lacked understanding in his youth.

412. "Caveat Emptor." *Viva*, October 21, 1973, 6.

When Momaday was twelve, his parents bought a dog for him from a Navajo man whose dogs always followed his wagon. Momaday tied up the dog in their garage that night, but it was gone the following morning. He concludes: "From that experience I learned something about the heart's longing." This essay, with some changes, appears as "The Indian Dog" in *The Man Made of Words* (1997), 172–73. "The Indian Dog" was reprinted in *In Brief: Short Takes on the Personal*, eds. Judith Kitchen and Mary Paumier Jones (1999), 169–70, and in *Seattle Review* 27, no. 1 (2005): 42–43.

413. "The Gourd Dancer: Mammedaty, 1880–1932." *Viva*, November 4, 1973, 6.

This prose poem about Momaday's grandfather appeared first in his poetry collection *The Gourd Dancer* (1976) and later in *In the Presence of the Sun* (1992).

414. "The Miraculous Comes So Close." *Viva*, November 11, 1973, 6.

Having studied the Russian language, traveled and visited in the country, and taught at its great university, Momaday recalls the strength of the people. He includes a poem about the human spirit by Russian poet Anna Akhmatova.

415. "Thoughts on Jemez and Billy the Kid." *Viva*, November 18, 1973, 8.

Looking out of his office window at Stanford University on November 12, Momaday recalls the annual Feast of San Diego held at Jemez Pueblo on that date and yearns to be there. He also wonders about particulars involving Billy the Kid's demise.

416. "How It Began." *Viva*, November 25, 1973, 4.

Momaday divulges "the strange and true story of my life with Billy the Kid." This story appeared in *The Ancient Child* (1989) and was also published with the title "The Man in Black," in *In the Presence of the Sun* (1992).

417. "Billy Offers a Kindness to an Old Man at Glorieta." *Viva*, December 9, 1973, 12.

After a long visit with an old, broken cowboy, The Kid offered him half of a plug of tobacco. He explained that he offered only half because it pleased the old man more to know that something had been shared rather than the whole piece given outright. This story was published in *The Ancient Child* (1989) and again in *In the Presence of the Sun* (1992).

Forewords, Introductions, Prefaces, and Afterword

Forewords

418. Foreword. *Famous American Indians of the Plains,* by S. Carl Hirsch. Chicago: Rand McNally, 1973. 11–12.

419. Foreword. *Windsinger,* by Frances Gillmor. A Zia Book. Albuquerque: University of New Mexico Press, 1976. v–vii.

420. Foreword. *A Coyote in the Garden,* by An Painter. Edited and with a foreword by N. Scott Momaday. Lewiston, Idaho: Confluence Press, 1988. v–vi.

421. Foreword. *Keepers of the Earth: Native American Stories and Environmental Activities for Children,* by Michael J. Caduto and Joseph Bruchac. Illustrations by John Kahionhes Fadden and Carol Wood. Golden, Colorado: Fulcrum, 1989. xvii.

422. Foreword. *Enduring Culture: A Century of Photography of the Southwest Indians,* by Marcia K. Keegan and Frontier Photographers Wesley Bradfield, Edward S. Curtis, Wyatt Davis, Burton Frasher, Odd Halseth, John K. Hillers, Charles Lummis, T. Harmon Parkhurst, George H. Pepper, Simeon Schwemberger, Matilde Coxe Stevenson, J. R. Willis, Ben Wittick, and Adam Clark Vroman. Santa Fe, New Mexico: Clear Light Publishers, 1990. 7.

423. Foreword. *David Johns on the Trail of Beauty,* by Lois Essary Jacka with photos by Jerry Jacka. Scottsdale, Arizona: Snailspace Publishing, 1991. vii.

424. Foreword. *Dancing with the Wind: The ArtsReach Literary Magazine.* Vol. III, edited by N. Scott Momaday. Tucson, Arizona: ArtsReach Imaginative Writing Program, 1991. 5–6. This magazine presented the poetry and fiction of Native American students of this program, sponsored by the Tucson-Pima Arts Council.

425. Foreword. *Native American Stories.* Told by Joseph Bruchac. From *Keepers of the Earth,* by Michael J. Caduto and Joseph Bruchac. Illustrations by John K. Fadden. Golden, Colorado: Fulcrum, 1991. vii–viii. Reprint, Fulcrum, 2005.

426. Foreword. *Between Sacred Mountains: Navajo Stories and Lessons from the Land,* edited by Claudeen Arthur et al. Sun Tracks, American Literary Series, vol. 11, ser. ed. Larry Evers. Tucson: University of Arizona Press, 1994. vii–viii.

427. Foreword. *A Sense of Mission: Historic Churches of the Southwest.* Photography by David Wakely; text by Thomas A. Drain. San Francisco: Chronicle Books,

1994. vii. This is a study of twenty-nine mission churches.

428. Foreword. *Earth Is My Mother, Sky Is My Father: Space, Time, and Astronomy in Navajo Sandpainting,* by Trudy Griffin-Pierce. Albuquerque: University of New Mexico Press, 1995. [xv]–xvii.

429. Foreword. *Navajo Place Names: An Observer's Guide,* compiled and written by Alan Wilson, with Gene Dennison, Navajo consultant. On-the-Green, Guilford, Connecticut: Jeffrey Norton Publishers, 1995. v–vii. This book serves as a geographical gazetteer to the Navajo Nation and the Four Corners Region and is accompanied by an audio cassette. This foreword appeared with a few changes under the title "Navajo Place-Names" in *The Man Made of Words,* Part 2 (1997), 124–26.

430. Foreword. *Sacred Images: A Vision of Native American Rock Art.* Text by Leslie G. Kelen and David Sucec. Photos by Craig Law et al. Layton, Utah: Gibbs Smith, 1996. 8.

431. Foreword. *Legacy: Southwest Indian Art at the School of American Research,* edited by Duane Anderson. Santa Fe: School of American Research Press, 1999. x–xi.

432. Foreword. *Sacred Legacy: Edward S. Curtis and the North American Indian,* edited by Christopher Cardozo. Photographs by Edward S. Curtis, essays by Christopher Cardozo and Joseph D. Horse Capture. Afterword by Anne Makepeace. New York: Simon & Schuster, 2000. [9]–10.

433. Foreword. *They Have a Saying For It . . . Multicultural Idioms and Their Navajo Equivalents,* by Alan Wilson, with Gene Dennison. Gallup, New Mexico; Fort Collins, Colorado: Hashké Publications, 2000. vii–viii.

434. Foreword. *At the Hems of the Lowest Clouds: Meditations on Navajo Landscapes,* by Gloria J. Emerson. Santa Fe, New Mexico: School of American Research, 2003. ix–xi.

435. Foreword. *The Road to Paradise: Collected Poems,* by Robert Emmons. A Robert Bason Book. Santa Barbara, California: Capra Press, 2003. 9.

436. Foreword. *Body, Mind & Spirit: Native Cooking of the Americas,* by Beverly Cox and Martin Jacobs. Published by *Native Peoples* (magazine), 2004. 8–9.

437. Foreword. *Native American Stories.* Told by Joseph Bruchac. Reprint, Golden, Colorado: Fulcrum, 2005. vii.

Introductions

438. Introduction. "A Note on Contemporary Native American Poetry." In *Carriers of the Dream Wheel,* edited by Duane Niatum. New York: Harper & Row, 1975. xix–xx. Reprint (pbk.), San Francisco: Harper & Row, 1981, ©1975.

439. Introduction. *With Eagle Glance: American Indian Photographic Images, 1868 to 1931: An Exhibition of Selected Photographs from the Collection of Warren Adelson and Ira Spanierman.* New York: Museum of the American Indian, 1982. 6–7.

440. Introduction. *The Strength of Art: Poets and Poetry in the Lives of Yvor Winters and Janet Lewis.* An exhibition of books and manuscripts prepared by Brigitte Hoy Carnochan. Louis R. Lurie Rotunda, Cecil H. Green Library, March 11–April 9, 1984. Stanford, California: Stanford University Libraries, 1984. 7–9.

441. Introduction. "Only an Appearance." In *Native American Literatures,* edited by Laura Coltelli. Forum, no. 1. Pisa, Italy: SEU (Servizio Editoriale Universitaria), 1989. 1–3. The introduction is followed by five drawings by N. Scott Momaday.

442. Introduction. *Sign Language: Contemporary Southwest Native America.* Photographs by Skeet McAuley. New York: Aperture Foundation; Burden Gallery, 1989. 11–12. This illustrated book was published to accompany an exhibition at the Burden Gallery, New York City, and the Amon Carter Museum, Fort Worth, Texas, in 1989. 78 pp.

443. Introduction. *Turtle Island Alphabet: A Lexicon of Native American Symbols and Culture,* by Gerald Hausman. New York: St. Martin's Press, 1992. vii–viii.

444. Introduction. *Native American Lives: Photographs from the Permanent Collection of the National Museum of the American Indian.* Washington, D.C.: Smithsonian Institution, 1994. 7–13.

445. Introduction. "Soy Nuevo Méxicano: An Introduction." *Mark Nohl: Photographs of New Mexico.* Santa Fe: New Mexico Magazine, 1997. 15–19.

446. Introduction. *Gifts of Pride and Love: Kiowa and Comanche Cradles,* edited by Barbara A. Hail. Studies in Anthropology and Material Culture, vol. 7. Bristol, Rhode Island: Haffenreffer Museum of Anthropology, Brown University, 2000. 13, 15. This book is based on an exhibition that traveled across the United States from the Haffenreffer Museum and ended at the Gilcrease Museum, Tulsa, Oklahoma. It was produced by the Haffenreffer Museum and members

of Kiowa and Comanche cradle-making families. Momaday was a member of the Kiowa and Comanche Consulting Committee.

447. Introduction. *A House for the Beginning of Life*, edited by Barbara A. Hail. Foreword by Shepard Krech III, with an afterword by Christina Hunt Simmons and J. Arterberry. Norman: University of Oklahoma Press, 2000. This book is based on *Gifts of Pride and Love* (2000), cited above.

448. Introduction. *The Way of Kinship*. A Special Issue, edited by Alexander Vaschenko and Claude Clayton Smith. *North Dakota Quarterly* 69, no. 3 (Summer 2002): 5–6.

Prefaces

449. Preface. *California Indian Characteristics and Centennial Mission to the Indians of Western Nevada and California*, by Stephen Powers, with a biographical essay, "Stephen Powers as Anthropologist," by Robert F. Heizer. Keepsake Series of the Friends of the Bancroft Library, no. 23. Berkeley, California: Bancroft Library, 1975.

450. Preface. *Lost Copper: Poems*, by Wendy Rose. Banning (Morongo Indian Reservation), California: Malki Museum Press, 1980. ix–x.

Afterword

451. Afterword. *To Walk in Beauty: A Navajo Family's Journey Home*, by Stacia Spragg-Braude. Santa Fe: Museum of New Mexico Press, 2009. 193–95.

Reviews of Published Works by Other Authors

452. "Pamphlets and Portraits, Re-appraisals and Reviews." *Southern Review,* n.s., 3, no. 2 (April 1967): 468–78. In this review essay, Momaday reviews two volumes of critical essays: *Re-Appraisals: Some Commonsense Readings in American Literature,* by Martin Green, and *The King of the Cats,* by F. W. Dupee.

453. "The Land Inspired the Artist." Rev. of *American Indian Paintings of the Southwest and Plains Areas,* by Dorothy Dunn. *New York Times Book Review,* July 28, 1968, 6–7.

454. "Tribal Spirit." Rev. of *The New Indians,* by Stan Steiner. *New York Times Book Review,* March 17, 1968, 22.

455. "Land of Many Frontiers." Rev. of *A History of the American Southwest,* by Odie B. Faulk. *New York Times Book Review,* February 2, 1969, 10.

456. "A Sad People, Lost, among the Anonymous Dead." Rev. of *How a People Die,* by Alan Fry. *New York Times Book Review,* November 15, 1970, 66–67.

457. "When the West Was Won and a Civilization Was Lost." Revs. of *Bury My Heart at Wounded Knee,* by Dee Brown, and *A History of the Indians of the United States,* by Angie Debo. *New York Times Book Review,* March 7, 1971, 46–47.

458. Rev. of *The White Dawn: An Eskimo Saga,* by James Houston. *New York Times Book Review,* May 16, 1971, 6.

459. "Bringing on the Indians." Revs. of *Indians* (play), by Arthur Kopit; *We Talk, You Listen* (book), by Vine Deloria, Jr.; *Custer Died for Your Sins* (book), by Vine Deloria, Jr.; *Man's Rise to Civilization as Shown by the Indians of North America from Primeval Times to the Coming of the Industrial State* (book), by Peter Farb. *New York Review of Books* 16, no. 6 (April 8, 1971): 39–42.

460. "In the Trail of the Wind." Rev. of *American Indian Poems and Ritual Orations,* edited by John Bierhorst. *New York Times Book Review,* October 3, 1971, 8.

461. "Indian Facts and Artifacts." Revs. of *The Girl Who Married a Ghost,* by Edward S. Curtis and edited by John Bierhorst; *The Art of the Southeastern Indian,* by Shirley Glubok; *Many Smokes, Many Moons,* by Jamake Highwater; and *Native American Testimony,* by Peter Nabokov. *New York Times Book Review,* April 30, 1978, 42.

462. "The Language of the Tribes." Rev. of *Hanto Yo,* by Ruth Beebe Hill. *Washington Post Book World,* January 28, 1979, Sunday final ed., 1.

463. "The Spirit in Words." Rev. of *Storyteller*, by Leslie Marmon Silko. *New York Times Book Review*, May 24, 1981, 8, 17.

464. "The Visible Indian." Rev. of *Now That the Buffalo's Gone*, by Alvin M. Josephy. *Natural History* 92, no. 1 (January 1983): 80–81.

465. "Sachem, Genius and Enigma." Rev. of *Joseph Brant, 1743–1807: Man of Two Worlds*, by Isabel Thompson Kelsay. *New York Times Book Review*, May 13, 1984, 7.

466. "The Missing American." Rev. of *Native Americans: Five Centuries of Changing Images*, by Patricia Trenton and Patrick T. Houlihan. *Natural History* 99, no. 11 (November 1990): 88–90.

467. Rev. of *Blood and Thunder: An Epic of the American West*, by Hampton Sides. *International Herald Tribune*, Feature section, October 28, 2006, 9.

468. "Cowboys and Indians." Rev. of *Blood and Thunder: An Epic of the American West*, by Hampton Sides. *New York Times Book Review*, October 29, 2006, 21. See also "Up Front," by The Editors, p. 6, commenting on this review.

469. "Review: *Blood and Thunder*." *Biography* 30, no. 2 (Spring 2007): 255.

Published Poetry and Prose Poems in Works by Momaday, Anthologies, and Published Works by Others

N. Scott Momaday's first published writing was a poem, "Earth and I Gave You Turquoise," written while he was a student at the University of New Mexico. It was published in the Summer 1959 issue of *New Mexico Quarterly*, a literary journal published by the University of New Mexico. Other poems were published later in 1959 and during the 1960s in issues of *New Mexico Quarterly*, *The Southern Review*, and other publications. A major selection of his poems was published for the first time in 1968: "Eight Poems." *New Mexico Quarterly* 38, no. 1 (Spring 1968): 102–109.

Momaday discusses American Indian poetry in "A Note on Contemporary Native American Poetry," which appears at the beginning of *Carriers of the Dream Wheel: Contemporary Native American Poetry*, edited by Duane Niatum. New York: Harper & Row, 1975; reprint, Harper & Row, 1981. xix–xx. Niatum's anthology was the first major gathering of contemporary Native American poetry. He borrowed the title of Momaday's poem, "Carriers of the Dream Wheel," for the main title of this anthology.

Momaday's published poetry and prose poems are listed below. Titles of poems are followed by brief citations that include the last names of authors or editors of books or other published works where the poems have appeared, the titles of the published works, dates of publication in chronological order, and page numbers. Full citations to the anthologies containing poems and prose by Momaday are found in the section "Anthologies and Literary Collections Containing Momaday's Writings" and in other sections in this part of the bio-bibliography. References to *In the Presence of the Sun* (1992) refer to *In the Presence of the Sun: Stories and Poems, 1961–1991*.

470. "Abstract: Old Woman in a Room" For Olga Sergeevna Akhmanova

    Momaday, *The Gourd Dancer*, Part III (1976), 56.

    Woodard, *Ancestral Voice* (1989), 159–60.

    Dictionary of Literary Biography, vol. 143 (1994), 166.

471. "Angle of Geese"

    Southern Review, n.s., 1, no. 2 (April 1965): 423.

    New Mexico Quarterly 38, no. 1 (Spring 1968): 105.

    Winters and Fields, *Quest for Reality* (1969), 189.

Fields, "More than Language Means," *Southern Review*, n.s., 6, no. 1 (January 1970): 198–99.

Haslam, ed., *Forgotten Pages of American Literature* (1970), 59–60.

Western American Literature 5 (Spring 1970): 25–27.

Sanders and Peek, eds., *Literature of the American Indian* (1973), 461.

Momaday, *Angle of Geese and Other Poems* (1974), 28.

Dodge and McCullough, eds., *Voices from Wah'Kon-Tah* (1974), 73.

Niatum, ed., *Carriers of the Dream Wheel* (1975, 1981), 106.

Momaday, *The Gourd Dancer*, Part I (1976), 31–32.

Dickinson-Brown, *Southern Review* 14, no. 1 (1978): 42–43.

Velie, ed., *American Indian Literature: An Anthology* (1979), 285.

Standiford essay in Baker, *Three American Literatures* (1982), 181.

Velie, *Four American Indian Literary Masters* (1982), 36–37.

Krupat, *Critical Inquiry* 10, no. 1 (September 1983): 161 (opening stanzas).

Dodge and McCullough, eds., *New and Old Voices of Wah'Kon-Tah* (1985), 79.

Berry, "Brilliant Son of the Kiowas," *Lincoln, Nebraska Journal Star*, March 16, 1986, H15.

Niatum, ed., *Harper's Anthology of 20th Century Native American Poetry* (1988), 67.

Krupat, *The Voice in the Margin* (1989), 123 (opening stanzas).

Woodard, *Ancestral Voice* (1989), 153.

Velie, ed., *American Indian Literature: An Anthology*, rev. ed. (1991), 229.

Arens and Braun, *Der Gesang des Schwarzen* (1992), 234–35.

Momaday, *In the Presence of the Sun*, Part I (1992), 21.

Anderson, *Bloomsbury Review* 13, no. 4 (July–August 1993): 14.

Dictionary of Literary Biography, vol. 143 (1994), 161.

Witalec, ed., *Native North American Literature* (1994), 435–36.

Giroux, ed., *Contemporary Literary Criticism*, vol. 85 (1995), 249.

Momaday, "A Divine Blindness," *The Man Made of Words*, Part I (1997), 86.

Napierkowski, ed., *Poetry for Students*, vol. 2 (1998), 2.

Keegan and McKusick, eds., *Literature and Nature*, Part IV (2001), 1036.

Purdy and Ruppert, eds., *Nothing but the Truth* (2001), 510.

472. "Anywhere Is a Street into the Night"

Momaday, *The Gourd Dancer,* Part III (1976), 54.

Lincoln, *Native American Renaissance* (1983), 98.

Schubnell, *N. Scott Momaday: The Cultural and Literary Background* (1985), 35.

Lincoln, "Introduction" to essay, "Tai-Me to Rainy Mountain," *American Indian Quarterly* 10, no. 2 (Spring 1986): 101 (epigraph).

Momaday, *In the Presence of the Sun,* Part I (1992), 34.

Lincoln, *Sing with the Heart of a Bear* (2000), 252.

473. "At Risk"

Momaday, *In the Presence of the Sun,* Part IV (1992), 143.

Witalec, ed., *Native North American Literature* (1994), 447.

Giroux, ed., *Contemporary Literary Criticism,* vol. 85 (1995), 282.

Momaday, "A Divine Blindness," *The Man Made of Words,* Part 1 (1997), 86.

Lincoln, *Sing with the Heart of a Bear* (2000), 255.

Purdy and Ruppert, eds., *Nothing but the Truth* (2001), 511.

Poetics and Politics Reading Series, University of Arizona, website: http://poeticsandpolitics.arizona.edu/momaday/momaday_top.html.

474. "The Bear" Winner of the Academy of American Poets Prize, 1962

New Mexico Quarterly 31, no. 1 (Spring 1961): 46.

Winters, *Forms of Discovery* (1967), 289.

New Mexico Quarterly 38, no. 1 (Spring 1968): 104.

Faderman and Bradshaw, eds., *Speaking for Ourselves* (1969), 515.

Momaday, *Angle of Geese and Other Poems* (1974), 5.

Dodge and McCullough, eds., *Voices from Wah'Kon-Tah* (1974), 72.

Imprint of the Stanford Libraries Associates 1, no. 2 (October 1975): 9.

Niatum, ed. *Carriers of the Dream Wheel* (1975, 1981), 91.

Momaday, *The Gourd Dancer,* Part I (1976), 11.

Velie, ed., *American Indian Literature: An Anthology* (1979), 283–84.

Bromley essay, "Renegade Wants the Word," *Literary Review* 23, no. 3 (Spring 1980): 418.

Velie, *Four American Indian Literary Masters* (1982), 41–42.

Roemer essay in P. G. Allen, ed., *Studies in American Indian Literature* (1983), 182–83.

Dodge and McCullough, eds., *New and Old Voices of Wah'Kon-Tah* (1985), 78.

Bruchac, ed., *Survival This Way: Interviews with American Indian Poets* (1987), 176.

Niatum, ed., *Harper's Anthology of 20th Century Native American Poetry* (1988), 63.

Velie, ed., *American Indian Literature: An Anthology*, rev. ed. (1991), 227.

Momaday, *In the Presence of the Sun*, Part I (1992), 3.

Anderson, *Bloomsbury Review* 13, no. 4 (July–August 1993): 14.

Dictionary of Literary Biography, vol. 143 (1994), 161.

Giroux, ed., *Contemporary Literary Criticism*, vol. 85 (1995), 224.

Witalec, ed., *Native North American Literature* (1994), 435.

Momaday, *In the Bear's House* (1999), 53.

Keegan and McKusick, eds., *Literature and Nature*, Part IV (2001), 1034–35.

Purdy and Ruppert, eds., *Nothing but the Truth* (2001), 511.

Roberts and Jacobs, eds., *Literature: An Introduction to Reading and Writing*, 3rd ed. (2006), 809.

475. "A Bear in Bronze" For Luis Jimenez, A drawing for a fountain

Momaday, *In the Bear's House* (1999), 56.

476. "Before an Old Painting of the Crucifixion" The Mission Carmel, June 1960

Southern Review, n.s., 1, no. 2 (April 1965): 421–22.

Winters, *Forms of Discovery* (1967), 291–92.

New Mexico Quarterly 38, no. 1 (Spring 1968): 106–107.

Winters and Fields, *Quest for Reality* (1969), 188.

Haslam, ed. *Forgotten Pages of American Literature* (1970), 58–59.

Sanders and Peek, eds., *Literature of the American Indian* (1973), 462.

Momaday, *Angle of Geese and Other Poems* (1974), 23–24.

———, *The Gourd Dancer*, Part I (1976), 28–29.

Velie, ed., *American Indian Literature: An Anthology* (1979), 284–85.

———, *Four American Indian Literary Masters* (1982), 46–47.

———, ed. *American Indian Literature: An Anthology*, rev. ed. (1991), 228.

Witalec, ed., *Native North American Literature* (1994), 434.

Giroux, ed., *Contemporary Literary Criticism*, vol. 85 (1995), 225.

477. "Believe This"

Ploughshares 20, no. 1 (Spring 1994): 37.

478. "The Blind Astrologers" Tucson, 1994

Momaday, *In the Bear's House* (1999), 58–59.

479. "The Burning"

Pembroke Magazine 6 (1975): 31.

Momaday, *The Gourd Dancer*, Part III (1976), 58.

Lincoln, *Native American Renaissance* (1983), 97–98.

Foss, ed., *The Clouds Threw This Light* (1983), 176.

Niatum, ed., *Harper's Anthology of 20th Century Native American Poetry* (1988), 69.

Woodard, *Ancestral Voice* (1989), 156.

Momaday, *In the Presence of the Sun*, Part I (1992), 35.

Nelson, ed., *Anthology of Modern American Poetry* (2000), 1005.

480. "But Then and There the Sun Bore Down"

Niatum, ed., *Carriers of the Dream Wheel* (1975, 1981), 105.

481. "Buteo Regalis"

New Mexico Quarterly 31, no. 1 (Spring 1961): 47.

Winters, *Forms of Discovery* (1967), 290.

New Mexico Quarterly 38, no. 1 (Spring 1968): 104.

Faderman and Bradshaw, eds., *Speaking for Ourselves* (1969), 515.

Momaday, *Angle of Geese and Other Poems* (1974), 6.

Dodge and McCullough, eds., *Voices from Wah'Kon-Tah* (1974), 77.

Momaday, *The Gourd Dancer*, Part I (1976), 12.

Velie, *Four American Indian Literary Masters* (1982), 44.

Dodge and McCullough, eds., *New and Old Voices of Wah'Kon-Tah* (1985), 81.

Momaday, *In the Presence of the Sun*, Part I (1992), 4.

Nelson, ed., *Anthology of Modern American Poetry* (2000), 1002–1003.

Keegan and McKusick, eds., *Literature and Nature*, Part IV (2001), 1035.

Schweninger, *Literary Masters*, vol. 12 (2001), 124.

McMaster and Trafzer, eds., *Native Universe: Voices of Indian America* (2004), 96.

482. "Carnegie, Oklahoma, 1919"

Elling, ed., *Southwestern Poetry Festival*. Paradise, Arizona: Mummy Mountain Press (1989).

Momaday, *In the Presence of the Sun*, Part IV (1992), 136.

———, "Sacred Places," *The Man Made of Words*, Part 2 (1997), 113–14.

Allen, Chadwick, *Blood Narrative* (2002), 179.

———, *Western American Literature* 41, no. 2 (Summer 2006): 150.

———, *Studies in American Indian Literatures* 19, no. 4 (Winter 2007): 5.

483. "Carriers of the Dream Wheel"

Niatum, ed., *Carriers of the Dream Wheel* (1975, 1981), 87.

Momaday, *The Gourd Dancer*, Part II (1976), 42.

Lincoln, ed., "Introduction: Native Literatures," Special Issue No. 2, *American Indian Culture and Research Journal* 4, no. 4 (1980): 4.

Lincoln essay in Houston A. Baker, Jr. ed., *Three American Literatures* (1982), 114.

Lincoln, *Native American Renaissance* (1983), 83–84.

Highwater, *Words in the Blood* (1984), 46.

Freydorf and Riese, *Die weiten Horizonte* (*The Vast Horizons*), (1985), 354–55.

Rhetoric Review 8, no. 1 (Fall 1989): 152.

Momaday, *In the Presence of the Sun*, Part I (1992), 26.

Parini, ed., *Columbia Anthology of American Poetry* (1995), 691.

Joyce essay in Litz, ed., *American Writers*, Supplement, IV, Part 2 (1996), 481.

Trout, comp., *Native American Literature: An Anthology* (1998), 79–80.

Lincoln, *Sing with the Heart of a Bear* (2000), 51, 128, 251.

Nelson, ed., *Anthology of Modern American Poetry* (2000), 1003.

Gioia, Mason, and Schoerke, *Twentieth-Century American Poetry* (2004), 868–69.

McMaster and Trafzer, eds., *Native Universe: Voices of Indian America* (2004), 96.

Bloom and Zuba, eds., *American Religious Poems: An Anthology* (2006), 454.

Parini, ed., *The Wadsworth Anthology of Poetry, Shorter Edition* (2006), 405.

Lincoln, *Speak Like Singing* (2007), 136–38. See under heading "Dream Wheel Names."

484. "Cave Painting" Altamira, 1995

Momaday, *In the Bear's House* (1999), 79.

485. "Cocoon"

Program of the Annual Phi Beta Kappa Dinner, Stanford University, June 7, 1961.

Schubnell, *N. Scott Momaday: The Cultural and Literary Background* (1985), 27.

486. "The Colors of Night"

Sequoia (Stanford University literary magazine) 19, no. 1 (Fall 1974): 22–23.

"Green" (fifth sequence of "Colors") in "Landscapes: N. Scott Momaday," interview conducted by William T. Morgan, Jr. *Sequoia* 19, no. 2 (Winter 1975): 39, and *Sequoia* 23, no. 1 (Autumn–Winter 1978): 21. Reprinted in Schubnell, ed., *Conversations* (1997), 45.

Momaday, *The Gourd Dancer*, Part II (1976), 44–47.

Bruchac, ed., *Songs from This Earth on Turtle's Back* (1983), 158–60.

"Green" (fifth sequence) in Lincoln, *Native American Renaissance* (1983), 99.

"Blue" (sixth sequence) in Momaday, *The Ancient Child* (1989), 266.

Olivier and Juliet, trans., *Poetes Indiens d'Amérique* 70–71 (1989), 100–107.

"White" (first sequence) in Woodard, *Ancestral Voice* (1989), 185.

Momaday, *In the Presence of the Sun*, Part I (1992), 28–30.

Reynolds, *Los Angeles Times Book Review*, December 27, 1992, 6.

Friebert and Young, eds., *Models of the Universe* (1995), 206–208.

Deming, *Poetry of the American West* (1996), 205–206.

"Brown" (third sequence) in Martin, *The Way of the Human Being* (1999), 51.

"Green" (fifth sequence) in Lincoln, *Sing with the Heart of a Bear* (2000), 132.

"Purple" (seventh sequence) in Nelson, ed., *Anthology of Modern American Poetry* (2000), 1004.

Purdy and Ruppert, eds., *Nothing but the Truth* (2001), 513–14.

"Green" (fifth sequence) in Lincoln essay, *American Indian Culture and*

Research Journal 29, no. 3 (2005): 12.

"Purple" (seventh sequence) in Schweninger, *Listening to the Land* (2008), 55.

Translation in French: "Les couleurs de la nuit." In *La poésie amérindienne: textes, choisis et traduits,* by Manuel Van Thienen. Les cahiers de Poésie-rencontres, no. 25. Saint-Symphorien d'Ozon, France: Poésie-rencontres, 1989. 82–85.

487. "Comparatives"

Momaday, *Angle of Geese and Other Poems* (1974), 8–9.

———, *The Gourd Dancer,* Part I, (1976), 13–14.

Dickinson-Brown in *Southern Review* 14, no. 1 (1978): 41–42.

Dacey and Jauss, eds., *Strong Measures* (1986), 241.

Momaday, *In the Presence of the Sun,* Part I (1992), 5.

Witalec, ed., *Native North American Literature* (1994), 435.

Giroux, ed., *Contemporary Literary Criticism,* vol. 85 (1995), 248.

488. "Concession"

Momaday, "Three Poems," *Paris Review,* no. 99 (Spring 1986): 161.

———, *In the Presence of the Sun,* Part IV (1992), 127.

489. "The Corporeal Bear" Jemez Springs, 1998

Momaday, *In the Bear's House* (1999), 55.

490. "A Cradle for This Child"

IAIA website, p. 2, www.iaia.edu/college/_1scottmomaday.php.

Momaday, "The Testament of Allan Houser," *Native Modernism: The Art of George Morrison and Allan Houser* (2004), 76.

491. "Crows in a Winter Composition"

Momaday, *The Gourd Dancer,* Part III (1976), 53.

Miller, J., ed., *United States in Literature* (1979), 586.

Lincoln, *Native American Renaissance* (1983), 100.

Momaday, *In the Presence of the Sun,* Part I (1992), 33.

Arens and Braun, eds., *Der Gesang des Schwarzen* (1992), 246–47.

Laskowski essay, *MELUS* 19, no. 3 (Fall 1994), 47.

Nelson, ed., *Anthology of Modern American Poetry* (2000), 1003.

Keegan and McKusick, eds., *Literature and Nature*, Part IV (2001), 1037.

492. "The Death of Beauty"

Momaday, *In the Presence of the Sun*, Part IV (1992), 112.

Dictionary of Literary Biography, vol. 143 (1994), 169.

493. "December 29, 1890, Wounded Knee Creek"

Momaday, *In the Presence of the Sun*, Part IV (1992), 139.

Witalec, ed., *Native North American Literature* (1994), 447.

Momaday, "The American West and the Burden of Belief," *The Man Made of Words*, Part 1 (1997), 98–99.

Trout, comp., *Native American Literature: An Anthology* (1998), 264–65.

Nelson, ed., *Anthology of Modern American Poetry* (2000), 1005–1006.

Purdy and Ruppert, eds., *Nothing but the Truth* (2001), 512.

494. "The Delight Song of Tsoai-talee" (This is Momaday's name poem, his celebration of self.)

Momaday, *Viva*, *Santa Fe New Mexican*, August 12, 1973, 8.

———, *Angle of Geese and Other Poems* (1974), 22.

Niatum, ed., *Carriers of the Dream Wheel* (1975, 1981), 89.

Momaday, *The Gourd Dancer*, Part I (1976), 27.

Dickinson-Brown in *Southern Review* 14, no. 1 (1978), 35.

Lincoln in Houston A. Baker, Jr., ed., *Three American Literatures* (1982), 117 (all but last six lines).

Smith, William J., comp., *A Green Place: Modern Poems* (1982), 57.

Bruchac, ed., *Songs from This Earth on Turtle's Back* (1983), 158.

Lincoln, *Native American Renaissance* (1983), 105 (part of poem).

Flood, *Through Native Eyes* (1985), 31.

Freydorf and Riese, *Die weiten Horizonte* (*The Vast Horizons*), (1985), 352–53.

Editorial Board of Rothman Publishing, *Survey of American Poetry*, vol. x (1986), 251.

Bruchac essay, "Survival Comes This Way," in Harris and Aguero, eds., *A Gift of Tongues* (1987), 203 (last four lines only).

Bruchac, ed., *Survival This Way: Interviews with American Indian Poets* (1987), 184–85.

Olivier and Juliet, trans., *Poetes Indiens d'Amérique*, 70–71 (1989), 98–99.

Rethinking Schools, Ltd., *Rethinking Columbus* (1991), 37.

Momaday, *In the Presence of the Sun*, Part I (1992), 16.

Arens and Braun, eds., *Der Gersang des Schwarzen* (1992), 112–13.

Anderson, *Bloomsbury Review* 13, no. 4 (July–August 1993): 14.

Nolan, James, "Introduction," *Poet-Chief* (1994), 3 (excerpt).

Witalec, ed., *Native North American Literature* (1994), 433.

Harvey, ed., *American Indian Voices* (1995), 102–103.

Deming, *Poetry of the American West* (1996), 204–205.

Momaday, "A Divine Blindness," *The Man Made of Words*, Part 1 (1997), 87–88.

Schubnell, ed., *Conversations with N. Scott Momaday* (1997), 104–105 (in Bruchac interview from *Survival This Way*).

Bigelow and Peterson, eds., *Rethinking Columbus: The Next Five Hundred Years* (1998), 72.

Trout, comp., *Native American Literature: An Anthology* (1998), 60–61.

Martin, *The Way of the Human Being* (1999), 210–11.

Lincoln, *Sing with the Heart of a Bear* (2000), 249.

Keegan and McKusick, eds., *Literature and Nature* (2001), 1035–36.

Vecchione, Patrice, *Whisper & Shout: Poems to Memorize* (2002), 70–71.

Gioia, Mason, and Schoerke, *Twentieth-Century American Poetry* (2004), 869.

Stone and Young, eds., *The Anthology: Poems for Poetry Out Loud: National Recitation Contest* (2005), 91.

Bloom and Zuba, eds., *American Religious Poems: An Anthology*, by Harold Bloom (2006), 453.

www.hanksville.org/voyage/poems/Tsoai-talee.html.

495. "The Eagle-Feather Fan"

Momaday, "To the Singing, To the Drums," *Natural History* 84 (February 1975), 45.

Niatum, ed., *Carriers of the Dream Wheel* (1975, 1981), 98.

Ternes, ed., *Ants, Indians, and Little Dinosaurs* (1975), 256.

Momaday, *The Gourd Dancer*, Part II (1976), 43.

Bruchac, ed., *Songs from This Earth on Turtle's Back* (1983), 162.

Barnet, Berman, and Burto, eds., *An Introduction to Literature: Fiction, Poetry, Drama*, 10th ed. (1993), 618.

Ferguson, Salter, and Stallworthy, eds., *Norton Anthology of Poetry*, 4th ed. (1996), 1756.

Purdy and Ruppert, eds., *Nothing but the Truth* (2001), 515.

Gioia, Mason, and Schoerke, *Twentieth-Century American Poetry* (2004), 870.

Ferguson, Salter, and Stallworthy, eds., *Norton Anthology of Poetry*, 5th ed. (2005), 1861.

496. "Earth and I Gave You Turquoise"

This is Momaday's first published poem. It appeared in the *New Mexico Quarterly*, a literary journal published at the University of New Mexico from 1931 to 1969.

New Mexico Quarterly 29, no. 2 (Summer 1959): 156.

Poetry for Pleasure: The Hallmark Book of Poetry (1960), 60–61.

New Mexico Quarterly 38, no. 1 (Spring 1968): 103.

Lowenfels, ed., *From the Belly of the Shark* (1973), 44.

Momaday, *Angle of Geese and Other Poems* (1974), 10–11.

Dodge and McCullough, eds., *Voices from Wah'Kon-Tah* (1974), 74–75.

Niatum, ed., *Carriers of the Dream Wheel* (1975, 1981), 96–97.

Brooks and Warren, eds., *Understanding Poetry*, 4th ed. (1976), 436–37.

Momaday, *The Gourd Dancer*, Part I (1976), 15–16.

Lincoln, *Native American Renaissance* (1983), 98.

Bergman and Epstein, eds., *The Heath Guide to Literature* (1984), 876.

Dodge and McCullough, eds., *New and Old Voices of Wah'Kon-Tah* (1985), 80.

Freydorf and Riese, *Die weiten Horizonte* (*The Vast Horizons*), (1985), 348–51.

Schubnell, *N. Scott Momaday: The Cultural and Literary Background* (1985), 190.

Niatum, ed., *Harper's Anthology of 20th Century Native American Poetry* (1988), 64–65.

Momaday, *In the Presence of the Sun*, Part I (1992), 6.

Guth and Rico, *Discovering Literature*, 2nd ed. (1997), 714–16.

Trout, comp., *Native American Literature: An Anthology* (1998), 581–82.

Guth and Rico, *Discovering Literature: Compact Edition* (2000), 500–501.

Lincoln essay in Padgett, ed., *World Poets*, vol. 2 (2000), 225.

Lincoln, *Sing with the Heart of a Bear* (2000), 103.

———, *Speak Like Singing* (2007), 143–44. Presented under the heading "Collaborative Art."

497. "Ernesto Maestas Instructs Ynocencia Saavedra in the Art of Acting"

Momaday, *The Gourd Dancer*, Part III (1976), 61.

498. "Eve My Mother, No"

Sequoia 5, no. 1 (Autumn 1959): 37.

Schubnell, *N. Scott Momaday: The Cultural and Literary Background* (1985), 64.

Lincoln, *Sing with the Heart of a Bear* (2000), 240.

499. "The Fear of Bo-talee" (prose poem)

Viva, Santa Fe New Mexican, August 12, 1973, 8.

Momaday, *Angle of Geese and Other Poems* (1974), 19.

———, *The Gourd Dancer*, Part I (1976), 25.

Hobson, ed., *The Remembered Earth* (1979, 1981), 174.

Velie, ed., *American Indian Literature: An Anthology* (1979), 286.

Velie, *Four American Indian Literary Masters* (1982), 48.

Bruchac, ed., *Songs from This Earth on Turtle's Back* (1983), 160.

Olivier and Juliet, trans., *Poetes Indiens d'Amérique*, 70–71 (1989), 97.

Velie, ed., *American Indian Literature: An Anthology*, rev. ed. (1991), 229.

Momaday, *In the Presence of the Sun*, Part I (1992), 14.

Witalec, ed., *Native North American Literature* (1994), 433.

Martin, *The Way of the Human Being* (1999), 174.

500. "A Fire at Thule"

Momaday, *In the Presence of the Sun*, Part IV (1992), 123.

501. "For the Old Man Mad for Drawing, Dead at Eighty-nine"

Pembroke Magazine 6 (1975): 31.

Momaday, *The Gourd Dancer*, Part III (1976), 55.

Woodard, *Ancestral Voice* (1989), 158–59.

502. "Forms of the Earth at Abiquiu" For Georgia O'Keeffe

Niatum, ed., *Carriers of the Dream Wheel* (1975, 1981), 88.

Momaday, *The Gourd Dancer*, Part III (1976), 60.

Schubnell, *N. Scott Momaday: The Cultural and Literary Background* (1985), 246–47.

Woodard, *Ancestral Voice* (1989), 185.

Momaday, *In the Presence of the Sun*, Part I (1992), 38.

Nohl, Introduction to *Photographs of New Mexico* (1997), 18.

Lincoln, "Native Poetics," *Modern Fiction Studies* 45, no. 1 (Spring 1999): 147.

———, *Sing with the Heart of a Bear* (2000), ix, 253, 401.

Hoberock, "New Poet Laureate Announced," *Tulsa World*, July 13, 2007, A11.

Lincoln, *Speak Like Singing* (2007), 139–40. Under heading, "Age with Grace and Beauty."

503. "Fort Sill: Set-angia" Tucson, 1991

Quiriva (Journal of Cameron University Honor Societies, Lawton, Oklahoma) 2, no. 1 (Spring 1992): 1.

Momaday, *In the Presence of the Sun*, Part IV (1992), 141.

Witalec, ed., *Native North American Literature* (1994), 447.

504. "Four Charms"

Momaday, *In the Presence of the Sun*, Part IV (1992), 131.

505. "Four Notions of Love and Marriage" For Judith and Richardson Morse, their wedding

Momaday, *Viva*, *Santa Fe New Mexican*, August 12, 1973, 8.

———, *Angle of Geese and Other Poems* (1974), 13–14.

———, *The Gourd Dancer*, Part I (1976), 18–19.

Niatum, ed., *Harper's Anthology of 20th Century Native American Poetry* (1988), 65–66.

Woodard, *Ancestral Voice* (1989), 192–93.

Witalec, ed., *Native North American Literature* (1994), 433.

Native American Literature, Prentice Hall Literature Library (2000), 75.

506. "The Gift" For Bobby Jack Nelson

Momaday, *The Gourd Dancer*, Part III (1976), 62.

Miller, ed., *United States in Literature* (1979), 591.

Schubnell, *N. Scott Momaday: The Cultural and Literary Background* (1985), 244–45.

Momaday, *In the Presence of the Sun*, Part I (1992), 39.

Ferguson, Salter, and Stallworthy, eds., *Norton Anthology of Poetry*, 4th ed. (1996), 1756.

Paschen and Lauer, eds., *Poetry in Motion from Coast to Coast: 120 Poems from the Subways and the Buses* (2002), 111.

Ferguson, Salter, and Stallworthy, eds., *Norton Anthology of Poetry*, 5th ed. (2005), 1861.

507. "The Gourd Dancer: Mammedaty, 1880–1932"

Viva, Santa Fe New Mexican, November 4, 1973, 6.

Niatum, ed., *Carriers of the Dream Wheel* (1975, 1981), 94–95.

Momaday, *The Gourd Dancer*, Part II (1976), 35–37.

Hobson, ed. *The Remembered Earth* (1979, 1981), 175–76.

Miller, ed., *United States in Literature* (1979), 606–607.

Bromley essay, "Renegade Wants the Word," *Literary Review* 23, no. 3 (Spring 1980): 415.

Strickland, R., Preface, *The Indians in Oklahoma* (1980), xiii (part 2 of poem).

Bruchac, ed., *Songs from This Earth on Turtle's Back* (1983), 161–62.

Wiget, *Native American Literature* (1985), 101 (part 4 of poem).

Survey of American Poetry (Rothman Publishing), vol. x (1986), 249–50.

Momaday, *In the Presence of the Sun*, Part I (1992), 22–23.

Arens and Braun, eds., *Der Gesang des Schwarzen* (1992), 72–75.

Witalec, ed., *Native North American Literature* (1994), 447.

Allen, Chadwick, *Western American Literature* 41, no. 2 (Summer 2006): 35–37.

508. "The Great Fillmore Street Buffalo Drive"

Freydorf and Riese, *Die weiten Horizonte* (*The Vast Horizons*), (1985), 346–47.

Velie, ed., *American Indian Literature: An Anthology*, rev. ed. (1991), 229–30.

Momaday, *In the Presence of the Sun*, Part IV (1992), 119.

Joyce essay in Litz, ed., *American Writers*, Supplement IV, Part 2 (1996), 493.

509. "Headwaters"

The Way to Rainy Mountain (1969), p. 2, facing Prologue.

Raymont, "A Novelist Fights for His People's Lore," *New York Times*, July 26, 1969, 22.

Santa Fe New Mexican, August 7, 1969, A15.

Momaday, *Angle of Geese and Other Poems* (1974), 26.

Turner, *Portable North American Indian Reader* (1974), 578.

Chapman, ed., *Literature of the American Indians* (1975), 101.

Momaday, *The Gourd Dancer*, Part I (1976), 30.

Hobson, ed., *The Remembered Earth* (1979, 1981), 173.

Wunder, *The Kiowa* (1989), 103.

Elliott, gen. ed., *American Literature: A Prentice Hall Anthology* (1991), 2089–2090.

Momaday, *In the Presence of the Sun*, Part I (1992), 19.

Lauter, gen. ed., *Heath Anthology of American Literature* (1994), 2723.

French translation, "À la source," in *Le Chemin de la montagne de pluie* (1995), 11.

Ferguson, Salter, and Stallworthy, eds., *Norton Anthology of Poetry*, 4th ed. (1996), 1756.

Jenseth and Lotto, eds., *Constructing Nature: Readings from the American Experience* (1996), 229.

Lincoln, *Sing with the Heart of a Bear* (2000), 250.

Dreese, *Ecocriticism: Creating Self and Place in Environmental and American Indian Literatures* (2002), 25.

Baym, ed., *Norton Anthology of American Literature*, 6th ed. (2003), 2321–22.

Bartlett, Price, and Edenfield, *In Company* (2004), 168.

Gioia, Mason, and Schoerke, eds., *Twentieth-Century American Poetry* (2004), 870.

Ferguson, Salter, and Stallworthy, eds., *Norton Anthology of Poetry*, 5th ed. (2005), 1861.

Parini, ed., *Wadsworth Anthology of Poetry, Shorter Edition* (2006), 405.

Lauter, ed., *Heath Anthology of American Literature*, vol. E (2006), 2480.

Lincoln, *Speak Like Singing* (2007), 128–29.

510. "The Horse That Died of Shame" (prose poem)

Momaday, *The Way to Rainy Mountain* (1969), 70. This is the first, or ancestral, voice of Story XX.

———, "Thoughts on Life," *Viva, Santa Fe New Mexican*, August 12, 1973, 8.

———, *Angle of Geese and Other Poems* (1974), 21.

———, *The Gourd Dancer*, Part I (1976), 26.

Hobson, ed., *The Remembered Earth* (1979, 1981), 174.

Freydorf and Riese, *Die weiten Horizonte* (*The Vast Horizons*), (1985), 356–57.

Momaday, *In the Presence of the Sun*, Part I (1992), 15.

Witalec, ed., *Native North American Literature* (1994), 433.

Momaday, "The Centaur Complex," *The Man Made of Words*, Part 1 (1997), 78.

511. "The Hotel 1829" For An Painter

Momaday, "Three Poems," *Paris Review*, no. 99 (Spring 1986): 160.

———, *In the Presence of the Sun*, Part IV (1992), 126.

512. "If It Could Ascend"

Momaday, *In the Presence of the Sun*, Part IV (1992), 134.

513. "The Khanty Bear Feast" For Yeremei Aipin, Tucson, 1997

Momaday, *In the Bear's House* (1999), 73.

514. "Krasnopresnenskaya Station" For Will Sutter

Momaday, *The Gourd Dancer*, Part III (1976), 63.

Hobson, ed., *The Remembered Earth* (1979, 1981), 176.

Survey of American Poetry, vol. x (1986), 252.

Dictionary of Literary Biography, vol. 143 (1994), 166.

515. "Lawrence Ranch"

Momaday, *In the Presence of the Sun*, Part IV (1992), 137.

516. "Long Shadows at Dulce"

Momaday, *The Gourd Dancer*, Part II (1976), 50.

———, *In the Presence of the Sun*, Part I (1992), 32.

517. "Los Alamos"

New Mexico Quarterly 29, no. 3 (Autumn 1959): 306.

New Mexico State Poetry Society, *Turquoise Land: Anthology of New Mexico Poetry* (1974), 63.

Schubnell, *N. Scott Momaday: The Cultural and Literary Background* (1985), 192.

Joyce essay in Litz, ed., *American Writers*, Supplement IV, Part 2 (1996), 482.

Schubnell, "N. Scott Momaday," in *American Nature Writers*, vol. 2, edited by J. Elder (1996), 646.

518. "Magpies" This poem is "Plainview: 1."

Halcyon: A Journal of the Humanities 11 (1989): 2.

519. "Marina Green" For Reina, Valentine's Day, 1981

Momaday, *In the Presence of the Sun*, Part IV (1992), 121.

520. "Meditation on Wilderness" Jemez Springs, 1997

Momaday, *In the Bear's House* (1999), 78.

521. "Mogollon Morning"

Sequoia (Centennial Issue) 31, no. 1 (1986): 46.

Momaday, *In the Presence of the Sun*, Part IV (1992), 129.

Lincoln, *Sing with the Heart of a Bear* (2000), 254–55.

522. "The Monoliths"

Momaday, *The Gourd Dancer*, Part II (1976), 47.

Panzer, ed., *Celebrate America: In Poetry and Art* (1994), 15.

523. "Moscow Circus" Santa Fe, 1995

Momaday, *In the Bear's House* (1999), 69–70.

524. "My Words Do Not Hold" For My Father

Momaday, *In the Presence of the Sun*, Part IV (1992), 135.

525. "New Orleans Vesper"

Sequoia 5, no. 2 (Winter 1960): 12.

526. "New World"

Momaday, *The Gourd Dancer*, Part II (1976), 38–40.

———, "A First American Views His Land," *National Geographic* (July 1976), 13–15, 18.

Momaday, *In the Presence of the Sun*, Part I (1992), 24–25.

Guth and Rico, *Discovering Literature*, 2nd ed. (1997), 516–17.

Momaday, "A First American Views His Land," *The Man Made of Words* (1997), Part 1 (of poem), 30; Part 2, 33; Part 3, 38–39; Part 4, 40–41.

Guth and Rico, *Discovering Literature, Compact Edition* (2000), 349.

Wormser and Cappella, *Teaching the Art of Poetry: The Moves*, Part 3 (2000), 2.

McKibben and Gore, eds., *American Earth: Environmental Writing since Thoreau* (2008), 570–71, 573, 579, 581.

527. "The Nickname of Nothing"

Schubnell, *N. Scott Momaday: The Cultural and Literary Background* (1985), 212.

528. "North Dakota, North Light"

Momaday, *The Gourd Dancer*, Part II (1976), 48.

Niatum, ed., *Harper's Anthology of 20th Century Native American Poetry* (1988), 68.

Woodard, *Ancestral Voice* (1989), 158.

Momaday, *In the Presence of the Sun*, Part I (1992), 31.

529. "Notes on a Hunting Scene" Tobolsk, 1997

Momaday, *In the Bear's House* (1999), 71.

530. "*Nous avons vu la mer*" (poem in English with title in French)

Momaday, *In the Presence of the Sun*, Part IV (1992), 122.

531. "Of Ambition"

Momaday, *In the Presence of the Sun*, Part IV (1992), 116.

Utah Law Review, no. 1 (2005): 169.

532. "Old Guerre (For Janet)"

Momaday, *In the Presence of the Sun*, Part IV (1992), 125.

533. "On Chastity"

Momaday, *In the Presence of the Sun*, Part IV (1992), 115.

Dictionary of Literary Biography, vol. 143 (1994), 169.

Utah Law Review, no. 1 (2005): 170.

534. "On Futility"

Momaday, *In the Presence of the Sun,* Part IV (1992), 113.

Utah Law Review, no. 1 (2005): 169.

535. "On the Cause of a Homely Death"

Momaday, *In the Presence of the Sun,* Part IV (1992), 117.

536. "Pit Viper"

New Mexico Quarterly 31, no. 1 (Spring 1961): 47.

New Mexico Quarterly 38, no. 1 (Spring 1968): 102.

Momaday, *Angle of Geese and Other Poems* (1974), 7.

Dodge and McCullough, eds., *Voices from Wah'Kon-Tah* (1974), 76.

Niatum, ed., *Carriers of the Dream Wheel* (1975, 1981), 100.

Momaday, *The Gourd Dancer,* Part I (1976), 12.

Dodge and McCullough, eds., *New and Old Voices of Wah'Kon-Tah* (1985), 81.

An unpublished version of the poem appeared in Schubnell, *N. Scott Momaday: The Cultural and Literary Background* (1985), 217.

Niatum, ed., *Harper's Anthology of 20th Century Native American Poetry* (1988), 64.

537. "Plainview: 1–4"

This is a cycle of poems. "Plainview: 1" is a sonnet in heroic couplets, and "Plainview: 2" was earlier titled "Remember My Horse."

"Plainview: 1" in Momaday, *Viva, Santa Fe New Mexican,* November 24, 1972, 2.

"Plainview: 2" with Abbott interview, *Puerto del Sol* 12, no. 2 (1973): 39.

"Plainview: 1 and 2" in Momaday, *Angle of Geese and Other Poems* (1974), 15, 16–17.

"Plainview: 3" in Niatum, ed., *Carriers of the Dream Wheel* (1975, 1981), 103.

"Plainview: 1–4" in Momaday, *The Gourd Dancer,* Part I (1976), 20–24.

"Plainview: 1" in Momaday, *The Names: A Memoir* (1976), 5.

"Plainview: 2" in Dickinson-Brown in *Southern Review* 14, no. 1 (1978): 35–36.

"Plainview: 1" in Lincoln, *Native American Renaissance* (1983), 96–97.

"Plainview: 1" in Highwater, *Words in the Blood* (1984), 44–45.

"Plainview: 1–4" in Flood, *Through Native Eyes* (1985), 30.

"Plainview: 1" in *Halcyon: A Journal of the Humanities* 11 (1989): 2.

"Plainview: 1" in Woodard, *Ancestral Voice* (1989), 75.

"Plainview: 1–4" in Arens and Braun, eds., *Der Gesang des Schwarzen* (1992), 240–41.

"Plainview: 1–4," Momaday, *In the Presence of the Sun*, Part I (1992), 8–13.

"Plainview: 2" in Witalec, ed., *Native North American Literature* (1994), 433–34.

"Plainview: 2" in Giroux, ed., *Contemporary Literary Criticism*, vol. 85 (1995), 247.

"Plainview: 2" in Isernhagen, *Momaday, Vizenor, Armstrong* (1999), 53.

"Plainview: 3" in Nelson, ed., *Anthology of Modern American Poetry* (2000), 1002.

"Plainview: 3" in Keegan and McKusick, eds., *Literature and Nature* (2001), 1035.

"Plainview: 1" in Rader and Gould, eds., *Speak to Me Words* (2003), 9.

538. "Planned Parenthood"

Momaday, *In the Presence of the Sun*, Part IV (1992), 111.

539. "Prayer" For Aho

Momaday, *In the Presence of the Sun*, Part IV (1992), 130.

540. "Prayer for Words" "My voice restore for me" Navajo

Momaday, *In the Bear's House* (1999), 60.

Read by Momaday on *All Things Considered*, National Public Radio (NPR), June 1, 1999. www.npr.org.

541. "The Print of the Paw" Jemez Springs, 1997

Momaday, *In the Bear's House* (1999), 61.

542. "Rainy Mountain Cemetery"

New Mexico Quarterly 38, no. 1 (Spring 1968): 107.

Santa Fe New Mexican, August 7, 1969, A15.

Momaday, *The Way to Rainy Mountain* (1969), 89.

Fields, *Southern Review*, n.s., 6, no. 1 (January 1970): 204.

Momaday, "The Man Made of Words," in R. Costo, ed., *Indian Voices* (1970), 53.

———, *Angle of Geese and Other Poems* (1974), 28.

———, "The Man Made of Words," in A. Chapman, ed., *Literature of the American Indians* (1975), 100–101.

Niatum, ed., *Carriers of the Dream Wheel* (1975, 1981), 99.

Momaday, *The Gourd Dancer,* Part I (1976), 30.

Morgan, "Landscapes: N. Scott Momaday," *Sequoia* 23, no. 1 (Autumn–Winter 1978): 26.

Hobson, ed., *The Remembered Earth* (1979, 1981), 173.

Lincoln in Houston A. Baker, Jr., ed., *Three American Literatures* (1982), 123.

———, *Native American Renaissance* (1983), 116.

Highwater, *Words in the Blood* (1984), 46.

Niatum, ed., *Harper's Anthology of 20th Century Native American Poetry* (1988), 66–67.

Halcyon: A Journal of the Humanities 11 (1989): 4.

Jahner, "Metalanguages," in Vizenor, *Narrative Chance* (1989, 1993), 175.

Elliott, gen. ed., *American Literature: A Prentice Hall Anthology* (1991), 2113.

Momaday, *In the Presence of the Sun,* Part 1 (1992), 20.

Slovic and Dixon, *Being in the World* (1993), 609.

Elder and Wong, eds., *Family of Earth and Sky* (1994), 297.

Witalec, ed., *Native North American Literature* (1994), 434.

French translation, "Le cimetière de la montagne de pluie," published by Rocher (1995), 105.

Jenseth and Lotto, eds., *Constructing Nature: Readings from the American Experience* (1996), 249.

Momaday, "An American Land Ethic," *The Man Made of Words* (1997), 46–47.

Lincoln, *Sing with the Heart of a Bear* (2000), 250–51.

Purdy and Ruppert, eds., *Nothing but the Truth* (2001), 85.

Baym, ed., *Norton Anthology of American Literature,* 6th ed. (2003), 2331.

Bartlett, Price, and Edenfield, *In Company* (2004), 168.

Lauter, ed., *Heath Anthology of American Literature,* vol. E (2006), 2489.

Lincoln, *Speak Like Singing* (2007), 148 (last stanza).

543. "The Remembering" Tucson, 1994

Momaday, *In the Bear's House* (1999), 62.

544. "Remember My Horse" (See "Plainview: 2" above.)

545. "Revenant" Tucson, 1997

Momaday, *In the Bear's House* (1999), 74.

546. "Rings of Bone"

Momaday, *In the Presence of the Sun*, Part IV (1992), 132.

Nelson, Cary, ed., *Anthology of Modern American Poetry* (2000), 1004.

547. "Scaffold Bear" "Bears love the taste of whiskey"—Esther Nahgahnub, Tucson, 1997

Momaday, *In the Bear's House* (1999), 54.

548. "Simile"

Sequoia 6, no. 1 (Autumn 1960): 39.

New Mexico Quarterly 38, no. 1 (Spring 1968): 108.

Quick, ed., *Poetry of the Desert Southwest* (1973), 32.

Momaday, *Angle of Geese and Other Poems* (1974), 12.

Niatum, ed., *Carriers of the Dream Wheel* (1975, 1981), 101.

Momaday, *The Gourd Dancer*, Part I (1976), 16.

Velie, ed., *American Indian Literature: An Anthology* (1979), 283.

———, *American Indian Literature: An Anthology*, rev. ed. (1991), 227.

Momaday, *In the Presence of the Sun*, Part I (1992), 7.

Witalec, ed., *Native North American Literature* (1994), 433.

Kennedy and Gioia, *An Introduction to Poetry*, 9th ed. (1998), 121.

Kennedy and Gioia, *Literature: An Introduction to Fiction, Poetry, and Drama*, 7th ed. (1998, © 1999), 771.

Gioia, Mason, and Schoerke, *Twentieth-Century American Poetry* (2004), 868.

Kennedy, X. J., Dorothy M. Kennedy, and Dana Gioia, *Literature: An Introduction to Fiction, Poetry, Drama, and Writing*, 5th compact ed. (2007), 528.

Lincoln, *Speak Like Singing* (2007), 159.

549. "Sonnet for a Mottled-Breasted Girl"

Momaday, "Three Poems," *Paris Review*, no. 99 (Spring 1986): 162.

550. "The Stalker"

Momaday, *The Gourd Dancer*, Part II (1976), 41.

Miller, ed., *United States in Literature* (1979), 608.

Velie, *Four American Indian Literary Masters* (1982), 49.

Momaday, *In the Presence of the Sun*, Part I (1992), 27.

Nelson, Cary, ed., *Anthology of Modern American Poetry* (2000), 1004.

551. "The Story of a Well-Made Shield"

Momaday, *Viva, Santa Fe New Mexican*, August 12, 1973, 8.

———, *Angle of Geese and Other Poems* (1974), 20.

Niatum, ed., *Carriers of the Dream Wheel* (1975, 1981), 104.

Momaday, *The Gourd Dancer*, Part I (1976), 25.

Hobson, ed., *The Remembered Earth* (1979, 1981), 174.

Smith, W. J., comp., *A Green Place: Modern Poems* (1982), 61.

Niatum, ed., *Harper's Anthology of 20th Century Native American Poetry* (1988), 66.

Momaday, *In the Presence of the Sun: A Gathering of Shields* (1991), vii.

———, *In the Presence of the Sun: Stories and Poems*, Part III (1992), 73.

Witalec, ed., *Native North American Literature* (1994), 433.

552. "Summons" For Yuri Vaella, Moscow, 1997

Momaday, *In the Bear's House* (1999), 72.

553. "Sun Dance Shield"

Momaday, *In the Presence of the Sun*, Part I (1992), 17.

———, "A Gathering of Shields," *Native Peoples* 5, no. 3 (Spring 1992): 32.

Joyce essay in Litz, ed., *American Writers*, Supp. IV (1996), 491.

554. "That Woman and This Woman"

Momaday, *The Gourd Dancer*, Part III (1976), 57.

Foss, ed., *The Clouds Threw This Light* (1983), 177.

555. "There, Outside, the Long Light of August"

Museum of the American Indian Newsletter 3, no. 2 (1978): n.p.

556. "To a Child Running with Outstretched Arms in Canyon de Chelly"

Niatum, ed., *Carriers of the Dream Wheel* (1975, 1981), 92.

Momaday, *The Gourd Dancer,* Part II (1976), 49.

Niatum essay in Schöler, ed., *Coyote Was Here.* The Dolphin, no. 9 (1984), 29–30.

Niatum, ed., *Harper's Anthology of 20th Century Native American Poetry* (1988), 68.

Napierkowski, ed., *Poetry for Students,* vol. 11 (1998), 173.

557. "To An Aged Bear" Santa Fe, 1995

Momaday, *In the Bear's House* (1999), 64.

558. "Tres Campos" Jemez Springs, 1997

Momaday, *In the Bear's House* (1999), 66–67.

559. "Two Figures" (See the following section, "Poems and Prose about Billy the Kid.")

560. "Ursa Major" Tucson, 1995

Momaday, *In the Bear's House* (1999), 63.

561. "Walk on the Moon" For Henry Raymont, July 21, 1969

Momaday, *Angle of Geese and Other Poems* (1974), 25.

———, *The Gourd Dancer,* Part I (1976), 17.

Ramsey, P., *Contemporary Religious Poetry* (1987), 172.

Olsen, *On the Wing* (2005), 185.

562. "We Have Been Lovers, You and I"

Momaday, Special limited edition of poem printed by Crepuscular Press (1980).

563. "Winter Holding off the Coast of North America"

Niatum, ed., *Carriers of the Dream Wheel* (1975, 1981), 93.

Momaday, *The Gourd Dancer,* Part II (1976), 49.

Woodard, *Ancestral Voice* (1989), 157.

Parini, ed., *Columbia Anthology of American Poetry* (1995), 691.

564. "Winter Solstice at Amoxiumqua" For Barbara, Jemez Springs, 1997

Momaday, *In the Bear's House* (1999), 76–77.

565. "Woman Waiting on a Porch"

Momaday, *In the Presence of the Sun,* Part IV (1992), 128.

566. "The Wound"

Momaday, *The Gourd Dancer*, Part III (1976), 59.

Foss, ed., *The Clouds Threw This Light* (1983), 178.

Momaday, "The Strange and True Story of My Life with Billy the Kid," *American West* 22, no. 5 (September–October 1985): 65.

———, *The Ancient Child* (1989), 180–81.

———, *In the Presence of the Sun*, Part I (1992), 37.

Ferguson, Salter, and Stallworthy, eds., *Norton Anthology of Poetry*, 4th ed. (1996), 1756.

567. "Wreckage"

Momaday, *In the Presence of the Sun*, Part IV (1992), 124.

Poems and Prose about Billy the Kid

The following poems and prose pieces about Billy the Kid were published in Momaday's second novel, *The Ancient Child, A Novel* (1989). Before the appearance of the novel, "The Strange and True Story of My Life with Billy the Kid" was published in a beautiful layout with color illustrations from Momaday's *Billy the Kid Suite* in *American West* 22, no. 5 (September–October 1985): 56–65. "The Strange and True Story" was reprinted in 1992 in the second part of *In the Presence of the Sun: Stories and Poems*, 1961–1991, 41–69. Some of the poems have also appeared in other published works.

Described by Momaday as a "memorial" or "an elegy and farewell," "The Strange and True Story of My Life with Billy the Kid" is composed of twenty-one poems and stories, one for each year of Billy the Kid's short life from his early childhood to his death. This explains why the poems and prose pieces are numbered from one to twenty-one in the second part of *In the Presence of the Sun* (1992) and in the section below.

An Italian translation of "The Strange and True Story of My Life with Billy the Kid" was published in Italy: "La strana e verace storia della mia vita con Billy the Kid e alter storias." By N. Scott Momaday, a cura de Gaetano Prampolini. Vaghe stele dell'orsa, no. 2. Rome: Salerno, ©1993. 100 pp. Illus., 20 pp. of plates, 21 cm. The original English text appears on facing pages.

The following section presents the poems and prose pieces in the order in which they appear in this "strange and true story." Momaday customarily begins the story with a short introduction, "A Word on Billy the Kid," presenting some of the known facts about this famous outlaw. The poem "Two Figures" begins and ends the story and is numbered once, at the end.

The Strange and True Story of My Life with Billy the Kid

"Two Figures"

These figures moving in my rhyme,
Who are they? Death and Death's dog, Time.

568. "Riding Is an Exercise of the Mind"

This prose piece first appeared with the title "Growing Up at Jemez Pueblo" in Momaday's column in *Viva, Santa Fe New Mexican*, June 25, 1972, 2.

Momaday, "The Pear-shaped Legend," *Stanford Magazine* 3, no. 1 (Spring–Summer 1975): 46–47.

———, *American West* 22, no. 5 (September–October 1985): 56–57.

A shortened version appears in *The Ancient Child* (1989), 177–78.

Momaday, *In the Presence of the Sun*, Part II (1992), 45–47.

Martin, *The Way of the Human Being* (1999), 185 (excerpt).

569. "Billy the Kid, His Rocking Horse: A Lullaby"

Momaday, *American West* 22, no. 5 (September–October 1985): 57.

———, *The Ancient Child* (1989), 175.

———, *In the Presence of the Sun*, Part II (1992), 48.

570. "Billy the Boy at Silver City"

Momaday, "The Pear-shaped Legend," *Stanford Magazine* 3, no. 1 (Spring–Summer 1975): 47.

———, *American West* 22, no. 5 (September–October 1985): 57.

Schubnell, *N. Scott Momaday: The Cultural and Literary Background* (1985), 253.

Momaday, *The Ancient Child* (1989), 178–79.

———, *In the Presence of the Sun*, Part II (1992), 49.

571. "Henry McCarty Witnesses His Mother's Marriage, 1 March 1873"

Momaday, *American West* 22, no. 5 (September–October 1985): 58.

———, *The Ancient Child* (1989), 179–80.

———, *In the Presence of the Sun*, Part II (1992), 50.

572. "The Man in Black"

Momaday, "How It Began," *Viva, Santa Fe New Mexican*, November 25, 1973, 4.

———, "The Pear-Shaped Legend," *Stanford Magazine* 3, no. 1 (Spring–Summer 1975): 47–48.

———, *American West* 22, no. 5 (September–October 1985): 59.

———, *The Ancient Child* (1989), 182–184.

———, *In the Presence of the Sun*, Part II (1992), 51–52.

Martin, *The Way of the Human Being* (1999), 185–86 (excerpt).

573. "He Reckons Geologic Time According to His Sign"

Momaday, *American West* 22, no. 5 (September–October 1985): 59.

———, *The Ancient Child* (1989), 187.

———, *In the Presence of the Sun*, Part II (1992), 53.

574. "A Prospector Catches Sight of Him in the Doña Anas"

Momaday, *American West* 22, no. 5 (September–October 1985): 60.

———, *The Ancient Child* (1989), 187–88.

———, *In the Presence of the Sun*, Part II (1992), 54.

575. "On the Simple Nature of His Lust"

Momaday, *American West* 22, no. 5 (September–October 1985): 60.

———, *In the Presence of the Sun*, Part II (1992), 55.

576. "The Girl at the Doll House"

Momaday, *American West* 22, no. 5 (September–October 1985): 60.

———, *The Ancient Child* (1989), 188–89.

———, *In the Presence of the Sun*, Part II (1992), 56.

577. "Billy's Boast to an Old Blind Woman at San Patricio"

Momaday, *In the Presence of the Sun*, Part II (1992), 57.

578. "He Counts Anacita the Weaver among His True Loves"

Momaday, *American West* 22, no. 5 (September–October 1985): 60.

———, *The Ancient Child* (1989), 189.

———, *In the Presence of the Sun*, Part II (1992), 58.

579. "Billy the Kid Offers a Kindness to an Old Man at Glorieta"

This story was first published in *Viva*, December 9, 1973, 12.

Momaday, "The Pear-shaped Legend," *Stanford Magazine* 3, no. 1 (Spring–Summer 1975): 48. This appears under the title "The Dying Cowboy."

———, *American West* 22, no. 5 (September–October 1985): 61.

———, *The Ancient Child* (1989), 190–192.

———, *In the Presence of the Sun*, Part II (1992), 59–60.

580. "He Encounters a Player at Words"

Momaday, "The Pear-shaped Legend," *Stanford Magazine* 3, no. 1 (1975): 48.

———, *American West* 22, no. 5 (September–October 1985): 61.

———, *The Ancient Child* (1989), 193.

———, *In the Presence of the Sun*, Part II (1992), 61.

———, "New Mexico: Passage into Legend," *The Man Made of Words* (1997), 154–55.

581. "He Would Place a Chair for Sister Blandina"

Momaday, *American West* 22, no. 5 (September–October 1985): 62.

Schubnell, *N. Scott Momaday: The Cultural and Literary Background* (1985), 251.

Momaday, *The Ancient Child* (1989), 197–198.

———, *In the Presence of the Sun*, Part II (1992), 62.

582. "Billy Fixes a Bully in His Gaze"

Momaday, "The Pear-shaped Legend," *Stanford Magazine* 3, no. 1 (1975): 48.

———, *American West* 22, no. 5 (September–October 1985): 63.

———, *The Ancient Child* (1989), 200–201.

———, *In the Presence of the Sun*, Part II (1992), 63.

Martin, *The Way of the Human Being* (1999), 187.

583. "Trees and Evening Sky"

Niatum, ed., *Carriers of the Dream Wheel* (1975, 1981), 102.

Momaday, *American West* 22, no. 5 (September–October 1985): 63.

———, *The Ancient Child* (1989), 217.

———, *In the Presence of the Sun*, Part II (1992), 64.

584. "He Foretells Disaster in a Dream"

Momaday, *American West* 22, no. 5 (September–October 1985): 63.

———, *The Ancient Child* (1989), 219–20.

———, *In the Presence of the Sun*, Part II (1992), 65.

585. "He Enters upon the Afternoon of His Last Day"

Momaday, *American West* 22, no. 5 (September–October 1985): 63.

———, *The Ancient Child* (1989), 226.

———, *In the Presence of the Sun*, Part II (1992), 66.

586. "Billy the Kid, the Departure of His Soul, 14 July 1881"

Momaday, "The Pear-shaped Legend," *Stanford Magazine* 3, no. 1 (1975): 48.

———, *American West* 22, no. 5 (September–October 1985): 64.

Schubnell, *N. Scott Momaday: The Cultural and Literary Background* (1985), 253–54.

Momaday, *The Ancient Child* (1989), 127.

———, *In the Presence of the Sun*, Part II (1992), 67.

587. "Wide Empty Landscape with a Death in the Foreground"

Niatum, ed., *Carriers of the Dream Wheel* (1975, 1981), 90.

Momaday, *American West* 22, no. 5 (September–October 1985): 65.

———, *The Ancient Child* (1989), 234.

Woodard, *Ancestral Voice* (1989), 160.

Momaday, *In the Presence of the Sun*, Part II (1992), 68.

Joyce essay in Litz, ed., *American Writers*, Supplement IV, Part 2 (1996), 492.

588. "Two Figures"

Momaday, *The Gourd Dancer*, Part III (1976), 64.

———, *American West* 22, no. 5 (September–October 1985): 56, 65.

———, *The Ancient Child* (1989), 163.

———, *In the Presence of the Sun* (1992), xix, 43, 69.

Ferguson, Salter and Stallworthy, eds., *Norton Anthology of Poetry*, 4th ed. (1996), 1756.

Lincoln, *Sing with the Heart of a Bear* (2000), 253.

Ferguson, Salter, and Stallworthy, eds., *Norton Anthology of Poetry*, 5th ed. (2005), 1862.

Lincoln, *Speak Like Singing* (2007), 141.

The poem "Two Figures" ends, as it begins, the legend of Billy the Kid.

Plays and Dialogues

Published Plays

The following plays were published in *Three Plays: The Indolent Boys, Children of the Sun, The Moon in Two Windows* by the University of Oklahoma Press in 2007. This is the first published collection of Momaday's plays.

589. *The Indolent Boys.* A play in two acts.

The play's setting is the Kiowa Boarding School located in Anadarko, Oklahoma Territory, in January 1891. It is based on a true story about three young boys who ran away from the boarding school in an attempt to reach the camps of their families. The oldest had been whipped by a teacher. They were overtaken by a severe snowstorm and froze to death on a small bluff south of present-day Carnegie, Oklahoma. This incident is marked in the pictographic calendar of the Kiowas, and it remains fixed in their cultural memory and the Kiowa oral tradition.

The Indolent Boys has been produced on the stage in several locations: Syracuse Stage, Syracuse, New York, 1989; Harvard University, 1992; Syracuse Stage, February 1994; Museum of Indian Arts and Culture, Santa Fe, August 22–25, 2002; and Rodey Theatre, University of New Mexico Performing Arts Center, Albuquerque, August 30–31, 2002. A reading was also performed in Phoenix, Arizona, at the Heard Museum in 2001.

The Southwest Repertory Theatre Company, in association with the Institute of American Indian Arts Museum, The Buffalo Trust, and the Heard Museum, presented a dramatic reading of *The Indolent Boys* in Santa Fe as part of its 2002–2003 Mainstage Season. This reading was directed by Jennifer Chavez with associate directors Jill Momaday, daughter of N. Scott Momaday, and Maria Redcorn. Jill Momaday was the "Storyteller."

A brief article in the July–August 2003 issue of *American Theatre* reported that the last mainstage production of the Southwest Repertory Theatre Company of Albuquerque was *The Indolent Boys.* The company closed in May 2003 because it had been unsuccessful in leveraging the success of the play, which had sold out in Albuquerque, Santa Fe, and Scottsdale (Arizona), into a financial commitment from sponsors to fund a Native American Theater Festival.

590. *Children of the Sun.* A play for the stage in twelve scenes.

Written primarily for children, the play tells a sacred story that is based on an ancient Kiowa narrative about the Twin Heroes, children of an earthly mother and the god who is the Sun. Through the Twin Heroes, the Kiowas are related to the deity of *Ka'do*, or Sun Dance. This is a story within the story of Aila, a young woman who brings color to the world. In creating this play, Momaday collaborated with his daughter Cael, who wrote the story of Aila for her first child.

An article in the May 1996 issue of *Stagebill*, titled "New Visions/New Voices," tells about a forum for works in progress for young audiences that featured stage performances of plays, including *Children of the Sun*. Commissioned by the John F. Kennedy Center for the Performing Arts, Washington, D.C., the play was presented in the Theatre Lab of the Kennedy Center on Sunday, May 26, 1996. The performance was directed by Tazewell Thompson.

The Barter Theatre, the State Theatre of Virginia, located at Abingdon, presented the play with choreographed dance from March 21 to May 21, 2001. This production was directed by Katy Brown.

591. *The Moon in Two Windows*. A screenplay in four acts.

This screenplay takes place at the Carlisle Indian Industrial School, in operation from 1879 to 1918, located at Carlisle Barracks, Pennsylvania. This was the first of the government Indian boarding schools established in the United States. It was founded by Richard Henry Pratt, who is remembered for his statement, "Kill the Indian, and save the Man." Children were sent long distances to Carlisle, separating them from family, home, and culture, and placing them in profoundly different and difficult situations. Besides Pratt, among the thirty-two characters in this screenplay are well-known names from American history, including Olympic champion Jim Thorpe, Coach Glen "Pop" Warner, Dwight D. "Ike" Eisenhower, Chief Spotted Tail, and Sitting Bull.

Published Dialogues

592. "The Bear-God Dialogues." *In the Bear's House*. New York: St. Martin's Press, 1999. 15–50.

Translation of *The Bear-God Dialogues*

Russian translation. Translated by Alexander Vaschenko. Moscow, Russia, 2005. 95 pp. A brief "Momaday Chronology," spanning the years from 1934 to 2004, is included at the end of this book. A black-and-white photograph of Momaday is on the frontispiece facing the title page. Momaday's painting of a pink bear on a yellow background is on the book's cover. Vaschenko wrote the first dissertation on American Indian literature at the University of Moscow.

In these dialogues, or short plays, Urset, the Original Bear, and Yahweh (God, the creator, the Great Mystery, the Supreme Being) are the only characters. Eight "Bear-God Dialogues" were published in *In the Bear's House*:

593. "You Are, Urset. I Am, Yahweh," 15–19.

594. "Berries," 21–24.

595. "Prayer," 25–27.

596. "Dreams," 29–32.

597. "Story," 33–37.

598. "Evolution," 39–41.

This dialogue was published in *The Epic of Evolution: Science and Religion in Dialogue,* edited by James B. Miller. Upper Saddle River, New Jersey: Pearson Prentice Hall, 2004. 206–208.

599. "Thought," 42–45.

600. "Time," 47–50.

Screenplays

601. "House Made of Dawn: Screen Play," by N. Scott Momaday and Richardson Morse. 1969. From the Pulitzer Prize–winning novel *House Made of Dawn,* by N. Scott Momaday. 122 pp. This screenplay has not been published. The original is in typewritten form.

602. "The Man Who Killed the Deer: Screen Play," by N. Scott Momaday. 1970. The screen adaptation of the classic novel by Frank Waters was filmed in New Mexico by Sagittarius Productions of New York. Momaday was on leave from the English Department of the University of California, Berkeley, while working on the script. This screenplay has not been published.

603. "The Moon in Two Windows: Screen Play," by N. Scott Momaday. 2006. Published in *Three Plays*. Norman: University of Oklahoma Press, 2007. 105–77. See also above under "Published Plays."

Paintings and Drawings in Works by Momaday and Others

Shortened bibliographic citations are presented in this listing. *In the Presence of the Sun*, Parts I–IV, refers to the book with the subtitle, *Stories and Poems, 1961–1991*, published in 1992 by St. Martin's Press.

604. *Ambition*. Graphite and wash, 1992.

Momaday, *In the Presence of the Sun*, Part IV (1992), 116.

605. *Antelope Killing Shield*. Etching, 21 × 25¼ in.

Nelson, Mary C. "One Fire, Three Flames," *Art West* 5, no. 5 (August–September 1982): 82.

606. *Anthracite*. Graphite and wash, 23 × 30 in., 1976.

Woodard, *Ancestral Voice* (1989), 65.

607. *Arfig*. Graphite and wash, 1979.

Momaday, *In the Presence of the Sun*, Part I (1992), 30.

608. *The Bear/Canyon*. Acrylic, 18 × 24 in., 1991.

Momaday, *In the Presence of the Sun*, Part I (1992), 2.

609. *Bear Mask*. Acrylic, 1990.

Momaday, *In the Presence of the Sun*, Part IV (1992), 133.

610. *Billy the Kid* (from *Billy the Kid Suite*). Ink and watercolor on Arches paper, 23 × 30 in., 1984.

Momaday, *American West* 22, no. 5 (September–October 1985): 55.

Woodard, *Ancestral Voice* (1989), 23.

Momaday, *In the Presence of the Sun*, Part II (1992), 41.

611. *Bote-talee's Shield*. Ink, 1991.

Momaday, *In the Presence of the Sun: A Gathering of Shields*, 1992, ©1991, n.p.

———, *In the Presence of the Sun*, Part III (1992), 82.

———, "A Gathering of Shields," *Native Peoples* 5, no. 3 (Spring 1992): 32. Reprinted in *Native Peoples* 11, no. 1 (Fall–Winter 1997): 60.

612. *Boy and Bear*. Monoprint, 1987.

Momaday, *In the Presence of the Sun*, Part I (1992), 25.

613. *Buffalo Tail Shield*. Etching, 23 × 30 in., 1988.

Woodard, *Ancestral Voice* (1989), 166.

Momaday, *In the Presence of the Sun,* Part I (1992), 17.

614. *Buffalo with Magpie*. Ink, 11 × 14 in., 1987.

Woodard, *Ancestral Voice* (1989), 169.

Momaday, *In the Presence of the Sun,* Part I (1992), 8.

615. *Catherine McCarty* (from *Billy the Kid Suite*). Ink and watercolor on Arches paper, 23 × 30 in., 1984.

Momaday, *American West* 22, no. 5 (September–October 1985): 58.

616. *Concession*. Graphite and wash, 1979.

Momaday, *In the Presence of the Sun,* Part IV (1992), 127.

617. *Crane Shield.*

Detail from this drawing appeared on the cover of the Spring 1999 issue of *Western American Literature.*

618. *Cristobal*. Ink, 23 × 30 in., 1976.

Woodard, *Ancestral Voice* (1989), 196.

619. *Dancing Boy*. Graphite and wash, 1989.

Momaday, *In the Presence of the Sun,* Part II (1992), 48.

620. *Death Mask*. Graphite and wash, 1992.

Momaday, *In the Presence of the Sun,* Part IV (1992), 112.

621. *Desert Form*. Graphite and wash, 1992.

Momaday, *In the Presence of the Sun,* Part II (1992), 54.

622. *Dog Horse*. Graphite and wash, 11 × 14, 1987.

Woodard, *Ancestral Voice* (1989), 56.

623. *Dog Horse*. Graphite, 1988.

Momaday, *In the Presence of the Sun,* Part I (1992), 15.

624. *Dragonfly* (Koi-khan-hole). Watercolor, n.d.

Cover illustration of *The Names: A Memoir.* Sun Tracks, An American Indian Literary Series, vol. 16, ser. ed. Lawrence Evers. Tucson: Sun Tracks/University of Arizona Press, ©1976 by N. Scott Momaday. Modeled on a photograph,

Kiowa Brave in War Dress, taken by Will Soule, frontier photographer.

625. *Dreaming Bear Shield: West,* 1984.

Andrews, Lynn V., *Flight of the Seventh Moon: The Teaching of the Shields.* Illustrations by N. Scott Momaday. San Francisco: Harper & Row, 1984. 94. Reprint (pbk.), 1985. New edition with different title: *Spirit Woman: The Teachings of the Shields.* New York: J. P. Tarcher, 2002, ©1984. 94. Reprint, 2007.

626. *Eagle Wing Shield.* Etching, 25¼ × 21 in.

Nelson, Mary C. "One Fire, Three Flames." *Art West* 5, no. 5 (August–September 1982): 82.

627. *Elder.* Pen and ink on Arches paper, 24 × 30 in., n.d.

Bartlett, *The New Native American Novel: Works in Progress* (1986), ii.

628. *Faces.* Graphite and wash, 11 × 14 in., 1985/1987.

Woodard, *Ancestral Voice* (1989), 5.

Momaday, *In the Presence of the Sun,* Part IV (1992), 109.

629. *Fire-That-Falls-From-The-Sky Shield,* 1984.

Andrews, *Flight of the Seventh Moon: The Teaching of the Shields.* Illustrations by Momaday. San Francisco: Harper & Row, 1984. 150. Reprint (pbk.), 1985. New edition with different title: *Spirit Woman: The Teachings of the Shields.* New York: J. P. Tarcher, 2002, ©1984. 150. Reprint, 2007.

630. *The Floating Feathers Shield.* Ink, 1991.

Momaday, *In the Presence of the Sun: A Gathering of Shields,* 1992, ©1991, n.p.

Villani, *Pasatiempo, Santa Fe New Mexican,* December 6–12, 1991, 9.

Momaday, *In the Presence of the Sun,* Part III (1992), 80.

Schweninger, *Literary Masters,* vol. 12 (2001), 91.

631. *Formal Mask.* Acrylic, 1989.

Momaday, *In the Presence of the Sun* (1992), title page.

632. *Girl with Umbrella.* Ink, 1976.

Momaday, *In the Presence of the Sun,* Part IV (1992), 120.

633. *Gourd Dancer.* Ink, 1976 (a line drawing representing Mammedaty as the Gourd Dancer).

Momaday, *The Gourd Dancer,* Part II (1976), 34.

Allen, C., *Western American Literature* 41, no. 2 (Summer 2006): 155.

634. *The Horned Horse Shield.* Etching, 23 × 30 in., 1976.

Coltelli, ed., *Native American Literatures* (1989), 8.

Woodard, *Ancestral Voice* (1989), 142.

Momaday, *In the Presence of the Sun,* Part I (1992), 11.

635. *Hunter.* Ink and wash, 22 × 30 in., 1985.

Woodard, *Ancestral Voice* (1989), 54.

Momaday, *In the Presence of the Sun,* Part I (1992), 26.

636. *Indian Angel.* Monoprint, 23 × 30 in., 1987.

Woodard, *Ancestral Voice* (1989), 172.

637. *Indolent Girl.* Graphite and wash, 1985.

Momaday, *In the Presence of the Sun,* Part II (1992), 56.

638. *La Posada.* Ink and watercolor, 1985.

Momaday, *In the Presence of the Sun,* Part I (1992), 38.

639. *L. G. Murphy* (from *Billy the Kid Suite*). Ink and watercolor on Arches paper, 23 × 30 in., 1984.

Momaday, *American West* 22, no. 5 (September–October 1985): 60.

Woodard, *Ancestral Voice* (1989), 130.

640. *Lincoln County Warrior.* Monoprint, 1987.

Momaday, *In the Presence of the Sun,* Part II (1992), 46.

641. *Lone Bull.* Ink and watercolor, 1990.

Momaday, *In the Presence of the Sun,* Part I (1992), 30.

642. *Mad Buffalo.* Watercolor, 11 × 14 in., 1985/1987.

Woodard, *Ancestral Voice* (1989), 84.

Momaday, *In the Presence of the Sun,* Part IV (1992), 118.

Schweninger, *Literary Masters,* vol. 12 (2001), 34.

643. *Mammedaty.* Graphite and wash, 23 × 30 in., 1976.

Cover illustration of paperback edition of *Approaches to Teaching Momaday's*

"*The Way to Rainy Mountain*," edited by Kenneth Roemer. New York: Modern Language Association of America, 1988.

Woodard, *Ancestral Voice* (1989), 70.

Momaday, *In the Presence of the Sun*, Part IV (1992), 135.

644. *Many Goats and Wife*. Watercolor and ink, 41 × 51 cm.

Coltelli, ed., *Native American Literatures* (1989), 5.

645. *Marriage at Huerfano*. Etching, 23 × 30 in., 1985.

Woodard, *Ancestral Voice* (1989), 180.

Momaday, *In the Presence of the Sun*, Part I (1992), 7.

646. *Medicine Doll Shield*. Monoprint, n.d.

Ellis, "Conversations with N. Scott Momaday," *Southwest Profile* 13, no. 1 (January 1990): 34.

647. *The Muddy Horses Shield*. Ink, 1991.

Momaday, *In the Presence of the Sun: A Gathering of Shields*, 1992, ©1991, n.p.

———, *In the Presence of the Sun*, Part III (1992), 102.

Clements, "image and word cannot be divided," *Western American Literature* 36, no. 2 (Summer 2001): 134.

648. *Pat Garrett* (from *Billy the Kid Suite*). Ink and watercolor on Arches paper, 23 × 30 in., 1984.

Momaday, *American West* 22, no. 5 (September–October 1985): 64.

649. *The Plainest of Shields*. Ink, 1991.

Momaday, *In the Presence of the Sun: A Gathering of Shields*, 1992, ©1991, n.p.

———, *In the Presence of the Sun*, Part III (1992), 86.

650. *Planned Parenthood*. Ink. Graphite and wash, 1992.

Momaday, *In the Presence of the Sun*, Part IV (1992), 111.

651. *Protector-of-Children Shield: South*, 1984.

Andrews, *Flight of the Seventh Moon* (1984), xiv. Reprint, 1985.

———, *Spirit Woman: The Teachings of the Shields* (2002), xvi. Reprint, 2007.

652. *Rainy Mountain Christmas Doll*. Watercolor, 9 × 12 in., 1986.

Woodard, *Ancestral Voice* (1989), 176.

Momaday, *In the Presence of the Sun*, Part IV (1992), 131.

653. *Reflection*. Graphite and wash, 1987.

Momaday, *In the Presence of the Sun*, Part IV (1992), 142.

654. *Rock Tree*. Graphite and wash, 11 × 14 in., 1987.

Woodard, *Ancestral Voice* (1989), 208.

Momaday, *In the Presence of the Sun*, Part I (1992), 18.

655. *Rodrigo*. Monoprint, 1991.

Momaday, *In the Presence of the Sun* (1992), xxi.

656. *Running Coyote*. Watercolor, 11 × 14 in., 1986.

657. *San Salvador*. Acrylic, 1990.

Momaday, *In the Presence of the Sun*, Part IV (1992), 138.

658. *Self Portrait*. Watercolor and ink, 41 × 51 cm. (portrait as a bear).

Coltelli, ed., *Native American Literatures* (1989), 4.

659. *Self Portrait*. Graphite and wash, 23 × 30 in., 1987 (profile with eyeglasses).

Woodard, *Ancestral Voice* (1989), 40.

Momaday, *In the Presence of the Sun* (1992), xvi, 144.

Schweninger, *Literary Masters*, vol. 12 (2001), 29.

660. *Self Portrait*. Watercolor, 1989 (as a standing bear).

Momaday, *In the Presence of the Sun*, Part IV (1992), 129.

661. *Self Portrait with Leaves*. Graphite and wash, 11 × 14 in., 1987/1988 (bear with leaves).

Woodard, *Ancestral Voice* (1989), 19.

Momaday, *In the Presence of the Sun*, Part I (1992), 1.

Schubnell, *American Indian Quarterly* 18, no. 4 (Fall 1994): 470.

Giroux, ed., *Contemporary Literary Criticism*, vol. 85 (1995), 260.

Schweninger, *Literary Masters*, vol. 12 (2001), 128.

662. *Set-anyga*. Watercolor, 11 × 14 in., 1984.

Woodard, *Ancestral Voice* (1989), 184.

Momaday, *In the Presence of the Sun*, Part IV (1992), 140.

663. *Shaman.* Graphite and wash, 23 × 30 in., 1978.

Woodard, *Ancestral Voice* (1989), 87.

664. *The Shattered Sky Shield.* Ink, 1991.

Momaday, *In the Presence of the Sun: A Gathering of Shields*, 1992, ©1991, n.p.

———, *In the Presence of the Sun*, Part III (1992), 76.

665. *Shield-Made-of-Shadows: Self.* 1984.

Andrews, *Flight of the Seventh Moon* (1984), 188. Reprint, 1985.

———, *Spirit Woman: The Teachings of the Shields* (2002), 188. Reprint, 2007.

666. *The Shield of Pai-matone's Brother.* Ink, 1991.

Momaday, *In the Presence of the Sun: A Gathering of Shields*, 1992, ©1991, n.p.

———, *In the Presence of the Sun*, Part III (1992), 96.

667. *The Shield of the Time of the Bluebonnets.* Ink, 1991.

Momaday, *In the Presence of the Sun: A Gathering of Shields*, 1992, ©1991, n.p.

———, *In the Presence of the Sun*, Part III (1992), 88.

668. *The Shield of Two Dreams.* Ink, 1991.

Momaday, *In the Presence of the Sun: A Gathering of Shields*, 1992, ©1991, n.p.

———, *In the Presence of the Sun*, Part III (1992), 106.

———, "A Gathering of Shields," *Native Peoples* 5, no. 3 (Spring 1992): 30. Reprinted in *Native Peoples* 11, no. 1 (Fall–Winter 1997): 58.

Giroux, ed., *Contemporary Literary Criticism*, vol. 85 (1995), 281.

669. *The Shield of Which the Less Said the Better.* Ink, 1991.

Momaday, *In the Presence of the Sun: A Gathering of Shields*, 1992, ©1991, n.p.

———, *In the Presence of the Sun*, Part III (1992), 90.

Giroux, ed., *Contemporary Literary Criticism*, vol. 85 (1995), 280.

670. *The Shield That Came Back.* Ink, 1991.

Momaday, *In the Presence of the Sun: A Gathering of Shields*, 1992, ©1991, n.p.

———, *In the Presence of the Sun*, Part III (1992), 78.

671. *The Shield That Died.* Ink, 1991.

Momaday, *In the Presence of the Sun: A Gathering of Shields*, 1992, ©1991, n.p.

———, *In the Presence of the Sun*, Part III (1992), 92.

Giroux, ed., *Contemporary Literary Criticism*, vol. 85 (1995), 280.

672. *The Shield That Was Brought Down from Tsoai.* Ink, 1991.

Momaday, *In the Presence of the Sun: A Gathering of Shields*, 1992, ©1991, n.p.

———, *In the Presence of the Sun*, Part III (1992), 104.

Charles, *Reading, Learning, Teaching: N. Scott Momaday* (2007), 89.

673. *The Shield That Was Looked After by Dogs.* Ink, 1991.

Momaday, *In the Presence of the Sun: A Gathering of Shields*, 1992, ©1991, n.p.

Momaday, *In the Presence of the Sun*, Part III (1992), 100.

674. *The Shield That Was Touched by Pretty Mouth.* Ink, 1991.

Momaday, *In the Presence of the Sun: A Gathering of Shields*, 1992, ©1991, n.p.

———, *In the Presence of the Sun*, Part III (1992), 98.

Giroux, ed., *Contemporary Literary Criticism*, vol. 85 (1995), 280.

675. *Sister Blandina* (from *Billy the Kid Suite*). Ink and watercolor on Arches paper, 23 × 30 in., 1984.

Momaday, *American West* 22, no. 5 (September–October 1985): 62.

676. *Sitting Bear Iá.* Ink and watercolor, 31 × 36 cm., 1985.

Coltelli, ed., *Native American Literatures* (1989), 6.

677. *Squaw Dance.* Graphite and wash, 14 × 12 in., 1978.

Woodard, *Ancestral Voice* (1989), 122.

678. *St. Aegidienkirche.* Watercolor, 1987.

Momaday, *In the Presence of the Sun*, Part IV (1992), 12.

679. *Standing Buffalo Shield.* 1984.

Andrews, *Flight of the Seventh Moon* (1984), 122. Reprint, 1985.

———, *Spirit Woman: The Teachings of the Shields* (2002), 122. Reprint, 2007.

680. *Star Shield.* Etching, 52.5 × 63.13 cm.

Coltelli, ed., *Native American Literatures* (1989), 7.

681. *Star Shield.* Graphite and wash, 11 × 14 in., 1987.

Woodard, *Ancestral Voice* (1989), 108.

Momaday, *In the Presence of the Sun*, Part III (1992), 71.

682. *Stone.* Graphite and wash, 23 × 30 in., 1976.

Woodard, *Ancestral Voice* (1989), 26.

Momaday, *In the Presence of the Sun,* Part I (1992), 14.

683. *The Story of a Well-Made Shield.* Ink and wash, 1979.

Guerard, ed., *Mirrors and Mirage: Fiction by Nineteen* (1980), 124.

Momaday, *In the Presence of the Sun,* Part III (1992), 75. The detail of this art is also used on this book's endpapers.

684. *Sun and Moon Shield.* Monoprint, n.d.

Ellis, "Conversation with N. Scott Momaday," *Southwest Profile* 13, no. 1 (January 1990): 34.

685. *The Sun Dance Shield.* Ink, 1991.

Momaday, *In the Presence of the Sun: A Gathering of Shields,* 1992, ©1991, n.p.

Momaday, *In the Presence of the Sun,* Part III (1992), 84.

———, "A Gathering of Shields." *Native Peoples* 5, no. 3 (Spring 1992): 33. Reprinted in *Native Peoples* 11, no. 1 (Fall–Winter 1997): 61.

Giroux, ed., *Contemporary Literary Criticism,* vol. 85 (1995), 280.

www.english.illinois.edu/maps/poets/m_r/momaday/shields1.htm.

686. *The Talyi-dai.* Acrylic on paper, 12 × 16 in., 2007.

Momaday, *Three Plays* (2007), 75.

———, "One Who Brings the Light." *World Literature Today* 81, no. 6 (November–December 2007): 37.

687. *Tsoai.* Ink and watercolor on paper, n.d.

Charles, Jim. *Reading, Learning, Teaching: N. Scott Momaday* (2007), 26.

688. *The Unicorn.* Pen and ink, 1980.

Cott and Gimbel, eds., *Wonders: Writings and Drawings for the Child in Us All* (1980), 429.

689. *Walking Bear's Shield.* Ink, 1991.

Momaday, *In the Presence of the Sun: A Gathering of Shields,* 1992, ©1991, n.p.

———, *In the Presence of the Sun,* Part III (1992), 94.

———, "A Gathering of Shields." *Native Peoples* 5, no. 3 (Spring 1992): 31. Reprinted in *Native Peoples* 11, no. 1 (Fall–Winter 1997): 59.

www.english.illinois.edu/maps/poets/m_r/momaday/shields1.htm.

690. *White Buffalo*. Ink and wash, 12 × 18 in.

Native Peoples 19, no. 3 (May–June 2006): 64. This drawing is the signature image of The Buffalo Trust. It appears on the website: www.buffalotrust.org.

691. *Wildflower*. Graphite and wash, 1979.

Momaday, *In the Presence of the Sun*, Part I (1992), 36.

692. *Window Woman*. Ink and wash, 1979.

Momaday, *In the Presence of the Sun*, Part I (1992), 34.

693. *Woman*. Graphite and wash, 1980.

Momaday, *In the Presence of the Sun*, Part IV (1992), 128.

694. *Woman in Red Hat*. Monotype, 30 × 40 in., 1988.

Clark, William. "Written Word Not Enough for Momaday," *Albuquerque Journal*, May 5, 1989, C1, C5.

695. *Word Woman*. Graphite and wash, 1977.

Momaday, *In the Presence of the Sun*, Part IV (1992), 114.

696. *Word Shield*. Graphite and colored pencil, 1992.

Momaday, *In the Presence of the Sun*, Part III (1992), 72.

Art Shows and Exhibits

Momaday's paintings, drawings, and other artwork have been shown across the United States and in several galleries abroad, including galleries in Heidelberg, Germany, and Basel, Switzerland, in 1986.

His first one-man show took place in March and April 1979 on the campus of the University of North Dakota at Grand Forks. The same show was exhibited later in Minneapolis, Minnesota, and Norman, Oklahoma. His work has also been exhibited in Norman at The Galleria. Several shows have taken place in Oklahoma City at the Oklahoma Center for Science and Art, Kirkpatrick Center, the Jacobson House Native Art Center (April–July 2006); and the JRB Art Gallery at the Elms (September 2006).

Other shows and exhibits have been held in Arizona at the Heard Museum in Phoenix, the Wrigley Mansion and the Lovena Ohl Gallery (1982, 1989–90) in Scottsdale, and at locations in Tucson. His work was also exhibited at the Native American Center for the Living Arts in Niagara Falls, New York, the Buffalo Bill

Historical Center at Cody, Wyoming, and in Idaho and several other states.

The first time all three Momadays showed their work together was in November 1979 at R. C. Gorman's Navajo Gallery in Albuquerque. Scott Momaday's work has been shown in Santa Fe, New Mexico, at the LewAllen-Butler Fine Art Gallery (1989) and the Horwitch-LewAllen Art Gallery (1995). He has also exhibited his paintings at the annual Santa Fe Festival of the Arts.

In late 1992 and early 1993, the Wheelwright Museum of the American Indian, Santa Fe, held a twenty-year retrospective exhibit of Momaday's drawings and paintings.

Interviews and Conversations with N. Scott Momaday

Books Devoted Entirely to Interviews with N. Scott Momaday

697. Schubnell, Matthias, ed. *Conversations with N. Scott Momaday.* With an introduction by Matthias Schubnell. Literary Conversations. Jackson: University Press of Mississippi, 1997. 237 pp. (port.) Schubnell has written an illuminating introduction, which appears on pp. ix–xviii. For interviews reprinted in this collection, citations listed below are in a shortened form: Reprint in Schubnell, ed., *Conversations* (1997), page numbers of specific interview.

698. Woodard, Charles L. *Ancestral Voice: Conversations with N. Scott Momaday.* American Indian Lives. Lincoln: University of Nebraska Press, 1989. 229 pp. The interviews, or conversations, took place during 1986 and 1987.

Interviews Published in Books, Journals, Newspapers, and Online

Interviews with Momaday are listed in alphabetical order by the last name of the interviewer, rather than by date. The date and place of the interview are included whenever available.

699. Abbott, Lee. "An Interview with N. Scott Momaday." *Puerto del Sol* 12, no. 2 (March 1973): 21–38. Reprint in Schubnell, ed., *Conversations* (1997), 19–35. This interview was conducted in 1972 at the time Momaday was serving as the first Visiting Distinguished Professor of Humanities at New Mexico State University, Las Cruces. Affixed to page 39, following the interview, is an 8½ × 14 inch folded sheet on which Momaday's poem "Plainview: 2" is superimposed on his charcoal sketch of a woman and horse.

700. Academy of Achievement, A Museum of Living History. "The Writer Warrior." Interview conducted on June 28, 1996, in Sun Valley, Idaho. Washington, D.C.: The Academy, ©2001. (ports.) See Academy of Achievement website: www.achievement.org/autodoc/page/mom0int-1.

701. Adkins, Camille. "Interview with N. Scott Momaday." *Conversations with N. Scott Momaday.* Literary Conversations. Edited by Matthias Schubnell. Jackson: University Press of Mississippi, 1997. 216–34. Conducted in Tucson on April 21, 1993.

702. Barry, Paul C. "N. Scott Momaday." *Canku Ota, A Newsletter Celebrating Native America*, no. 9, May 6, 2000. This profile-interview is accompanied by

a portrait. www.turtletrack.org. To access the information, find Issue 2000 in the Archives and click on May 6.

703. Bataille, Gretchen. "An Interview with N. Scott Momaday." *Iowa English Bulletin* 29, no. 1 (1979): 28–32. Conducted in April 1977. Reprint in Schubnell, ed., *Conversations* (1997), 57–63, by permission of Gretchen Bataille.

704. ———. "Interview with N. Scott Momaday." *Studies in American Indian Literatures: A Journal of Literary Art, Criticism, and Reviews/ASAIL Newsletter*, n.s., 4, no. 1 (Winter 1980): 1–3. Conducted on April 11, 1979. Reprint in Schubnell, ed., *Conversations* (1997), 64–66, with the permission of John Purdy, ed. This interview focuses on the filming of *House Made of Dawn*.

705. Bonetti, Kay. "N. Scott Momaday: Interview." American Audio Prose Library, ©1983. In Schubnell, ed., *Conversations* (1997), 130–48. This is a print version of Bonetti's interview of Momaday at his Tucson home in 1983 for the American Audio Prose Library. See also the following section, "Nonprint Media: Audio Recordings."

706. Brown, Lenora I. "The Indolent Boys: First Play by Pulitzer Prize Recipient N. Scott Momaday." *Native Playwrights Newsletter*, Winter 1994, 28–29. This also appeared in *StageView* (Syracuse Stage, Syracuse, New York), February–March 1994, 6–7.

707. Bruchac, Joseph. "N. Scott Momaday: An Interview." *American Poetry Review* 13, no. 4 (July–August 1984): 13–18. This interview was conducted in December 1982 in Momaday's office in the English Department of the University of Arizona. Reprinted with the title "The Magic of Words: An Interview with N. Scott Momaday," in *Survival This Way: Interviews with American Indian Poets*, edited by Joseph Bruchac. Sun Tracks, vol. 15. Tucson: Sun Tracks and the University of Arizona Press, 1987. 173–91. Reprint in Schubnell, ed., *Conversations* (1997), 96–110, with permission of University of Arizona Press.

708. Bunge, Nancy, ed. "N. Scott Momaday." *Finding the Words: Conversations with Writers Who Teach*. Athens, Ohio: Swallow; Ohio University Press, 1985. 87–95. At the end of this interview, Momaday repeats a passage beginning "I grew up in a very rich and exotic world" (95).

709. ———. "I Grew Up in a Very Rich and Exotic World." In "Theory: Interviews with Writer-Teachers." *Master Class: Lessons from Leading Writers*. Iowa City: University of Iowa Press, 2005. 47–52. Conducted in February 1981.

710. Cabbell, Paul. "Dr. Momaday: Notes on a Pulitzer Prize Winner; Interview

with N. Scott Momaday." *Christian Science Monitor*, June 20, 1969, 19. This interview is cited in the Momaday biographical article in *Current Biography Yearbook*. 1975 ed. New York: H. W. Wilson, 1976.

711. Coltelli, Laura, ed. "N. Scott Momaday." *Winged Words: American Indian Writers Speak*. American Indian Lives. Lincoln: University of Nebraska Press, 1990. 89–100. (port.) See also Introduction, 2–4. Conducted on September 25, 1985, at Momaday's Tucson home. Reprint in Schubnell, ed., *Conversations* (1997), 157–67, with permission of University of Nebraska Press, ©1990. Reprinted in Italian with the title, *Parole fatte d'alba: gli scrittori indiani d'America parlamo*. Rome: Castelvecchi, 1995.

712. Costo, Rupert, ed. "Discussion [with N. Scott Momaday]: The Man Made of Words." *Indian Voices: The First Convocation of American Indian Scholars*. San Francisco: Indian Historian Press, 1970. 63–84. This discussion took place after Momaday's seminal address to the Convocation assembly, held at Princeton University in March 1970. Reprint in Schubnell, ed., *Conversations* (1997), 3–18.

713. Ellis, Nancy. "Conversation with N. Scott Momaday." *Southwest Profile* 13, no. 1 (January 1990): 33–35. A discussion about Plains Indian shields is included.

714. Evers, Lawrence J. "A Conversation with N. Scott Momaday." *Sun Tracks: An American Indian Literary Magazine* 2, no. 2 (Spring 1976): 18–21. This conversation was transcribed from a videotape made of a session attended by Momaday, Dr. Larry Evers, and students of American Indian literature at the University of Arizona on November 1, 1974. Reprint in Schubnell, ed., *Conversations* (1997), 36–44, with permission of Lawrence J. Evers. See also the following section, "Nonprint Media."

715. Fiorentino, Daniele. "The American Indian Writer as a Cultural Broker: An Interview with N. Scott Momaday." In special issue "European Writings on Native American Literatures," guest ed. Birgit Hans. *Studies in American Indian Literatures* 8, no. 4 (Winter 1996): 61–72. Conducted in Rome in June 1991 when Momaday was lecturing and touring in Italy.

716. Fletcher, Kenneth R. "Q & A." *Smithsonian* 39, no. 10 (January 2009): 25. Momaday answers questions about aspects of Native American culture that inspire his work, the goals of The Buffalo Trust, and oral traditions and language. Online at www.smithsonianmag.com/specialsections/heritage/QA-Scott-Momaday.html.

717. Garrait-Bourrier, Anne. "Entretien privé, avec N. Scott Momaday." *N. Scott Momaday, l'homme-ours, voix et regard*. Clermont-Ferrand, France: Presses Universitaires Blaise Pascal, 2005. [14]–19 (in French). Conducted in France in July 2003.

718. Givens, Bettye. "A *MELUS* Interview: N. Scott Momaday—A Slant of Light." *MELUS* (Journal of the Society for the Study of Multi-ethnic Literature in the United States) 12, no. 1 (Spring 1985): 79–87. This issue focuses on Native American literature. This interview took place on the campus of Texas Tech University in Lubbock on March 26, 1982, during the Kiowa Symposium. Reprint in Schubnell, ed., *Conversations* (1997), 87–95, with permission.

719. Hansen, Liane. "N. Scott Momaday Interview." *Weekend Edition,* National Public Radio (NPR), Sunday, December 12, 1999. Hansen speaks with the author about his children's story *Circle of Wonder: A Native American Christmas Story.* www.npr.org.

720. Hearne, Joanna. "N. Scott Momaday Interview: *House Made of Dawn*." Native Networks, 2005. Conducted in March 2003 at the University of Arizona. This interview discusses the film adaptation of the novel. http://.nativenetworks.si.edu/eng/rose/momaday_n_interview.htm.

721. Isernhagen, Hartwig. Chapter 1, "N. Scott Momaday." In *Momaday, Vizenor, Armstrong: Conversations on American Indian Writing.* American Indian Literature and Critical Studies, vol. 32. Norman: University of Oklahoma Press, 1999. 29–75. This interview was taped in July 1994 at La Fonda in Santa Fe, New Mexico. The questions asked by the interviewer are provided on pp. 21–27.

722. King, Tom. "A *MELUS* Interview: N. Scott Momaday—Literature and the Native Writer." *MELUS* 10, no. 4 (Winter 1983): 66–72. Reprint in Schubnell, ed., *Conversations* (1997), 149–56, with permission.

723. Kuralt, Charles (TV anchor). *This I Believe* (television series), February 1969. Momaday was among several distinguished guests interviewed individually in five-minute segments of this program aired on national television. This was the first program of the new series patterned on an earlier series anchored by Edward R. Murrow. Each person spoke about his or her philosophy of life. See also the *Washington Post* article, February 5, 1996, under "Newspaper Articles and Press Releases" in Part III.

724. Low, Denise, ed. "A Conversation with N. Scott Momaday and Luci Tapahanso." *The Wakarusa Wetlands in Word and Image.* Lawrence, Kansas:

Committee on Imagination and Place, 2005. 12–14. This conversation took place in April 1999 during Momaday's visit to speak at the University of Kansas in Lawrence. It appeared in an earlier version in *Cottonwood* 55 (Spring 2000): 19–24. The Committee on Imagination and Place is affiliated with the Lawrence Arts Center.

725. MacPherson, Myra. "Interview with N. Scott Momaday." *Washington Post*, November 21, 1969, B1, and December 7, 1974, B1.

726. Modern American Poetry: An Online Journal and Multimedia Companion to *Anthology of Modern American Poetry*, edited by Cary Nelson. "Online Interview with N. Scott Momaday." www.english.illinois.edu/maps/poets/m_r/momaday/interview.htm.

727. Morgan, William T., Jr. "Landscapes: N. Scott Momaday." *Sequoia* 19, no. 2 (Winter 1975): 38–49. This interview took place at Stanford University. It appeared again in *Sequoia* 23, no. 1, The Best of *Sequoia* Prose (Autumn–Winter 1978): 21–31. Reprint in Schubnell, ed., *Conversations* (1997), 45–56, with permission.

728. Nizalowski, John. "N. Scott Momaday: Globetrotting Author Comes Home to 'Center of the World.'" *New Mexico Magazine* 68, no. 8 (August 1990): 21–25. This interview took place in Santa Fe, New Mexico, in 1990.

729. Owens, Louis. "N. Scott Momaday." Chapter 5 of *This Is about Vision: Interviews with Southwestern Writers*, edited by William Balassi, John F. Crawford, and Annie O. Eysturoy. New American Studies in the American West. Albuquerque: University of New Mexico Press, 1990. 59–69. (port.) Conducted in Tucson, Arizona, in April 1986. Reprint in Schubnell, ed., *Conversations* (1997), 178–91, with permission of the University of New Mexico.

730. *Persona*. "Shouting at the Machine: An Interview with N. Scott Momaday." *Persona: The University of Arizona Undergraduate Magazine of Literature and Art*, Spring 1982, 24–44. Accompanied by a self-portrait in pencil by Momaday. This interview took place at Momaday's Tucson home while he was a professor at the University of Arizona. It begins and ends with excerpts from *House Made of Dawn*. Reprint in Schubnell, ed., *Conversations* (1997), 111–29, with permission of Lawrence J. Evers.

731. Prampolini, Gaetano. "*The Ancient Child*: A Conversation with N. Scott Momaday." *Native American Literatures*, edited by Laura Coltelli. Forum, nos. 2–3 (1990–1991): 77–100. Pisa, Italy: SEU (Servizio Editoriale Universitaria),

1992. Conducted by Prampolini at Momaday's Tucson, Arizona, home in November 1990. Reprint in Schubnell, ed., *Conversations* (1997), 192–215, with permission of Gaetano Prampolini.

732. Quay, Jim. "The Confirmation of the Earth: Writer N. Scott Momaday on the Power of Place." *Humanities Network* (quarterly of the California Council for the Humanities) 15, no. 2 (Spring 1993): 1–2. Quay, executive director, interviewed Momaday in preparation for the Council's community project in San Diego, where he delivered the 1993 Public Humanities Lecture in June. The third paragraph in the Preface of *In the Presence of the Sun* (1992) is quoted on p. 1: "I have been called 'the man of words.' . . . Words inform the element in which I live my daily life" (xviii).

733. Ray, Rachel. "A Candid Chat with N. Scott Momaday." *Santa Fean* 33, no. 7 (August 2005): 230–31. This interview was conducted in Santa Fe, New Mexico, during the summer of 2005.

734. Reising, Robert W. "The Voice and the Vision: A Visit with N. Scott Momaday." *Pembroke Magazine* 19 (1987): 120–24.

735. Ross, Jean W. "*Contemporary Authors* Interview." In *Contemporary Authors,* New Revision Series, vol. 14, edited by Linda Metzger et al. Detroit: Gale Research, ©1985. 338–40. This interview follows a biographical article about Momaday beginning on p. 335.

736. Rostkowski, Joëlle. "Looking Back: *House Made of Dawn* as the Portrait of a Lost Generation." *Q/W/E/R/T/Y: Arts, littératures, & civilisations du monde Anglophone* (Pau, France) 7 (October 1997): 145–50. This interview took place in Tucson, Arizona, in August 1997.

737. Schubnell, Matthias. "An Interview with N. Scott Momaday." In Schubnell, ed., *Conversations with N. Scott Momaday* (1997), 67–86. This interview was conducted in December 1981 at Momaday's Tucson home and is referred to numerous times by Schubnell in his book *N. Scott Momaday: The Cultural and Literary Background*. Norman: University of Oklahoma Press, 1985.

738. Tayac, Gabrielle. "Native Voices: N. Scott Momaday." *Northeast Indian Quarterly* 7, no. 3 (Fall 1990): 6–7. This interview, conducted in July 1989, focuses on American Indian perspectives pertaining to the Quicentenary.

739. Underwood, Von. "Interview with N. Scott Momaday." *Quivira, Journal of the Cameron University Honor Societies* 2, no. 1 (Spring 1992): 2–3, 23–25. Conducted in February 1992 at Cameron University, Lawton, Oklahoma,

where Momaday spoke during the celebration of the university's Year of the Renaissance.

740. Walker, Carla. "A Virtual Visit with N. Scott Momaday." Walker, editor of *Oklahoma Humanities Magazine*, interviewed Momaday in Oklahoma City in July 2007 following his appointment by Governor Brad Henry as the Oklahoma Centennial State Poet Laureate. www.okhumanitiescouncil.org/momaday-interview.

741. Weiler, Dagmar. "N. Scott Momaday: Storyteller." *Journal of Ethnic Studies* 16, no. 1 (Spring 1988): 118–26. This interview was conducted at Washington State University in April 1986 and focused on various aspects of *House Made of Dawn* and its characters. Reprint in Schubnell, ed., *Conversations* (1997), 168–77, with permission.

742. Wiegner, Kathleen. "Interview with N. Scott Momaday." *Seattle Review* 27, no. 1 (2005): 12–35. (ports.) This interview was conducted in February 2003 at Momaday's home in Jemez Springs, New Mexico. Reprinted in *Page to Page: Retrospectives of Writers from the* Seattle Review, edited by Colleen J. McElroy. Seattle: University of Washington Press, 2006. 356–77.

743. Wise, Suzanne. "Of Magic and Morality: An Interview with M.[*sic*] Scott Momaday." *Poetry Society of America Newsletter*, no. 34 (Fall 1990): 1, 23–28. Conducted by telephone in July 1990.

Nonprint Media: A Selected List Involving Momaday

Motion Pictures

744. "House Made of Dawn." Produced and directed by Richardson Morse. Screenplay by N. Scott Momaday and Richardson Morse. With Larry Littlebird as Abel and John Saxon as Tosamah. Firebird Productions/New Line Cinema, 1972. The filming was done on location in Los Angeles and New Mexico. The original film was archived by the Smithsonian Institution. A new print was made in Los Angeles in 1992 through the support of the Smithsonian and other organizations. These were the only two prints in existence until a videotape became available in 1996 through New Line Home Video and Turner Home Entertainment.

Audio Recordings

745. Sound recording. "The Indian Oral Tradition." North Hollywood, California: Pacifica Radio Archive, 1969. This recording was made shortly after Momaday received the Pulitzer Prize.

746. Sound recording. "The C.A.T.E. Presents 'A Day of Poets Reading Their Own Poetry,'" with N. Scott Momaday reading his poems. San Francisco: California Association of Teachers of English, 1970. Sound disc (1), analog, 33⅓ rpm, mono., 12 in. This is part of the Bancroft poetry archive sound recordings, University of California, Berkeley.

747. Sound recording. "Address before Congress." Vital History Cassettes Series, no. 1, June 1976. New York: Encyclopedia Americana/CBS News Audio Resource Library; Grolier Educational Corp., 1976. Sound cassette (1), 22 min., 1⅞ ips. This tape, made at the time of the Bicentennial events in the United States, includes the address made by Juan Carlos, king of Spain, to the U.S. Congress on June 2, and a recording of Momaday speaking about "Tradition, Arts, and Future of the American Indian" on June 9, 1976.

748. Sound recording. "Land as Symbol: The American Indian." Washington, D.C.: National Public Radio (NPR), 1981, ©1979. Sound cassette (1), 59 min., analog, 1⅞ ips, mono. Author Peter Nabokov interviews Momaday about the Indian's relationship with the earth.

749. Sound recording. "N. Scott Momaday Interview with Kay Bonetti." Columbia, Missouri: American Audio Prose Library, 1983. Sound cassette (1), 69 min., analog, 1⅞ ips, mono., AAPL No. 3092. Recorded in 1983 in Tucson, Arizona,

Momaday talks about the process of writing and his identity as an American Indian.

750. Sound recording. "N. Scott Momaday Reads from *House Made of Dawn, The Gourd Dancer, The Names* . . . ." Columbia, Missouri: American Audio Prose Library, 1983. Sound cassette (1), 40 min., analog, mono., AAPL No. 3091.

751. Sound recording. "N. Scott Momaday: Storyteller." Music and sound effects by Rusty Crutcher. Santa Fe, New Mexico: Lotus Press, 1989. Sound cassette (1), 60 min., analog. Momaday reads from *The Ancient Child, House Made of Dawn, The Way to Rainy Mountain,* and poetry collections. He also talks about his Kiowa name. This was reviewed by Alan Cheuse in the March 1992 issue of *Forbes,* pp. S25–S26.

752. Sound recording. "An Evening with N. Scott Momaday." Recorded February 26, 1993. This recording is cataloged in the University of California Libraries Online Catalog.

753. Sound recording. Accompanies *Navajo Place Names: An Observer's Guide,* compiled and written by Alan Wilson, with Gene Dennison, Navajo consultant. Foreword by N. Scott Momaday. Guilford, Connecticut: J. Norton Publishers, 1995. Cassette (1), 54 min., analog, mono.

754. Sound recording—Audiobook. "StoryLines Southwest: *House Made of Dawn.*" Hosted by Rachel Maurer and Jack Loeffler. StoryLines America, no. 5. Albuquerque, New Mexico: KUNM, 1997. Cassettes (2), 2 hrs., analog. Funded by the National Endowment for the Humanities and the American Library Association. *House Made of Dawn* is discussed by the late Paula Gunn Allen, Susan Scarberry-García, and Momaday. Originally broadcast in October 1997 by KUNM 89.9 (Public Radio for Central and Northern New Mexico).

755. Sound recording—Audiobook. *House Made of Dawn.* Narrated by George Guidall. Classics on Cassette series. Prince Frederick, Maryland: Recorded Books, 1999. Cassettes (5), 7 hrs., analog. Also available on CD.

756. Sound recording—Cassette. "The Best American Essays of the Century." Vol. 2. Compiled by Joyce Carol Oates et al. Boston: Houghton Mifflin, 2001. The "Introduction" to *The Way to Rainy Mountain* is included in this selection of essays.

757. Sound recording. "Circle of Wonder: A Native American Christmas Story," read by N. Scott Momaday. Albuquerque: University of New Mexico Press,

2001. Cassette (1), 60 min., analog, stereo, 1⅞ ips. Also on CD. Momaday reads from his first children's book.

758. Sound recording—CD. "The Radio Adaptation of N. Scott Momaday's *The Indolent Boys*." This is the full production presented by the Autry Museum of Western Heritage and Wells Fargo Radio Theater. Los Angeles: Tubert Productions, 2003. Sound disc (1), 60 min., digital, 4¾ in.

759. Sound recording—CD. "Voices of the Southwest 2004." Voices of the Southwest Literature Series, no. 2. Albuquerque: University of New Mexico Press, ©2004. Sound discs (5), digital, stereo, 4¾ in. Disc no. 3 includes Momaday's lecture given during this series held at the university in 2004.

760. Sound recording—CD. "Poetry Out Loud: National Recitation Contest; Performing Poetry, An Audio Guide." Presented by the National Endowment for the Arts and The Poetry Foundation. Produced by Dan Stone. Washington, D.C.: NEA, 2005. Sound disc (1), 60 min. Introduced by Dana Gioia, poet and director of the National Endowment for the Arts. Poetry is read by well-known speakers and performers. Momaday reads his and others' poems. See also the sections "Anthologies and Literary Collections" and "Internet and Online Resources."

761. Sound recording—CD. "A Multicultural Reader, Collection Two," by Julie A. Schumacher and Rebecca Christian. Princeton, New Jersey: Recording for the Blind and Dyslexic, 2006. This is only one example of numerous recordings containing writings by Momaday from anthologies and other sources that have been produced by this organization.

762. Sound recording—Audiobook. "An Introduction to *The Death of Ivan Ilyich* by Leo Tolstoy." Written and produced by Dan Stone; narrated by Dana Gioia. Washington, D.C.: National Endowment for the Arts, 2007. Sound disc (1), 41 min., digital, 4¾ in. This reading is part of the national "Big Read" series. Momaday participates in the reading of excerpts from the book.

763. Sound recording—CD. *Pulling Down the Clouds*. N. Scott Momaday et al. Edited by Tanya Thrasher. Washington, D.C.: National Museum of the American Indian, Smithsonian Institution, 2007. Sound disc (1), 70 min., digital, 4¾ in., with music. Fifteen contemporary American Indian writers read and discuss their work in this anthology. Momaday reads "Sacagawea" from his *The Voices of Encounter*.

Video Recordings (VHS/DVD)

764. Video recording (VHS). *A Conversation with N. Scott. Momaday.* Interview conducted by Dr. Larry Evers and University of Arizona students of American Indian literature in the studios of KUAT-TV (PBS), Tucson, Arizona, in November 1974. Produced by KUAT-TV. Momaday was a guest of the University of Arizona Poetry Center, the Amerind Club, and the American Indian Studies Program. See also the preceding section, "Interviews and Conversations with N. Scott Momaday."

765. Video recording (VHS). *The Lakota: One Nation on the Plains.* Produced and directed by Frank Cantor; written by Julia Welch. Based on a script by Robert Reilly. Great Plains Experience Series, no. 2. Lincoln, Nebraska: Great Plains National Instructional Library (GPN), 1978.

766. Video recording (VHS). *White Man's Way.* Produced, written, and directed by Christine Lesiak; Native American Public Broadcasting Consortium, Inc. Lincoln, Nebraska: GPN, ©1986. The subject is the establishment by the U.S. government of off-reservation boarding schools.

767. Video recording (VHS and DVD). *Distant Voices, Thunder Words.* Native American Public Broadcasting Consortium, Nebraska Educational Television Council for Higher Education (NETCHE); produced, directed, and edited by Luis Peon Casanova, written by Lori Maass Vidlak, and narrated by N. Scott Momaday. Lincoln, Nebraska: GPN, 1990, ©2000. Videocassette (1), 60 min., sound, color, ½ in. This was published in DVD by GPN in 2000.

768. Video recording (VHS). *Winds of Change: A Matter of Promises.* Host and narrator, N. Scott Momaday. Produced by Carol Cotter et al., through the facilities of WHA-TV, the Wisconsin Educational Communications Board, and the Board of Regents of the University of Wisconsin System. Alexandria, Virginia: PBS Home Video, 1990; distributed by Pacific Arts Video. Videocassette (1), 60 min., sound, color, ½ in. Music by R. Carlos Nakai. Originally shown on television, this program is about three American Indian Nations, Onondaga, Navajo, and Lummi, and how these societies are meeting the challenges of preserving their cultures.

769. Video recording (VHS). *Last Stand at Little Big Horn.* Produced and directed by Paul Stekler, written by Paul Stekler and James Welch, and edited by Michael Goldman. Executive producer, Judy Crichton. Narrated by N. Scott Momaday. Presented by WGBH/Boston, WNET/New York, and KCET/Los

Angeles. Alexandria, Virginia: PBS Home Video, ©1992. Videocassette (1), 60 min., sound, mostly black and white, ½ in. Originally broadcast by PBS in 1983 as part of *The American Experience* (television series), this program won an Emmy Award.

770. Video recording (VHS). *Our Vanishing Forests.* A production of Public Communications, Inc., and Public Interest Video Network. Producer-director, Arlen J. Slobodow; producer, Pamela Westfall–Rosen. Narrated by N. Scott Momaday. Bethesda, Maryland: Public Interest Video Network, 1992. Videocassette (1), 58 min., sound, color, ½ in. This program focuses on how the national forests of the United States have been mismanaged.

771. Video recording (VHS). *Cry of the Earth.* Executive producers, Carina Cowtright and John Phillip Santos; producers, Lavina Adamson and Lou Delemos; editing by Jon Fordham. Music by R. Carlos Nakai. New York: Crescentera, 1993. Videocassettes (3), 326 min. total, sound, color, ½ in. In 1993 spiritual leaders of seven indigenous nations of North America came to the United Nations to deliver their traditional prophecies relating to the earth. Momaday made a presentation at this gathering.

772. Video recording (VHS and DVD). *More Than Bows and Arrows.* A film by Conrad Denke et al. Produced by Camera One Productions and directed by Gray Warriner. Narrated by N. Scott Momaday. Ancient America Series. Seattle, WA: Camera One Productions; 13th Regional Corp., 1994. Videocassette (1), 54 min., sound, color, ½ in. Released in DVD by Camera One, ©2007. Numerous ways in which American Indians have contributed to and shaped American culture are presented.

773. Video recording (VHS and DVD). *Native American Novelists: N. Scott Momaday.* A film by Matteo Bellinelli; written by Andrea Belloni in collaboration with Claudio Belotti et al. Produced by Radiotelevisione della Svizzera italiana. Native American Novelists Series, vol. 1. Princeton, New Jersey: Films for the Humanities and Sciences, 1995. Videocassette (1), 50 min., sound, color, ½ in. Momaday speaks on what it means as a Native American to be an American citizen and discusses his work. Released in DVD in 2004.

774. Video recording (VHS). *Momaday: Voice of the West.* Produced and directed by Jean Walkinshaw; KCTS Television, Seattle. Distributed by PBS Video, ©1996. Videocassette (1), 30 min., sound, color, ½ in. Profiles Momaday and presents readings by him. A release of a 1995 television production.

775. Video recording (VHS and DVD). *The West.* A film by Ken Burns. Produced

and directed by Stephen Ives; written by Geoffrey C. Ward and Dayton Duncan. Videodiscs (5), 720 min., 4¾ in. On-screen commentary by N. Scott Momaday. Alexandria, Virginia: PBS Video; Burbank, California: Warner Home Video, ©2003. Originally televised on PBS in 1996.

776. Video recording (DVD). "Billy the Kid." Produced by Kurtis Productions. New York: A&E Television Networks; distributed by New Video Group, 2004. Videodisc (1), 50 min., sound, color, 4¾ in. Momaday provides commentary. The original broadcast appeared on The History Channel® in 2004. This DVD was distributed by New Video in 2007, ©2004.

777. Video recording (DVD). "Remembered Earth: New Mexico's High Desert." Written and produced by John Grabowska. Narrated by Irene Bedard, with interpretative remarks by N. Scott Momaday. Boise: Idaho Public Television, ©2006. Videodisc (1), 27 min., sound, color, 4¾ in. Landscape and land ethics are the subjects. Momaday recites "The Remembered Earth."

778. Video recording (DVD). "Kit Carson." Written by Michelle Ferrari and narrated by Michael Murphy. Produced and directed by Stephen Ives. N. Scott Momaday participates as an on-camera interview subject. *The American Experience* series; New Perspectives on the West. PBS Video, ©2008. Videodisc (1), 90 min., sound, color, 4¾ in.

Musical Scores (Printed Music)

779. Musical Score. *Dream of the Morning Sky.* (1982–83). In three parts for large orchestra, with soprano voice in Part III. By Aaron Jay Kernis and N. Scott Momaday. New York: Associated Music Publishers, 1983. 78 pp.

780. Musical Score. *Beyond the Silence of Sorrow: For Soprano and Orchestra,* by Roberto Sierra with words by N. Scott Momaday. Verona, New Jersey: Subito Music, 2002. 62 pp.

Locations of Special Collections and Archives Containing Information about Momaday and His Works

Special collections and archives containing archived materials by and about Momaday are housed at a number of university libraries. A list of such libraries is provided below. Correspondence and other special materials pertaining to Momaday are also found in the papers of other persons. Information regarding archival collections should be directed to special collections or reference departments by mail, e-mail, or phone. Many libraries require written requests for information. Researchers will also want to contact other libraries, public and private, particularly at locations where Momaday has lived and taught. A growing number of online archives and other electronic resources are available for research.

New Mexico State University, Las Cruces

Pennsylvania State University, University Park

Stanford University, Palo Alto, California

Texas State University, San Marcos

University of Arizona, Tucson

University of California, Berkeley

University of California, Los Angeles

University of California, Santa Barbara

University of Minnesota, Minneapolis

University of New Mexico and Center for Southwest Research, Albuquerque

University of Southern California, Los Angeles

Examples of contents of archival collections related to Momaday are provided below:

Stanford University Special Collections, housed in the Cecil H. Green Library on the Stanford campus, include an uncorrected manuscript of the first edition of *The Ancient Child: A Novel*, correspondence in the Yvor Winters and Janet Lewis Papers, and miscellaneous items in the papers of Albert J. Guerard and Wallace Stegner.

University of California, Berkeley, Archive and Manuscript Collections include the N. Scott Momaday Papers, 1963–1972, composed of correspondence with publishers, essays and poems, a manuscript of *House Made of Dawn,* a publisher's typescript and two sets of revised galleys of *The Names,* and a musical score manuscript of *Dream of the Morning Sky* (1983).

Part III

Works about N. Scott Momaday and His Works

A Bibliography

Books

1973 Trimble, Martha Scott. *N. Scott Momaday.* Boise State College Western Writers, no. 9. Boise, Idaho: Boise State College. 46 pp.

1985 Schubnell, Matthias. *N. Scott Momaday: The Cultural and Literary Background.* Norman: University of Oklahoma Press. 336 pp. Schubnell, a native of Freiburg, Germany, studied as a Rhodes Scholar at the University of Oxford, where he was awarded the PhD degree. He has taught in academic positions in the United States and written essays about Momaday, in addition to the two books listed.

1986 Georgi-Findlay, Brigitte. *Tradition und Moderne in der zeitgenössischen indianischen Literatur der USA: N. Scott Momaday's Roman "House Made of Dawn."* Serie Literatur und Geschichte; Pahl-Rugenstein Hochschulschriften Gesellschafts und Naturwissenschaften, no. 219. Cologne, Germany: Pahl-Rugenstein. 352 pp.

1988 Roemer, Kenneth M., ed. *Approaches to Teaching Momaday's "The Way to Rainy Mountain."* Approaches to Teaching World Literature, no. 17, edited by Joseph Gibaldi. New York: Modern Language Association of America. 172 pp.

1989 Woodard, Charles L. *Ancestral Voice: Conversations with N. Scott Momaday.* Edited by Charles L. Woodard. Lincoln: University of Nebraska Press. 229 pp.

1990 Scarberry-García, Susan. *Landmarks of Healing: A Study of "House Made of Dawn."* Foreword by Andrew Wiget. Albuquerque: University of New Mexico Press. 208 pp.

1997 Pellerin, Simone. *N. Scott Momaday.* Collection Première Leçon sur. Paris: Ellipses. 112 pp. (in French)

1997 Rigal-Cellard, Bernadette, ed. *"House Made of Dawn": N. Scott Momaday.* Paris: Ellipses, 176 pp. This collection of essays in French and English includes a biographical essay about Momaday in French.

1997 ———, ed. *N. Scott Momaday: "House Made of Dawn."* Collection CNED-Didier Concours. Paris: Didier Érudition-CNED (Centre National d'Enseignement à Distance). 216 pp. (in English)

1997 Schubnell, Matthias, ed. *Conversations with N. Scott Momaday.* Literary Conversations. Jackson: University of Mississippi Press. 237 pp.

2001 Schweninger, Lee. *N. Scott Momaday.* Literary Masters, vol. 12. Detroit: Gale Group. 175 pp.

2005 Garrait-Bourrier, Anne. *N. Scott Momaday, l'homme-ours: Voix et regard.* Collection Littératures. Clermont-Ferrand, France: Presses Universitaires Blaise Pascal. 394 pp. (in French)

2007 Charles, Jim. *Reading, Learning, Teaching: N. Scott Momaday.* Confronting the Text, Confronting the World, vol. 5, edited by P. L. Thomas. New York: Peter Lang. 150 pp.

Critical, Literary, and Other Essays in Books and Journals

Most of the citations that follow are accompanied by an annotation, except when the title of an essay describes a primary subject or subjects and includes the title of the work or works by Momaday that are discussed in the essay.

1967

781. Winters, Yvor. "Post-Symbolist Methods." Chapter 5 in *Forms of Discovery: Critical and Historical Essays on the Forms of the Short Poem in English*. Chicago: Alan Swallow, 1967. 288–94, 296–97, 368. Winters discusses Momaday's poetry, in particular "The Bear," and explains the meaning of "post-Symbolist." This essay, in a slightly different form, appeared as the foreword to *The Complete Poems of Frederick Goddard Tuckerman*, edited by N. Scott Momaday (Oxford University Press, 1965).

1970

782. Fields, Kenneth. "More than Language Means." *Southern Review*, n.s., 6, no. 1 (January 1970): 196–204. Included in this review essay about *The Way to Rainy Mountain* are comments about Momaday's writing and published poetry.

783. Haslam, Gerald. "American Indians: Poets of the Cosmos." *Western American Literature* 5, no. 1 (Spring 1970): 25–27. Haslam critiques *House Made of Dawn* and remarks about its reception by some critics. In discussing poetry, he describes "Angle of Geese" as "a combination of discipline, imagination, and esthetic symmetry" (26).

1971

784. Kaye, Howard. "The Post-Symbolist Poetry of Yvor Winters." *Southern Review*, n.s., 7, no. 1 (January 1971): 176–97. In his discussion of Winters's poetry, Kaye comments about Momaday's years of study as Winters's doctoral student.

1972

785. Garrett, Roland. "The Notion of Language in Some Kiowa Folk Tales." *Indian Historian* 5, no. 2 (Summer 1972): 32–37, 42. The first six stories from the Kiowa oral tradition in *The Way to Rainy Mountain* are presented to demonstrate the role of language in each story.

786. Hylton, Marion Willard. "On a Trail of Pollen: Momaday's *House Made of Dawn*." *Critique: Studies in Modern Fiction* 14, no. 2 (Summer 1972): 60–69.

Focuses on Abel, the novel's protagonist, and the clash of cultures in his struggle toward spiritual healing.

1973

787. Oleson, Carole. "The Remembered Earth: Momaday's *House Made of Dawn*." *South Dakota Review* 11, no. 1 (Spring 1973): 59–78. Oleson considers landscape of central importance to Abel's recovery of self.

788. Porter, Mark. "Mysticism of the Land and the Western Novel." *South Dakota Review* 11, no. 1 (Spring 1973): 79–91. Porter includes in Part 3 of this essay, pp. 82–83, the Navajo Night Chant, which provided the title of *House Made of Dawn*.

789. Sanders, Thomas E., and Walter W. Peek. "Anguish, Angry, Articulate: Current Voices in Poetry, Prose, and Protest." *Literature of the American Indian*, edited by Sanders and Peek. Beverly Hills, California: Glencoe Press, 1973. 445–51. Two critical reviews of *House Made of Dawn* are compared: a negative review by William James Smith and a positive one by Marshall Sprague. These reviews are cited in the section "Reviews of Books in Journals and Periodicals."

1974

790. McAllister, Harold S. "Incarnate Grace and the Paths of Salvation in *House Made of Dawn*." *South Dakota Review* 12, no. 4 (Winter 1974–75): 115–25. This essay focuses on the character of Angela Grace St. John.

1975

791. Billingsley, R. G. "*House Made of Dawn*: Momaday's Treatise on the Word." *Southwestern American Literature*, vol. 5 (1975): 81–87.

792. Finlay, John. "N. Scott Momaday's *Angle of Geese*." *Southern Review* n.s., 11, no. 3 (Summer 1975): 658–61. This essay critiques Momaday's first published poetry collection. Finlay also comments about *The Way to Rainy Mountain*.

793. Lincoln, Kenneth. "Native American Tribal Poetics." *Southwest Review* 60, no. 2 (Spring 1975): 101–16. Lincoln paraphrases "The Story of the Arrowmaker" and quotes "The Man Made of Words" in this essay about the oral literatures of Native Americans.

794. McAllister, Harold S. "Be a Man, Be a Woman: Androgyny in *House Made of Dawn*." *American Indian Quarterly* 2, no. 1 (Spring 1975): 14–22.

795. Nicholas, Charles A. "*The Way to Rainy Mountain*: N. Scott Momaday's Hard

Journey Back." *South Dakota Review* 13, no. 4 (Winter 1975–76): 149–58. Nicholas explores "the many journeys in the one" and concludes that much of Momaday's writing represents "a continuing commentary on the journey" (149).

796. Strelke, Barbara. "N. Scott Momaday: Racial Memory and Individual Imagination." In *Literature of the American Indians: Views and Interpretations; A Gathering of Indian Memories, Symbolic Contexts, and Literary Criticism,* edited by Abraham Chapman. New York: New American Library, 1975. 348–57. Strelke explores Momaday's combining of elements of American Indian culture and art with elements of Western literature and philosophy in *House Made of Dawn* and *The Way to Rainy Mountain.*

797. Trimmer, Joseph F. "Native Americans and the American Mix: N. Scott Momaday's *House Made of Dawn.*" *Indiana Social Studies Quarterly* 28, no. 2 (Autumn 1975): 75–91.

1976

798. Davis, Jack L. "The Whorf Hypothesis and Native American Literature." *South Dakota Review* 14, no. 2 (Summer 1976): 59–72. This hypothesis of linguistic relativity, named for Benjamin Lee Whorf, postulates that one's perception of the world and ways of thinking are greatly influenced by the structure of his or her language. Davis examines *House Made of Dawn* (1968) and Frank Waters's *The Man Who Killed the Deer* (1942).

799. Lincoln, Kenneth. "Tribal Poetics of Native America." *American Indian Culture and Research Journal* 1, no. 4 (1976): 14–21. Lincoln discusses the distinctive elements of the oral literatures of American Indians and includes "The Story of the Arrowmaker."

800. Robinson, David E. "Angles of Vision in N. Scott Momaday's *House Made of Dawn.*" In *Selected Proceedings of the Third Annual Conference on Minority Studies, April 1975,* edited by George E. Carter and James R. Parker. LaCrosse, Wisconsin: Institute for Minority Studies, 1976. 129–41.

1977

801. Davis, Jack L. "Language and Consciousness in *House Made of Dawn.*" *New America* 3 (Summer–Fall 1977): 56–59.

802. Evers, Lawrence J. "Words and Place: A Reading of *House Made of Dawn.*" *Western American Literature* 11, no. 4 (Winter 1977): 297–320. Reprinted in *Critical Essays on Native American Literature,* edited by Andrew Wiget.

Boston: G. K. Hall, 1985. 211–30. Reprinted in *Critical Perspectives on Native American Fiction*, edited by Richard F. Fleck. Washington, D.C.: Three Continents Press, 1993. 114–33. Reprinted in *Native-American Writers*, edited and with an introduction by Harold Bloom. Modern Critical Views. Philadelphia: Chelsea House, 1998. 5–23.

803. Ramsey, Paul. "Faith and Form: Some American Poetry of 1976." *Sewanee Review* 85 (Summer 1977): 532–40. *The Gourd Dancer*, Momaday's second book of poetry, is critiqued within this essay.

804. Roemer, Kenneth M. "Bear and Elk: The Nature(s) of Contemporary American Indian Poetry." *Journal of Ethnic Studies* 5, no. 2 (Summer 1977): 69–79. A revised version of this essay appeared in *Studies in American Indian Literature: Critical Essays and Course Designs*, edited by Paula Gunn Allen. New York: Modern Language Association of America, 1983. 178–89. Roemer compares Momaday's "The Bear" and Leslie Marmon Silko's "Snow Elk" in this overview of poetry.

805. Watkins, Floyd C. "Culture versus Anonymity in *House Made of Dawn*." *In Time and Place: Some Origins of American Fiction*. Athens: University of Georgia Press, 1977. 133–71.

806. Young, Jim. "Tradition and the Experimental." *The Compass* (Edmonton, Alberta, Canada) no. 1 (1977): 99–107. This essay comments on the structure of *The Way to Rainy Mountain*.

1978

807. Barry, Nora Baker. "'The Bear's Son Folk Tale' in *When the Legends Die* and *House Made of Dawn*." *Western American Literature* 12, no. 4 (Winter 1978): 275–87. Barry concludes that Hal Borland and Momaday used elements of the ancient tale in creating a quality of heroic legend in these novels.

808. Bloodworth, William. "Neihardt, Momaday, and the Art of Indian Autobiography." In *Where the West Begins: Essays on Middle Border and Siouxland Writings in Honor of Herbert Krause*, edited by Arthur R. Huseboe and William Geyer. Sioux Falls, South Dakota: Center for Western Studies Press, Augustana College, 1978. 152–60. This essay also appeared in *Teaching English in the Two-Year College* 4, no. 2 (1978): 137–43.

809. ———. "Varieties of American Indian Autobiography." *MELUS* (Journal of the Society for the Study of the Multi-ethnic Literature of the United States) 5, no. 3 (Autumn 1978): 67–81.

810. Dickinson-Brown, Roger. "The Art and Importance of N. Scott Momaday." *Southern Review*, n.s., 14, no. 1 (January 1978): 30–45. While he compliments Momaday on his genius and exceptional range, Dickinson-Brown describes *House Made of Dawn* as "a memorable failure" (30). He praises *The Way to Rainy Mountain* and Momaday's poetry, stating that "Angle of Geese" is the best example of Momaday's "importance to contemporary literature." (45).

811. Espey, David B. "Endings in Contemporary American Indian Fiction." *Western American Literature* 13, no. 2 (Summer 1978): 133–39. *House Made of Dawn* and its protagonist are included in this study of novels with endings having to do with death and funeral rituals.

812. Kerr, Baine. "The Novel as Sacred Text: N. Scott Momaday's Myth-making Ethic." *Southwest Review* 63, no. 2 (Spring 1978): 172–79. Kerr explores this ethic in *House Made of Dawn*.

813. Larson, Charles R. "The Emergence of American Indian Fiction." Chapter 1 in *American Indian Fiction*. Albuquerque: University of New Mexico Press, 1978. 1–16. This is the first book-length study of novels by American Indians. It presents fiction writers from three generations.

814. ———. "Rejection: The Reluctant Return." Chapter 4 in *American Indian Fiction*. Albuquerque: University of New Mexico Press, 1978. 66–96. Larson examines *House Made of Dawn* and D'Arcy McNickle's *The Surrounded* (1936) and finds these two novels, separated by thirty-two years, share a number of structural and thematic similarities.

815. ———. "The Figure in the Dark Forest." Chapter 7 in *American Indian Fiction*. Albuquerque: University of New Mexico Press, 1978. 165–72. Larson presents fiction writers from the 1920s to contemporary times, including Momaday.

816. Lincoln, Kenneth. "(Native) American Poetries." *Southwest Review* 63, no. 4 (Autumn 1978): 367–84. Lincoln continues his discussion about American Indian literature begun in the Spring 1975 issue.

817. McAllister, Mick. "The Topology of Remembrance in *The Way to Rainy Mountain*." *Denver Quarterly* 12, no. 4 (Winter 1978): 19–31.

818. Nabokov, Peter. "American Indian Literature: A Tradition of Renewal." *ASAIL Newsletter*, ser. 1, vol. 2, no. 3 (Autumn 1978): 31-40. *House Made of Dawn* and *The Names* are included in this essay about Indian writers' "abiding devotion to the traditional tribal past" (38–39).

819. Standiford, Lester A. "Worlds Made of Dawn: Characteristic Image and Incident in Native American Imaginative Literature." In *Ethnic Literatures since 1776: The Many Voices of America,* edited by Wolodymyr T. Zyla and Wendell M. Aycock. Comparative Literature Symposium (9th: 1976). Lubbock: Texas Tech Press, 1978. 327–52. Reprinted in *Three American Literatures,* edited by Houston A. Baker, Jr. New York: Modern Language Association of America, 1982. 168–96. Standiford examines *House Made of Dawn, The Way to Rainy Mountain,* and Momaday's poetry, including "Angle of Geese," in this study.

820. Velie, Alan R. "Cain and Abel in N. Scott Momaday's *House Made of Dawn.*" *Journal of the West* 17 (April 1978): 55–62.

821. Woodard, Charles L. "Momaday's *House Made of Dawn.*" *Explicator* 36, no. 2 (Winter 1978): 27–28. Woodard proposes an alternative interpretation of the conclusion of *House Made of Dawn.*

1979

822. Beidler, Peter G. "Animals and Human Development in the Contemporary American Indian Novel." *Western American Literature* 14, no. 2 (Summer 1979): 133–48. This essay explores the role of animals in helping Abel of *House Made of Dawn* and other protagonists to find their way to peace and a meaningful place in the world. In particular, see pp. 134–39.

823. Berner, Robert L. "N. Scott Momaday: Beyond Rainy Mountain." *American Indian Culture and Research Journal* 3, no. 1 (1979): 57–67. This essay focuses on the structure and language of *The Way to Rainy Mountain.*

824. Doudoroff, Michael. "N. Scott Momaday y la novela indigenista en inglés." *Texto Critico* (Xalapa, Mexico) 5, no. 15 (October–December 1979): 180–85. *House Made of Dawn* is included in Doudoroff's study.

825. Lattin, Vernon E. "The Quest for Mythic Vision in Contemporary Native American and Chicano Fiction." *American Literature* 50, no. 4 (January 1979): 625–40. Lattin explores the mythic quest in *House Made of Dawn* and in Rudolfo A. Anaya's *Bless Me, Ultima* (1972).

826. Rosen, Kenneth. "American Indian Literature: Current Condition and Suggested Research." *American Indian Culture and Research Journal* 3, no. 2 (1979): 57–66. Rosen emphasizes the need for increased scholarly and critical research, citing Charles R. Larson's *American Indian Fiction* (1978) as the only scholarly full-length study of novels by Native American writers at the time of this essay's publication.

827. Schneider, Jack W. "The New Indian: Alienation and the Rise of the Indian Novel." *South Dakota Review* 17, no. 4 (Winter 1979–80): 67–76. In his survey of fifteen works of fiction, including *House Made of Dawn,* Schneider did not find one case of an Indian protagonist successfully existing in Anglo society.

828. Zachrau, Thekla. "N. Scott Momaday: Towards an Indian Identity." *American Indian Culture and Research Journal* 3, no. 1 (1979): 39–56. This essay also appeared in *Dutch Quarterly Review of Anglo-American Letters* (Amsterdam, The Netherlands) 9 (1979): 52–70. In examining the search for identity in *House Made of Dawn, The Way to Rainy Mountain,* and *The Names,* Zachrau concludes that *The Names* completes a cycle begun by the first book.

1980

829. Allen, Paula Gunn. "A Stranger in My Own Life: Alienation in American Indian Prose and Poetry." *MELUS* 7, no. 2 (Summer 1980): 3–19. Allen presented three categories of responses to alienation. She included *House Made of Dawn* and its protagonist in her discussion on pp. 11–13.

830. Bromley, Anne. "Renegade Wants the Word: Contemporary Native American Poetry." *Literary Review* 23, no. 3 (Spring 1980): 413–21. This essay critiques poetry by Momaday, Janet Campbell Hale, Wendy Rose, and James Welch.

831. Brumble, H. David, III. "Anthropologists, Novelists, and Indian Sacred Material." *Canadian Review of American Studies* 11, no. 1 (Summer 1980): 32–48. This essay was published with changes in *Smoothing the Ground: Essays on Native American Oral Literature,* edited by Brian Swann. Berkeley: University of California Press, 1983. 283–300.

832. Buller, Galen. "New Interpretations of Native American Literature: A Survival Technique." *American Indian Culture and Research Journal* 4, nos. 1–2 (1980): 165–77. Buller argues that American Indian literature differs as a body of literature from that designated as American literature in five critical aspects, including a significantly different worldview. His discussion includes *House Made of Dawn, The Way to Rainy Mountain,* and Momaday's address "The Man Made of Words."

833. Chambers, Mary P. "White Man, White Whale: Albinism in *House Made of Dawn.*" *ASAIL Newsletter,* ser. 1, 4, no. 4 (Autumn 1980): 54–57.

834. Hogan, Linda. "Who Puts Together." *Denver Quarterly* 14, no. 4 (1980): 103–11. Reprinted in *Studies in American Indian Literature: Critical Essays and Course Designs,* edited by Paula Gunn Allen. New York: Modern

Language Association of America, 1983. 169–77. Reprinted in *American Indian Quarterly* 10, no. 2 (1986): 101–17. Reprinted in *Critical Perspectives on Native American Fiction,* edited by Richard F. Fleck. Washington, D.C.: Three Continents Press, 1993. 134–42. Hogan discusses Momaday's use of the Navajo Night Chant in *House Made of Dawn* and the importance of language and creative visualization in the healing process.

835. Lincoln, Kenneth. "Introduction: 'Trans—:' 'To the Other Side of, Over, Across.'" "Word Senders: Special Issue on American Indian Translation," edited by K. Lincoln. *American Indian Culture and Research Journal* 4, nos. 1–2 (1980): 1–17. Momaday's essay, "The Morality of Indian Hating" (1964), is quoted in Lincoln's introduction concerning the translation of traditional forms of American Indian literatures.

836. ———. "Introduction: Native Literatures." "Special Issue No. 2 on American Indian Translation," edited by K. Lincoln. *American Indian Culture and Research Journal* 4, no. 4 (1980): 1–4. In his discussion about Indian poets and poetry, Lincoln includes remarks about Momaday's belief that being Indian is an idea of oneself.

837. McAllister, Mick. "The Color of Meat, the Color of Bone." *Denver Quarterly* 14, no. 4 (1980): 10–18. McAllister considers issues associated with classifying books about American Indians as American Indian literature. He focuses on Frank Waters's *The Man Who Killed the Deer* and on *House Made of Dawn,* books about Pueblo Indians by authors who are outsiders to them.

838. Mason, Kenneth C. "Beautyway: The Poetry of N. Scott Momaday." *South Dakota Review* 18, no. 2 (Summer 1980): 61–83. This review essay provides an analysis of the poems published in *The Gourd Dancer* (1976).

839. Prampolini, Gaetano. "On N. Scott Momaday's *House Made of Dawn.*" *Dismisura, Rivista Bimestrale di Produzione and Crit. Culturale* (Alatri, Italy) 9, nos. 39–50 (1980): 58–75.

840. Ruppert, James. "The Uses of Oral Tradition in Six Contemporary Native American Poets." *American Indian Culture and Research Journal* 4, no. 4 (1980): 87–110. This essay begins with an excerpt from Momaday's "A Note on Contemporary Native American Poetry," first published in Duane Niatum's *Carriers of the Dream Wheel* (1975). The six poets studied are Elizabeth Cook-Lynn, Liz Sohappy Bahe, Wendy Rose, Peter Blue Cloud, Maurine Kenny, and Ray Young Bear. Ruppert confirms Momaday's insights concerning the continuance of oral tradition in contemporary Native American poetry.

841. Vecsey, Christopher. "American Indian Environmental Religions." Chapter 1 in *American Indian Environments: Ecological Issues in Native American History,* edited by C. Vecsey and Robert W. Venables. Syracuse, New York: Syracuse University Press, 1980. 6–7. Vecsey believes that the two most famous Indian writers who have steadily expressed an Indian ecologist image have been Momaday and Vine Deloria, Jr.

842. Waniek, Marilyn Nelson. "The Power of Language in N. Scott Momaday's *House Made of Dawn.*" *Minority Voices* 4, no. 1 (Spring 1980): 23–28. Waniek refers to Momaday's essay, "The Story of the Arrowmaker," published in the *New York Times* in 1969, reflecting his belief in the power of language that was evident in his award-winning novel.

1981

843. Giordano, Fedora. "Translating the Sacred: The Poet and the Shaman." In *North American Indian Studies: European Contributions,* edited by Pieter Hovens. Göttingen, Germany: Edition Herodot, 1981. 109–21. Giordano quotes Momaday from *The Way to Rainy Mountain* on the power of the word.

844. Jahner, Elaine. "Introduction: American Indian Writers and the Tyranny of Expectations." *Book Forum* 5, no. 3 (1981): 343–48. Jahner comments on Momaday being one of the small number of American Indian writers to become a public figure.

845. Ortiz, Simon J. "Towards a National Indian Literature: Cultural Authenticity in Nationalism." *MELUS* 8, no. 2 (Summer 1981): 7–12. Ortiz maintains that the continuing use of the oral tradition is evidence of ongoing resistance and that it has spurred the outpouring of works by Indian authors and created a nationalistic aspect to their voices. He draws upon *House Made of Dawn* and Abel, its protagonist, in his discussion. This essay is also the Appendix of *American Indian Literary Nationalism,* by Jace Weaver, Craig Womack, and Robert Warrior. Foreword by Simon Ortiz. Albuquerque: University of New Mexico Press, 2006. 253–60.

1982

846. Cederstrom, Lorelei. "Myth and Ceremony in Contemporary North American Native Fiction." *Canadian Journal of Native Studies* 2, no. 2 (1982): 285–301. Cederstrom examines how Momaday and others use myth and ceremony in structuring their novels and in giving meaning to protagonists' lives.

847. Clements, William M. "Momaday's *House Made of Dawn.*" *Explicator* 41, no. 1

(Fall 1982): 60–62. This critique provides an analysis of plot, characters, and primary themes.

848. Lincoln, Kenneth. "A Contemporary Tribe of Poets." *American Indian Culture and Research Journal* 6, no. 1 (1982): 79–101. Lincoln comments on anthologies of works by Native American poets published in the 1970s, including Duane Niatum's *Carriers of the Dream Wheel* (1975) and Geary Hobson's *Remembered Earth* (1979, 1981). Both titles are from Momaday's writings. A bibliography of twenty-two anthologies is on pp. 100–101.

849. ———. "Native American Literatures: 'old like hills, like stars.'" In *Three American Literatures: Essays in Chicano, Native American, and Asian American Literatures for Teachers of American Literature,* edited by Houston A. Baker, Jr. New York: Modern Language Association of America, 1982. 80–167. See "Tribal Poetics," 88–106, and "Momaday's Way," 114–23, which discusses the making of *The Way to Rainy Mountain.*

850. Sharma, R. S. "Vision and Form in N. Scott Momaday's *House Made of Dawn.*" *Indian Journal of American Studies* (Hyderabad, India) 12, no. 1 (January 1982): 69–79. Sharma examines Momaday's depiction of the native vision of the world.

851. Velie, Alan R. "*House Made of Dawn*: Nobody's Protest Novel." Chapter 4 in *Four American Indian Literary Masters: N. Scott Momaday, James Welch, Leslie Marmon Silko, and Gerald Vizenor.* Norman: University of Oklahoma Press, 1982. 51–64.

852. ———. "Post-Symbolism and Prose Poems: Momaday's Poetry." Chapter 3 in *Four American Indian Literary Masters* (1982), 33–49.

853. ———. "The Search for Identity: N. Scott Momaday's Autobiographical Works." Chapter 2 in *Four American Indian Literary Masters* (1982), 11–31. (port.) Velie includes discussion of *The Names, The Way to Rainy Mountain,* and *House Made of Dawn.*

1983

854. Brumble, H. David, III. "Indian Sacred Materials: [Alfred L.] Kroeber, [Theodora] Kroeber, [Frank] Waters, and Momaday." In *Smoothing the Ground: Essays on Native American Oral Literature,* edited by Brian Swann. Berkeley: University of California Press, 1983. 283–300. Brumble focuses on attitudes related to the use of Indian materials, particularly the nonapologetic use by anthropologists and others. After surveying Momaday's primary

works, Brumble maintains that Momaday is not willing to reveal matters sacred to his forebears. See pp. 293–96.

855. ———. "Reasoning Together." In *Smoothing the Ground*, edited by Brian Swann. Berkeley: University of California Press, 1983. 347–64. Karl Kroeber, son of Alfred and Theodora Kroeber, comments on pp. 347–53 that Brumble overlooked some critical issues relating to Momaday and others. Brumble responds on pp. 353–64.

856. Castro, Michael. "The 1970s: An Uprising of Indian Writers." *Interpreting the Indian: Twentieth-Century Poets and the Native American*. Albuquerque: University of New Mexico Press, 1983. 155–73. On pp. 155–58, Castro includes *The Way to Rainy Mountain* and *The Names* in his discussion about autobiography and the merging of Native American literary traditions with techniques of Western autobiography.

857. Hirsch, Bernard. "Self-hatred and Spiritual Corruption in *House Made of Dawn*." *Western American Literature* 17, no. 4 (Winter 1983): 307–20. Hirsch delineates American Indian characters Martinez, Tosamah, and Benally and their relationships with and treatment of the protagonist Abel.

858. Hogan, Linda. "Who Puts Together." In *Studies in American Indian Literature: Critical Essays and Course Designs*, edited by Paula Gunn Allen. New York: Modern Language Association of America, 1983. 169–77. Published in *Denver Quarterly* in 1980. Hogan deals with the subject of healing and the inclusion of the Navajo Night Chant in *House Made of Dawn*.

859. Jahner, Elaine. "A Cultural Approach to American Indian Literature: Intermediate Genres and the Novel." In *Studies in American Indian Literature: Critical Essays and Course Designs*, edited by Paula Gunn Allen. New York: MLA, 1983. 216–23. Jahner presents an analysis of works that derive from both oral and written modes, including *House Made of Dawn* and *The Way to Rainy Mountain*.

860. ———. "Intermediate Forms between Oral and Written Literatures." In *Studies in American Indian Literature*, edited by Paula Gunn Allen (MLA, 1983). 66–74. Jahner describes *The Way to Rainy Mountain* as "an example of an intermediate or intermediary form of the highest literary quality" (74, n.4).

861. Krupat, Arnold. "Native American Literature and the Canon." "Special Issue on the Canon." *Critical Inquiry* 10, no. 1 (September 1983): 145–71. Most of this essay appeared later in Krupat's *The Voice in the Margin* (1989). *House*

Made of Dawn, *The Names*, *The Way to Rainy Mountain*, and “Angle of Geese” are included in Krupat’s essay.

862. Lincoln, Kenneth. “Introduction: ‘Sending a Voice.’” *Native American Renaissance*. Berkeley: University of California Press, 1983. 1–14. Momaday is among contemporary writers in Lincoln’s discussion of the Native American Renaissance, which he defines as “a written renewal of oral traditions translated into Western literary forms” (8).

863. ———. “A Contemporary Tribe of Poets.” Chapter 4 in *Native American Renaissance* (1983). Lincoln discusses poetry by Momaday and a number of his contemporaries. In particular, see pp. 62, 69, 76–77. This chapter originally appeared as a review essay in *American Indian Culture and Research Journal* 6, no. 1 (1982): 79–101.

864. ———. “Word Senders: Black Elk and N. Scott Momaday.” Chapter 5 in *Native American Renaissance* (1983), 82–121. The section “Momaday’s Way,” 95–116, focuses on his poetry, *The Journey of Tai-me*, and *The Way to Rainy Mountain*. It is followed by “‘In Beauty It Is Finished,’” 117–21, which discusses *House Made of Dawn* and its protagonist.

865. Lincoln, Kenneth. “Native American Literatures: ‘—old like hills, like stars.’” In Part One, “Context and Overview,” *Smoothing the Ground: Essays on Native American Oral Literature*, edited by Brian Swann. Berkeley: University of California Press, 1983. 3–38. Parts of this essay about the poetic traditions and literatures of Native Americans appeared earlier in *Southwest Review* (1975) and *American Indian Culture and Research Journal* (1976, 1980).

866. Ramsey, Jarold. “Tradition and Individual Talents in Modern Indian Writing.” *Reading the Fire: Essays in the Traditional Indian Literatures of the Far West*. Lincoln: University of Nebraska Press, 1983. 181–82, 187–89. Ramsey discusses the writing of *The Way to Rainy Mountain*. See also rev. ed. under 1999.

867. Raymond, Michael W. “Tai-me, Christ, and the Machine: Affirmation through Mythic Pluralism in *House Made of Dawn*.” *Studies in American Fiction* 11, no. 1 (Spring 1983): 61–71.

868. Roemer, Kenneth M. “Bear and Elk: The Nature(s) of Contemporary American Indian Poetry.” In *Studies in American Indian Literature: Critical Essays and Course Designs*, edited by Paula Gunn Allen. New York: Modern Language Association of America, 1983. 178–91. This is a revised version of Roemer’s essay in *Journal of Ethnic Studies* (1977).

869. ———. "Native American Oral Narratives: Context and Continuity." In *Smoothing the Ground: Essays on Native American Oral Literature*, edited by Brian Swann. Berkeley: University of California Press, 1983. 39–42, 50–55. Roemer includes discussion of "The Man Made of Words," "An American Land Ethic," and *The Way to Rainy Mountain.*

1984

870. Allen, Paula Gunn. "All the Good Indians." In *The 60s, without Apology*, edited by Sohnya Sayers et al. Minneapolis, Minnesota: University of Minnesota Press, 1984. 226–29. Allen remembered receiving a copy of *House Made of Dawn*, the only book about an Indian by an Indian that she read in the 1960s. She believed it saved her life.

871. Berner, Robert L. "Trying to Be Round: Three American Indian Novels." *World Literature Today* 58, no. 3 (Summer 1984): 341–44. Berner presents an analysis of structural similarities in and the use of Black Elk's vision in *House Made of Dawn*, Leslie Marmon Silko's *Ceremony*, and James Welch's *Winter in the Blood.*

872. Macaruso, Victor. "Cowboys and Indians: The Image of the Indian in American Literature." *American Indian Culture and Research Journal* 8, no. 2 (1984): 13–21. *House Made of Dawn* and *The Way to Rainy Mountain* are included in this presentation of the multifaceted images of the American Indian.

873. Mariani, Giorgio. "'Art Made of Dawn': An Introduction to Contemporary Native American Poetry." In *North American Indian Studies 2: European Contributions; Society and Art*, edited by Pieter Hovens. Göttingen, Germany: Edition Herodot, 1984. 174–89. Focuses on poetry by Momaday and others as expressions of their bicultural experiences.

874. Niatum, Duane. "History in the Colors of Song: A Few Words on Contemporary Native American Poetry." In *Coyote Was Here: Essays on Contemporary Native American Literary and Political Mobilization*, edited by Bo Schöler. The Dolphin, no. 9. Aarhus, Denmark: SEKLOS, 1984. 25–34. Includes an excerpt on pp. 29–33 from Momaday's introduction to Niatum's *Carriers of the Dream Wheel.*

875. Velie, Alan R. "Indians in Indian Fiction: The Shadow of the Trickster." *American Indian Quarterly* 8, no. 4 (Fall 1984): 315–29. Velie studies the protagonists of *House Made of Dawn* and James Welch's *Winter in the*

Blood and *The Death of Jim Loney*. He concludes that they are from the long tradition of tricksters in Indian cultures.

876. Warner, Nicholas O. "Images of Drinking in 'Woman Singing,' *Ceremony*, and *House Made of Dawn*." *MELUS* 11, no. 4 (Winter 1984): 15–30. Warner examines images of "the drunken Indian" and finds that these three works by Simon J. Ortiz, Leslie Marmon Silko, and Momaday have "complementary visions of Indian drinking" (30).

877. Wiget, Andrew. "Sending a Voice: The Emergence of Contemporary Native American Poetry." *College English* 46, no. 6 (October 1984): 598–609. Wiget tells about a growing number of writers publishing their poetry through small presses and other publishing venues, and discusses John R. Milton's special edition, *The American Indian Speaks* (1969). A listing of contemporary Native American poets is included. See also the section "Anthologies and Literary Collections" in Part II.

1985

878. Aithal, S. K. "The Redemptive Return: Momaday's *House Made of Dawn*." *North Dakota Quarterly* 52, no. 3 (Spring 1985): 160–72.

879. Anderson, Lauri. "Fusion and Statis in Momaday's *The Way to Rainy Mountain*." *Notes on Contemporary Literature* 15, no. 1 (January 1985): 6–15.

880. Clements, William M. "Folk Historical Sense in Two Native American Authors." *MELUS* 12, no. 1 (Spring 1985): 65–78. The two authors are Leslie Marmon Silko and Momaday.

881. Evers, Lawrence J. "The Killing of a New Mexican State Trooper: Ways of Telling an Historical Event." *Wicazo Sa Review* 1, no. 1 (Spring 1985): 17–25. Reprinted in *Critical Essays on Native American Literature*, edited by Andrew Wiget. Boston: G. K. Hall, 1985. 246–60. Evers examines the ways in which a particular event is treated in fiction, focusing on *House Made of Dawn* and works by Leslie Marmon Silko and Simon J. Ortiz.

882. Schubnell, Matthias. *N. Scott Momaday: The Cultural and Literary Background*. Norman: University of Oklahoma Press, 1985. This book is devoted to Momaday and his works, beginning with Schubnell's introduction on pp. 3–11 and "A Biographical Sketch" on pp. 13–39, which ends with Momaday's academic appointment at the University of Arizona in 1981. The following chapters focus on Momaday's books, essays, poetry, and other works to the early 1980s. This book is available in electronic form through

NetLibrary at libraries providing this and other e-content services.

883. ———. *N. Scott Momaday: The Cultural and Literary Background* (1985). Chapter 2, "The Man Made of Words: N. Scott Momaday's Theory of Language and the Imagination," 40–62. Schubnell examines Momaday's seminal address on the nature of oral tradition and some of the important themes underlying this and other works.

884. ———. *N. Scott Momaday: The Cultural and Literary Background* (1985). Chapter 3, "The American Earth," 63–92. This chapter presents Momaday's depiction of the earth, nature, and the American landscape in terms of his understanding of American Indian perceptions and beliefs. Schubnell also discusses Momaday's knowledge of the writings of other authors, including Isak Dinesen, William Faulkner, and D. H. Lawrence.

885. ———. *N. Scott Momaday: The Cultural and Literary Background* (1985). Chapter 4, "The Crisis of Identity: *House Made of Dawn*," 93–139. After a brief introduction to the novel, Abel, the protagonist, is the primary subject.

886. ———. *N. Scott Momaday: The Cultural and Literary Background* (1985). Chapter 5, "The Indian Heritage: *The Way to Rainy Mountain*," 140–66. Schubnell provides an in-depth analysis of this book.

887. ———. *N. Scott Momaday: The Cultural and Literary Background* (1985). Chapter 6, "Myths to Live By: *The Names: A Memoir*," 167–88. Imagination and language are crucial for mythmaking.

888. ———. *N. Scott Momaday: The Cultural and Literary Background* (1985). Chapter 7, "Momaday's Poetry," 189–254. Schubnell presents an illuminating discussion of poems from *Angle of Geese* and *The Gourd Dancer*. A few unpublished poems are included.

889. Wiget, Andrew. "The Study of Native American Literature: An Introduction." *Critical Essays on Native American Literature*, edited by Andrew Wiget. Critical Essays on American Literature. Boston: G. K. Hall, 1985. 1–20. In his introduction, Wiget comments on Momaday's Pulitzer Prize–winning novel and its influence in drawing the attention of the literary world to Native American literature.

890. ———. "Contemporary Fiction: N. Scott Momaday." In chapter 4, "Modern Fiction," of *Native American Literature*, edited by Andrew Wiget. Twayne's United States Author Series, 467. Boston: Twayne, 1985. 82–85. The power of language is presented as an important theme in *House Made of Dawn*.

891. ———. "The Formalists." In chapter 5, "Contemporary Poetry," of *Native American Literature* (Twayne, 1985), 98, 100–103. Wiget examines Momaday's poetry in *Angle of Geese* and *The Gourd Dancer.*

892. ———. "Looking Sunward." Chapter 6 in *Native American Literature* (Twayne, 1985), 121–22. These pages, on the topic of nonfictional prose, briefly discuss Momaday's personal narratives, *The Names* and *The Way to Rainy Mountain.*

1986

893. Allen, Paula Gunn. "The Ceremonial Motion of Indian Time: Long Ago, So Far." *The Sacred Hoop: Recovering the Feminine in American Indian Traditions.* Boston: Beacon Press, 1986. 147–54. Reprinted with a new preface by Allen (Beacon Press, 1992); first digital print edition, 2004. Allen examined time as a structuring device used in American Indian novels, in particular *House Made of Dawn,* concluding that achronology is the favored structuring device.

894. ———. "N. Scott Momaday and James Welch: Transition and Transcendence," in Allen's essay, "Whose Dream Is This Anyway? Remythologizing and Self-definition in Contemporary American Indian Fiction." *The Sacred Hoop* (Beacon Press, 1986; repr. 1992) 80–82, 86–94. Allen maintained that of all the Indian men who have major novels among their works, Momaday is "the clearest in denying that cultural conflict must result in either genocide or deicide" (87), and that "the most important theme in Native American novels is not conflict and devastation, but transformation and continuance" (101).

895. ———. "Word Warriors—A Stranger in My Own Life." *The Sacred Hoop* (Beacon Press, 1986; repr. 1992.) 138–39, 144–45. In her analysis of novels by Momaday, Leslie Marmon Silko, and James Welch, Allen found that the inability to speak is a prime symbol of powerlessness.

896. Fischer, Michael M. J. "Ethnicity and the Post-Modern Arts of Memory." In *Writing Culture: The Poetics and Politics of Ethnography,* edited by James Clifford and George E. Marcus. Berkeley: University of California Press, 1986. 194–233. In this study of ethnic autobiographies, Fischer presents a brief discussion of *House Made of Dawn, The Way to Rainy Mountain,* and *The Names,* authored by "a skillful experimenter with multiple voices and perspectives" (225–26).

897. Gross, Konrad. "Erzahlen als Ritual: Die Funktion indianischer Tradition in N. Scott Momaday's *House Made of Dawn.*" *Theorie und Praxis im Erzahlen des 19. und 20.* Jahrhunderts: Studien zur enlischen und amerikanischen

Literatur zu Ehren von Willi Erzgraber. Tübingen, Germany: Narr, 1986. 345–57. (in German)

898. Lincoln, Kenneth. "Tai-Me to Rainy Mountain: The Makings of American Indian Literature." *American Indian Quarterly* 10, no. 2 (Spring 1986): 101–17. Excerpts from *The Way to Rainy Mountain* appear in Lincoln's illuminating essay about the making of this classic book.

899. Papovich, J. Frank. "Landscape, Tradition, and Identity in *The Way to Rainy Mountain*." *Perspectives on Contemporary Literature* 12 (1986): 13–19.

900. Ruppert, James. "Mediation and Multiple Narrative in Contemporary Native American Fiction." *Texas Studies in Literature and Language* 28 (1986): 209–25. This essay appeared later in *Genre: Forms of Discourse and Culture* 25, no. 4 (Winter 1992): 321–37. Ruppert demonstrates how Native American writers, including Momaday, are mediators between Indian and Anglo cultural traditions.

1987

901. Allen, Paula Gunn. "Bringing Home the Fact: Tradition and Continuity in the Imagination." In *Recovering the Word: Essays on Native American Literature*, edited by Brian Swann and Arnold Krupat. Berkeley: University of California Press, 1987. 563–79. In this analysis of "homing" plots in novels by Native Americans, Allen described *House Made of Dawn* as "an act of the imagination designed to heal" (571).

902. Barnes, Jim. "On Native Ground." In *I Tell You Now: Autobiographical Essays by Native American Writers*, edited by Brian Swann and Arnold Krupat. Lincoln: University of Nebraska Press, 1987. 93–94, 97. Barnes includes *House Made of Dawn* and Momaday in his discussion of the practice of labeling writers.

903. Bevis, William. "Native American Novels: Homing In." In *Recovering the Word*, edited by Brian Swann and Arnold Krupat. Berkeley: University of California Press, 1987. 580–609, 618. Reprinted in *Critical Perspectives on Native American Fiction*, edited by Richard F. Fleck. Washington, D.C.: Three Continents Press, 1993. 15–45. Reprinted in *Defining Travel: Diverse Visions*, edited by Susan Roberson. Jackson: University Press of Mississippi, 2001. 244–57. Bevis draws from *House Made of Dawn* and *The Ancient Child* to demonstrate the patterns of homing, return, and the connection between place and self.

904. Boelhower, William. "What Is the Ethnic? A Model of Ethnic Semiosis." *Through a Glass Darkly: Ethnic Semiosis in American Literature*. New York: Oxford University Press, 1987. 81–83. Boelhower examines *The Names* in his analysis and concludes that "the foundations of ethnicity are based on the general elaboration of the story behind one's name" (83). An earlier edition was published in Italy in 1984.

905. Bruchac, Joseph. "Survival Comes This Way: Contemporary Native American Poetry." In *A Gift of Tongues: Critical Challenges in Contemporary American Poetry*, edited by Marie Harris and Kathleen Aguero. Athens: University of Georgia Press, 1987. 196–205. Momaday is included among the poets discussed.

906. Forbes, Jack. "Colonialism and Native American Literature: Analysis." *Wicazo Sa Review* 3, no. 2 (Autumn 1987): 17–23. In examining works of Native American writers, including Momaday's, Forbes states that "it is not easy to be an Indian writer writing for Indians" (22).

907. Nabokov, Peter. "Taos to Santa Fe, 5 August: Lawrence, Waters, and Momaday on Pueblo Races." *Indian Running: Native American History and Tradition*, by Peter Nabokov. Santa Fe, New Mexico: Ancient City Press, 1987, ©1981. In this reprint of an earlier edition published by Capra Press, Nabokov explores the ancient, symbolic roots of Indian running, giving readers a better understanding of the significance of the protagonist running in *House Made of Dawn*.

908. Niatum, Duane. "On Stereotypes." In *Recovering the Word*, edited by Brian Swann and Arnold Krupat. Berkeley: University of California Press, 1987. 552–62. In this thoughtful essay, Niatum offers his views on the labeling of Native Americans in general and writers and artists in particular. He refers to the labeling of Momaday and *House Made of Dawn*.

1988

909. Antell, Judith A. "Momaday, Welch, and Silko: Expressing the Feminine Principle through Male Alienation." *American Indian Quarterly* 12, no. 3 (Summer 1988): 213–20. Antell explores the role and power of women in tribal communities in *House Made of Dawn*, James Welch's *The Death of Jim Loney*, and Leslie Marmon Silko's *Ceremony*.

910. Brumble, H. David, III. "N. Scott Momaday: Oral to Written Tradition." *American Indian Autobiography*. Berkeley: University of California Press,

1988. 165–80. Reprinted with a new introduction by Brumble: Lincoln: University of Nebraska Press, 2008, ©1988. 165–80.

911. Hanson, Elizabeth I. "N. Scott Momaday: Evocations of Disruption and Defeat." In *American Literature in Belgium*, edited and with a preface by Gilbert Debusscher. Amsterdam: Rodopi, 1988. 197–204. Discussion of *House Made of Dawn* is included in this essay.

912. Hirsch, Bernard A. "'The Telling Which Continues': Oral Tradition and the Written Word in Leslie Marmon Silko's *Storyteller*." *American Indian Quarterly* 12, no. 1 (Winter 1988): 1–26. See pp. 4–10 for discussion about Momaday and *The Way to Rainy Mountain*.

913. Roemer, Kenneth M., ed. *Approaches to Teaching Momaday's "The Way to Rainy Mountain."* New York: Modern Language Association of America, 1988. See citations to the essays in this book in the section "Teaching Momaday's Writings."

914. Swann, Brian. "Introduction: Only the Beginning." In *Harper's Anthology of 20th Century Native American Poetry*, edited by Duane Niatum. New York: Harper Collins, 1988. xiii–xxxii. Swann presents a survey of Native American poetry and literature, reminding readers that Indians were writing in English for over two centuries. He also quotes a familiar statement made by Momaday: "The oral tradition is always but one generation from extinction" (xxvii).

915. Wong, Hertha D. "Contemporary Native American Autobiography: N. Scott Momaday's *The Way to Rainy Mountain*." *American Indian Culture and Research Journal* 12, no. 3 (1988): 15–31. Wong, like others, believes this book defies generic classification.

1989

916. Blaeser, Kimberly. "*The Way to Rainy Mountain*: Momaday's Work in Motion." Chapter 3 in *Narrative Chance: Postmodern Discourse on Native American Indian Literatures*, edited by Gerald Vizenor. Albuquerque: University of New Mexico Press, 1989. 39–54. Reprinted (pbk.) with same title. American Indian Literature and Critical Studies, vol. 8. Norman: University of Oklahoma Press, 1993. 39–54. Blaeser describes the book as one that can involve the reader in the performance of the text.

917. Cox, Jay. "Dangerous Definitions: Female Tricksters in Contemporary Native American Literature." *Wicazo Sa Review* 5, no. 2 (Autumn 1989): 17–21. Cox refers to Momaday as a "trickster-novelist" (18) in this study that includes

remarks about *The Ancient Child, House Made of Dawn,* and *The Way to Rainy Mountain.*

918. Hobson, Geary. "General Introduction to Indian Country: A Survey of American Indian Literature, 1968–1988." Special issue, "Native American Literatures," edited by James Ruppert. *Wicazo Sa Review* 5, no. 1 (Spring 1989): 36–46. Hobson points out in this survey that Momaday was not the first Indian to publish a novel.

919. Jahner, Elaine A. "Metalanguages." Chapter 10 in *Narrative Chance: Postmodern Discourse on Native American Indian Literatures,* edited by Gerald Vizenor. Albuquerque: University of New Mexico Press, 1989. 155–85. Reprint, University of Oklahoma Press, 1993. 155–85. In this critical study of *The Way to Rainy Mountain* and the dynamics of the reading process, Jahner describes it as a "performance" that exemplifies "the oral traditions living beneath the surface of the written word" (156).

920. Kroeber, Karl. "Technology and Tribal Narrative." Chapter 2 in *Narrative Chance: Postmodern Discourse on Native American Indian Literatures,* edited by Gerald Vizenor. Albuquerque: University of New Mexico Press, 1989. 17–37. Reprint, University of Oklahoma Press, 1993. 17–37. Kroeber critiques *House Made of Dawn* (17–22) and devotes the rest of the chapter to an analysis of *The Golden Women: The Colville Narrative of Peter J. Seymour,* edited by Anthony Mattina and translated by Mattina and Madeline deSautel (University of Arizona Press, 1985). In the process, he demonstrates the difficulties faced in translation and the successes achieved by Momaday and others.

921. Krupat, Arnold. "Native American Literature and the Canon." *The Voice in the Margin: Native American Literature and the Canon,* edited by Arnold Krupat. Berkeley: University of California Press, 1989. 96–131. See also his earlier essay published in 1983.

922. ———. "Monologue and Dialogue in Native American Autobiography." *The Voice in the Margin* (1989). 132–201. Krupat states his belief that Momaday, more than any other Native American writer, is "committed to hegemonic monologue, to the all-encompassing voice of lyric or epic, romantic or modernist art-speech in his writing" (177).

923. McAllister, Mick. "Homeward Bound: Wilderness and Frontier in American Indian Literature." In *The Frontier Experience and the American Dream: Essays on American Literature,* edited by David Mogen, Mark Busby, and

Paul Bryant. College Station: Texas A&M University Press, 1989. 149–58. *House Made of Dawn* and Leslie Marmon Silko's *Ceremony* are examined for approaches to frontier mythology. The author also discusses how westering's linearity, or leaving home, conflicted with circularity, or return, in the culture and tradition of American Indians.

924. Nelson, Robert M. "Snake and Eagle: Abel's Disease and the Landscape of *House Made of Dawn*." *Studies in American Indian Literatures* 1, no. 2 (Fall 1989): 1–20.

925. Turner, Frederick. "Voice Out of the Land: Leslie Marmon Silko's *Ceremony*." Chapter 10 in *Spirit of Place: The Making of an American Literary Landscape*, 324–28. San Francisco: Sierra Club Books, 1989. Reprint (pbk.): Washington, D.C.: Island Press, 1992. The pages cited are devoted to Momaday as an example of writers who write out of their tribal backgrounds and experiences.

926. Ude, Wayne. "Forging an American Style: The Romance-Novel and Magical Realism as Response to the Frontier and Wilderness Experiences." In *The Frontier Experience and the American Dream*, edited by David Mogen, Mark Busby, and Paul Bryant. College Station: Texas A&M University Press, 1989. 50–64. See pp. 60–63 for Ude's discussion about Momaday, Leslie Marmon Silko, and James Welch writing within the tradition of the American romance novel and at the same time within an American Indian literary tradition that was old when the Europeans arrived.

927. Vaschenko, Alexander. "Some Russian Responses to Native American Indian Cultures." In *Indians and Europe: An Interdisciplinary Collection of Essays*, edited by Christian F. Feest. Forum, no. 11. Aachen, Germany: Edition Herodot; Alano Verlag, 1987. 307–20. Vaschenko recalls meeting Momaday at the Moscow airport and being asked by him about Russians' interest in American Indians. This was Momaday's first trip, in 1974, to the Soviet Union to lecture at Moscow State University, also known as the University of Moscow.

928. Volborth, Judith Mountain Leaf. "Pollen Breath under the Tongue." In *Native American Literatures*, edited by Laura Coltelli. Forum, no. 1. Pisa, Italy: SEU (Servizio Editoriale Universitaria), 1989, 67–69. This essay is about the power of words and sounds.

1990

929. Duryea, Polly. "Rainwatch Ritual in Cather, Lawrence, Momaday, and Others." *Journal of Ethnic Studies* 18, no. 2 (Summer 1990): 59–75. The term

"rainwatch" refers to a woman with magical powers to bring about rain. Angela of *House Made of Dawn* and Grey of *The Ancient Child* are included in this study on pp. 70–72.

930. Ellis, Clyde. "Truly Dancing Their Own Way: Modern Revival and Diffusion of the Gourd Dance." *American Indian Quarterly* 14, no. 1 (Winter 1990): 19–33. Ellis presents an informative essay on the Gourd Dance, which has great significance for Momaday.

931. Hobson, Geary. "The Literature of Indian Oklahoma: A Brief History." "University of Oklahoma Centennial Issue, 1890–1990." *World Literature Today* 64, no. 3 (Summer 1990): 427–31. Hobson presents a significant number of poets and fiction writers of Oklahoma and includes remarks about Momaday's influence on the growth of the literature.

932. Meli, Franco. "Los Angeles: Citta di angeli? La prospettiva nativa americana N. S. Momaday." *Rivista di Studi Anglo Americani* 6, no. 8 (1990): 213–24. Meli is the Italian translator of *House Made of Dawn.*

933. Meredith, Howard. "N. Scott Momaday: A Man of Words." "University of Oklahoma Centennial Issue, 1890–1990." *World Literature Today* 64, no. 3 (Summer 1990): 405–407. (port.) Meredith focuses on the sacred Tai-me in Momaday's works.

934. Rigal-Cellard, Bernadette. "*House Made of Dawn* de Scott Momaday: La course d'Abel ou comment franchir le mur du silence." *Annales du CRAA* (Centre de Recherches sur l'Amérique Anglophone), no. 15. Bordeaux, France: MSHA, 1990. 63–78. This essay also appeared in *Multilinguisme et multiculturalisme en Amerique du Nord*, edited by Jean Beranger, Jean Cazemajou, Jean Michel Lacroix, and Pierre Spriet. Bordeaux, France: Morillier, 1990. 63–78.

935. Schein, Marie M. "Alienation and Art in *The Ancient Child*." *Studies in American Indian Literatures*, 2nd ser., 2, no. 4 (1990): 11–14.

936. Zolla, Elémire. "American Indian Literature from 1970 to 1990: The Redemptive Mountain." *European Review of Native American Studies* 4, no. 2 (1990): 3–8. Rainy Mountain is one of the sacred mountains included by Zolla.

1991

937. Bottalico, Michele. "A Place for All: Old and New Myths in the Italian Appreciation of American Literature." *As Others Read Us: International Perspectives on American Literature*, edited by Huck Gutman. Amherst:

University of Massachusetts Press, 1991. 148–60. Bottalico remarks that Momaday, James Welch, and Leslie Marmon Silko are the Native American writers who have received the most attention from Italian critics.

938. Fleck, Richard F. "Sacred Land in the Writings of Momaday, Welch, and Silko." In *Entering the 90s: The North American Experience*, edited by Thomas Schirer. Proceedings from the Native American Studies Conference, October 1989. Sault Ste. Marie, Michigan: Lake Superior State University Press, 1991. 125–33. Fleck confines his commentary on Momaday to *The Way to Rainy Mountain.*

939. Krupat, Arnold. "Native American Autobiography and the Synecdochic Self." In *American Autobiography: Retrospect and Prospect*, edited by Paul John Eakin. Madison: University of Wisconsin Press, 1991. Also published in Krupat's *Ethnocriticism: Ethnography, History, Literature*. Berkeley: University of California Press, 1991. 201–31. Krupat concludes after studying *The Way to Rainy Mountain* and *The Names* that, in general, the majority of Native American autobiographies are synecdochic in their presentation of the self, while Momaday's seem to be metonymic. In particular, see pp. 230–31.

940. Murray, David. "Autobiography and Authorship: Identity and Unity." *Forked Tongues: Speech, Writing, and Representation in Native American Indian Texts*. Bloomington: Indiana University Press, 1991. 80–82, 92–96. Murray examines writers' approaches to American Indian autobiography and remarks about Momaday's use of continuity, community, and kinship in *The Way to Rainy Mountain* and *The Names.*

1992

941. Berner, Robert L. "Columbus, Indians, and American Literature." *World Literature Today* 66, no. 2 (Spring 1992): 292–96. As the 500th anniversary of Columbus's first voyage approached, Berner undertook a study of the interrelatedness of Indians and non-Indians in American culture, drawing from a statement made by Momaday about the American Indian being indispensable to the dreams and the destinies of America.

942. Bierhorst, John. "The Chantway Novels," in "Incorporating the Native Voice: A Look Back from 1990." *On the Translation of Native American Literatures*, edited by Brian Swann. Washington, D.C.: Smithsonian Institution Press, 1992. Bierhorst describes *House Made of Dawn* as "a distant variant on the basic Navajo chantway myth" and the Navajo Night Chant as "the ceremony that serves as the story's turning point" (55–56).

943. Blaeser, Kimberly M. "Learning 'the Language the Presidents Speak': Images and Issues of Literacy in American Indian Literature." *World Literature Today* 66, no. 2 (Spring 1992): 230–35. (port.) Examines selections from *House Made of Dawn* and works by others to find various ways in which historical struggles connected to literacy may be viewed. In particular, see pp. 232–33.

944. ———. "The New 'Frontier' of Native American Literature: Dis-arming History with Tribal Humor," in "Native American Perspectives on Literature and History," edited by Alan R. Velie and Gerald Vizenor. *Genre: Forms of Discourse and Culture* 25, no. 4 (Winter 1992): 351–64. Blaeser quotes on p. 362 a statement about the act of imagination that Momaday made during a lecture at the Library of Congress in January 1974. See "The Writing of Nonfiction Prose," *Teaching Creative Writing* (1974), in Part II, entry no. 44.

945. Cahill, Gloria, and Chad Galts. "N. Scott Momaday: An Introduction; 'The Bear Comes Forth.'" Graduate students wrote this essay about Momaday's participation and reading at the Poetics and Politics reading series held at the University of Arizona in 1992. This essay can be accessed at http://poeticsandpolitics.arizona.edu/english/poetics/main.html.

946. Monahan, Kristin. "Mergence of Myth and Reality in N. Scott Momaday's *The Ancient Child*." In *Quincentennial: A Critical Exploration (1492–1992)*, by Tarcisio Beal et al. San Antonio, Texas: College of the Incarnate Word, 1992.

947. Owens, Louis. "Acts of Imagination: The Novels of N. Scott Momaday." *Other Destinies: Understanding the American Indian Novel*. American Indian Literature and Critical Studies, vol. 3. Norman: University of Oklahoma Press, 1992. 90–127. Reprint (pbk.), University of Oklahoma Press, 1994. Owens focused on *House Made of Dawn* and its main characters in this chapter, followed by a shorter discussion about *The Ancient Child*. See also "An Introduction to Indian Novels," 3–31.

948. Rigal-Cellard, Bernadette. "A Reading of the Prologue of *House Made of Dawn*." In *Native American Literatures*, edited by Laura Coltelli. Forum, nos. 2–3, 1990–91. Pisa, Italy: SEU (Sevizio Editoriale Universitaria), 1992. 39–56. Reprinted in "*House Made of Dawn*": *N. Scott Momaday*, edited by Bernadette Rigal-Cellard. Paris: Ellipses, 1997. 55–72.

949. Ruppert, James. "Mediation in Contemporary Native American Writing," in "Native American Perspectives on Literature and History," edited by Alan R. Velie and Gerald Vizenor. *Genre: Forms of Discourse and Culture* 25, no. 4

(Winter 1992): 321–37. Ruppert maintains that Native American writers, including Momaday, are mediators.

950. Secco, Anna. "The Search for Origins through Storytelling in Native American Literature: Momaday, Silko, Erdrich." *RSA Journal (Rivista di Studi Nord Americani)* 3 (1992): 59–71.

951. Simard, Rodney. "American Indian Literatures, Authenticity, and the Canon." *World Literature Today* 66, no. 2 (Spring 1992): 243–48. Simard believes *House Made of Dawn* and "The Man Made of Words" were influential in changing "the compartmentalized academic process" that ignored the literatures of American Indians.

952. Taylor, Paul Beekman. "Native Americans Translating Culture: Momaday and Anaya." In *Writing Culture*, edited by Balz Engler. Swiss Papers in English Language and Literature, vol. 6. Tübingen, Germany: Gunter Narr, 1992. 133–50. Taylor discusses *The Way to Rainy Mountain* and Rudolfo A. Anaya's *Tortuga*.

953. Trafzer, Clifford E. "The Word Is Sacred to a Child: American Indians and Children's Literature." *American Indian Quarterly* 16, no. 3 (Summer 1992): 381–95. In this review essay, Trafzer discusses the state of children's books about Native Americans and recommends a number of outstanding ones.

954. Velie, Alan R. "American Indian Literature in the Nineties: The Emergence of the Middle-Class Protagonist." *World Literature Today* 66, no. 2 (Spring 1992): 264–68. Velie includes Locke Setman of *The Ancient Child* as an example of a middle-class protagonist in this study of the "new breed" of protagonists.

955. Vizenor, Gerald. "Native American Indian Identities: Autoinscriptions and the Cultures of Names," in "Native American Perspectives on Literature and History," edited by Alan R. Velie and Gerald Vizenor. *Genre: Forms of Discourse and Culture* 25, no. 4, (Winter 1992): 431–40. Vizenor includes quotes from *The Way to Rainy Mountain* and *The Names* on pp. 434–35. See also this issue's introduction, by Velie and Vizenor, 315–19.

956. ———. "Native American Indian Literature: Critical Metaphors of the Ghost Dance." *World Literature Today* 66, no. 2 (Spring 1992): 223–27. Vizenor includes remarks about *House Made of Dawn* and comments made by Charles Larson and Andrew Wiget. See pp. 224–25.

957. Wong, Hertha D. "Contemporary Innovations of Oral Traditions: N. Scott Momaday and Leslie Marmon Silko." *Sending My Heart Back across the Years:*

Tradition and Innovation in Native American Autobiography. New York: Oxford University Press, 1992. 153–99. *The Way to Rainy Mountain* and *The Names* constitute the focus of the essay.

1993

958. Bevis, William. "Native American Novels: Homing In." In *Critical Perspectives on Native American Fiction*, edited by Richard Fleck. Critical Perspectives. Washington, D.C.: Three Continents Press, 1993. 15–45. Bevis examines *House Made of Dawn* and novels by D'arcy McNickle, Leslie M. Silko, and James Welch that tell of return and of homing by protagonists who experienced the white world.

959. Evers, Lawrence J. "Words and Place: A Reading of *House Made of Dawn*." In *Critical Perspectives on Native American Fiction*, edited by Richard F. Fleck. Washington, D.C.: Three Continents Press, 1993. 114–33. This essay was originally published in *Western American Literature* in 1977.

960. Fleck, Richard F. "Introduction." *Critical Perspectives on Native American Fiction*, edited by Fleck. Washington, D.C.: Three Continents Press, 1993. 1–11. Fleck introduces Momaday, "the dean of American Indian letters" (6), and five other Native American novelists (D'arcy McNickle, Louise Erdrich, Leslie Marmon Silko, Gerald Vizenor, and James Welch), about whom the critical essays in this collection were written.

961. Hochbruck, Wolfgang. "Mystery Novels to Choctaw Pageant: Todd Downing and Native American Literatures." In *New Voices in Native American Literary Criticism*, edited by Arnold Krupat. Smithsonian Series of Studies in Native American Literatures, ser. eds. Arnold Krupat and Brian Swann. Washington, D.C.: Smithsonian Institution Press, 1993. 205–21. Hochbruck presents issues relating to the problem of defining Native American literature and includes *House Made of Dawn* in his discussion. He suggests a model for a definition consisting of seven categories, using Downing as a case in point.

962. Hogan, Linda. "Who Puts Together." In *Critical Perspectives on Native American Fiction*, edited by Richard F. Fleck. Washington, D.C.: Three Continents Press, 1993. 134–42. In her study of *House Made of Dawn*, Hogan maintains that Momaday is like the oral poet or singer who "creates harmony out of alienation and chaos" (134). This essay originally appeared in 1980 in *Denver Quarterly*.

963. Lincoln, Kenneth. "Comic Accommodations: Momaday and Norman." *Indi'n Humor: Bicultural Play in Native America*. New York: Oxford University Press, 1993. 280–308. Lincoln examines the use of humor, irony, and trickster

figures in *House Made of Dawn* and Howard Norman's *The Northern Lights.*

964. Moss, Maria. "N. Scott Momaday: Angela and First Woman." In Part IV, "Mythological Women in Contemporary Literature." *We've Been Here Before: Women in Creation Myths and Contemporary Literature of the Native American Southwest.* North American Studies, no. 1. Münster and Hamburg, Germany: Lit, ©1993. 66–100. This study focuses on Angela of *House Made of Dawn.* See also Moss under "Dissertations—1993."

965. ———. "N Scott Momaday: Grey and Changing Woman." In Part IV, "Mythological Women in Contemporary Literature." *We've Been Here Before,* ©1993. This is about Grey, the medicine woman of *The Ancient Child.*

966. Nelson, Robert M. "The Function of the Landscape of *House Made of Dawn.*" *Place and Vision: The Function of Landscape in Native American Fiction.* American Indian Studies, no. 1, gen. ed. Rodney Simard. New York: Peter Lang, 1993. 41–89. See also pp. 183–84 of the book's index for other references to Momaday.

967. Neneve, Miguel. "The Significance of Oral Language in Momaday's *The Way to Rainy Mountain.*" *UNILETRAS* (Brazil) 15 (December 1993): 133–37.

968. Rigal-Cellard, Bernadette. "Analyse de deux mises en scène interculturelles du sujet: Les Pactes autobiographiques de Momaday dans *The Names* et de Vizenor dans *Interior Landscapes.*" *Annales du CRAA,* no. 18. Bordeaux, France: MSHA, 1993. 161–74.

969. Roemer, Kenneth M. "Ancient Children at Play—Lyric, Petroglyphic, and Ceremonial." In *Critical Perspectives on Native American Fiction,* edited by Richard F. Fleck. Washington, D.C.: Three Continents Press, 1993. 99–113. Reprinted in *Native American Writers,* edited and with an introduction by Harold Bloom. Modern Critical Views. Philadelphia: Chelsea House, 1998. 57–72. This essay explores types and concepts of play, focusing on *The Ancient Child,* but also including pertinent remarks about *House Made of Dawn* and *The Way to Rainy Mountain.*

970. Schweninger, Lee. "Writing Nature: Silko and Native Americans as Nature Writers." *MELUS* 18, no. 2 (Summer 1993): 47–60. Focusing primarily on Leslie Marmon Silko and Momaday, this essay explores his essays, "An American Land Ethic" and "Native American Attitudes to the Environment." Also discussed is Momaday's phrase "reciprocal appropriation," which relates to a person investing himself or herself in the landscape.

971. Sequoya, Jana. "How(!) Is an Indian? A Contest of Stories." In *New Voices in Native American Literary Criticism*, edited by Arnold Krupat. Smithsonian Series of Studies in Native American Literatures, ser. eds. Arnold Krupat and Brian Swann. Washington, D.C.: Smithsonian Institution Press, 1993. 453–73. In examining the question of who is and how is an Indian, Sequoya draws from *House Made of Dawn* and Leslie Marmon Silko's *Ceremony.* See also "Round 2" of this essay under the year 2000 and the name Sequoya Magdaleno, Jana, entry no. 1090.

972. Vizenor, Gerald. "The Ruins of Representation: Shadow Survivance and the Literature of Dominance." *American Indian Quarterly* 17, no. 1 (Winter 1993): 7–30. Vizenor includes *House Made of Dawn, The Way to Rainy Mountain,* and *The Ancient Child* in this essay about critical responses to American Indian literature.

973. ———. "Shadow Survivance." Chapter 3 in *Manifest Manners: Postindian Warriors of Survivance.* Hanover, New Hampshire: University Press of New England, 1993, ©1994. Vizenor includes excerpts from *The Names* and *The Way to Rainy Mountain* in his discussion about "shadows, memories, and imagination," pp. 73–74, 93, and quotes others about *House Made of Dawn* and *The Ancient Child,* pp. 78–79, 84–85. He defines "manifest manners."

1994

974. Bartelt, Guillermo. "American Indian English in Momaday's *House Made of Dawn.*" *Language and Literature* 19 (1994): 19, 37–53.

975. Bruchac, Joseph. "Contemporary Native American Writing: An Overview." In *Dictionary of Native American Literature*, edited by Andrew Wiget. New York: Garland, 1994. 311–28. Reprinted with title, *Handbook of Native American Literature*, edited by Wiget (Garland, 1996). 311–28. In particular, see "Roots of a Renaissance," pp. 311–16, about the period of the late 1960s, when *House Made of Dawn* was published.

976. Coltelli, Laura. "European Responses to Native American Literatures." In *Dictionary of Native American Literature*, edited by Andrew Wiget. New York: Garland, 1994. 339–45. Reprint, *Handbook of Native American Literature*, edited by Wiget (Garland, 1996). 339–45. Coltelli describes the growth of interest in Europe in contemporary studies of American Indians and their literatures and in the critical analysis of works by Momaday and other established Native American authors.

977. Domina, Lynn. "Liturgies, Rituals, Ceremonies: The Conjunction of Roman Catholic and Native American Religious Traditions in N. Scott Momaday's *House Made of Dawn*," in "The World of N. Scott Momaday: Special Issue," edited by Richard F. Fleck. *Paintbrush* 21 (Autumn 1994): 7–27.

978. Donovan, Kathleen M. "'A Menace among the Words': Women in the Novels of N. Scott Momaday." *Studies in American Indian Literatures* 6, no. 4 (Winter 1994): 51–76. Reprinted in Donovan's *Feminist Readings of Native American Literature: Coming to Voice.* Tucson: University of Arizona Press, 1998. 69–98. This essay focuses on women characters in *House Made of Dawn* and *The Ancient Child,* which Donovan asserts are "linked by an underlying misogyny" (72).

979. Hobson, Geary. "On a Festival Called Returning the Gift." In *Returning the Gift: Poetry and Prose from the First North American Native Writers' Festival,* edited by Joseph Bruchac. Sun Tracks, vol. 29. Tucson: University of Arizona Press, 1994. xxiii–xxix. Hobson recalls an anecdote about Georgia O'Keeffe told by Momaday during the festival in 1992.

980. Jay, Paul. "Posing: Autobiography and the Subject of Photography." In *Autobiography and Postmodernism,* edited by Kathleen Ashley, Leigh Gilmore, and Gerald Peters. Amherst: University of Massachusetts Press, 1994. 191–92, 203–11. Jay explores the role of "visual memory," or the "reading" of images in photographs in autobiography, and the ideas of self-identity that such images embody. He uses three texts in this study: *La chambre,* by Roland Barthe; *L'amant,* by Marguerite Duras; and Momaday's *The Names.* Photographs from *The Names* are included.

981. Kracht, Benjamin R. "Kiowa Powwows: Continuity in Ritual Practice." *American Indian Quarterly* 18, no. 3 (Summer 1994): 321–28. This essay traces the history of the Gourd Dance and includes other information about this sacred dance that is integral to Kiowa identity.

982. Laskowski, Timothy. "Naming Reality in Native American and Eastern European Literatures." *MELUS* 19, no. 3 (Autumn 1994): 47–59. The author finds parallels between the literatures of American Indians and Eastern Europeans, cultures that have lived with the threat of extinction. In particular, he examines the writings of Momaday and Polish-Lithuanian exile Czeslaw Milosz.

983. Manley, Kathleen E. B. "Decreasing the Distance: Contemporary Native American Texts, Hypertext, and the Concept of Audience." *Southern Folklore*

51, no. 2 (1994): 121–35. This essay examines the "orally-influenced" writing of Momaday and other contemporary writers, with references to *House Made of Dawn*, *The Way to Rainy Mountain*, and *The Names.*

984. Portelli, Alessandro. "Houses of Dawn." In chapter 1 of Part 1, "Foundation: The Text beneath the Voice." *The Text and the Voice: Writing, Speaking, and Democracy in American Literature.* New York: Columbia University Press, 1994. 2–26. In particular, see pp. 11–12, 22, 25. Portelli includes *House Made of Dawn* in his review of theories on the relationship of orality and writing. This book was published earlier in Italy as *Testo e la voce.*

985. ———. "Writing Silence: [Henry] James, Momaday, and [Edith] Wharton." In chapter 5 of Part 2, "The Text in the Voice." *The Text and the Voice* (1994). 111–15. Momaday's use of silence as an articulation of speech is examined.

986. ———. "The Man Made of Words: Momaday, Silko, Welch." In chapter 9 of Part 3, "Second Foundation: The Voice upon the Text." *The Text and the Voice* (1994). 213–17. Portelli discusses "The Man Made of Words," tribal memory, and the old woman Ko-shan as a figure integrating orality and writing.

987. Prampolini, Gaetano. "'Many Journeys in the One': *The Way to Rainy Mountain* and N. Scott Momaday's Literary Work." In *Native American Literatures,* edited by Laura Coltelli. Forum, nos. 4–5. Pisa, Italy: SEU (Servizio Editoriale Universitaria), 1994. 3–30.

988. Roemer, Kenneth M. "Contemporary American Indian Literature: The Centrality of Canons on the Margins." *American Literary History* 6, no. 3 (Autumn 1994): 583–99. Anthologies and collections of American Indian literature are the focus of this essay.

989. ———. "Returning the Gift of Identity," in "The World of N. Scott Momaday: Special Issue," edited by Richard F. Fleck. *Paintbrush* 21 (Autumn 1994): 31–48.

990. Schubnell, Matthias. "Locke Setman, Emil Nolde and the Search for Expression in N. Scott Momaday's *The Ancient Child.*" *American Indian Quarterly* 18, no. 4 (Fall 1994): 468–80. Discussion of Momaday's venture into painting and drawing is included in this essay.

991. Taylor, Paul Beekman. "Repetition as Cure in Native American Story: Silko's *Ceremony* and Momaday's *The Ancient Child.*" In *Repetition,* edited by Andreas Fischer. Tübingen, Germany: Narr, 1994. 221–42. This essay also appeared in *Swiss Papers in English Language and Literature,* no. 7 (1994): 221–42.

992. Velie, Alan R. "The Return of the Native: The Renaissance of Tribal Religions as Reflected in the Fiction of N. Scott Momaday." *Religion & Literature* 26, no. 1 (Spring 1994): 135–46.

993. Wong, Hertha D. "Plains Indian Names and 'the Autobiographical Act': N. Scott Momaday's *Names*." In *Autobiography and Postmodernism*, edited by Kathleen Ashley, Leigh Gilmore, and Gerald Peters. Amherst: University of Massachusetts Press, 1994. 212–39. Wong uses statements made by Momaday in *The Names* to affirm the importance of names for Plains Indian identity. In particular, see pp. 213, 232–37.

1995

994. Henry, Gordon. "Cultural Relationships in American Indian Literature: The Power of Word in the Works of Four American Indian Novelists." In *Jornadas de estudios ingleses*, edited by Carmelo Medina-Casado. Jaen, Spain: Universidad de Jaen, 1995. Momaday is one of the novelists included in this study.

995. Kauffman, Stuart. *At Home in the Universe: The Search for the Laws of Self-Organization and Complexity*. New York: Oxford University Press, 1995. Kauffman recounts hearing Momaday speak at a meeting about serious issues facing humanity and stating his belief that the central issue people must address is the need to reinvent the sacred, a sense of the sacred whereby we hold things precious and ourselves as being of worth. See also Kauffman under 2008.

996. Rainwater, Catherine. "Planes, Lines, Shapes, and Shadows: N. Scott Momaday's Iconological Imagination." *Texas Studies in Literature and Language* 37, no. 4 (Winter 1995): 376–93. The four references to art in this essay's title are the titles of the four "books," or parts, of *The Ancient Child*.

997. Ruppert, James. "Intricate Patterns of the Universe: *House Made of Dawn*." Chapter 3 in *Mediation in Contemporary Native American Fiction*. American Indian Literature and Critical Studies, vol. 15. Norman: University of Oklahoma Press, 1995. 36–55. Ruppert argues that Momaday "mediates through the embedding of non-Native psychological elements in a Native mythic story" (54).

998. Scheick, William J. "Structures of Belief/Narrative Structures: Mojtabai's *Ordinary Time* and Erdrich's *The Bingo Palace*." *Texas Studies in Literature and Language* 37, no. 4 (Winter 1995): 363–73. The author includes *The Ancient Child* in exploring ways in which narrative structures register structures of belief.

999. Tessman, Lisa. "Beyond Communitarian Unity in the Politics of Identity." *Socialist Review* 94, nos. 1–2 (1995): 55–83. The author maintains that "the unresolved ideological tension" at the end of *House Made of Dawn* may be "restated in terms of a friction between two models of identity," one that sees "home" as a place of return (tribal identity) and the other that sees it as a point of departure (75–77). This essay is cited below in Giorgio Mariani's *Post-Tribal Epics* (1996).

1000. Tissut, Anne Laure. "*The Ancient Child* of N. Scott Momaday: A Redeeming Disorder?" *Ideologies dans le monde Anglo Saxon* 8 (1995): 167–85.

1001. Vizenor, Gerald. "Authored Animals: Creature Tropes in Native American Fiction." *Social Research* 62, no. 3 (Fall 1995): 661–83. Vizenor discusses the authored bears as metaphors in the narratives of *The Ancient Child* and *House Made of Dawn.*

1002. ———. "Native American Indian Identities: Autoinscriptions and the Cultures of Names." In *Native American Perspectives on Literature and History,* edited by Alan R. Velie. American Indian Literature and Critical Studies, vol. 19. Norman: University of Oklahoma Press, 1995. 117–26. Previously published in 1992. Vizenor quotes from *The Way to Rainy Mountain* and *The Names.* In particular, see pp. 120–21.

1996

1003. Browdy de Hernandez, Jennifer. "The Plural Self: The Politicization of Memory and Form in Three American Ethnic Autobiographies." In *Memory and Cultural Politics: New Approaches to American Ethnic Literatures,* edited by Amritjit Singh, Joseph T. Skerrett, Jr., and Robert E. Hogan. Boston: Northeastern University Press, 1996. 41–59. The author examines Momaday's *The Names,* Gloria Anzaldua's *Borderlands/La Frontera,* and Audre Lorde's *Zami: A New Spelling of My Name,* and concludes that these works give "new meanings and new possibilities to the term autobiography" (57).

1004. Burnham, Philip. "The Return of the Native: The Politics of Identity in American Indian Fiction of the West." In *Reading the West: New Essays on the Literature of the American West,* edited by Michael Kowalewski. Cambridge Studies in American Literature and Culture, no. 98. New York: Cambridge University Press, 1996. 199–212. Momaday is included in Burnham's discussion about a variety of works and perspectives of Native writers who have written on the mythical place of the West in American history. In particular, see pp. 204–207.

1005. Cook-Lynn, Elizabeth. "American Indian Intellectualism and the New Indian Story." *American Indian Quarterly* 20, no. 1 (Winter 1996): 57–82. The author comments on reasons why *House Made of Dawn* is a classic.

1006. ———. "The American Indian Fiction Writers: Cosmopolitanism, Nationalism, the Third World, and First Nation Sovereignty." Chapter 8 of *Why I Can't Read Wallace Stegner and Other Essays: A Tribal Voice*. Madison: University of Wisconsin Press, 1996. 78–96. Includes references to "The Man Made of Words," on pp. 80, 83, 84.

1007. Davis, Randall C. "'Something Other and Irresistible and Wild': Bear in the Work of N. Scott Momaday." *Journal of the Association for the Interdisciplinary Study of the Arts* 1, no. 2 (Spring 1996): 79–87.

1008. Gish, Robert F. "The Word Medicine of James Welch: *The Death of Jim Loney*." In Part 2, "Indian Voices," of *Beyond Bounds: Cross-cultural Essays on Anglo, American Indian, and Chicano Literature*. Albuquerque: University of New Mexico Press, 1996. 65–67, 69. Gish finds "a longing for transcendence" in the story of Loney that parallels Momaday's descriptions in *House Made of Dawn*. See also Gish's "Introduction" to Part 2, 54–55, regarding Momaday and the Pulitzer Prize.

1009. Hindman, Jane E. "I Think of That Mountain as My Maternal Grandmother: Constructing Self and Other through Landscape." *Interdisciplinary Studies in Literature and Environment* 3, no. 2 (Fall 1996): 63–72.

1010. Krupat, Arnold. "Postcolonialism, Ideology, and Native American Literature." Chapter 2 in *The Turn to the Native: Studies in Criticism and Culture*. Lincoln: University of Nebraska Press, 1996. 30–55. Krupat discusses the term "postcolonial" as it is applied to *House Made of Dawn* and Native American literature. In particular, see pp. 30, 37, 40–44.

1011. Landrum, Larry N. "The Shattered Modernism of Momaday's *House Made of Dawn*." *Modern Fiction Studies* 42, no. 4 (Winter 1996): 763–86.

1012. Mariani, Giorgio. "Timelessness and the Invention of Tradition in Scott Momaday's *House Made of Dawn*." *Post-Tribal Epics: The Native American Novel between Tradition and Modernity*. Native American Studies, vol. 3. Lewiston, New York: Edwin Mellen Press, 1996. 49–80.

1013. ———. "Back to the Future: Apocalypse and Utopia in Recent Native American Novels." *Post-Tribal Epics*. Lewiston, New York: Edwin Mellen

Press, 1996. 188–89. Mariani discusses *The Ancient Child* and its protagonist, Locke Setman.

1014. Slater, Renee, and Kate Fullbrook. "Revisioning the American Landscape: From Utopia to Eco-critique." Chapter 9 in *Writing and America*, edited by Gavin Cologne-Brookes, Neil Sammells, and David Timms. London: Longman, 1996. 216–31. References to Momaday are included in the section titled "The Contemporary Situation."

1015. Strong, Pauline Turner, and Barrik Van Winkle. "'Indian Blood': Reflections on the Reckoning and Refiguring of Native North American Identity." *Cultural Anthropology* 11, no. 4 (November 1996): 547–76. See the section "'Blood Memory' and 'Crossblood Survivors': Refigurations and Critiques of Essentialized Identities," 560–65, in reference to Momaday's trope, "memory in the blood," which the authors describe as "a vehicle of connection and integration" (562).

1016. Wallace, Karen Lynn. "Liminality and Myth in Native American Fiction: *Ceremony* and *The Ancient Child*." *American Indian Culture and Research Journal* 20, no. 4 (Fall 1996): 91–119. Wallace studies the use of myth and how Momaday weaves together past and present to create the perception of one blending into the other. See also Wallace in the section "Theses—1996."

1997

1017. Bennett, Robert. "The Artist as Shaman: Ritual, Healing, and Art in N. Scott Momaday's *House Made of Dawn*." *Q/W/E/R/T/Y: Arts, littératures, & civilisations du monde Anglophone* 7 (October 1997): 151–61.

1018. Berthier-Foglar, Susanne. "Le contexte historique de *House Made of Dawn*." In *"House Made of Dawn": N. Scott Momaday*, edited by Bernadette Rigal-Cellard. Paris: Ellipses, 1997. 17–25 (in French).

1019. Besson, Françoise. "Murs visibles et invisibles ou le paysage mémoire dans *House Made of Dawn* de N. Scott Momaday." In *"House Made of Dawn": N. Scott Momaday*, edited by Bernadette Rigal-Cellard. Paris: Ellipses, 1997. 101–14 (in French).

1020. Castillo, Susan. "Naming into Being: Ethnic Identities in N. Scott Momaday's *House Made of Dawn*." *Q/W/E/R/T/Y: Arts, littératures, & civilisations du monde Anglophone* 7 (October 1997): 163–66.

1021. Dunsmore, Roger. "Inside Out—Outside In: The Arrowmaker and the Child."

Earth's Mind: Essays in Native Literature. Albuquerque: University of New Mexico Press, 1997. 123–33. Dunsmore observes that some readers have questioned the focus on killing the enemy, which he thinks is central to what the arrowmaker does. He feels there is a need for stories that tell of events in which a man goes beyond the patterns of warrior identity. He asks whether there can be no doubt about the identity of the man outside the tipi, or tepee, as an enemy. Momaday's response to this question is a definitive "yes." There is no doubt. "The Story of the Arrowmaker" is on pp. 123–24 of Dunsmore's book.

1022. Feith, Michel. "Entre deux voi(es)x: 'Double-voicedness' dans *House Made of Dawn.*" In *"House Made of Dawn": N. Scott Momaday,* edited by Bernadette Rigal-Cellard. Paris: Ellipses, 1997. 140–57 (in French and English).

1023. Fourtina, Hervé. "Entre chien et loup: Aires transitionnelles et jeux sur l'origine dans *House Made of Dawn.*" In *"House Made of Dawn": N. Scott Momaday,* edited by Bernadette Rigal-Cellard. Paris: Ellipses, 1997. 45–54 (in French and English).

1024. Gish, Robert F. "N. Scott Momaday." In *Updating the Literary West,* edited by Thomas Lyon et al. Sponsored by the Western Literature Association. Fort Worth: Texas Christian University Press, 1997. 537–40.

1025. Hardy, Mireille. "'A Small Silversided Fish': From Relocation to Dislocation in *House Made of Dawn.*" *Q/W/E/R/T/Y: Arts, littératures, & civilisations du monde Anglophone* 7 (October 1997): 167–73.

1026. Heldrich, Philip. "Constructing the Self through Language and Vision in N. Scott Momaday's *The Ancient Child.*" *Southwestern American Literature* 22, no. 2 (Spring 1997): 11–19.

1027. Hill, Randall T. G. "Methodological Approaches to Native American Narrative and the Role of Performance." *American Indian Quarterly* 21, no. 1 (Winter 1997): 111–47. In the section "Content Analysis/Ethnic Criticism," Hill discusses how Charles Larson, Andrew Wiget, and Jamake Highwater categorize Momaday's fiction writing.

1028. Kracht, Benjamin R. "Kiowa Religion in Historical Perspective." "Special Issue on Native American Spirituality," edited by Lee Irwin. *American Indian Quarterly* 21, no. 1 (Winter 1997): 15–33. An excerpt from *The Way to Rainy Mountain* is presented at the beginning of this essay. Kracht believes that Momaday has recounted Kiowa prayer best in his description of his grandmother Aho praying in her native language.

1029. Kurjatto-Renard, Patrycja. "The Native American Concept of the Word in *House Made of Dawn*." In *"House Made of Dawn": N. Scott Momaday*, edited by Bernadette Rigal-Cellard. Paris: Ellipses, 1997. 125–39.

1030. Isernhagen, Hartwig. "N. Scott Momaday and the Use(s) of Modernism: Some Remarks on the Example of Yvor Winters." In *Aspects of Modernism: Studies in Honour of Max Nänny*, edited by Andreas Fischer, Martin Heusser, and Thomas Hermann. Tübingen, Germany: Narr, 1997. 313–28.

1031. Marty, Myron A. *Daily Life in the United States, 1960–1990: Decades of Discord*. Daily Life through History. Westport, Connecticut: Greenwood Press, 1997. 92. This social history series briefly mentions two books, *House Made of Dawn* and Vine Deloria, Jr.'s, *Custer Died for Your Sins*, in connection with the conditions faced by Native Americans during the period of the Civil Rights Movement, the Vietnam War, and Watergate.

1032. Mielle de Prinsec, Annie-Paule. "Sur le fil du rasoir." In *"House Made of Dawn": N. Scott Momaday*, edited by Bernadette Rigal-Cellard. Paris: Ellipses, 1997. 90–100 (in French).

1033. Moser, Irene. "Native American Imaginative Spaces." Chapter 14 in *American Indian Studies: An Interdisciplinary Approach to Contemporary Issues*, edited by Dane Morrison. New York: Peter Lang, 1997. 285–97. Moser explores how Momaday and other writers construct social spaces in their fiction and poetry. *House Made of Dawn*, *The Way to Rainy Mountain*, and *The Ancient Child* are discussed.

1034. Nelson, Robert M. "Grounded in Place: The Houses Made of Dawn in *House Made of Dawn*." In *"House Made of Dawn": N. Scott Momaday*, edited by Bernadette Rigal-Cellard. Paris: Ellipses, 1997. 76–89.

1035. ———. "Place, Vision, and Identity in Native American Literatures." Chapter 13 in *American Indian Studies: An Interdisciplinary Approach to Contemporary Issues*, edited by Dane Morrison. New York: Peter Lang, 1997. 265–83. *House Made of Dawn* is among the contemporary novels included in this study of critical approaches to Native American literatures. A list, "Some Novels (U.S. and Canadian) Published since *House Made of Dawn* and *Ceremony*," is included on pp. 282–83.

1036. Pellerin, Simone. "Espace et temps: *House Made of Dawn*." In *"House Made of Dawn": N. Scott Momaday*, edited by Bernadette Rigal-Cellard. Paris: Ellipses, 1997. 115–21 (in French and English).

1037. Peters, Darrell J. "Diving Home: Centering in Louis Owens's *Wolfsong.*" *American Indian Quarterly* 21, no. 3 (Summer 1997): 471–81. This essay pertains to the reconstructing of one's lost center, and includes discussion of *House Made of Dawn* and its protagonist, Abel. Peters quotes a frequently repeated statement from Momaday's "The Man Made of Words": "An Indian is an idea which a given man has of himself" (*Indian Voices,* 1970, 49).

1038. Purdy, John. "'perspective, proportion, design': The Moral Lesson of *House Made of Dawn.*" In *"House Made of Dawn": N. Scott Momaday,* edited by Bernadette Rigal-Cellard. Paris: Ellipses, 1997. 34–42.

1039. Rekow, Alec. "Telling about Bear in N. Scott Momaday's *The Ancient Child.*" *Wicazo Sa Review* 12, no. l (Spring 1997): 149–64.

1040. Rigal-Cellard, Bernadette. "A Reading of the Prologue of *House Made of Dawn* by Momaday." In *"House Made of Dawn": N. Scott Momaday,* edited by Bernadette Rigal-Cellard. Paris: Ellipses, 1997. 55–72. This is a revised version of her article, originally published in *Native American Literatures,* edited by Laura Coltelli. *Forum,* nos. 2–3, 1990–91. Pisa, Italy: SEU (Servizio Editoriale Universitaria), 1992. 39–56.

1041. Scenters-Zapico, John. "Cross-cultural Mediation: Language, Storytelling, History, and Self as Enthymematic Premises in the Novels of N. Scott Momaday." *American Indian Quarterly* 21, no. 3 (Summer 1997): 499–514. The author uses "the epistemological view of the enthymeme" in his study of Abel in *House Made of Dawn* and of Set in *The Ancient Child.* He also brings the Kiowas' Tai-me into his discourse on the sense of self.

1042. Tidwell, Paul L. "Imagination, Conversation, and Trickster Discourse: Negotiating an Approach to Native American Literary Culture." *American Indian Quarterly* 21, no. 4 (Fall 1997): 621–31. Tidwell discusses his own dialogical approach to contemporary Native American literature, focusing primarily on *House Made of Dawn,* Leslie Marmon Silko's *Ceremony,* and James Welch's *Winter in the Blood.*

1043. Valtat-Comet, Nelly. "La narration dans *House Made of Dawn.*" In *"House Made of Dawn": N. Scott Momaday,* edited by Bernadette Rigal-Cellard. Paris: Ellipses, 1997. 26–33 (in French).

1044. Van Wynsberghe, Patricia. "De la voix à la letter: Émergence d'une écriture de l'entre-deux." In *"House Made of Dawn": N. Scott Momaday,* edited by Bernadette Rigal-Cellard. Paris: Ellipses, 1997. 158–70 (in French).

1045. Velie, Alan R. "Identity and Genre in *House Made of Dawn*." *Q/W/E/R/T/Y: arts, littératures, & civilisations du monde Anglophone* 7 (October 1997): 175–81.

1046. ———. "Indian Identity and Indian Literature." *European Review of Native American Studies* 11, no. 1 (1997): 5–10. Velie points out that determining Indian identity has not been a simple matter. He discusses how Momaday has addressed the issue of identity.

1047. Weaver, Jace. "Indian Literary Renaissance and the Continuing Search for Community (1968–)." *That the People Might Live: Native American Literatures and Native American Community*. New York: Oxford University Press, 1997. 121–59. Beginning with the publication of *House Made of Dawn*, Weaver writes about Momaday and other authors whose works have appeared since 1968 and who, Weaver believes, offer a "communitist" view. He coined "communitist" by combining "community" and "activism."

1048. Wilson, Michael. "Speaking of Home: The Idea of the Center in Some Contemporary American Indian Writing." *Wicazo Sa Review* 12, no. 1 (Spring 1997): 129–47. Wilson presents an analysis of the centers of identity in *The Way to Rainy Mountain*.

1998

1049. Bartelt, Guillermo. "American Indian Geopiety in Scott Momaday's Discourse of the Moral Landscape." *Language and Literature* 23 (1998): 19–31.

1050. Broecke, Kim-van-den. "The Shadow of Tsoai: The Land, the Stories, and the People in N. Scott Momaday's *The Ancient Child*." *Cycnos* (France) 15, no. 1 (1998): 71–85.

1051. Cook-Lynn, Elizabeth. "American Indian Intellectualism and the New Indian Story." In *Natives and Academics: Researching and Writing about American Indians*, edited by Devon A. Mihesuah. Lincoln: University of Nebraska Press, 1998. 126, 131–32, 136. Cook-Lynn discusses the qualities of *House Made of Dawn* that make this novel a classic.

1052. Deville, Michel. *The American Prose Poem: Poetic Form and Boundaries of Genre*. Gainesville: University Press of Florida, 1998. 247. In this study, Deville makes only one reference, albeit a noteworthy one, to Momaday: "The speech-based tradition of the prose poem has found . . . its most remarkable expressions in the works of several North American writers, most notably Momaday, Luci Tapahanso, and Joy Harjo."

1053. Donovan, Kathleen M. "'A Menace among the Words': Women in the Novels of N. Scott Momaday." *Feminist Readings of Native American Literature: Coming to Voice*. Tucson: University of Arizona Press, 1998. 69–98. Donovan finds an "underlying misogyny" in Momaday's *House Made of Dawn* and *The Ancient Child*.

1054. Miller, Carol. "Telling the Indian Urban: Representations in American Indian Fiction." "Special Issue on American Indians and the Urban Experience," edited by Susan Lebo and Kurt Peters. *American Indian Culture and Research Journal* 22, no. 4 (Fall 1998): 43–65. Post–World War II America, a period of dislocation, is discussed as it is presented in *House Made of Dawn* and Leslie Marmon Silko's *Ceremony*, pp. 52–61.

1055. Owens, Louis. "Blood Trails: Missing Grandmothers and Making Worlds." Chapter 10 in *Mixedblood Messages: Literature, Film, Family, Place*. American Indian Literature and Critical Studies, vol. 26. Norman: University of Oklahoma Press, 1998. 150–66. Owens explored Momaday's "memory in the blood" and Owens's own phrase "blood trails." Owens disagreed with Arnold Krupat's comments about such phrases being racist and explained that these are tropes, or figurative notions.

1056. ———. "'Everywhere There Was Life': How Native Americans Can Save the World." Chapter 16 in *Mixedblood Messages*. University of Oklahoma Press, 1998. 218–36. Owens cited passages from the works of Momaday, D'Arcy McNickle, and Luther Standing Bear in discussing Native Americans' worldview and their image as "the ultimate ecologist." Owens also explained the significance of a "truly remarkable thing" seen by Mammedaty in *The Way to Rainy Mountain* (73).

1057. ———. "Through an Amber Glass: Chief Doom and the Native American Novel Today." Chapter 6 in *Mixedblood Messages*. University of Oklahoma Press, 1998. 56–61. *House Made of Dawn* was used as Owens's beginning point for his discussion of where the Native American novel stood at the end of the twentieth century.

1058. Roberson, Susan L. "Translocations and Transformations: Identity in N. Scott Momaday's *The Ancient Child*." *American Indian Quarterly* 22, nos. 1–2 (Winter–Spring 1998): 31–45.

1059. Schwendener, Peter. "In Quest of Graham Hough." *American Scholar* 67, no. 1 (Winter 1998): 139–45. Schwendener, an admirer of Yvor Winters, comments on Winters's views of Momaday's poetry.

1060. Spellmeyer, Kurt. "'Too Little Care': Language, Politics, and Embodiment in the Life-World." *Rhetoric in an Antifoundational World: Language, Culture, and Pedagogy,* edited by Michael Bernard-Donals and Richard R. Glejzer. New Haven, Connecticut: Yale University Press, 1998. 254–91. The importance of "The Man Made of Words" is considered in this study of the politics of speech and writing. In particular, see pp. 256–63, 271–73.

1061. Toy, Phyllis. "Racing Them Homeward: Myth and Ritual in *House Made of Dawn.*" *Etudes Anglaises: Grande-Bretagne, Etats-Unis* (Paris) 51, no. 1 (January–March 1998): 27–38.

1062. Vickers, Scott B. "The Storytellers: Transforming the Oral Tradition." In chapter 9 of *Native American Identities: From Stereotype to Archetype in Art and Literature.* Albuquerque: University of New Mexico Press, 1998. 128, 133–35. Vickers includes discussion of *House Made of Dawn, The Way to Rainy Mountain,* and *The Names.* He places Momaday among the foremost Native American autobiographers.

1063. Vizenor, Gerald. "Literary Animals." In chapter 3 of *Fugitive Poses: Native American Indian Scenes of Absence and Presence.* Abraham Lincoln Lecture Series. Lincoln: University of Nebraska Press, 1998. 132–43. Vizenor calls Momaday "an author of memorable animals," especially of bears and eagles, "the creatures of native survivance."

1064. Warrior, Robert Allen. "Literature and Students in the Emergence of Native American Studies." In *Studying Native America: Problems and Prospects,* edited by Russell Thornton. Madison: University of Wisconsin Press, 1998. 111–15, 121–22. This essay discusses how Native American literary studies since Momaday's Pulitzer Prize have affected Native American studies and the ways in which the literature was institutionalized in English departments and literary texts.

1999

1065. Allen, Chadwick. "Blood (and) Memory." *American Literature* 71, no. 1 (March 1999): 92–116. Allen examines the articulation of indigenous memories in literature and culture.

1066. Anderson, Eric Gary. "Mobile Homes: Migration and Resistance in American Indian Literature." *American Indian Literature and the Southwest: Contexts and Dispositions.*Austin: University of Texas Press, 1999. 17, 21, 29–31. The pages cited focus on *The Way to Rainy Mountain.*

1067. Berner, Robert L. "What Is an American Indian Writer?" *Defining American Indian Literature: One Nation Divisible.* Native American Studies, vol. 6. Lewiston, New York: Edwin Mellen Press, 1999. 1–18. In particular, see pp. 12–14 of Berner's essay.

1068. Besson, Françoise. "The Doll, the Zodiac, and the Deer of Lascaux: The Essence of the World in Scott Momaday's Pictorial Language." *European Review of Native American Studies* (Budapest) 13, no. 1 (1999): 35–46. Besson explores the visual imagery in *House Made of Dawn* and *The Ancient Child.*

1069. Brill de Ramírez, Susan Berry. "Semiotic Significance, Conversive Meaning, and N. Scott Momaday's *House Made of Dawn.*" Chapter 2 in *Contemporary American Indian Literatures and the Oral Tradition.* Tucson: University of Arizona Press, 1999. 41–64. See also "Introduction: Orality and Conversivity in Relation to American Indian Literatures," 16–17.

1070. Caffey, David L. *Land of Enchantment, Land of Conflict: New Mexico in English-language Fiction.* Tarleton State University Southwestern Studies in the Humanities, no. 11. College Station: Texas A&M University Press, 1999. (port.) This book includes brief discussions of the following works: *House Made of Dawn,* chapter 3, 40–42, 49; *The Ancient Child,* chapter 8, 121–22; and the film based on *House Made of Dawn,* chapter 11, 182.

1071. Elder, Arlene A. "'Dancing the Page': Orature in N. Scott Momaday's *The Way to Rainy Mountain.*" *Narrative* 7, no. 3 (October 1999): 272–88.

1072. Fast, Robin Riley. "'Still Talking Indian.'" *The Heart as a Drum: Continuance and Resistance in American Indian Poetry.* Ann Arbor: University of Michigan Press, 1999. 31–46. Fast includes an analysis of Momaday's address, "The Man Made of Words," which she believes is the key text for reading and understanding him on language. She states: "The contemporary American Indian writers who most persistently and searchingly make language their subject are N. Scott Momaday and Gerald Vizenor" (32–33).

1073. Frischkorn, Craig. "The Shadow of Tsoai: Autobiographical Bear Power in N. Scott Momaday's *The Ancient Child.*" *Journal of Popular Culture* 33, no. 2 (Fall 1999): 23–29.

1074. Hafen, P. Jane. "Pan-Indianism and Tribal Sovereignties in *House Made of Dawn* and *The Names.*" *Western American Literature* 34, no. 1 (Spring 1999): 6–24.

1075. Lincoln, Kenneth. "Native Poetics." *Modern Fiction Studies* 45, no. 1 (Spring

1999): 146–84. Lincoln explains the term "native poetics," cross-referencing American Indian and Anglo-American literatures as they have evolved over a century. His discussion includes references to Momaday's essay, "A Love Affair with Emily Dickinson," in *Viva, Santa Fe New Mexican*, August 6, 1972, 2.

1076. Martin, Calvin Luther. ". . . to the Skin of the World." *The Way of the Human Being*. New Haven, Connecticut: Yale University Press, 1999. 32–51. Martin begins with a passage from "The Man Made of Words," about Americans needing a land ethic. He also draws from *The Way to Rainy Mountain* and *The Gourd Dancer* in this essay about stories relating to kinship.

1077. Mjoberg, Joran Nestor. "Bland Native Americans: Indianen och forfattaren N. Scott Momaday." *Kulturtidskriften-HORISONT* (Vasa, Finland) 46, no. 4 (1999): 31–43.

1078. Peterson, Nancy J. "Introduction: Native American Literature: From the Margins to the Mainstream." *Modern Fiction Studies* 45, no. 1 (Spring 1999): 1–9.

1079. Ramsey, Jarold. "Tradition and Individual Talents in Modern Indian Writing." Essay 15 in *Reading the Fire: The Traditional Indian Literatures of America*. Rev. ed. Seattle: University of Washington Press, 1999. 252–53, 258–60. *The Way to Rainy Mountain* is included in Ramsey's discussion.

1080. Schnabel, William. "Conservation and Innovation in *House Made of Dawn*." *Idéologies dans le monde Anglo Saxon* 11 (1999): 47–66.

1081. Selinger, Bernard. "*House Made of Dawn*: A Positively Ambivalent *Bildungsroman*." *Modern Fiction Studies* 45, no. 1 (Spring 1999): 38–68.

1082. Taylor, Paul Beekman. "Silko's Reappropriation of Secrecy." In *Leslie Marmon Silko: A Collection of Critical Essays*, edited by Louise K. Barnett and James L. Thorson. Albuquerque: University of New Mexico Press, 1999. 23–32, 39–40. Momaday is among writers who have influenced Silko's writing. *House Made of Dawn* and *The Way to Rainy Mountain* are included in Beekman's discussion. See also p. 308 of the book's index for additional references to Momaday.

1083. Warrior, Robert A. "The Native American Scholar: Toward a New Intellectual Agenda." "Issue on Emerging Ideas in Native American Studies." *Wicazo Sa Review* 14, no. 2 (Autumn 1999): 46–54.

2000

1084. Adams, Timothy Dow. "We Have All Gone into the World of Light: N. Scott

Momaday." *Light Writing and Life Writing: Photography in Autobiography.* Chapel Hill: University of North Carolina Press, 2000. 81–102. Adams's emphasis is on *The Names,* with some remarks about *The Way to Rainy Mountain.*

1085. Giles, James R. "Redemptive Landscape, Malevolent City: Scott Momaday's *House Made of Dawn.*" *Violence in the Contemporary American Novel: An End to Violence.* Columbia: University of South Carolina Press, 2000. 100–112.

1086. Hurst, David Thomas. *Skull Wars: Kennewick, Archaeology, and the Battle for Native American Identity.* New York: Basic Books, 2000. 256–57. Hurst quotes from "Disturbing the Spirits" in the November 2, 1966, issue of the *New York Times,* in which Momaday writes about the desecration of Indian spiritual life and his belief in the Bering Strait migration theory.

1087. Krupat, Arnold, and Brian Swann. "Introduction." In *Here First: Autobiographical Essays by Native American Writers,* edited by Krupat and Swann. New York: Modern Library; Random House, 2000. xv–xvii. Although Momaday does not have an essay in this volume, the editors include him in their discussion of collections of interviews and autobiographical works.

1088. Lincoln, Kenneth. "Old Songs Made New: Momaday." In chapter 8, "Seer, Shaman, Clown," of *Sing with the Heart of a Bear: Fusions of Native and American Poetry, 1890–1999.* Berkeley: University of California Press, 2000. 240–55. Lincoln presents the poetics of this poet-writer and his book *In the Presence of the Sun: Stories and Poems, 1961–1991* (1992). See also "Afterword: The Bear's Tail," 401–409.

1089. Schnell, Steven M. "The Kiowa Homeland in Oklahoma." *Geographical Review* 90, no. 2 (April 2000): 155–76. Reprinted in *Homelands: A Geography of Culture and Place across America,* edited by Richard L. Nostrand and Lawrence E. Estaville. Baltimore: Johns Hopkins University Press, 2001. 139–54. This essay includes quotes from *The Names* and *The Way to Rainy Mountain,* including Momaday's "The Story of Tsoai" (Rock Tree). In particular, see pp. 146–50.

1090. Sequoya Magdaleno, Jana. "How (!) Is an Indian? A Context of Stories, Round 2." In *Postcolonial Theory and the United States: Race, Ethnicity, and Literature,* edited by Amritjit Singh and Peter Schmidt. Jackson: University Press of Mississippi, 2000. 279–99. Discusses ethnic identity, the question of who is an Indian, and how Momaday and Leslie Marmon Silko approach this subject. An earlier essay appeared in 1993 under Sequoya, Jana.

1091. Warrior, Robert Allen. "Packing and Unpacking 'The Man Made of Words.'" *Genre: Forms of Disclosure and Culture* 33, nos. 3–4 (Fall–Winter 2000): 257–68.

1092. Wong, Hertha D. "Native American Visual Autobiography: Figuring Place, Subjectivity, and History." *Iowa Review* 30, no. 3 (Winter 2000–2001): 149–53. Wong considers *The Way to Rainy Mountain* a good example of a visual autobiography and thinks it has four narrative modes—mythical, historical, personal, and visual—rather than three.

2001

1093. Adamson, Joni. *American Indian Literature, Environmental Justice, and Ecocriticism: The Middle Place.* Tucson: University of Arizona Press, 2001. Includes comments about Momaday and *House Made of Dawn* on p. 131.

1094. Bevis, William W. "Native American Novels: Homing In." In *Defining Travel: Diverse Visions,* edited by Susan L. Roberson. Jackson: University Press of Mississippi, 2001. 244–57.

1095. Clements, William M. "'image and word cannot be divided': N. Scott Momaday and Kiowa Ekphrasis." *Western American Literature* 36, no. 2 (Summer 2001): 134–52. Clements examines Momaday's poems in *In the Presence of the Sun* (1992) to demonstrate an affinity of the verbal and visual in his artistic expression.

1096. Evers, Larry, and Felipe Molina. "Coyote Songs." Issue titled "Native American Literature: Boundaries and Sovereignties," edited by Kathryn W. Shanley. *Paradoxa: Studies in World Literary Genres,* no. 15 (2001): 9–10. In their introduction to this essay, the authors discuss the three directions that works by American Indian writers took following Momaday's winning of the Pulitzer Prize.

1097. Owens, Louis. "As If an Indian Were Really an Indian: Native American Voices and Postcolonial Theory." *I Hear the Train: Reflections, Inventions, Refractions.* American Indian Literature and Critical Studies, vol. 40. Norman: University of Oklahoma Press, 2001. 210, 213, 222–26. Owens discussed identity and authenticity, and remarked about *House Made of Dawn* being "superbly subversive" (225). Reprinted in *Native American Representations: First Encounters, Distorted Images, and Literary Appropriations,* edited by Gretchen M. Bataille. Lincoln: University of Nebraska Press, 2001. 11–24. Reprinted with different subtitle in *Paradoxa,* no. 15 (2001): 170–83.

1098. Stevens, Jason W. "Bear, Outlaw, and Storyteller: American Frontier

Mythology and the Ethnic Subjectivity of N. Scott Momaday." *American Literature* 73, no. 3 (September 2001): 599–631.

1099. Wilson, Norma C. "Affirmations of Identity: The Poetry of N. Scott Momaday." *The Nature of Native American Poetry.* Albuquerque: University of New Mexico Press, 2001. 31–43.

2002

1100. Allen, Chadwick. "Blood/Land/Memory: Narrating Indigenous Identity in the American Indian Renaissance." Chapter 4 in *Blood Narrative: Indigenous Identity in American Indian and Maori Literary and Activist Texts.* Durham, North Carolina: Duke University Press, 2002. 160–93. In particular, see pp. 162, 178–92. Allen examines Momaday's "signature trope," memory in the blood, which he coined in *House Made of Dawn* (1968, 129).

1101. Celi, Ana, and María Cristina Boiero. "The Heritage of Stories: A Traditional Wisdom." *American Studies International* 40, no. 2 (June 2002): 57–72. The co-authors quote "The Man Made of Words" in their essay about the efficacy of language and the magic of words.

1102. Clements, William M. "Preface." *Oratory in Native North America.* Tucson: University of Arizona Press, 2002. ix–xii. Clements opens his preface with Momaday's response to a question asked by Charles Woodard (*Ancestral Voice*, 1989) regarding the most powerful statements he knew. Momaday replied that those statements are in the Bible, works of Shakespeare, and orations made by Indian leaders.

1103. Dreese, Donelle N. "N. Scott Momaday: The Great Plains." In chapter 2, "Mythic Reterritorializations in Ecocriticism." *Ecocriticism: Creating Self and Place in Environmental and American Indian Literatures.* American Indian Studies, vol. 15. New York: Peter Lang, 2002. 23–33, 40, 44–45. Dreese presents *The Way to Rainy Mountain* as an example of works that contribute to ecocritical approaches to literary texts.

1104. Hestetun, Øyunn. "The Land of Myth, Story, and History in Contemporary American Indian Writing: N. Scott Momaday and James Welch." *Angles on the English-Speaking World*, n.s., vol. 2, edited by Clara Juncker and Russell Duncan (2002). 105–16. Hestetun examines *The Way to Rainy Mountain* and James Welch's *Fool's Crow* (1986) to learn how the authors "envision—through the use of language—a landscape that constitutes more than a physical setting, and a history that represents more than a backdrop, for the stories they tell" (105–106). She includes a familiar Momaday statement: "The landscape of the American West has to be seen to be believed. And perhaps, conversely, it has to be believed in order to be seen."

1105. Konevich, John. "Momaday's *House Made of Dawn*." *Explicator* 60, no. 4 (Summer 2002): 236–38. Konevich explicates Abel's killing of the albino in *House Made of Dawn*, concluding that it was not done out of vengeance, but because Abel did not fully understand the rituals and customs of the tribe.

1106. Krupat, Arnold. Chapter 5, "The 'Rage Stage': Contextualizing Sherman Alexie's Indian Killer." In *Red Matters: Native American Studies*. Rethinking the Americas. Philadelphia: University of Pennsylvania, 2002. 107–11. In his discussion of *House Made of Dawn* and its protagonist, Krupat considers Momaday as a writer who resists violence.

1107. Mariani, Andrea. "Reading Momaday's Visual Art: An European Perspective." In *Literature and the Visual Arts in Twentieth-Century America*, edited and with an introduction by Michele Bottalico. Palomar Eupalinos: Letteratura Artistica, 6. Bari, Italy: Palomar, 2002. 137–55. Mariani focuses on the role of syncretism in Momaday's art and writing.

1108. Nabokov, Peter. "Old Stories, New Ways: Writing, Power, and Indian Histories." *A Forest of Time: American Indian Ways of History*. New York: Cambridge University Press, 2002. 215–16. Nabokov describes *The Way to Rainy Mountain* as a "disarmingly minimalist prose collage" and states that Momaday "blazed a trail for one kind of modern Indian history" (216).

2003

1109. Anderson, Eric Gary. "Situating American Indian Poetry: Place, Community, and the Question of Genre." In *Speak to Me Words: Essays on Contemporary American Indian Poetry*, edited by Dean Rader and Janice Gould. Tucson: University of Arizona Press, 2003. 34–55. In particular, see pp. 36–39 for references to Momaday.

1110. Breinig, Helmbrecht, ed. *Imaginary (Re)-locations: Tradition, Modernity, and the Market in Contemporary Native American Literature and Culture*. Tübingen, Germany: Stauffenburg Verlag, 2003. This collection of essays by German and American scholars examines what it has meant to be an indigenous writer in North America since the late 1960s, with a focus on cultural and political identity formation.

1111. Douglas, Christopher. "The Flawed Design: American Imperialism in N. Scott

Momaday's *House Made of Dawn* and Cormac McCarthy's *Blood Meridian*." *Critique: Studies in Contemporary Fiction* 45, no. 1 (Fall 2003): 3–21.

1112. Garroutte, Eva Marie. "Allowing the Ancestors to Speak: Radical Indigenism and New/Old Definition of Identity." Chapter 6 of *Real Indians: Identity and the Survival of Native America*. Berkeley: University of California Press, 2003. 118–26. Garroutte discusses Momaday's statements, made during conversations with Charles Woodard (*Ancestral Voice*, 1989), about "memory in the blood" and "racial memory."

1113. Gray, Richard. "Negotiating the American Century: American Literature since 1945." *A History of American Literature*. Malden, Massachusetts: Blackwell Publishing, 2003. 804–808. Gray remarks about Momaday's influence in the emergence of a major movement in Native American writing.

1114. Kang, Yong-Ki. "N. Scott Momaday's *House Made of Dawn*: The Politics of 'Running.'" *Journal of English Language and Literature/Yongo Yongmunhak* 49, no. 2 (2003): 271–88 (in Korean with English summary).

1115. Lee, A. Robert. *Multicultural American Literature: Comparative Black, Native, Latino/a, and Asian American Fictions*. Jackson: University Press of Mississippi, 2003. Three chapters contain discussion of Momaday's works: chapter 1, "Landmarks: Ellison, Momaday, Anaya, Kingston," 20–36; chapter 2, "Selves: Autobiography, Autoethnicity, and Autofiction," 37–66; and chapter 4, "Fictions of the Indian, Native Fictions?" 90–119.

1116. Lewis, Nathaniel. "Introduction: The Legacy of Authenticity." Postwestern Horizons, gen. ed. William R. Handley. *Unsettling the Literary West: Authenticity and Authorship*. Lincoln: University of Nebraska Press, 2003. 1–18. Lewis examines the elusive subjects of "authenticity" and the "meaning of the West." In particular, see pp. 7–8, 11, 14.

1117. Lyons, Greg. "Native American Images and Voices." Chapter 7 in *Literature of the American West: A Cultural Approach*. New York: Longman, 2003. See "Introduction," 365–69, and "Biography," 380–83.

1118. Palmer, Gus, Jr. *Telling Stories the Kiowa Way*. Tucson: University of Arizona Press, 2003. 57–58. In his discourse on the Kiowa oral storytelling tradition, Palmer refers to Momaday as "perhaps the best spokesman and advocate for oral traditions." He also remarks that Momaday is a storyteller, "though not in the Kiowa sense, not insofar as the term applies to the oral Kiowa world" (58).

1119. Parker, Robert Dale. "The Reinvention of Restless Young Men." *The Invention of Native American Literature*. Ithaca, New York: Cornell University Press, 2003. 128–67. In this study of novels about "restless young men with nothing to do," Parker includes comments relating to Abel of *House Made of Dawn*.

1120. Perreten, Peter F. "Eco-Autobiography: Portrait of Place/Self Portrait." *A/B: Auto/Biography Studies* 18, no. 1 (Summer 2003): 1–22. Although writing primarily about author Lisa Dale Norton, Perreten includes *The Names* in a discussion of self, place, landscape, and ecocriticism.

1121. Pulitano, Elvira. "Crossreading Texts, Bridging Cultures." Chapter 3 in *Toward a Native American Critical Theory*. Lincoln: University of Nebraska Press, 2003. 124–43. Pulitano discusses the theoretical approach employed by Louis Owens in exploring Momaday's ideas about language and how messages of cultural survival are written and read across cultures.

1122. Rader, Dean, and Janice Gould. "Introduction: Generations and Emanations." *Speak to Me Words: Essays on Contemporary American Indian Poetry*, edited by Rader and Gould. Tucson: University of Arizona Press, 2003. 3–20. This is a dialogue between the editors and includes quotes from writings by Momaday. See also a bibliography, "Collections of Poems by Native Authors," 269–76, listing books of poetry by over fifty authors, including four by Momaday.

1123. Schröder, Nicole. *Kulturelle Selbstentwürfe in zeitgenössischer indianischer Literatur: N. Scott Momaday, Sherman Alexie, und Wendy Rose*. Series Beiträge aus Anglistik und Amerikanistik, no. 13. Frankfurt am Main, Germany; New York: Peter Lang, 2003. 174 pp. (in German). Schröder compares the treatment of cultural identity by these three authors. *The Way to Rainy Mountain* was selected for this study.

1124. Schweninger, Lee. "Claiming Europe: Native American Literary Responses to the Old World." *American Indian Culture and Research Journal* 27, no. 2 (2003): 61–76. In writing about their travels to and experiences in Europe, Schweninger declares that Native American writers are claiming Europe. Momaday's travel essays are used as examples.

1125. Vizenor, Gerald. "Introduction." *Wordarrows: Native States of Literary Sovereignty*, with a new introduction by Vizenor. Lincoln: University of Nebraska Press, 2003. vii–viii, xii. Vizenor begins with the importance of words, employing Momaday's "Story of the Arrowmaker."

2004

1126. Besson, Françoise. "Arts and Crafts in N. Scott Momaday's Fiction: The

Timeless Language of Memory." *European Review of Native American Studies* 18, no. 2 (2004): 33–40.

1127. Gradoli, Marina. "Telling History." In *Indian Stories, Indian Histories,* edited by Fedora Giordano and Enrico Comba. Collana Nova Americana in English. Turin, Italy: Otto, 2004. 127–32. The recovery of native history and the treatment of storytelling in works by Momaday and in D'Arcy McNickle's *The Surrounded* (1936) are discussed. Presented at the American Indian Workshop, held in 2003 in Italy.

1128. Graulich, Melody. "Prepositional Spaces: Family Photographs, History, and Storytelling in Memoirs by Contemporary Western Writers." Chapter 13 in *Western Subjects: Autobiographical Writing in the North American West,* edited by Kathleen A. Boardman and Gioia Woods. Salt Lake City: University of Utah Press, 2004. 388–89. Graulich comments on the pages cited about Momaday's family photographs in *The Names* and their significance in locating the personal story within a historical space.

1129. Hebebrand, Christina M. *Native American and Chicano/a Literature of the American Southwest: Intersections of Indigenous Literature.* Indigenous Peoples and Politics. New York: Routledge, 2004. See this book's index for numerous references pertaining to Momaday and *House Made of Dawn.*

1130. Padget, Martin. "Travels in the American Southwest." *Journal of the Southwest* 46, no. 2 (2004): 430–32. Briefly discusses Benally, a Navajo character in *House Made of Dawn,* who plays an important role in helping Abel, the novel's protagonist.

1131. Pulitano, Elvira. "Crossreading Texts, Crossreading Identity: Hybridity, Diaspora, and Transculturation in Louis Owens's *Mixedblood Messages.*" Chapter 3 in *Louis Owens: Literary Reflections on His Life and Work,* edited by Jacquelyn Kilpatrick. American Indian Literature and Critical Studies, vol. 46. Norman: University of Oklahoma Press, 2004. 79–102. Pulitano includes *House Made of Dawn* and "The Man Made of Words" in her discussion on pp. 83, 89–91.

1132. Ransom, James. "Perpetuating Remembrance: N. Scott Momaday and Kiowa Storytelling." *p.o.v.: A Danish Journal of Film Studies* 18 (December 2004): 68–77.

1133. Rigal-Cellard, Bernadette. *Le mythe et la plume: La littérature Indienne contemporaine en Amérique du Nord.* Nuage Rouge series. Monaco: Éditions du Rocher, 2004. 417 pp. (in French). See this book's index for references to Momaday.

1134. Roemer, Kenneth M. "The Kiowa-Matsue Connection: Inventive Modeling and American Indian Literature Teach Japanese Identity." In *Crossing Oceans: Reconfiguring American Literary Studies in the Pacific Rim,* edited by Noelle Brada-Williams and Karen Chow. Hong Kong: Hong Kong University Press, 2004. 79–87.

1135. Turner, Dale. "Oral Traditions and the Politics of (Mis) Recognition." Chapter 18 in *American Indian Thought: Philosophical Essays,* edited by Anne Waters. Malden, Massachusetts: Blackwell, 2004. 231–32. Turner comments on a theme found in Momaday's works that presents "the incommensurable nature of European and Indigenous ways of understanding the world" (231).

2005

1136. Allen, Chadwick. "N. Scott Momaday: Becoming the Bear." Chapter 10 in *The Cambridge Companion to Native American Literature,* edited by Joy Porter and Kenneth M. Roemer. Cambridge, United Kingdom; New York: Cambridge University Press, 2005. 207–19.

1137. Bartelt, Guillermo. "Hegemonic Registers in Momaday's *House Made of Dawn.*" *Style* 39, no. 4 (Winter 2005): 469–79.

1138. Carlson, David J. "Conclusion: Toward Self-Sovereignty." *Sovereign Selves: American Indian Autobiography and the Law.* Urbana: University of Illinois, 2005. 171–78. This study seeks to prove that autobiographical acts of storytelling have the potential to enable political resistance and to lay a foundation for legal change. *The Names* is presented as an example of such an act of storytelling.

1139. Cutter, Martha J. "Linguistic Recovery in N. Scott Momaday's *House Made of Dawn* and *The Way to Rainy Mountain.*" In chapter 3, "Translation as Revelation: The Task of the Translator in the Fiction of N. Scott Momaday, Leslie Marmon Silko, Susan Power, and Sherman Alexie." *Lost and Found in Translation: Contemporary Ethnic American Writing and the Politics of Language Diversity,* edited by M. J. Cutter. Chapel Hill: University of North Carolina Press, 2005. 89–103.

1140. Katanski, Amelia V. "Replaying the Returned Student in Momaday's *Indolent Boys.*" In chapter 5, "Runaways, Rebels, and Indolent Boys in Contemporary Re-visions of Boarding-School Narratives." *Learning to Write "Indian": The*

Boarding-School Experience and American Indian Literature. Norman: University of Oklahoma Press, 2005. 179–94.

1141. Powell, Paul Andrew. "On the Conceivability of Artifically Created Enlightenment." *Buddhist-Christian Studies,* no. 25 (2005): 123–32. Powell quotes a passage about a cricket from the "Introduction" (p. 12) to *The Way to Rainy Mountain,* describing it as "the poetic experience of Momaday's complex soul," and opines that in terms of enlightenment, "we may be better off in poetry than in technology" (131).

1142. Siemerling, Winfried. "Native Writing, Orality, and Anti-Imperial Translation: Thomas King and Gerald Vizenor." *The New North American Studies: Culture, Writing, and the Politics of Re/Cognition.* London: Routledge, 2005. 59–119. In this survey of writings by Thomas King and Gerald Vizenor, the author explores Momaday's trope, "memory in the blood," and includes statements from *House Made of Dawn, The Way to Rainy Mountain,* and the essay "Personal Reflections." In particular, see pp. 64–67, 104–10.

1143. Valaskakis, Gail Guthrie. "Indian Country: Claiming Land in Native America." Chapter 4 in *Indian Country: Essays on Contemporary Native Culture.* Aboriginal Studies. Waterloo, Ontario, Canada: Wilfrid Laurier University Press, 2005. 107–24. The author frequently quotes from Momaday's books and essays. While the book focuses on Canada's indigenous people, Valaskakis discusses issues pertinent to many Native North Americans. See also chapter 5, "Blood Borders."

1144. Warrior, Robert. "Momaday in the Movement Years: Rereading 'The Man Made of Words.'" Chapter 4 in *The People and the Word: Reading Native Nonfiction.* Indigenous Americas, ser. eds. Robert Warrior and Jace Weaver. Minneapolis: University of Minnesota Press, 2005. 143–80. Warrior describes this keynote address as one of Momaday's most enduring works and focuses on his intellectual contribution to twentieth-century nonfiction.

2006

1145. Abouddahab, Rédouane. "L'écriture et la vie: N. Scott Momaday et le texte stéréoscopique." *Revue Française d'Etudes Américaines,* no. 107 (March 2006): 89–106 (in French).

1146. Allen, Chadwick. "Engaging the Politics and Pleasures of Indigenous Aesthetics." *Western American Literature* 41, no. 2 (Summer 2006): 146–75. Described as an experiment in indigenous literary studies, Allen's analysis of the poem "Carnegie, Oklahoma, 1919," draws upon Kiowa, Navajo, and Maori systems of aesthetics.

1147. Claviez, Thomas. "Enigmatic Circles: Approaching the Ethics of Myth through N. Scott Momaday." *Amerikastudien/American Studies* 51, no. 4 (2006): 523–38.

1148. Czarnecki, Kristin. "'A House Made with Stones/Full of Stories': Anthologizing Native American Literature." Chapter 3 in *Multiethnic Literature and Canon Debates,* edited by Mary Jo Bona and Irma Maini. Albany: State University of New York Press, 2006. 61–82. The author traces a history of exclusion of Native American literature in the large, popular anthologies of American literature and its increasing inclusion in such anthologies since 1990. She focuses primarily on editions of *The Heath Anthology of American Literature* and *The Norton Anthology of American Literature.*

1149. DiZerega, Gus. "Civil Society, Philanthropy, and Institutions of Care." *The Good Society* 15, no. 1 (2006): 43–50. In differentiating "the market order" and "the market place," the author discusses Momaday's statement about how the Indian views the land and his use of it in "A First American Views His Land."

1150. Haseltine, Patricia. "Becoming Bear: Transposing the Animal Other in N. Scott Momaday and Joy Harjo." *Concentric: Literary and Cultural Studies* 32, no. 1 (January 2006): 81–106. This essay compares the treatment of bear by Momaday and Harjo. It examines Momaday's *The Ancient Child* and *In the Bear's House.*

1151. Huang, Hsinya. "Blood/Memory in N. Scott Momaday's *The Names: A Memoir* and Linda Hogan's *The Woman Who Watches Over the World: A Native Memoir.*" *Concentric: Literary and Cultural Studies* 32, no. 1 (January 2006): 171–95.

1152. Kupperman, Kim Dana. "Of Miracles, Nested Dolls, and the Unlimited: The Physics of Dimensionality in Three Works of Literary Nonfiction." *Interdisciplinary Studies in Literature and Environment* 13, no. 2 (Summer 2006): 33–56. "The Man Made of Words" is the nonfiction work by Momaday included in this study.

1153. Lim, Shirley Geok-Lin. "The Native and the Diasporic: Owning America in Native American and Asian American Literatures." *Women's Studies Quarterly* 34, nos. 1–2 (Spring–Summer 2006): 295–308. This essay examines symbolic spatialization and geospatial imagination in *The Way to Rainy Mountain* and Maxine Hong Kingston's *China Men* (1980), both mixed-genre books.

1154. Low, Denise. "Composite Indigenous Genres." *Studies in American Indian Literatures* 18, no. 2 (Summer 2006): 83–104. Low presents the circular structure of *House Made of Dawn* as an example of strategies used by American Indian writers.

1155. Rio, David, and Mina Soroosh. *Exploring the American Literary West: International Perspectives*. Bilbao, Spain: Servicio Editorial de la Universidad del País Vasco=Euskal Herriko Unibertisitateko Argitalpen Zerbitzua, 2006.

1156. Weaver, Jace, Craig S. Womack, and Robert Warrior. Chapter 1, Part III, "Seeing Red, Reading Red." *American Indian Literary Nationalism*. Albuquerque: University of New Mexico Press, 2006. 50–55, 64–66.

2007

1157. Allen, Chadwick. "Rere Ke/Moving Differently: Indigenizing Methodologies for Comparative Indigenous Literary Studies." *Studies in American Indian Literatures* 19, no. 4 (Winter 2007): 1–26. Allen juxtaposes Maori poetry texts with Momaday's poem, "Carnegie, Oklahoma, 1919."

1158. Besson, Françoise. "Commentary on Scott Momaday's 'Angle of Geese.'" *Introduction to Poetry in English*. Toulouse, France: Presses Universitaries du Mirail, 2007. 171–72.

1159. Dyck, Reginald. "'Interpretation Is a Perilous Venture': Petroglyphs, Maps, DNA." *Studies in American Indian Literatures* 19, no. 1 (Spring 2007): 49–65. Dyck discusses the differing points of view of Momaday and Vine Deloria, Jr., concerning the Bering Strait migration theory.

1160. Isernhagen, Hartwig. "'They Have Stories, Don't They?': Some Doubts Regarding an Overused Theorem." Chapter 1 in *Transatlantic Voices: Interpretations of Native North American Literatures*, edited by Elvira Pulitano. Lincoln: University of Nebraska Press, 2007. 3–23. Isernhagen examines the notion of story or narrative, and describes "The Man Made of Words" as "the single most influential text in establishing the centrality of a notion of story to any definition of *Indianness*" (3).

1161. Jang, Jung-Hoon. "Native American Writer: Overturned Native/Foreign Consciousness." *Journal of English Language and Literature/Yongo Yongmunhak* 53, no. 1 (2007): 99–128.

1162. Lincoln, Kenneth. “Plains Ways: N. Scott Momaday.” Chapter 7 in *Speak Like Singing: Classics of Native American Literature.* Albuquerque: University of New Mexico Press, 2007. 125–49. Lincoln presents Momaday as a Native formalist and provides a detailed reading of several of his poems and prose poems.

1163. McClure, John A. “Narratives of Turning in Native American Fiction: N. Scott Momaday, Leslie Marmon Silko, and Louise Erdrich.” Chapter 4 in *Partial Faiths: Postsecular Fiction in the Age of Pynchon and Morrison.* Athens: University of Georgia Press, 2007. 131–61. The postsecular elements in the fiction of these three Native American writers are discussed.

1164. Pulitano, Elvira. “Introduction.” In *Transatlantic Voices: Interpretations of Native North American Literatures,* edited by Elvira Pulitano. Lincoln: University of Nebraska Press, 2007. xiii–xxvii. The introduction to this collection of essays by European scholars includes references to Momaday and some of the scholars who have written about or translated his writings.

1165. Tillett, Rebecca. “Seminal Writers: N. Scott Momaday, James Welch, and Leslie Marmon Silko.” *Contemporary Native American Literature.* British Association for American Studies Series. Edinburgh, United Kingdom: Edinburgh University Press, 2007. 34–45. The section on Momaday presents an overview of his published books through 1999 and his contributions to American literature.

1166. Twomey, Tish Eshelle. “More Than One Way to Tell a Story: Rethinking the Place of Genre in Native American Autobiography and the Personal Essay.” *Studies in American Indian Literatures* 19, no. 2 (Summer 2007): 22–51. Twomey discusses *The Way to Rainy Mountain* and the views of H. David Brumble III on Momaday’s autobiographical writing. See the sections titled “Autobiographical Writing as Situated Response,” 34–39, and “Native American Writers and the Art of the Personal Essay,” 40–42.

2008

1167. Brumble, H. David, III. Chapter 8, “N. Scott Momaday: Oral to Written Tradition.” *American Indian Autobiography.* Lincoln: University of Nebraska Press, 2008. 165–80. This paperback printing has a new introduction by Brumble. The paging is the same as that in the original edition published by the University of California Press in 1988. A listing of the American Indian autobiographies in this new printing is on pp. 211–57, with Momaday’s on p. 243.

1168. Claviez, Thomas. "N. Scott Momaday: *House Made of Dawn.*" Chapter 11 in Part IV, "Toward an Ethics of Literature." *Aesthetics and Ethics: Otherness and Moral Imagination from Aristotle to Levinas and from "Uncle Tom's Cabin" to "House Made of Dawn."* Heidelberg, Germany: Universitätsverlag Winter, 2008. 393–445.

1169. Gruber, Eva. *Humor in Contemporary Native North American Literature.* Rochester, New York: Camden House, 2008. Gruber demonstrates how humor promotes intercultural understanding and agrees wholeheartedly with Momaday that words are powerful. In particular, see pp. 224–28.

1170. Kauffman, Stuart A. *Reinventing the Sacred: A New View of Science, Reason, and Religion.* New York: Basic Books, 2008. 286–87. In the main title of his book, Kauffman incorporates Momaday's statement, "we must reinvent the sacred," which is less concerned with the concept of the divine than with the expression of deep reverence and respect.

1171. Schweninger, Lee. "'From the Land Itself': Momaday's Language, Landscape, and Land Ethic." *Listening to the Land: Native American Literary Responses to the Landscape.* Athens: University of Georgia Press, 2008. 131–48. Emphasis is on Momaday's nonfiction writing about his beliefs and concepts connected to a land ethic. Included are numerous quotes from Momaday's books and essays connected to the land.

1172. Teuton, Sean K. "Embodying Lands: Somatic Place in N. Scott Momaday's *House Made of Dawn.*" *Red Land, Red Power: Grounding Knowledge in the American Indian Novel.* New Americanists, edited by Donald E. Pease. Durham: Duke University Press, 2008. 43–78. See also Teuton's "Introduction: Imagining an American Indian Center," 1–40, in which he explores the "Red Power novel" and includes Momaday as "a founding Indian voice at the rise of Red Power" (7–8).

1173. Weaver, Jace. "The Mystery of Language: N. Scott Momaday, An Appreciation." *Studies in American Indian Literatures* 20, no. 4 (2008): 76–86. On the fortieth anniversary of the publishing of *House Made of Dawn,* Weaver surveys the works and influence of Momaday. He remarks on early critical reviews by historian Marshall Sprague and writer William James Smith that drew the attention of others. Weaver emphasizes Momaday's overarching belief, held throughout these years, in the importance of words, language, and story.

1174. Wilson, Michael. "Centers of Identity in *The Way to Rainy Mountain.*" In chapter 1, "Assimilation or Appropriation? The Idea of the Center in N. Scott

Momaday's *Way to Rainy Mountain* and Leslie Marmon Silko's *Ceremony.*" *Writing Home: Indigenous Narratives of Resistance.* American Indian Studies. East Lansing: Michigan State University Press, 2008. 9–20. An earlier version of this essay appeared with the title "Speaking of Home: The Idea of the Center in Some Contemporary American Indian Writing." *Wicazo Sa Review* 18, no. 1 (1997): 129–47.

2009

1175. Douglas, Christopher. Chapter 7, "Blood and Identity," in *A Genealogy of Literary Multiculturalism.* Ithaca, New York: Cornell University Press, 2009. 220–59. This scholarly work covers the history of multicultural writing in the United States in three periods beginning with the 1920s. Momaday is included in the third, most recent period with other contemporary writers associated with literary multiculturalism. Douglas focuses on *House Made of Dawn,* but also refers to *The Way to Rainy Mountain* and *The Names.*

1176. Lincoln, Kenneth. "N. Scott Momaday: Word Bearer." *American Indian Culture and Research Journal* 33, no. 2 (2009): 89–102. Lincoln reminds readers in this thoughtful, poetical tribute that many Native writers, like Momaday, begin as poets. He presents an overview of Momaday's poetry and prose written during the half century since his poem "Earth and I Gave You Turquoise" became his first published work.

1177. McWilliams, John. "Inscribing the Prairie Sunset: Cooper, Cather, and Momaday." In *Leather-stocking Redux; or, Old Tales, New Essays,* edited by Jeffrey Walker. New York: AMS Press, 2009. 150–69. *The Way to Rainy Mountain* is McWilliams's primary focus. See, in particular, pp. 165–67.

Reviews of Books in Journals and Periodicals

Anonymously written reviews begin with the title of the publication.

Reviews of *The Ancient Child: A Novel* (1989)

1178. *American Indian Culture and Research Journal* 20 (Annual 1996): 91.

1179. Ballard, Charles. "Planes of Reality: A Review." *Studies in American Indian Literatures*, 2nd ser., 2, no. 4 (1990): 10–11.

1180. Bennett, Kate. "A Powerful Story." *Santa Fe* (New Mexico) *Reporter*, October 12–18, 1989, 25.

1181. *Booklist* 86 (September 1, 1989): 3.

1182. Bradford, Richard. "Momaday Takes Poetic Journey to Fresh Literary Region." *Albuquerque Journal*, September 17, 1989, G7.

1183. DeFlyer, Joseph E. *Choice: Current Reviews for College Libraries* 27, no. 10 (June 1990): 1679.

1184. Jaskoski, Helen. "*The Ancient Child*: A Note on Background." *Studies in American Indian Literatures*, 2nd ser., 2, no. 4 (1990): 14–15.

1185. Lesley, Craig. "The Mythology of Fiction: From an Indian Story, Momaday's Magic Vision." *Washington Post Book World*, November 28, 1989, final ed., C3.

1186. Marston, Ed. "Splendor in the Grasslands." *New York Times Book Review*, December 31, 1989, final late ed., 14.

1187. McAllester, David P. *Parabola* 15, no. 2 (Summer 1990): 110–14.

1188. Meredith, Howard. "World Literature in Review: Native American." *World Literature Today* 64, no. 3 (Summer 1990): 510–12.

1189. Owens, Louis. "Acts of Imagination: N. Scott Momaday's *The Ancient Child*." *World and I*, vol. 5 (March 1990): 434–44.

1190. Roemer, Kenneth M. "N. Scott Momaday: *The Ancient Child, a Novel*." *American Indian Quarterly* 15, no. 2 (Spring 1991): 269–71.

1191. Steinberg, Sybil, ed. "Forecasts: Fiction." *Publishers Weekly* 236, no. 7 (August 18, 1989): 48.

1192. St. John, Edward B. *Library Journal* 114, no.13 (August 1989): 165.

1193. Warrior, Robert Allen. "The Ancient Child." *Christianity and Crisis* 50, nos. 14–15 (October 22, 1990): 313.

Reviews of *Angle of Geese and Other Poems* (1974)

1194. Bromwich, David. "New Poetry Made a Little Less Private." *New York Times Book Review*, June 16, 1974, 6–7. Reviews the Godine series that includes *Angle of Geese and Other Poems.*

1195. *Choice: Current Reviews for College Libraries* 11, nos. 5–6 (July–August 1974): 755.

1196. Finlay, John. "N. Scott Momaday's *Angle of Geese*." *Southern Review*, n.s., 11, no. 3 (July 1975): 658–61.

1197. Gioia, Dana. "Momaday: A Cultural Vision." *Stanford Daily*, April 30, 1976, 5.

1198. Inez, Colette. "Especially for Meter Readers." *Parnassus: Poetry in Review* 3, no. 2 (Spring–Summer 1975): 173–82.

1199. *New Republic* 170 (April 6, 1974): 33.

1200. Ramsey, Paul. "Some American Poetry of 1974: Three Traditions." *Sewanee Review* 83 (1975): 348–56.

1201. "Reserves of Energy." *Times Literary Supplement* (London) 73 (August 30, 1974): 932.

1202. Shaw, Robert B. "Godine's Chapbooks: *Angle of Geese*." *Poetry* 126, no. 6 (September 1975): 356–57.

1203. Swann, Brian. "Reviewer's Corner." *Library Journal*, June 1, 1974, 1551.

Reviews of *Circle of Wonder: A Native American Christmas Story* (1994)

1204. Allen, Steven Robert. "N. Scott Momaday's *Circle of Wonder: A Native American Christmas Story*." *Alibi* (Albuquerque weekly) December 9–15, 1999, 24.

1205. Arndt, Katy. *Bloomsbury Review* 14, no. 6 (November–December 1994): 25.

1206. Cheuse, Alan. "Alan Cheuse's Annual Book Reviews." *All Things Considered*, National Public Radio (NPR), December 18 and 19, 2001.

1207. Devereaux, Elizabeth, ed. "Tidings of the Season: Christmas." *Publishers Weekly* 241, no. 38 (September 19, 1994): 28.

1208. Fauntleroy, Gussie. "Vivid Memories of Christmas Form Momaday's Pueblo Tale." *Pasatiempo* (weekly magazine of arts, entertainment, and culture), *Santa Fe New Mexican*, December 17–23, 1993: 30–31. Also tells about an exhibit of Momaday's paintings that appeared in the book and a book signing at LewAllen Gallery in Santa Fe.

1209. Rector, Leta. *News from Indian Country* (Hayward, Wisconsin), December 31, 2002, 13B.

1210. Tack, Alan. *Native Peoples* 8 (Fall 1994): 82.

1211. *Tribune Books* (*Chicago Tribune*), December 4, 1994, 9.

1212. Streitfeld, David. "Book Report: On Native Ground." *Washington Post Book World*, December 11, 1994, X15. (port.)

Review of *Colorado: Summer, Fall, Winter, Spring* (1974)

1213. *Book Talk* (New Mexico Book League, Albuquerque) 2, no. 6 (January 1974): 3.

Reviews of *The Complete Poems of Frederick Goddard Tuckerman* (1965)

1214. *American Literature* 37, no. 3 (November 1965): 357–61.

1215. *Choice: Books for College Libraries* 2, no. 9 (November 1965): 584.

1216. Cutler, Bruce. "An American Heart of Darkness." *Poetry* 107, no. 6 (March 1966): 401–403.

1217. Donoghue, Dennis. "The Store of the Human." *Hudson Review* 18, no. 4 (Winter 1965–66): 601–607.

1218. Eberhart, R. "Review." *New York Times Book Review*, June 20, 1965, 5.

1219. Francis, Richard Lee. "Book Reviews." *New England Quarterly* 39, no. 1 (March 1966): 98–100.

1220. Gullans, Charles. "Tuckerman's Poems Edited by Momaday." *Santa Barbara* (California) *News-Press*, April 4, 1965, A18.

1221. Howe, Irving. "An American Poet." *New York Review of Books* 4, no. 4 (March 25, 1965): 17–19.

1222. Kenny, Herbert A. "Poet Tuckerman Likely to Eclipse Cleric Uncle." *Boston Sunday Globe*, March 7, 1965, 30A.

1223. Lensing, George. “The Lyric Plenitude: A Time of Rediscovery.” *Southern Review*, n.s., 3, no. 1 (January 1967): 197–202.

1224. Marcus, Mordecai. “The Text of Tuckerman’s Poems.” *Massachusetts Review* 7, no. 2 (Spring 1966): 403–406.

1225. Sandeen, Ernest. “Book Reviews.” *Thought* 41 (Spring 1966): 139–40.

1226. *Times Literary Supplement* (London), December 2, 1965, 1102.

Reviews of *The Gourd Dancer* (1976)

1227. *Choice: Current Reviews for College Libraries* 13, no. 9 (November 1976): 1138.

1228. Daum, Timothy. *Library Journal* 101, no. 20 (November 15, 1976): 2378.

1229. Hobson, Geary. *New Mexico Humanities Review* 2, no. 2 (1979): 59–60.

1230. Matthiessen, Peter. *Book Talk*, November 1976, 6.

1231. Ramsey, Paul. “Faith and Form: Some American Poetry of 1976.” *Sewanee Review* 85, no. 3 (July–September 1977): 535.

1232. Sisco, Ellen, and Rose Moorachian. *School Library Journal* 23, no. 2 (October 1976): 125.

1233. Ward, P. “Noted: *The Gourd Dancer*.” *World Literature Today* 51, no. 3 (Summer 1977): 487.

1234. Wiegner, Kathleen. “Books: Poetry as Ritual.” *American Poetry Review* 6, no. 1 (1977): 46.

Reviews of *House Made of Dawn* (1968)

1235. Adams, Phoebe L. “Short Reviews: Books.” *The Atlantic* (later *The Atlantic Monthly*) 222, no. 1 (July 1968): 106.

1236. *Amerindian* 17, no. 1 (September–October 1968): 8.

1237. Bannon, Barbara A., ed. “Forecasts.” *Publishers Weekly* 193 (April 1, 1968): 34.

1238. Bennett, John Z. “Reviews: *House Made of Dawn*.” *Western American Literature* 5, no. 1 (Spring 1970): 69.

1239. Blackburn, Sara. “Book Marks.” *Nation* 207 (August 5, 1968): 91.

1240. *Booklist* 90, no. 15 (April 1, 1994): 1463.

1241. Borg, Mary. "Victims." *New Statesman* 77 (May 16, 1969): 696.

1242. *Critique: Studies in Contemporary Fiction* 45, no. 1 (Fall 2003): 3.

1243. Dollen, Charles. *Best Sellers* 28 (June 15, 1968): 131.

1244. Fields, Kenneth. "More than Language Means." *Southern Review*, n.s., 6, no. 1 (January 1970): 196–204.

1245. Fleischer, Leonore. "Paperbacks: Fiction." *Publishers Weekly* 196 (September 22, 1969), 86.

1246. Ford, Richard J. "The Indian in America's Closet." *Natural History* 79 (June 1970): 78–84.

1247. Gottlieb, Ann. "A Sense of the Land." *Village Voice*, January 29, 1970, 8, 33–34, 48.

1248. Graham, Kenneth. "Wind and Shadow." *Listener* 81 (May 15 1969): 686.

1249. Halio, Jay L. "Fantasy and Fiction." *Southern Review*, n.s., 7, no. 2 (April 1971): 635–47. This review briefly covers sixteen different titles; *House Made of Dawn* is reviewed on p. 635.

1250. Henry, Jeanette. "Momaday's Novel Wins Pulitzer Award." *Indian Historian* 2, no. 2 (Summer 1969): 38.

1251. Illick, Joseph E. "Looking Westward." *American West* 6, no. 6 (November 1969): 50, 52.

1252. Smith, William James. *Commonweal* 88 (September 20, 1968): 636–37. For a critique of this negative review, see Lester A. Standiford's essay, "Worlds Made of Dawn," *Three American Literatures*, edited by Houston A. Baker, Jr. New York: Modern Language Association of America, 1982. 187–88.

1253. Sprague, Marshall. "Anglos and Indians." *New York Times Book Review*, June 9, 1968, 5.

1254. Stevenson, Joan W. *Library Journal* 93 (June 15, 1968): 2522.

1255. Tube, Henry. "New Novels." *Spectator* 222 (May 23, 1969): 687–88.

Reviews of *In the Bear's House* (1999)

1256. Cheuse, Alan. "Alan Cheuse's Top Ten Books for Summer." *All Things Considered*, National Public Radio (NPR), February 7, 2002.

1257. *Kirkus Reviews* 67, no. 6 (March 15, 1999): 411.

1258. Olson, Ray. *Booklist* 95, no. 11 (February 1, 1999): 957–58.

1259. Pearson, J. Diane. *Wicazo Sa Review* 18, no. 2 (Fall 2003): 168–70. Pearson also reviews *The Indolent Boys.*

1260. *Publishers Weekly* 246, no. 8 (February 22, 1999): 91.

1261. "A Thousand Words." *Book,* September 2000, 15. A brief review is included in a listing of new paperbacks with exceptional illustrations.

Reviews of *In the Presence of the Sun: Stories and Poems, 1961–1991* (1992)

This book was included in the "Top Fiction & Poetry List" of the *New York Times Book Review* in 1992.

1262. Allen, Frank. *Library Journal* 117, no 14 (September 1, 1992): 175–76.

1263. Anderson, Scott Edward. *Bloomsbury Review* 13, no. 4 (July–August 1993): 14, 22.

1264. Bode, Barbara. "Imagination Man." *New York Times Book Review,* March 14, 1993, 15.

1265. Graeber, Laurel. "New & Noteworthy Paperbacks." *New York Times Book Review,* November 28, 1993, 32. Reviews the paperback issue and mentions Bode's review above.

1266. Matthiessen, Peter. *Book Talk,* January 1992, 5.

1267. Meredith, Howard. *World Literature Today* 67, no. 3 (Summer 1993): 650.

1268. Olson, Ray. *Booklist* 89, no. 4 (October 15, 1992): 392–93.

1269. Reynolds, Susan Salter. "In Brief: Poetry." *Los Angeles Times Book Review,* December 27, 1992, 6.

1270. Smith, William F. *American Indian Quarterly* 19, no. 2 (Spring 1995): 267–68.

1271. Steinberg, Sybil. "Forecasts: Fiction." *Publishers Weekly* 239, no. 42 (September 21, 1992): 80.

Reviews of *The Man Made of Words: Essays, Stories, Passages* (1997)

1272. Allen, Rodney F. "The Man Made of Words." *Social Studies* 89, no. 4 (July–August 1998): 189–90.

1273. Franzi, Emil. "Native Treasure: A New Collection of Essays and Other Works by One of America's Greatest Living Writers." *Tucson Weekly*, July 17–23, 1997, 26.

1274. *Kirkus Reviews* 65, no. 5 (March 1, 1997), 360.

1275. Knowles, Joe. "The Theft of the Sacred." *Nation* 264, no. 25 (June 30, 1997): 31.

1276. Mitchell, Caroline A. *Library Journal* 122, no. 8 (May 1, 1997): 104.

1277. Monaghan, Patricia. "Adult Books: Nonfiction." *Booklist* 93, no. 16 (April 15, 1997): 1376–77.

1278. Motyka, John. *New York Times Book Review*, June 15, 1997, 23.

1279. *Publishers Weekly* 244, no. 45 (November 3, 1997): 55.

1280. Sax, Boria. "Man Made Out of Words." *H-Net Reviews in the Humanities and Social Sciences*, January 1998.

1281. Schmitz, Neil. *Buffalo* (New York) *News*, June 8, 1997, F8.

1282. Stuttaford, Genevieve, and Maria Simson. "Forecasts: Nonfiction." *Publishers Weekly* 244, no. 12 (March 24, 1997): 67.

1283. *Voice of Youth Advocates* 21 (October 1998): 255.

Reviews of *The Names: A Memoir* (1976)

1284. Abbey, Edward. "Memories of an Indian Childhood." *Harper's* 254, no. 1521 (February 1977): 94–95.

1285. Adams, Phoebe L. *Atlantic Monthly* 239, no. 1 (January 1977): 93.

1286. Anderson, Terry. "Momaday's 'Names' Told through Childhood's Impressionistic Eyes." *Denver Post*, January 16, 1977, 23.

1287. *Booklist* 73, no. 8 (December 15, 1976): 582.

1288. Burrows, Jack. *American West* 14, no. 4 (July–August 1977): 49.

1289. *Choice: Current Reviews for College Libraries* 4, no. 3 (May 1977): 376.

1290. Fuller, Edmund. "Loving Account of Indian Upbringing." *Wall Street Journal,* January 11, 1977, 20.

1291. Grant, William E. "Voices from the Indian Past." *Courier-Journal* (Louisville, Kentucky), April 17, 1977, D5.

1292. Harper, Josie Morris. "My Name Is Tsoai-talee." *Detroit Free Press,* March 20, 1977, C5.

1293. Huntsman, Jeffrey. *ASAIL Newsletter,* n.s., 4, no. 2 (Spring 1980): 19–21. This review also includes comments about *The Names.*

1294. Johnson, Diane. "Ghosts." *New York Review of Books* 24, no. 1 (February 3, 1977): 19–20, 29. Johnson compares *The Names* with autobiographies by Maxine Hong Kingston and Carolbeth Laird.

1295. *Kirkus Reviews* 44 (November 1, 1976): 1206, and 44 (November 15, 1976): 1231.

1296. Marken, Jack W. "Critic Calls Momaday's New Book Autobiographical." *South Dakota State University Entertainment Collegian,* January 18, 1978, 7.

1297. ———. "*The Names: A Memoir.*" *American Indian Quarterly* 4, no. 2 (May 1978): 178–80.

1298. Matthiessen, Peter. *Book Talk* 6, no. 1 (January 1977): 4.

1299. McAllister, Mick. "*The Names.*" *Southern Review* n.s., 14, no. 2 (Spring 1978): 387–89.

1300. McPheron, Judith. *Library Journal* 102, no. 2 (January 15, 1977): 194.

1301. Miles, Elton. *Western American Literature* 12, no. 1 (May 1977): 86–87.

1302. *Natural History* 86, no. 2 (February 1977): 99.

1303. Nicholls, Richard. *Best Sellers* 37 (April 1977): 13.

1304. Rothfield, Lawrence. "The 'Autobiography of an Imagination.'" *Stanford Daily,* May 6, 1977. (port.)

1305. Stegner, Wallace. "My Name is Tsoai-talee." *New York Times Book Review,* March 6, 1977, 6–7. Stegner founded Stanford University's Creative Writing Program.

1306. Wilson, Norma. *World Literature Today* 51, no. 4 (Autumn 1977): 663.

1307. *Wilson Library Bulletin* 51, no. 9 (May 1977): 711.

Reviews of *Three Plays* (2007)

1308. Chadwick, Allen. *Western American Literature* 43, no. 4 (2009): 413.

1309. Godwin, Laura Grace. *American Book Review* 29, no. 4 (2008): 26–27.

1310. Hafen, P. Jane. *Multicultural Review* 17, no. 2 (Summer 2008): 56.

1311. Teuton, Chris. *World Literature Today* 82, no. 4 (July–August 2008): 79.

1312. Watts, James D., Jr. "Momaday's 'Three Plays' Tells Straightforward Tales in Magical Language." *Tulsa* (Oklahoma) *World*, October 21, 2007, H7.

Reviews of *The Way to Rainy Mountain* (1969)

1313. Adams, Phoebe L. "Short Reviews: Books." *Atlantic Monthly* 223 (June 1969): 117.

1314. *Amerindian* 18, no. 1 (November–December 1968): 8.

1315. Bennett, John Z. *Western American Literature* 5 (Spring 1970): 69.

1316. Bullock, Alice. "A Review." *Santa Fe New Mexican*, May 18, 1969, D4. Accompanies article "Pulitzer Champ Stays in Touch with Parents."

1317. *Choice: Current Reviews for College Libraries* 6, no. 7 (September 1969): 798.

1318. *Christian Century* 94 (May 11, 1977): 460.

1319. Dickey, Roland F. "Books." *Western Humanities Review* 24 (Summer 1970): 290–91.

1320. Egan, Ferral. "Books in Brief." *American West* 3 (September 1969): 83–84.

1321. Fields, Kenneth. "More Than Language Means: A Review of N. Scott Momaday's *The Way to Rainy Mountain*." *Southern Review*, n.s., 6, no. 1 (Winter 1970): 196–204.

1322. Fleischer, Leonore. "Forecasts: Paperbacks." *Publishers Weekly* 197, no. 5 (February 2, 1970): 91.

1323. Fontana, Bernard L. "Book Reviews." *Arizona Quarterly* 25 (Winter 1969): 377–78.

1324. Gard, Wayne. "Review of Books." *Southwest Review* 54, no. 3 (Summer 1969): vii.

1325. Huntsman, Jeffrey. *ASAIL Newsletter*, n.s., 4, no. 2 (Spring 1980): 19–21.

1326. Lask, Thomas. "End Papers." *New York Times Book Review*, May 16, 1969, 45.

1327. "Legends of Kiowas Reverently Told in 'Way to Rainy Mountain.'" *Albuquerque Tribune*, April 19, 1969, A4.

1328. Milton, John R. *Saturday Review*, June 21, 1969, 51–52.

1329. *New York Times Book Review*, August 9, 1970, 27.

1330. *New Yorker* 45 (May 17, 1969): 150.

1331. Renner, F. G., et al. "A Roundup of Western Reading by the Old Bookaroos." *Arizona and the West* 11 (Autumn 1969): 309–10.

1332. Robbins, J. Albert, ed. *American Literary Scholarship: An Annual/1969*. Durham, North Carolina: Duke University Press, 1971. 327.

1333. "Scott Momaday's Book is 'End of a Big Lie.'" *Santa Fe New Mexican*, June 1, 1969, C5.

1334. Stevenson, Joan W. "The Book Review." *Library Journal* 94, no. 16 (September 15, 1969): 3079.

1335. Taylor, J. Golden. "The Editor's Essay Review." *Western American Literature* 5 (Summer 1970): 166–68.

1336. Toelken, Barre. "The Native American: A Review Article." *Western Folklore* 29 (1970): 269–70.

1337. Trimble, Walt. "Scott Momaday: *The Way to Rainy Mountain*." *New Mexico Cultural News* (later became *Encanto*) 2, no. 4 (July 1969): 12.

1338. "Western Book Roundup by the Old Bookaroos." *American Book Collector* 20 (October 1969): 12.

1339. Wilks, Flo. "'Way to Rainy Mountain' Tells Migration of the Kiowa Indians." *Albuquerque Journal*, December 29, 1968, C3.

1340. Winters, Yvor. "Correspondence: 'Rainy Mountain.'" *The Reporter* 36 (February 23, 1967), 8.

1341. Wynn, Dudley. "Book Reviews." *New Mexico Historical Review* 45, no. 1 (January 1970): 89–90. This is a review of the first edition of *The Way to Rainy Mountain* (1969). Wynn later reviewed the paperback edition (1976) in *New Mexico Historical Review*, 51, no. 3 (July 1976): 259–60.

Reviews of Nonprint Media

1342. Cheuse, Alan. Rev. of "N. Scott Momaday: Storyteller" (sound cassette/ audiotape). *Forbes* (*Forbes FYI*) 149, no. 6 (March 16, 1992): S25–S26.

1343. Dick, Jeff. Rev. of "More than Bows and Arrows" (video recording). *Booklist* 92, no. 15 (April 1, 1996): 1376. The reviewer also includes remarks on the videos "Cahokia Mounds, Ancient Metropolis" and "Legacy of the Mound Builders," narrated by Momaday.

1344. Dipple, Brian W. Rev. of "Last Stand at Little Bighorn" (video recording of television series). *Public Historian* 15, no. 4 (Fall 1993): 134.

1345. Mcdougall, Walter A. "Bury My Heart at PBS." Rev. of *The West* (video recording of documentary television series). *Commentary* 102, no. 6 (December 1996): 41–46. Mcdougall expresses some dissatisfaction with the series, in particular the historical analysis, but finds Momaday "genuinely engaging" as a commentator.

1346. Noriega, Jorge A. Rev. of "Taking Tradition to Tomorrow" (film). Special issue, "Native American Literatures," edited by James Ruppert. *Wicazo Sa Review* 5, no. 1 (Spring 1989): 57.

1347. Paul, Nancy. Rev. of "N. Scott Momaday: Storyteller" (sound cassette/ audiotape). "Audio Reviews." *Library Journal* 115, no. 4 (March 1, 1990): 132.

1348. Shepard, Richard F. Rev. of "The Search for Ancient Americans" (video recording). This is the first episode of *The Infinite Voyage*, a PBS series. *New York Times*, September 7, 1988, C22. Momaday narrated this episode.

1349. Thibodeaux, A. Rev. of "N. Scott Momaday: Storyteller" (sound cassette/ audiotape). *Book Report* 10, no. 5 (March–April 1992): 57.

Reviews of *The Indolent Boys* (stage play)

1350. *Back Stage* 40, no. 45 (November 12, 1999): 25.

1351. Foster, Miranda. "N. Scott Momaday's 'The Indolent Boys.'" *IndianMarket 2002*, Official SWAIA Santa Fe Indian Market Supplement, *Santa Fe New Mexican*, August 14, 2002. 42.

1352. "N. Scott Momaday's 'Indolent Boys' Still Vital." *Pasatiempo* (weekly magazine), *Santa Fe New Mexican*, February 23–March 1, 2001, 32.

1353. Outlaw, Marpessa Dawn. "Connecting the Circles." *American Theatre*, 11, no. 8 (October 1994): 82–85. *The Indolent Boys* and another Native American play, both running in New York City theaters at the same time, are critiqued and described as "remarkable achievements."

1354. Pearson, J. Diane. *Wicazo Sa Review* 18, no. 2 (Fall 2003): 171–79.

1355. Persson-Reeves, C. H. "Momaday's Powerful Play of Assimilation and Genocide." *Crosswinds Weekly* (Albuquerque, New Mexico), August 8–15, 2002, 11.

1356. Shively, L. A. "Momaday's 'The Indolent Boys.'" *Indian Country Today*, August 28, 2002, D1.

Magazine Articles

1357. "First Novelists." *Library Journal* 93, no. 11 (June 1, 1968): 2270 (port.), 2271.

1358. "Currents." *Publishers Weekly* 195, no. 20 (May 19, 1969): 25–26. This article appeared shortly after Momaday received the Pulitzer Prize. It begins: "'Momaday' is a name derived from a Kiowa Indian word that means 'sky walker.' That's not a bad description these days for the 35-year-old Indian author who with his first novel, *House Made of Dawn* (Harper & Row), just won the Pulitzer Prize in fiction" (25).

1359. "Pulitzer Prize Won by Alumnus, American Indian." *UNM Alumnus* (University of New Mexico Alumni Association) 42, no. 2 (Summer 1969): 16. (port.)

1360. Dunn, Dorothy. "About Al Momaday: An Artist and His Family." *New Mexico Magazine* 48, nos. 1–2 (January–February 1970): 36–39. (port.)

1361. "Scott Momaday: New Major, Course in American Literature to Begin." *Journal of Educational Change* (University of California, Berkeley) 1, no. 2 (February 1970): 1, 4. (port.) A follow-up article in vol. 2, no 7 (July 1971) reports that the American Indian literature major would be established in the coming fall semester.

1362. Thayer, Paul. "Man of Two Worlds: A Profile of N. Scott Momaday." *California Monthly*, February 1970, 23–24. (port.)

1363. "Moviemaking Flourishes in New Mexico." *Encanto Magazine: New Mexico Cultural News* 3, no. 5 (November 1970): 2–6. This article, accompanied by eight photographs, is about the filming of *House Made of Dawn*. It includes an interview of producer-director Richardson Morse. The magazine's cover photo is of actor Larry Littlebird (Abel) on horseback.

1364. "First Winner Picked for Roger Klein Young Editors' Award." *Publishers Weekly* 199, no. 17 (April 26, 1971): 22–23. This article is about editor Frances McCullough, who brought Momaday and his first novel, *House Made of Dawn*, to Harper & Row.

1365. "Five Stanford Authors Converse." *Stanford University Alumni Almanac* 10, no. 1 (1971): 2–6. Momaday is among the authors.

1366. "'A Revolution of Consciousness among Indian People' Seen." *Wassaja* (American Indian Historical Society) 1, no. 8 (November 1973): 18. Momaday spoke in California on a rising consciousness about Indians in both the Indian and non-Indian worlds.

1367. Love, Marion F. "N. Scott Momaday." *Santa Fean* 8, no. 9 (October 1980): 36–38.

1368. Martin, Russell. "Writers of the Purple Sage: Voices in Western Literature." *New York Times Magazine*, December 27, 1981, 18–22, 40–42.

1369. "Living with Art: On-going Exhibitions." In *Arizona Living* (Phoenix) 13, no. 1. (January 1, 1982): 14–15. (ports.) Announces a special memorial art show, beginning in mid-January, in honor of recently deceased Al Momaday. The Lovena Ohl Gallery in Scottsdale, Arizona, exhibited the art of the late Al Momaday, Natachee Scott Momaday, and N. Scott Momaday.

1370. Nelson, Mary Carroll. "One Fire, Three Flames: A Visit with the Momadays." *Art West* 5, no. 5 (August–September 1982): 80–83. (ports.) This interview was conducted before Al Momaday's death in 1981.

1371. Riggan, William. "The 1984 Jurors and Their Candidates for the Neustadt International Prize for Literature." *World Literature Today* 58, no. 1 (Winter 1984): 51. Momaday served as a juror.

1372. Denton, Joan F., and Sanford L. Mauldin, Jr., photographer. "Kiowa Murals: 'Behold, I Stand in Good Relation to All Things.'" *Southwest Art,* 17, no. 2 (July 1987): 68–75. Describes a mural project at the Kiowa Tribal Museum in Carnegie, Oklahoma. Momaday is among Kiowa painters mentioned.

1373. Wild, Peter. "N. Scott Momaday: Gentle Maverick." *American West* 25, no. 1 (February 1988): 12–13.

1374. "N. Scott Momaday Is Visiting Scholar at the Library of Congress." *Library of Congress Information Bulletin* 48, no. 16 (April 17, 1989): 145–46. Momaday spent a week at the Library of Congress in March 1989. He read his poetry in the Coolidge Auditorium, accompanied by slides of his paintings. This was the first time in the fifteen years he had been painting that such a presentation was made.

1375. Ellis, Nancy. "Conversation with N. Scott Momaday." *Southwest Profile* 13, no. 1 (January 1990): 33–35. Momaday talks about the shields of the Plains Indians.

1376. Momaday, Natachee. "Alumni Profiles: A Thumbnail Sketch of N. Scott Momaday." *Mirage* (University of New Mexico Alumni Association magazine) Winter 1990, 28. (port.)

1377. Nizalowski, John. "N. Scott Momaday: Globe-trotting Author Comes Home to 'Center of the World.'" *New Mexico Magazine* 68, no. 8 (August 1990): 21–25. (port.)

1378. Fleming, Walter C. "Native American Literature Comes of Age." *Montana* 42, no. 2 (1992): 73–76. This article includes comments regarding Momaday and *House Made of Dawn.*

1379. Peterson, Andrew. "Native Voices." *Tucson Weekly,* January 22–28, 1992, 24–25. Reports on the University of Arizona reading series, "Poetics and Politics," in which Momaday participated. See also the section "Internet and Online Resources."

1380. Goode, Stephen. "Dead or Alive? Poetry at Risk." *Insight on the News* 9, no. 34 (August 23, 1993): 18–21. Goode finds there are still places where poetry thrives. The Poetry Center of Chicago, for instance, holds readings by Momaday and other poets throughout the year.

1381. Zeisler, Peter. "To Have or Have Not." *American Theatre* 10, no. 12 (December 1993): 5. Zeisler comments on the state of art across the nation and on Broadway, where serious dramatic work, he says, is no longer flourishing. He does find that, even with scarcity of funds, challenging works such as Momaday's *The Indolent Boys* are still being produced in other parts of the country.

1382. Mulrine, Anna. "Student Aid." *U.S. News and World Report* 121, no. 10 (September 9, 1996): 63. Mulrine comments on recently published *Cliffs Notes,* including the first about *House Made of Dawn,* and asks in reference to the twenty-eight years since the book's publication, "What took *Cliffs* so long?"

1383. Deloria, Vine, Jr. "OK, Scott, Where's the Beef?" *RED INK* (student magazine of the University of Arizona's American Indian Studies Program) 5, no. 2 (Spring 1997): 11. This article relates to Momaday's op-ed piece in the November 2, 1996 *New York Times,* reprinted in this issue of *RED INK.* Deloria's article originally appeared in the Late December 1996 issue of *News from Indian Country.* The three items cited below also relate to Momaday's and Deloria's comments.

1384. Moore, Marijo. "'Scientific Folklore': A Conversation with Vine Deloria, Jr.; Tilting the Reader to a Pro-Science Stance." *RED INK* 5, no. 2 (Spring 1997): 12–15. This interview originally appeared in the Mid January 1997 issue of *News from Indian Country.*

1385. Burshia, Jodi, and Michael A. Holm. "*RED INK* Talks with N. Scott Momaday." *RED INK* 5, no. 2 (Spring 1997): 16–17. Momaday responds to comments made by Vine Deloria, Jr., regarding his op-ed piece and his views on the Bering Strait migration theory.

1386. Tieri (Two Horse), Michael. "What Kind of Beef Are We Talking Here?" *RED INK* 5, no. 2 (Spring 1997): 18–21.

1387. Franzi, Emil. "Native Treasure: A New Collection of Essays and Other Works by One of America's Greatest Living Writers." *Tucson Weekly*, July 17–23, 1997, 26. Franzi writes about Momaday and newly published *The Man Made of Words*.

1388. "The Buffalo Trust: Sharing the Dream." *Native Peoples* 11, no. 3 (May–July 1998): 5.

1389. Beebe, Katharine. "Author N. Scott Momaday: Traveler through Place and Time on a Craft of Words." *Mirage* (University of New Mexico Alumni Association magazine) 15, no. 2 (Winter 1998): 16–20. The cover photograph shows Momaday at Jemez Monument near his Jemez Springs, New Mexico, home.

1390. Parsons, Scott. "Concrete America: An Indigenous Star Map Resurfaces the Downtown Grid." *Leonardo* 32, no. 3 (1999): 179–81. Parsons describes celestial artwork constructed in Denver and quotes "The Man Made of Words."

1391. Abbott, Larry, Rosemary Diaz, Michael Hice, and Daniel Gibson. "Artists of Change: Breaking through the Millennium." *Native Peoples* 13, no. 4 (June–July 2000): 55–56. This is Part III of a three-part series by these four authors. Daniel Gibson contributed a biographical sketch of N. Scott Momaday.

1392. Riggan, William. "The 2000 Neustadt International Prize for Literature: Jurors and Candidates." *World Literature Today* 74, no. 1 (Winter 2000): 91–100. Among ten candidates for the 2000 Prize, Momaday was the only one from the United States.

1393. Dustin, Daniel L, and Ingrid E. Schneider. "Collaborative Conflict Resolution at Devils Tower National Monument." *Parks & Recreation* 36, no. 7 (July 2001): 80. This article begins with Momaday's recounting of the Kiowa story of Tsoai (Rock Tree).

1394. Vendler, Helen Hennessey. "On WLT's Top 40." *World Literature Today* 75, no. 3 (Summer–Autumn 2001): 79. Critic Vendler comments about *WLT*'s selection of "the forty top works of world literature." *House Made of Dawn* is among the top forty.

1395. Pearl, Nancy, ed., with Jennifer Young. "The Reader's Shelf: Native Voices, Old and New." *Library Journal* 127, no. 14 (September 1, 2002): 244. Pearl comments that Momaday has been "exercising his visual voice for thirty years."

1396. "Goodbye to All That." In "Trends & Events," *American Theatre* 20, no. 6 (July–August 2003): 15. Reports on the last main-stage production of the Southwest Repertory Theater Company of Albuquerque. Its last production was *The Indolent Boys*. The company closed its doors in May 2003.

1397. Gibson, Daniel. "A Bear of a Man: N. Scott Momaday." *Native Peoples* 17, no. 1 (November–December 2003): 45–46. (port.)

1398. Cox, Beverly, and Martin Jacobs. "'Slow Cooking' with N. Scott Momaday." *Native Peoples* 17, no. 2 (January–February 2004): 24–25. Momaday is known for his tasty soups and stews.

1399. Van Deventer, M. J. "N. Scott Momaday: The Consummate Storyteller." *Persimmon Hill*, Thirty-second Anniversary Year Issue, Summer 2004. 57–61.

1400. Hearne, Betsy. "The Bones of Story." *Horn Book Magazine* 81, no. 1 (January–February 2005): 39–47. In this essay about the art of storytelling, Hearne reflects on the importance of a balance, "a balance of telling, of listening, and of sound and silence" (47). It begins with a quote from *House Made of Dawn* and includes other references to the book.

1401. Lynn, Mary. "Market Q&A." *The Writer* 118, no. 4 (April 2005): 54. In response to a question directed to author Tony Hillerman concerning how a writers' conference "worked" for him, Hillerman told how Momaday's remarks at a conference about "remembering the earth" impressed him and provided direction that he used over the years in writing about the settings chosen for his books.

1402. Roffman, Seth. "Momaday Builds Bridges with Siberian Native Peoples." *Native Peoples* 18, no. 4 (July–August 2005): 13. The author reports on a visit to Santa Fe made by western Siberian tribal leaders for a reunion hosted by The Buffalo Trust.

1403. Tall Chief, Russ. "Galleries: The Visual Voice of N. Scott Momaday; Jacobson House Native Art Center." *Native Peoples* 19, no. 3 (May–June 2006): 64. Surveys an exhibition of paintings and drawings by Momaday at the University of Oklahoma campus.

1404. Gibson, Daniel. "Arts & Lifeways." *Native Peoples* 19, no. 2 (March–April 2006): 18. Momaday is a featured speaker at the Fifth Annual Native American Film Festival, held at Palm Springs, California.

Newspaper Articles and Press Releases

1405. "Kiowa Indian Student at UNM." *Albuquerque Journal*, April 20, 1956, 11. (port.)

1406. "Momaday Wins Poetry Fellowship." *Albuquerque Journal*, May 17, 1959, 10.

1407. "Dr. Momaday to Speak on Steinbeck." *Santa Barbara* (California) *News-Press*, September 22, 1964, B9. At the time of this article, Momaday was beginning his second year at UC Santa Barbara.

1408. "Momaday Offers Tuckerman's Complete Poems." Press Release, Office of Public Information, University of California, Santa Barbara, March 9, 1965. Reports on new book, *The Complete Poems of Frederick Goddard Tuckerman*, edited by Momaday.

1409. "Tuckerman's Poems Edited by Momaday." *Santa Barbara News-Press*, March 14, 1965, C11. On the book *The Complete Poems of Frederick Goddard Tuckerman*, edited by Momaday.

1410. "Tales of Indian Warriors and Sun Priests Preserved by Professors." Press Release, Office of Public Information, University of California, Santa Barbara, March 1, 1966. 3 pp. Announces a limited edition book planned by Momaday to be titled *The Journey of Tai-me*.

1411. "Professor to Tell of Kiowa Indians on Radio." Press Release, Office of Public Information, University of California, Santa Barbara, March 28, 1966. Announces Momaday talk, "The Last Sun Dance," on University of California's radio program, *The University Explorer*.

1412. "Dr. Scott Momaday Is Recipient of Guggenheim Award." *Santa Barbara News-Press*, April 4, 1966, A12.

1413. "'Poetry of Resistance' Studied by UCSB Scholar." Press Release, Office of Public Information, University of California, Santa Barbara, April 19, 1966. Tells about Momaday's research carried out under the terms of his Guggenheim Fellowship.

1414. "Professor's Novel Tells of Indian Life." *Santa Barbara News-Press*, July 21, 1968, B6. Announces the publishing of Momaday's *House Made of Dawn*.

1415. "Dr. N. Scott Momaday Visits Jemez Springs, Goes to N.Y." *Santa Fe New Mexican*, January 5, 1969, C5.

1416. Bryan, Howard. "'Hard to Believe' Says Momaday after Winning a Pulitzer Prize." *Albuquerque* (New Mexico) *Tribune*, May 6, 1969, A7.

1417. "Momaday Is Long Shot Pulitzer Winner." *Albuquerque Tribune*, May 6, 1969, A8.

1418. "Biographical Sketches of Persons Selected for the Pulitzer Prize." *New York Times*, May 6, 1969, 34. Momaday is included in a photo gallery of winners.

1419. "Gets Pulitzer Prize for Fiction for Novel *House Made of Dawn*; Reportedly First American Indian to Win Prize," *New York Times*, May 6, 1969, 1.

1420. Raymont, Henry. "Award Surprises an Indian Author." *New York Times*, May 6, 1969, 35.

1421. "Man in the News: His Pride Is in His Tribe." *San Francisco Examiner*, May 6, 1969, 10.

1422. "Resident's Novel Wins Pulitzer Prize." *Santa Barbara News-Press*, May 6, 1969, A1, A4.

1423. "UNM Graduate Receives Pulitzer." *Albuquerque Journal*, May 6, 1969, B5.

1424. News release of the Office of Public Information, University of California, Berkeley, May 7, 1969. Announces that Momaday, recently awarded a Pulitzer Prize, would be joining the faculty of UC Berkeley in the coming fall.

1425. "Momaday to Teach at Berkeley." *San Francisco Chronicle*, May 8, 1969, 4.

1426. Raymont, Henry. "Berkeley Post to Winner of Pulitzer," *San Francisco Examiner*, May 8, 1969, 4.

1427. "Pulitzer Champ Stays in Touch with Parents." *Santa Fe New Mexican*, May 18, 1969, D4.

1428. Hogan, William. "A Kiowa Writer and His Editor from Stanford." *San Francisco Chronicle*, June 1, 1969, 36.

1429. Cabbell, Paul. "Dr. Momaday: Notes on a Pulitzer Prize Winner." *Christian Science Monitor*, June 20, 1969, 19.

1430. Raymont, Henry. "A Novelist Fights for His People's Lore." *New York Times*, July 26, 1969, 22. Reports that Momaday will begin a program in American Indian literature at the University of California, Berkeley, aimed at preserving legends and folktales of the Kiowa and other tribes.

1431. "N. Scott Momaday to Speak at College." *Santa Fe New Mexican,* August 7, 1969, A15. Momaday was the special guest at a public reception held at St. John's College in Santa Fe.

1432. Lucas, Urith. "Pulitzer Prize Winner Comes Home to New Mexico Honors." *Albuquerque Tribune,* August 9, 1969, A7.

1433. "Autograph Party to Honor Momaday." *Lawton* (Oklahoma) *Constitution Morning Press,* August 10, 1969, D3.

1434. "Party to Honor Indian Novelist." *Albuquerque Journal,* August 12, 1969, A11.

1435. Dungan, Eloise. "Berkeley Gets a Winner: It's a Year of 'Firsts' for Author Scott Momaday." *California Living* (Sunday supplement), *San Francisco Sunday Examiner and Chronicle,* September 21, 1969, 6–7, 9. A full-page color photograph shows Momaday at home. He was an associate professor at the University of California, Berkeley, at that time.

1436. "Scott Momaday to Get UNM's Highest Accolade." *Albuquerque Journal* November 9, 1969, D2. The Zimmerman Award, the University of New Mexico's highest honor for alumni, was presented to Momaday in recognition of his Pulitzer Prize for fiction.

1437. Lucas, Urith. "More Honors in Store for N. Scott Momaday." *Albuquerque Tribune,* November 14, 1969, A10. In addition to the article, a photo of Momaday and his wife Gaye is centered on p. A1, and a family photo including Momaday, his wife and daughters, mother, and father is on p. F1.

1438. MacPherson, Myra. "Blending Two Worlds." *Washington Post,* November 21, 1969, B1, B5. (port.) Reports that Momaday will be in Washington, D.C., to talk about his prize-winning novel.

1439. "Momaday Book Gets More National Honors." *Albuquerque Journal,* February 18, 1970, C6. *The Way to Rainy Mountain* quickly became the best-selling book published by the University of New Mexico Press. The book was selected for inclusion in the Western Book Show and the Southern Books of the Year event.

1440. "Momaday to Get Literary Honor." *Albuquerque Journal,* May 10, 1970, C2. Reports about award from the American Academy of Arts and Letters and the National Institute of Arts and Letters.

1441. "Pulitzer Prize Winning Indian Addresses Grads." *Daily Times-News* (Mount Pleasant, Michigan), June 8, 1970, 1. Momaday receives his first honorary

Doctor of Humane Letters degree from Central Michigan University at Mount Pleasant.

1442. "Pulitzer Winner to Study Navajo at Gallup Branch [University of New Mexico]." *Albuquerque Tribune*, June 8, 1970, B3.

1443. "'The Man Who Killed the Deer' Screenplay to Be Written in SF [Santa Fe]." *Santa Fe New Mexican*, June 14, 1970, D5. Momaday works on a screenwriting project based on Frank Waters's acclaimed book.

1444. Rothstein, Raphael. "In the White Man's Tongue." *New York Times Book Review*, August 9, 1970, 4–5, 26–27. Momaday is quoted in this article reporting on the newly founded American Indian Educational Publishers, which used the imprint of the Indian Historian Press. Later that year, the Press published *Indian Voices*, in which "The Man Made of Words" was first published.

1445. "Momaday and Ballard Write Opera." *Albuquerque Tribune*, August 27, 1970, B1. Momaday and Louis W. Ballard collaborate on an opera with an American Indian theme, partly based on *The Way to Rainy Mountain* and the figure of Ko-shan. The production would have its premiere at the John F. Kennedy Center for the Performing Arts in Washington, D.C.

1446. "Momaday Book Basis for Movie." *Albuquerque Tribune*, September 10, 1970, A1, A6. Refers to *House Made of Dawn*.

1447. "Movie of Momaday Novel May Be Filmed at Jemez." *Albuquerque Journal*, September 10, 1970, C2. Announces Richardson Morse would be the producer and director of the film version of *House Made of Dawn*.

1448. Briggs, Walter. "Momaday? You Mean the Painter?" *Christian Science Monitor*, October 15, 1970, 19. Briggs remarks: "Mention the name Momaday . . . and you're likely to be asked: 'Which one?'"

1449. "The Second Half of the 1970–71 Season of Literary Programs." *Library of Congress Information Bulletin* 30, no. 1 (January 7, 1971): 1–2. Momaday was featured in this series at the Library of Congress and read from his works in a program titled "Rainy Mountain Cemetery."

1450. "Pulitzer Novelist—Tribe Exploitation Decried by Kiowa." *Denver Post*, January 14, 1971, 21.

1451. "Honored Author to Give Speech on UCSB Campus." *Santa Barbara News-Press*, April 18, 1971, A5. Momaday, a professor at the University of California,

Berkeley, returned to UC Santa Barbara to give a speech on campus during National Library Week.

1452. Irving, Carl. "Saving Indian Tongues." *San Francisco Examiner,* November 1, 1971, 18.

1453. "Dr. N. Scott Momaday Named Visiting Professor for NMSU [New Mexico State University]." *Albuquerque Journal,* April 27, 1972, B12.

1454. "Momaday to Teach at Stanford." *San Francisco Examiner,* May 2, 1972, 18.

1455. "An American Indian Writer and Poet, N. Scott Momaday, Has Been Appointed Professor of English and Comparative Literature." *Stanford University Daily,* May 3, 1972, 1.

1456. "N. Scott Momaday Honored by NMSU." *Santa Fe New Mexican,* November 5, 1972. This United Press International story reports that Momaday was selected as New Mexico State University's first Visiting Distinguished Professor of English.

1457. Leonard, John. "The Pulitzer Prizes: Fail-Safe Again." *New York Times Book Review,* May 14, 1972, 47. Leonard discusses the Pulitzer Prizes for fiction.

1458. "Momaday Discusses Indians' Image." *Albuquerque Journal,* Sunday, September 17, 1972, G1.

1459. Donham, Nancy. "Scott Momaday's Course Attracts 200." *Campus Report,* Stanford University, October 10, 1973.

1460. "Kiowa History Lives Again on Commemorative Occasion." *Kiowa County Star Review,* October 25, 1973, 1, 10.

1461. Joffee, Robert. "American Literature, Soviet Style." *Washington Post,* December 7, 1974, B1. Joffe reports on Momaday's teaching experience in Moscow.

1462. Baumann, Melissa. "Native American Storyteller and Poet: English Professor Shares His Experience." *Stanford* (California) *Daily,* January 14, 1975, 3.

1463. Sekaquaptewa, Ken. "N. Scott Momaday Visits B.Y.U." *Eagle's Eye* (Brigham Young University, Utah), February 1975, 1–2.

1464. "Scott Momaday to Speak at Exercises." *Daily Lobo* (University of New Mexico student newspaper), April 17, 1975, 3. Announces that Momaday would give the address at the university's eighty-third commencement in May.

1465. "Commencement Speaker Named." *New Mexico Alumnus* 47 (April 1975): 6. N. Scott Momaday was named the featured speaker at the commencement exercises on May 18, 1975. Momaday's mother, author-educator Natachee Scott Momaday, received the honorary Doctor of Humane Letters degree at this commencement.

1466. Wilcox, Gregory J. "Pulitzer Meant Good and Bad for Author." *Thousand Oaks* (California) *News-Chronicle*, April 20, 1975, 11.

1467. "A Truly American Issue: Land, Indians, and Poetry." *San Francisco Examiner*, September 26, 1975, 6.

1468. Johns, Judith Clancy. "An All-American Experience." This World sec. *San Francisco Sunday Examiner & Chronicle*, October 10, 1976, 6. Johns writes about the first Western Film Conference, held in Sun Valley, Idaho. In a sidebar, she includes her own pen-and-ink sketch of Momaday, a conference attendee, and his comments about the state of the portrayal of the Indian in Western movies.

1469. Gallagher, Hugh. "N. Scott Momaday: Young Native Americans 'Know Who They Are, Which Was Not True Twenty-five Years Ago. They Knew Then Who They Were Told They Were.'" *Albuquerque Journal*, November 17, 1977, B1.

1470. "Family Affair: The Momadays Gather for a Unique Exhibition of Art," by Allan Pearson. *Albuquerque Journal*, November 23, 1979, B1. Momaday, father Al Momaday, and mother Natachee Scott Momaday exhibited their art at R. C. Gorman's Navajo Gallery in Albuquerque, New Mexico.

1471. "N. Scott Momaday, Professor of English and Comparative Literature at Stanford Received Honorary Degree." *Campus Report* (Stanford University), June 25, 1980.

1472. "Unique Exhibit of Family Talent." *Four Winds*, no. 3 (Summer 1980): 42.

1473. Clayton, Trisha Stanton. "Momaday on Art and Philosophy." *Navajo Times* (Window Rock, Arizona), February 12, 1981.

1474. "Momaday Joins UA [University of Arizona] Faculty." *Navajo Times*, March 26, 1981. Announces Momaday will join the faculty in the fall of 1981.

1475. Tucker, Chris. "Scott Momaday, Writing Little but Writing Well." *Dallas Morning News*, November 8, 1981, G5.

1476. Lucas, Urith. "World Known Artist Al Momaday from Jemez Springs Dies." *Albuquerque Tribune*, November 12, 1981, A1.

1477. "Renowned Artist Al Momaday Dies." *Albuquerque Journal,* November 13, 1981, A1. (port.)

1478. Bowman, Jon. "170 Graduate from CSF." *Santa Fe New Mexican,* May 10, 1982, A1, A9. Momaday received the honorary Doctor of Humane Letters degree and delivered the commencement address at the College of Santa Fe.

1479. "Momaday Not Constrained by Time." *Arizona Daily Star* (Tucson), Sunday, March 10, 1985, J1.

1480. Berry, John Stevens. "Brilliant Son of the Kiowas: N. Scott Momaday." *Lincoln, Nebraska Sunday Journal-Star,* March 16, 1986, H15.

1481. Russell, Inez. "Author's Pleasures Are Reading, Santa Fe." *Santa Fe New Mexican,* November 9, 1986, B1, B3.

1482. Clark, William. "Written Word Not Enough for Momaday." *Albuquerque Journal,* May 5 1989, C1, C5. (port.)

1483. Celine, Bonny. "Momaday: Writing for the Joy of It." *Pasatiempo* (weekly magazine), *Santa Fe New Mexican,* October 13, 1989, 9. Tells about Momaday in residence as a visiting scholar at the School of American Research in Santa Fe.

1484. Watts, James. "Momaday Interested in Untold Stories." *Tulsa World,* October 18, 1989, B1. About Momaday's newly released novel, *The Ancient Child,* and his other activities.

1485. Gamarekian, Barbara. "25 Named Trustees of Museum of Indian." National Desk. *New York Times,* January 30, 1990, 16. Momaday was among the Heye Foundation nominees.

1486. Nizalowski, John. "Momaday: American Indian Voice Speaks in Moscow." *Pasatiempo* (weekly magazine), *Santa Fe New Mexican,* February 9–15, 1990, 30. About Momaday's third trip to Moscow, where he spoke at a conference on the global environment.

1487. "Momaday Selected to Receive Jay Silverheels Achievement Award." *Navajo Times,* September 20, 1990, A5.

1488. "Harvard Native American Program Commissions N. Scott Momaday Play." *News from Indian Country* (Hayward, Wisconsin), October 15, 1991, 25. Reports that Momaday is working on a full-length play, *The Indolent Boys,* for a staged reading at Harvard University.

1489. Villani, John. "Momaday Uses Words, Images to Explain the Indian Shield."

Pasatiempo (weekly magazine), *Santa Fe New Mexican*, December 6–12, 1991, 9–10. This article is about Momaday's *In the Presence of the Sun: A Gathering of Shields* (1991).

1490. Seyda, Barbara. "Native Americans Exploring Legacy of Columbus' 'Discovery.'" *Pasatiempo, Santa Fe New Mexican*, December 6–12, 1991, 16, 18. Seyda describes Momaday's three-panel painting, "Columbian Triad," which creates three angles of vision on explorer Christopher Columbus. It was shown in an exhibition, "Native American Political Art," in Santa Fe.

1491. ———. "N. Scott Momaday's Memories of a Little Room in the Earth." *Santa Fe New Mexican*, January 24, 1992, 4, 6. Momaday talks about *The Ancient Child* and recalls his memories of the storm cellar at his grandmother's home in Oklahoma.

1492. Rede, George. "Prize-winning Author Sees Spiritual Crisis." *Portland Oregonian*, June 12, 1992, Dl.

1493. "Indians Gaining Unity Author Momaday Says." *Santa Fe New Mexican*, October 2, 1992, B6. This article is about the "Healing the Hoop" conference held at the University of Nebraska, Lincoln. Momaday opened the conference, stating that American Indians across the United States are developing a greater sense of community.

1494. Berger, Yves. "Moi, l'Indien." *Le Monde* (Paris), April 16, 1993, 31. This article in the newspaper section, "Lettres Étrangères," announces the Nuage Rouge collection by Éditions du Rocher that includes a French translation of *House Made of Dawn*.

1495. Edmo-Suppah, Lori. "Author N. Scott Momaday Says He Has One Story to Tell, It Continues from One Book to the Next." *Sho-Ban News* (Fort Hall, Idaho), May 6, 1993, 1.

1496. Bezdek, Michael. "American Indian Writing Hits Stride." *Santa Fe New Mexican*, August 22, 1993, D8. This Associated Press article focuses on several prominent writers, including Momaday.

1497. Gussow, Mel. "Director Shakes Up Syracuse Stage." *New York Times*, February 24, 1994, C13, C18. Primarily about the director of the Syracuse Stage, Tazewell Thompson, this article tells about his first full season, which included the premiere of *The Indolent Boys*.

1498. "Author Presents World Premiere Play." *Indian Country Today* (Oneida, New

York), March 16, 1994, B16. Tells about the premiere of *The Indolent Boys* at the Syracuse Stage in Syracuse, New York.

1499. "Momaday Wins Lifetime Award." *Tulsa World*, March 27, 1994, BK6. The Gibson Lifetime Achievement Award is presented by the Oklahoma Center for the Book.

1500. Madrigal, Alix. "Voice of the Turtle." In "Sunday Review," *San Francisco Chronicle*, July 24, 1994, 3, 4. This article about author Paula Gunn Allen includes her comments about Momaday's influence on her professional career.

1501. Bensley, Lis. "Witnessing the Power and Mystery of Shields." *Pasatiempo* (weekly magazine), *Santa Fe New Mexican*, December 23–29, 1994, 22, 45.

1502. Zad, Martie. "Kuralt Hosts 'This I Believe' Revival." *Washington Post TV Week*, February 25, 1996, Y04. Reports on a new series, "This I Believe," based on Edward R. Murrow's radio program of the 1950s. The half-hour program, hosted by Charles Kuralt, consisted of five-minute segments in which prominent people discussed their personal philosophies of life. Momaday was featured on the opening program.

1503. Brennan, Patricia. "A Place of Dreams and Disasters: Stories of the Land, Its Peoples, and Their Struggles." *Washington Post TV Week*, September 15, 1996, Y08. About the television series, *The West*, shown on the Public Broadcasting System. The article includes a statement by Momaday about the American West: "It's a landscape that has to be seen to be believed, and it may have to be believed to be seen."

1504. Grimes, William. "Headline: Spotlight; The Wild Frontier." *New York Times*, September 15, 1996, final late edition, sec. 12, 26. Announces that Momaday will be a commentator for the television series, *The West*.

1505. Chang, Richard. "Sculptor, Painter, Writer among Six to Receive Awards." *Santa Fe New Mexican*, November 1, 1996, B4. Momaday received the 1996 Governor's Award for Literature during a ceremony held in Santa Fe the following month.

1506. Ozer, Courtney E. "Lecture Focuses on the Vision of Words." *Arizona Daily Wildcat* (University of Arizona student newspaper), January 30, 1997, 1. Momaday, Regents Professor of English, spoke at the first program in a new Speaker Series.

1507. Reed, Ollie, Jr. "Return to Jemez." *Albuquerque Tribune*, November 27, 1997, B1. Momaday returns to Jemez Springs to live in the home where his parents once lived.

1508. Lopez, Ruth. "Ready for Bear." *Santa Fe New Mexican*, August 23, 1998, Outlook sec., F2.

1509. ———. "Write of Springs." *Pasatiempo* (weekly magazine), *Santa Fe New Mexican*, February 26–March 4, 1999, 32–33. This issue's cover is a color photograph by Craig Fritz of Momaday standing near the Jemez River close to his home in Jemez Springs.

1510. Sullivan, Craig. "Momaday to Read New Work." *Journal North* (*Albuquerque Journal*), February 28, 1999, 3. Announces a book signing and reading from his *In the Bear's House* at St. John's College in Santa Fe, New Mexico.

1511. Rector, Leta. "Momaday 'Treasured' by His Homestate." *News from Indian Country* (Hayward, Wisconsin), December 15, 1999, B9.

1512. Nemy, Enid. "The Delight Song of Beryl Chung, 12 Years Old." Metropolitan Diary. *New York Times*, January 24, 2000, 2. A young girl writes her own name poem inspired by Momaday's "The Delight Song of Tsoai-talee."

1513. Naedele, Walter F. "Remembering a Bitter Lesson, Native Americans Pay Tribute to the Children Who Attended the White-run Indian School in Carlisle." *Philadelphia Inquirer*, May 28, 2000, Sunday City ed., B1. Naedele writes about a special ceremony at the Carlisle Indian Industrial School about which Momaday wrote in *The Moon in Two Windows*, published in *Three Plays* by the University of Oklahoma Press in 2007.

1514. Henderson, Jane. "American Indian Writer Will Receive the St. Louis Literary Award." *St. Louis Post-Dispatch*, October 4, 2000, E1.

1515. "Author, Architect to Be Honored at Graduation." *Daily Lobo* (University of New Mexico student newspaper), May 7–11, 2001, 1, 11. Momaday received a Doctor of Letters honorary degree at the university's 2001 spring commencement.

1516. "UNM Graduation Ceremony Will Honor Momaday, Predock." *Albuquerque Tribune*, May 10, 2001, A2. Honorary degrees were bestowed on both men.

1517. Dudick, J. Mark. "Grandfather's Words: Native Literary Pioneer N. Scott Momaday Preserves Wisdom." *Anchorage* (Alaska) *Daily News*, October 26, 2001, final ed., F1.

1518. Cummings, Jeff. "Actor Says He Relates to 'Americanized' Indians in Play." *Albuquerque Tribune*, August 16, 2002, C5. This article refers to *The Indolent Boys*.

1519. Shively, L. A. "Momaday's 'The Indolent Boys.'" *Indian Country Today,* August 28, 2002, D1.

1520. "St. John's Board Appoints Momaday." *Santa Fe New Mexican,* April 1, 2003, B3.

1521. Roberts, Roxanne. "You Have a Dream; Achievement Summiteers Bask in the Past and Presence of Greatness." *Washington Post,* May 4, 2003, Sunday final ed., D1. Roberts describes the forty-second International Achievement Summit, in which Momaday participated.

1522. Summer, Polly. "New Shelf Life; Contemporary Books That Are Standing the Test of Time Have Redefined the Literary 'Classics.'" *Albuquerque Journal,* September 14, 2003, E1, E6. Momaday's *The Way to Rainy Mountain* is among the books named.

1523. Johnson, Jean. "Momaday Calls Lewis and Clark Expedition a Great Epic Odyssey." *Indian Country Today,* October 20, 2004, D1. Momaday speaks during the Lewis and Clark College's bicentennial symposium, "Encounters."

1524. Reynolds, Jerry. "An Honor Song in the Old Style." *Indian Country Today,* January 10, 2005. Momaday wrote a poem in honor of his friend Vine Deloria, Jr. The poem is archived at www.indiancountrytoday.com/archive/28172394.html.

1525. "St. John's to Host Campus Lectures." *Journal North* (*Albuquerque Journal*), January 26, 2005, 8. Momaday gives a lecture titled "Language, the Fifth Element: Remarks on Language and on Oral Tradition" at the Great Hall of St. John's College in Santa Fe, New Mexico.

1526. Harrelson, Barbara. "A Time for Tradition—A Time for Family." *Santa Fe New Mexican,* November 26, 2005, SS8 (special sec.). Jill Momaday Gray, daughter of N. Scott Momaday, tells how she and her three sisters continue in their own families some of the Christmas traditions begun when they were growing up. Each Christmas the family has gathered to hear him read a story or poem written for their holiday celebration.

1527. "Up Front." (editorial from The Editors) *New York Times Book Review,* October 29, 2006, 6. This piece by the editors references Momaday's review of Hampton Sides's *Blood and Thunder* in the same issue. They discuss an e-mail from Momaday in which he decries "the deprivation of American Indians' land as 'the theft of the sacred.'"

1528. Gwinn, Mary Ann. "Book Buzz: 'The Dean of American Indian Writers.'" *Seattle Times,* February 4, 2007, K7. Announces talk to be given by Momaday at the University of Washington's Dana Lecture Series.

1529. Storey, Natalie. "Laureate Offers Graduates Words of Wisdom." *Santa Fe New Mexican*, May 20, 2007, C1, C6. Momaday addresses the 2007 graduating class of St. John's College, speaking on the importance of keeping the oral storytelling traditions alive.

1530. Haven, Cynthia. "Writers N. Scott Momaday, Lucille Clifton, Nancy Huddleston Packer to Speak to Incoming Freshmen; Public Invited." *Stanford Report*, May 31, 2007, 1. *The Way to Rainy Mountain* was selected for the 2007 "Three Books" program, an annual summer reading program for incoming freshmen, who hear the authors speak at the New Student Orientation held on campus every September.

1531. Hoberock, Barbara. "New Poet Laureate Announced: N. Scott Momaday Won a Pulitzer Prize in 1969 for His Debut Novel." *Tulsa World*, July 13, 2007, A11, A13. (port.) Governor Brad Henry named Momaday Oklahoma's Centennial Poet Laureate. His term as the state's sixteenth laureate runs until January 1, 2009. He read his poem "Forms of the Earth at Abiquiu" at the announcement ceremony.

1532. Miller, Jay. "Take a Look at Exhibit of the Kid." *Santa Fe New Mexican*, July 22, 2007, Editorials sec., F1. Miller highlights the first-of-its-kind Billy the Kid exhibit on display at the Albuquerque Museum. The impressive collection of hundreds of books, posters, documents, and memorabilia included a first edition of *The Ancient Child* and an audiotape about Billy the Kid narrated by Momaday.

1533. Van Deventer, M. J. "Centennial: Poet Laureate Shares Commemorative Poem; Verse Traces State's 100 Years." *The Oklahoman* (Oklahoma City), November 10, 2007, 13A.

1534. "Medal of Arts Winners." Arts/Cultural Desk. *New York Times*, November 15, 2007, late edition, 2. Reports on Momaday and others receiving the National Medal of Arts.

1535. "Momaday to Get Medal of Arts." *Santa Fe New Mexican*, November 15, 2007, C1. The National Medal of Arts was presented by President and Mrs. Bush in the East Room of the White House on the day of this issue.

1536. "People: Recipients of the National Medal of Arts." *International Herald Tribune*, November 16, 2007, 10.

1537. Reynolds, Jerry. "Culture by Momaday at the Rasmuson Theater." *Indian Country Today* (Oneida, New York), January 9, 2008, A7, A8. Momaday speaks at the National Museum of the American Indian in Washington, D.C.

1538. Van Deventer, M. J. "N. Scott Momaday—An American Voice—An Oklahoma Voice." *The Oklahoman* (Oklahoma City), February 10, 2008, D1. This article reports on the honors and awards given Momaday in recent months and years.

1539. Watts, James D., Jr. "Momaday to Be Honored." *Tulsa World*, February 11, 2008, D2. The Oklahoma Humanities Council awards Momaday the 2008 Oklahoma Humanities Award.

1540. Brossy, Chee. "Momaday Says Poetry Embraces Native Song Tradition." *Navajo Times*, March 6, 2008, C4. (port.) Momaday talks about poetry and writing following his recounting of stories and legends pertaining to water at a water conservation and xeriscape conference held in Albuquerque, New Mexico.

1541. Adcock, Clifton. "Tribes Gather for Symposium on American Indian." *Tulsa World*, April 19, 2008, A15. The Oklahoma Centennial Poet Laureate read his poetry at Northeastern State University's thirty-sixth annual Symposium of the American Indian. The university is located at Tahlequah, Oklahoma.

1542. "Native American Oral Tradition: The Stories and the Storytellers." *The Ojibwe News* (St. Paul, Minnesota), November 1, 2008, 1. The article reports that "the dean of American Indian writers" told his audience: "If I do not speak with care, my words are wasted. If I do not listen with care, words are lost."

1543. "Obituaries: Barbara Glenn Momaday." *Jemez Thunder* (Jemez Springs, New Mexico), December 1, 2008, p. 3.

1544. Warlick, Heather. "State Lauds Momaday for Poet Laureate Term." *The Oklahoman* (Oklahoma City), January 4, 2009, D4. Momaday is honored at a gathering to commemorate the close of his two-year term.

1545. Reed, Martin. "Inspiring Minds with Momaday." *Wind River News* (Lander, Wyoming), April 9, 2009, pp. 1, 2. Momaday talks with college and high school students about his life, the process of writing, and his pride in his Indian heritage.

Biographical, Literary, and Bibliographic Reference Sources

1546. *100 Native Americans Who Shaped American History*. By Bonnie Juettner. San Mateo, California: Bluewood Books, 2003. 87.

1547. *American Ethnic Literatures: Native American . . . Writers and Their Backgrounds*. By David R. Peck. Magill Bibliographies. Pasadena, California: Salem Press, 1992. Chapter 5, "Native American Literature," 48–72, contains information about Momaday and selected lists of primary and secondary works. For specific subjects, see the book's index at p. 212.

1548. *American Ethnic Writers*. Rev. ed., vol. 2. Edited by David R. Peck et al. Magill's Choice. Pasadena, California: Salem Press, 2009. 792–96. A biographical sketch is accompanied by brief summaries of *The Ancient Child* and *House Made of Dawn*.

1549. *American Indian and Eskimo Authors: A Comprehensive Bibliography*. Compiled by Arlene B. Hirschfelder. New York: Association on American Indian Affairs, 1973. 62 (three entries for Momaday). This is a revised, enlarged edition of a bibliography published by the association in 1970.

1550. *American Indian Authors*. Compiled and written by Natachee Scott Momaday. Boston: Houghton Mifflin, 1971, ©1972. 119. (port.) A brief sketch of Momaday, written by his mother.

1551. *American Indian Biographies*. Rev. ed. Edited by Carole Barrett and Harvey Markowitz. Magill's Choice. Pasadena, California: Salem Press, 2005. 320–22. (port.) The biographical essay about Momaday is by Michael R. Meyers.

1552. *American Indian Chronology*. By Phillip M. White. Chronologies of the American Mosaic. Westport, Connecticut: Greenwood Press, 2006. 128. An entry about Momaday is under the subject category "Publications—1969."

1553. *The American Indian in Language and Literature*. Compiled by Jack W. Marken. Goldentree Bibliographies in Language and Literature. Arlington Heights, Illinois: AHM Publishing, 1978. See p. 194 for entry numbers to specific information about Momaday.

1554. *American Indian Literatures: An Introduction, Bibliographic Review, and Selected Bibliography*. By A. LaVonne Brown Ruoff. Indians of North America. New York: Modern Language Association of America, 1990. References to

Momaday and his published works before 1990 are found in the three parts of this book. See the book's index on p. 198.

1555. *American Indian Novelists: An Annotated Critical Bibliography.* Edited by Tom Colonnese and Louis Owens. New York: Garland, 1985. 38–61.

1556. *American Indian Portraits.* Macmillan Profiles. Farmington Hills, Michigan: Macmillan Reference USA, 2000. 160–62. The "portraits" are biographical sketches of notable Native Americans.

1557. *American Indian Quotations.* Compiled and edited by Howard J. Langer. Westport, Connecticut: Greenwood Press, 1996. 162–63 (entry nos. 594–97). Four Momaday quotations are related to several topics: Native vision (from *Contemporary American Indian Leaders,* 1972); Columbus and the Quincentenary (*Northeast Indian Quarterly,* Fall 1990); "the remembered earth" (*The Way to Rainy Mountain*); and "we are what we imagine" ("The Man Made of Words").

1558. *American Indian Reference and Resource Books for Children and Young Adults.* By Barbara J. Kuipers. 2nd ed. Englewood, Colorado: Libraries Unlimited, 1995. Includes *The Way to Rainy Mountain* in Part 2, "Annotated Bibliography of American Indian Books," 172 (entry no. 186).

1559. *American Nature Writers.* Edited by John Elder. Vol. 2. New York: Simon & Schuster and Prentice Hall, 1996. 639–49. (port.) The essay "N. Scott Momaday" is by Matthias Schubnell.

1560. *American Novelists since World War II.* See *Dictionary of Literary Biography,* vol. 143.

1561. *American Writers: A Collection of Literary Biographies.* A. Walton Litz, editor in chief. Supplement IV, Part 2. New York: Macmillan Library Reference USA, 1996. 479–96. The literary biography of Momaday is by Sally L. Joyce.

1562. *An Annotated Bibliography of American Indian and Eskimo Autobiographies.* By H. David Brumble III. Lincoln: University of Nebraska Press, 1981. This book was followed by "A Supplement to *An Annotated Bibliography of American Indian and Eskimo Autobiographies,*" *Western American Literature* 17, no. 3 (November 1982): 243–60. Three entries (nos. 343–45) relating to Momaday are on p. 243. An updated annotated listing was included in Brumble's *American Indian Autobiography.* Berkeley: University of California Press, 1988. 211–57. This book was reprinted with a new introduction by Brumble in 2008 by the University of Nebraska Press. It includes "The

Autobiographies," 211–57, a listing of the autobiographies mentioned in the new printing. Momaday's works (*The Journey of Tai-me, The Names,* and *The Way to Rainy Mountain*) appear again on p. 243.

1563. *Authors & Artists for Young Adults.* Dwayne D. Hayes, project ed. Vol. 64. Detroit: Thomson Gale, ©2005. 117–27. (ports.) Includes biographical information with summaries and critiques of Momaday's major published works through 1999. A shorter presentation on Momaday, with an essay by Michelle M. Motowski, appeared earlier in vol. 11, 1993, 137–46. (port.)

1564. *Bartlett's Familiar Quotations.* 17th ed. John Bartlett; Justin Kaplan, gen. ed. Boston: Little, Brown, 2002. 830. The quotation in this edition is from chapter "January 26," in Part 2, "The Priest of the Sun," *House Made of Dawn* (1968), 96.

1565. *Beacham's Encyclopedia of Popular Fiction.* Edited by Kirk H. Beetz. Vol. 2. Osprey, Florida: Beacham Publishing, 1996, ©2001. 1299–1304. The encyclopedia article about Momaday is by Lynne Facer.

1566. *Benét's Reader's Encyclopedia of American Literature.* See *HarperCollins Reader's Encyclopedia of American Literature,* 2nd ed.

1567. *A Bibliographical Guide to the Study of Western American Literature.* Edited by Richard W. Etulain and N. Jill Howard. 2nd ed. Albuquerque: University of New Mexico Press, 1995. A bibliography of works about Momaday is on pp. 314–16.

1568. *Biographical Dictionary of Indians of the Americas.* Vol. 1. Newport Beach, California: American Indian Publishers, 1991. 432.

1569. *Biographical Directory of Native American Painters.* By Patrick D. Lester. Tulsa, Oklahoma: SIR Publications, ©1995 by Servant Education & Research Foundation. Information about Momaday is at pp. 365–66 and about his father, Alfred M. (Al) Momaday, at p. 365. Previously published as *American Indian Painters: A Biographical Directory.*

1570. *A Broken Flute: The Native Experience in Books for Children.* Edited by Doris Seale and Beverly Slapin. Walnut Creek, California: AltaMira Press, 2005. 347–48. *House Made of Dawn* is recommended for advanced high school and older readers. See also the online reference tool, Oyate, maintained by Beverly Slapin, in the section "Internet and Online Resources."

1571. *The Cambridge Companion to Native American Literature.* Edited by Joy Porter and Kenneth M. Roemer. Cambridge Companions to Literature. New

York: Cambridge University Press, 2005. Chapter 10, "N. Scott Momaday: Becoming a Bear," is by Chadwick Allen. 207–19. Also, see the index to this reference source for other pertinent references to Momaday and his works.

1572. *The Cambridge Dictionary of American Biography.* Edited by John S. Bowman. New York: Cambridge University Press, 1995. 508. Includes Momaday, *House Made of Dawn* and *The Way to Rainy Mountain.*

1573. *The Cambridge History of the Native Peoples of the Americas.* Vol. 1, *North America.* Edited by Bruce G. Trigger and Wilcomb E. Washburn. New York: Cambridge University Press, 1996. See chapter 1, "Native Views of History," by Peter Nabokov. 52–53.

1574. *Chronology of American Indian History.* By Liz Sonneborn. Facts on File Library of American History. New York: Facts on File, 2007. 306, 371.

1575. *The Chronology of American Literature: America's Literary Achievements from the Colonial Era and Modern Times.* Edited by Daniel S. Burt. Boston: Houghton Mifflin, 2004. See p. 738 of the book's index for references to Momaday in Part V, "Modernism and Postmodernism, 1950–1999."

1576. *Chronology of Native North American History: From Pre-Columbian Times to the Present.* Edited by Duane Champagne. Detroit: Gale Research, 1994. This listing of historical and cultural events from 50,000 B.C. to 1993 includes references to Momaday on pp. 294, 351, and 356–58.

1577. *The Columbia Guide to American Environmental History.* Edited by Carolyn Merchant. New York: Columbia University Press, 2002. See p. 426 of the book's index for references to Momaday in several essays.

1578. *The Columbia Guide to American Indian Literatures of the United States since 1945.* Edited by Eric Cheyfitz. Columbia Guides to Literature since 1945. New York: Columbia University Press, 2006. This collection of long essays with lengthy bibliographies includes Momaday in chapter 2, "Cannons and Canonization: American Indian Poetries through Autonomy, Colonization, Nationalism, and Decolonization," by Kimberly M. Blaeser, 183–287; and chapter 5, "Imagining Self and Community in American Indian Autobiography," by Kendall Jackson, 357–409. This chapter includes "Chronology of U.S. American Indian Autobiographies Published Since 1945," 401–409. The most recent citation is dated 2004.

1579. *The Columbia History of American Poetry.* Edited by Jay Parini. New York: Columbia University Press, 1993. 731–32, 843, 857, 870.

1580. *The Columbia History of the American Novel.* Edited by Cathy N. Davidson et al. New York: Columbia University Press, 1991. Brief entry about Momaday, 795–96. *House Made of Dawn, The Way to Rainy Mountain,* and *The Ancient Child* are discussed in the section titled "Fiction of the West," by James H. Maguire, 453–57.

1581. *The Columbia Literary History of the United States.* Emory Elliott, gen. ed. New York: Columbia University Press, 1988. 795–96. The essay, "American Indian Fiction, 1968–83," was written by Paula Gunn Allen.

1582. *A Companion to American Indian History.* Edited by Philip J. Deloria and Neal Salisbury. Blackwell Companions to American History, no. 4. Malden, Massachusetts: Blackwell, 2002. References to Momaday are found in chapter 13, "Native American Literatures," by P. Jane Hafen, 234–40.

1583. *Contemporary American Indian Leaders.* By Marion E. Gridley. New York: Dodd, Mead, 1972. 136–42. (port.) This is among the earliest published biographical essays about Momaday. It includes a discussion of *House Made of Dawn* and *The Way to Rainy Mountain.* See also photo gallery, 76–77.

1584. *Contemporary Authors: A Bio-Bibliographical Guide to Writers.* First revision. Vols. 25–28 in one volume. Edited by Christine Nasso et al. Detroit: Gale Research, 1977. 500–501. This is the first appearance of Momaday in this important series.

1585. *Contemporary Authors.* New revision Series. Vol. 68. Edited by Daniel Jones and John D. Jorgenson. Detroit: Gale Research, 1998. 347–52. There are short sketches in two earlier volumes in this series: vol. 14, 1985, and vol. 34, 1991.

1586. *Contemporary Authors.* New Revision Series. Vol. 134. Tracey L. Matthews, project ed. Detroit: Thomson Gale, 2005. 338–44. (port.)

1587. *Contemporary Authors Online.* Gale Group, 2007– . The *Contemporary Authors* series is reproduced online and is generally available at larger public libraries and at college and university libraries.

1588. *Contemporary Literary Criticism.* Vol. 2. Edited by Carolyn Riley and Barbara Harte. Detroit: Gale Research, 1974. 289–90. (port.) Beginning with a short entry in this volume, the coverage of Momaday and his works, in particular *House Made of Dawn,* increased significantly in later volumes of the *CLC* series. This resource includes biographical information and discussion about plots, major characters, and themes. Selected published critical essays and reviews of an author's major works are also included.

1589. *Contemporary Literary Criticism.* Vol. 19. Edited by Sharon R. Gunton. Detroit: Gale Research, 1981. 317–21.

1590. *Contemporary Literary Criticism.* Vol. 85. Edited by Christopher Giroux. Detroit: Gale Research, 1995. 222–83. (ports.) This volume presents an overview of Momaday's career and works through 1993. A selection of his poems and artwork is also included.

1591. *Contemporary Literary Criticism.* Vol. 95. Edited by Brigham Narins and Deborah A. Stanley. Detroit: Gale, 1997. 213–81. The long essay by Carole Oleson is devoted to *House Made of Dawn.* It presents an in-depth analysis of the novel's structure and symbolism.

1592. *Contemporary Literary Criticism.* Vol. 160. Edited by Tom Burns and Jeffrey W. Hunter. Farmington Hills, Michigan: Gale Group, 2002. 236–89. A special commissioned essay, "An Analysis of *House Made of Dawn* by N. Scott Momaday," is by Lee Schweninger.

1593. *Contemporary Native American Authors: A Biographical Dictionary.* By Kay Juricek and Kelly J. Morgan. Golden, Colorado: Fulcrum, 1997. 167–68.

1594. *Contemporary Novelists.* 7th ed. Edited by Neil Schlager and Josh Lauer. Detroit: St. James Press, 2001. 715–16. The essay about Momaday is by Tom Colonnese.

1595. *Contemporary Popular Writers.* Edited by Dave Mote. Detroit: St. James Press, 1997. 291–92. The sketch about Momaday is by Tammy J. Bronson.

1596. *The Continuum Encyclopedia of American Literature.* Steven R. Serafin, gen. ed., and Alfred Bendixen, associate ed. New York: Continuum, 2000. 780–81. The encyclopedia article about Momaday is by John W. Crawford.

1597. *Current Biography Yearbook.* 1975 ed. New York: H.W. Wilson Co., 1975. 281–83. Through 2009 there has not been an updated biographical article about Momaday published in this annual.

1598. *Cyclopedia of World Authors II.* Edited by Frank N. Magill. Vol. 3. Pasadena, California: Salem Press, 1989. 1061–63. The essay, "N. Scott Momaday," is by Richard M. Leeson.

1599. *Dictionary of American History.* 3rd ed. By Stephanie Gordon; editor in chief, Stanley I. Kutler. New York: Charles Scribner's Sons, 2003. Brief mention of *House Made of Dawn,* vol. 4, 179, and about Momaday and the Pulitzer Prize under "Native American Literature," vol. 5, 129.

1600. *Dictionary of Literary Biography.* Vol. 143, *American Novelists since World War II,* 3rd ser. Edited by James R. Giles and Wanda H. Giles. Detroit: Gale, 1994. 159–70. (port.) The essay, "N. Scott Momaday," is by Alan R. Velie.

1601. *Dictionary of Literary Biography.* Vol. 175, *Native American Writers of the United States.* Edited by Kenneth M. Roemer. Detroit: Gale Research, 1997. 174–86. (port.) The essay about Momaday and his works is by Matthias Schubnell.

1602. *Dictionary of Literary Biography.* Vol. 256, *Twentieth-Century American Western Writers,* 3rd ser. Edited and with an introduction by Richard H. Cracroft. Detroit: Gale Group, 2002. 203–18. (port.) An essay about Momaday by Susan Evertsen Lundquist is included. This and other volumes of the *DLB* are also available online.

1603. *Dictionary of Literary Themes and Motifs.* Vol. 2. Edited by Jean-Charles Seigneuret et al. Westport, Connecticut: Greenwood Press, 1988. 1007. In a brief article, "Psychic Landscape," Richard F. Fleck quotes from Momaday's passage, "The Remembered Earth."

1604. *Dictionary of Native American Literature.* Edited by Andrew Wiget. Garland Reference Library of the Humanities, vol. 1815. New York: Garland, 1994. 463–77. The essay "N(avarre) Scott Momaday" is by Susan Scarberry-García. See also p. 576 of the book's index for other references to Momaday and his works. This book was reissued with the same paging by Garland in 1996 as *Handbook of Native American Literature.*

1605. *Encyclopedia of American Indian History.* Vol. 3. Edited by Bruce E. Johansen and Barry M. Pritzker. Santa Barbara, California: ABC-CLIO, 2008. 792–93. The article about Momaday is by Jennifer L. Bertolet.

1606. *Encyclopedia of American Indian Literature.* By Jennifer McClinton-Temple and Alan Velie. Facts on File Library of American Literature. New York: Facts on File, 2007. Included in this resource is information on the following subjects: Biography, 235–37; *The Ancient Child* (1989), 35; *Angle of Geese and Other Poems* (1974), 35–36; *The Gourd Dancer* (1976), 146; *House Made of Dawn* (1968), 172–73; *In the Bear's House* (1999), 187; *In the Presence of the Sun* (1992), 188; and *The Way to Rainy Mountain* (1969), 387–88. See also index, p. 459, for additional references.

1607. *Encyclopedia of American Literature.* See *Continuum Encyclopedia of American Literature.*

1608. *Encyclopedia of American Poetry: The Twentieth Century*. Edited by Eric L. Haralson. Chicago: Fitzroy Dearborn, 2001. 495–98. Momaday is among a number of Native American poets discussed in the article "Native American Poetry," by Donna L. Potts.

1609. *Encyclopedia of Frontier and Western Fiction*. Edited by Jon Tuska and Vicki Piekarski. New York: McGraw-Hill, 1983. 239–41. The biographical article about Momaday is by Deane Mansfield-Kelley.

1610. *Encyclopedia of Frontier Literature*. By Mary Ellen Snodgrass. ABC-CLIO Literary Companion series. Santa Barbara, California: ABC-CLIO, 1997. 220–22.

1611. *The Encyclopedia of Native American Biography*. By Bruce E. Johansen and Donald A. Grinde, Jr. New York: Henry Holt, 1997. 254.

1612. *The Encyclopedia of North American Indians*. D. L. Birchfield, gen. ed. Vol. 7. New York: Marshall Cavendish, 1997. 916–17. (port.)

1613. *Encyclopedia of North American Indians*. Edited by Frederick E. Hoxie. Boston: Houghton Mifflin, 1996. References to Momaday are included in the following articles: "Arts, Contemporary (Since 1960)," by Suzan Shawn Harjo, 52; "Kiowa," by Benjamin R. Kracht, 318; and "Literature by Indians," by Betty L. Bell, 339.

1614. *Encyclopedia of the Essay*. Edited by Tracy Chevalier. Chicago: Fitzroy Dearborn Publishers, 1997. 565–66. In his essay, John T. Price refers to Momaday as a well-known essayist and places him in the postmodern essay tradition.

1615. *Encyclopedia of the Great Plains Indians*. Edited by David J. Wishart. Lincoln: University of Nebraska Press, 2007. 129–30. The biographical article is by Kenneth M. Roemer. See also the book's index for related articles, including "Oral Tradition," "Fiction by Native Peoples," and "Plains Poetry."

1616. *Encyclopedia of World Biography*. Vol. 11, 2nd ed. Detroit: Gale Research, 2004. 92–94. (port.) Presents a profile of Momaday's life and professional career.

1617. *Environmental Literature: An Encyclopedia of Works, Authors, and Themes*. Compiled by Patricia D. Netzley. Santa Barbara, California: ABC-CLIO, 1999. 175–76. The article about Momaday contains comments by Matthias Schubnell about Momaday's nature-related writings in prose and poetry. See the index for additional references in other articles.

1618. *Fifty Western Writers: A Bio-Bibliographical Sourcebook.* Edited by Fred Erisman and Richard W. Etulain. Westport, Connecticut: Greenwood Press, 1982. 313–24. The essay, "N. Scott Momaday, 1934– ," by Martha S. Trimble, presents an overview of his life, major works and themes, and critical reception to 1980.

1619. *Great Plains Indian Illustration Index.* Compiled by John Van Balen. Jefferson, North Carolina: McFarland, 2004. See p. 233 of the book's index for references pertaining to N. Scott Momaday and Alfred M. Momaday.

1620. *Handbook of Native American Literature.* Edited by Andrew Wiget. Garland Reference Library of the Humanities, vol. 1815. New York: Garland, 1996. 463–77. The essay about Momaday, on the pages cited, is by Susan Scarberry-García and is the same as the essay published in *Dictionary of Native American Literature* in 1994. This is also an electronic resource through NetLibrary.

1621. *A Handbook to Literature.* 9th edited by William Harmon. Upper Saddle River, New Jersey: Prentice Hall, 2003. 616. Brief information about Momaday is included under "Native American Literature" and "Pulitzer Prizes for Fiction."

1622. *Harper Handbook to Literature.* 2nd rev. ed. By Northrop Frye et al. New York: Longman, 1997. 17–19. Information about Momaday is included under "American Indian Literature."

1623. *HarperCollins Reader's Encyclopedia of American Literature.* 2nd ed. Edited by George Perkins, Barbara Perkins, and Phillip Leininger. New York: HarperCollins, 2002. 692. Previously published as *Benét's Reader's Encyclopedia of American Literature.*

1624. *Identities and Issues in Literature.* Edited by David Peck. In three vols. Pasadena, California: Salem Press, 1997. The main entry on Momaday, written by Michael R. Meyers, is in vol. 2, 668–69. See also, "Native American Identity," by Wesley Britton, vol. 2, 702–706, and the index in vol. 3 for additional references.

1625. *Indians of Today.* Edited and compiled by Marion E. Gridley. 4th ed. ICFP, Inc., 1971. 355–59. (ports.) All three Momadays are included in this edition, Gridley's last. All biographical sketches are accompanied by a portrait. Of the three, Scott has the longest sketch on pp. 356–57. A sketch about Natachee Scott Momaday is on p. 355, and one about Alfred Morris Momaday is on pp. 358–59. The parents were included together in Gridley's third edition of *Indians of Today.* Chicago: Indian Council Fire and Association of American Indian Affairs, 1960. 152–54.

1626. *The Kiowa.* By John R. Wunder. Indians of North America. New York: Chelsea House, 1989. 13–14, 100–101. (port.)

1627. *The Kiowas.* By Mildred P. Mayhall. 2nd ed. The Civilization of the American Indian series. Norman: University of Oklahoma Press, 1971. 325. This edition includes information about Momaday and his father. The first edition mentions only Al Momaday on p. 277.

1628. *Larousse Dictionary of Writers.* Edited by Rosemary Goring. Edinburgh, United Kingdom: Larousse, 1994. A brief sketch is on p. 675.

1629. *A Literary History of the American West.* J. Golden Taylor, editor in chief, and Thomas J. Lyon, ser. ed. Sponsored by the Western Literary Association. Fort Worth: Texas Christian University Press, 1987. References to Momaday are in the essays "Native Oral Traditions," by Larry Evers and Paul Pavich, 11–28, and "American Indian Fiction, 1968–1983," by Paula Gunn Allen, 1058–66. See the book's index for additional references.

1630. *Literary Masters: N. Scott Momaday.* Compiled and written by Lee Schweninger. Gale Study Guides to Great Literature, no. 12. Detroit: Gale Group, 2001. 175 pp. (ports.)

1631. *Magill's Survey of American Literature.* Rev. ed., vol. 4. Edited by Steven G. Kellman. Pasadena, California: Salem Press, ©2007. 1759–68. (port.) A biographical essay by Kathleen Mills, updated and with a bibliography by Gina Macdonald, is accompanied by summaries of "The Bear" (poem), *House Made of Dawn, The Way to Rainy Mountain, The Names, The Ancient Child,* and *In the Presence of the Sun.*

1632. *Native America: Portrait of the Peoples.* Edited by Duane Champagne, with a foreword by Dennis Banks. Detroit: Visible Ink, 1994. 690–91.

1633. *The Native American Almanac: A Portrait of Native Americans Today.* By Arlene Hirschfelder and Martha Kreipe de Montaño. New York: Prentice Hall General Reference, 1993. See p. 335 of the book's index for brief references to Momaday.

1634. *Native American Biographies.* Edited by Virginia Seeley et al. Paramus, New Jersey: Globe Fearon, 1994. 16–24. Information about Momaday is in parts of Unit 1 under "Native Americans in Literature and Drama," 16–21, and

"Biography," 17–24. This book is primarily for junior and senior high school students. A photograph shows Momaday coloring an etching of a shield.

1635. *The Native American in American Literature: A Selectively Annotated Bibliography.* By Roger O. Rock. Bibliographies and Indexes in American Literature, no. 3. Westport, Connecticut: Greenwood Press, 1985. See the author index, p. 193, and the subject index, p. 204, for references to Momaday scattered throughout this bibliography.

1636. *The Native American in Long Fiction: An Annotated Bibliography.* By Joan Beam and Barbara Branstad. Native American Bibliography Series, no. 18, gen. ed. Jack W. Marken. Lanham, Maryland: Scarecrow Press, 1996. Includes *The Ancient Child,* entry no. 261, pp. 194–95, and entry no. 262, pp. 195–96.

1637. *Native American Literatures: An Encyclopedia of Works, Characters, Authors, and Themes.* By Kathy J. Whitson. Santa Barbara, California: ABC-CLIO, 1999. 153–55. (port.) The main entry about Momaday presents biographical information. Other references to characters, themes, and major works are listed in the index at pp. 288–89.

1638. *Native American Literatures: An Introduction.* By Suzanne Evertsen Lundquist. Continuum Studies in Literary Genre. New York: Continuum, 2004. An essay, "N. Scott Momaday (b. 1934)," is in chapter 4, "The Best and the Best Known in Native American Literatures: An Introduction," 55–70. See also chapter 5, "Themes in Native American Literatures," 202–205, and the book's index for additional information.

1639. *Native American Writers of the United States.* See earlier in this listing under *Dictionary of Literary Biography,* vol. 175.

1640. *Native Americans: An Annotated Bibliography.* Compiled by Frederick E. Hoxie and Harvey Markowitz. Magill Bibliographies. Pasadena, California: Salem Press, 1991. 310.

1641. *The Native North American Almanac: A Reference Work on Native North Americans in the United States and Canada.* Edited by Duane Champagne. Detroit: Gale Group, 2001. Includes a Momaday chronology on p. 56 and biographical sketch on p. 1303.

1642. *Native North American Firsts.* By Karen Gayton Swisher and AnCita Benally. Foreword by Billy Mills. Detroit: Gale Research, 1998. Information about Momaday is in sections "Education," 48; "Literature—1969," 106; and "Literature—1989," 109. (port.)

1643. *Native North American Literature: Biographical and Critical Information on Native Writers and Orators from the United States and Canada from Historical Times to the Present.* Edited by Janet Witalec et al. Detroit: Gale Research, 1994. Coverage is to the early 1990s. Momaday and his writing are presented in Part II, "Written Literature," 432–48.

1644. *The New Encyclopedia of the American West.* Rev. ed. Edited by Howard R. Lamar. New Haven, Connecticut: Yale University Press, 1998. 529, 728–29. See first edition under *The Reader's Encyclopedia of the American West.*

1645. *Notable Native Americans.* Edited by Sharon Malinowski. Detroit: Gale Research, 1995. 273–75. (port.) A biographical essay about Momaday is by JoAnn di Filippo.

1646. *The Oxford Companion to American Literature.* 6th ed. By James D. Hart, with revisions and additions by Phillip W. Leininger. New York: Oxford University Press, 1995. 440. This edition includes a brief entry about Momaday.

1647. *The Oxford Encyclopedia of American Literature.* Jay Parini, editor in chief. New York: Oxford University Press, 2004. An essay about Momaday by Arnold E. Sabatelli is in vol. 3, 156–59 (port.); information about *House Made of Dawn* and the Pulitzer Prize is in vol. 4, 335.

1648. *The Oxford Encyclopedia of Children's Literature.* Vol. 3. Jack Zipes, editor in chief. New York: Oxford University Press, 2006. 137. Momaday is mentioned in the essay "Native American Children's Literature," by Debbie Reese.

1649. *Poetry Criticism.* Vol. 25. Detroit: Gale Group, 2007; Cengage Learning, 2009. 186–222.

1650. *Poetry for Students: Presenting Analysis, Context, and Criticism on Commonly Studied Poetry.* Edited by Marie Rose Napierkowski and Mary K. Rudy. Detroit: Gale Research, 1998. Analysis of poems by Momaday is in vol. 2, 1–13, and vol. 11, 172–85.

1651. *Portrait Index of North American Indians in Published Collections.* 2nd ed., rev. and enlarged. Compiled by Patrick Frazier. Washington, D.C.: Library of Congress, 1996. 58. (port.) This resource provides a short list of works containing a portrait of Momaday.

1652. *The Reader's Encyclopedia of the American West.* Edited by Howard R. Lamar. New York: Thomas Y. Crowell, 1977. 765. See rev. ed. under *The New Encyclopedia of the American West.*

1653. *Reference Encyclopedia of the American Indian.* 13th ed. By Barry T. Klein. Boca Raton, Florida: Todd Publications, 2007. 773–74.

1654. *Reference Guide to American Literature.* 4th ed. Edited by Thomas Riggs. Detroit, Michigan: St. James Press, 2000. 610–11. The brief sketch on Momaday is by Jay Ann Cox.

1655. *The Scribner Encyclopedia of American Lives: The 1960s.* Vol. 2. Edited by William L. O'Neill and Kenneth T. Jackson. New York: Charles Scribner's Sons, 2003. 82–84. (port.) The biographical essay is by Brad Agnew, ser. ed.

1656. *Smoke Rising: The Native North American Literary Companion.* Edited by Janet Witalec, with Sharon Malinowski; Joseph Bruchac, managing ed. Detroit: Visible Ink Press, 1995. 325–34. (port.) Includes an essay by JoAnn di Filippo and excerpts from *The Way to Rainy Mountain.*

1657. *Something about the Author: Facts and Pictures about Authors and Illustrators of Books for Young People.* Vol. 48. Edited by Anne Commire. Detroit: Gale, ©1987. 158–62. (ports.) There has been no update through vol. 194, 2009.

1658. *Southwest Heritage: A Literary History, with Bibliographies.* Edited by Mabel Major and T. M. Pearce. 3rd ed., rev. and enlarged. Albuquerque: University of New Mexico Press, 1972. Annotated citations are in Part 4, "Literature from 1948–1970," for *House Made of Dawn,* 235, and *The Way to Rainy Mountain,* 256. This reference source was one of the first to list these two titles.

1659. *St. James Encyclopedia of Popular Culture.* Vol. 3. Edited by Sara Pendergast and Tom Pendergast. Detroit: St. James Press, 2000. 392. Includes a concise summary of Momaday's contributions to American popular culture.

1660. *St. James Guide to Native North American Artists.* Edited by Roger Matuz. Detroit: St. James Press, 1998. Includes an informative sketch about Momaday's father, artist Alfred Morris (Al) Momaday, by Gerhard and Gisela Hoffman, 384–85, but none about N. Scott Momaday.

1661. *St. James Guide to Young Adult Writers.* 2nd ed. Edited by Tom Pendergast and Sara Pendergast, with a preface by Richard Peck. St. James Guide to Writers Series. Detroit: St. James Press, 1999. 600–602. The essay about Momaday is by Charmaine Allmon Mosby.

1662. *Twentieth-Century Western Writers.* 2nd ed. Edited by Geoff Sadler. Chicago: St. James Press, 1991. 470–71.

1663. *Updating the Literary West.* Edited by Thomas Lyon et al. Sponsored by the

Western Literary Association. Fort Worth: Texas Christian University Press, 1997. 537–40. The essay "N. Scott Momaday" is by Robert F. Gish.

1664. *Who's Who in America.* 63rd ed., vol. 2. New Providence, New Jersey: Marquis Who's Who, 2009, ©2008. 3456–57.

1665. *Who's Who in the West.* 36th ed. New Providence, New Jersey: Marquis Who's Who, 2009, ©2008. 421.

1666. *Who's Who of Pulitzer Prize Winners.* By Elizabeth A. Brennan and Elizabeth C. Clarage. Phoenix, Arizona: Oryx Press, 1999. 233. (port.)

1667. *Words of Power: Voices from Indian America.* Edited by Norbert S. Hill, Jr. Golden, Colorado: Fulcrum, 1994. 1. Momaday contributed a quotation about values to this book of quotations.

1668. *World Poets.* Ron Padgett, editor in chief. Scribner Writers Series, vol. 2. New York: Charles Scribner's Sons; Gale Group, 2000. 217–27. (port.) The essay, "N. Scott Momaday," is by Kenneth Lincoln.

1669. *The Writers Directory 2009.* 24th ed., vol. 2, edited by Lisa Kumar. Detroit: St. James Press, 2008. 1520–21. Momaday has been included in this directory since the third edition, 1976–78.

Internet and Online Resources

A number of websites provide a wide range of information about N. Scott Momaday and his works. The list below serves as a useful starting point for accessing information about him, his works, and related topics.

1670. Academy of Achievement: A Museum of Living History. Washington, D.C.

www.achievement.org

Momaday was inducted into the Academy of Achievement in 1993. Included on this website is a biography, "The Writer Warrior," and a long interview conducted in June 1996. The interview is accompanied by a number of photographs and portraits. This site also provides links to other websites, including The Buffalo Trust, Literary Encyclopedia, and PBS. ©The Academy. Web address for the interview: www.achievement.org/autodoc/page/mom0int-1

1671. ASAIL/SAIL (Association for the Study of American Indian Literatures/ *Studies in American Indian Literatures*)

www.oncampus.richmond.edu/faculty/ASAIL/sail-hp.html

ASAIL has published different versions of its newsletter and journal since 1973. Its website offers free access to the full text of its publications, including essays and reviews: series 1, 1977–87, and series 2, 1988–current issue.

1672. The Buffalo Trust

www.buffalotrust.org

This is the official website of the nonprofit foundation established by Momaday for the preservation of the oral tradition and cultural heritage of Native Americans and indigenous peoples around the world. Its content includes the foundation's vision and mission statements and a biography of Momaday.

1673. *Canku Ota*: An Online Newsletter Celebrating Native America

www.turtletrack.org

Canku Ota (Many Paths) features a two-page essay, "N. Scott Momaday," presenting biographical information with quotes of Momaday, an excerpt from *House Made of Dawn* (1968), and two portraits. ©Vicki Lockard and Paul Barry. For Momaday, find Issue 2000 and click on May 6.

1674. Columbia Granger's World of Poetry (Columbia University Press)

www.columbiagrangers.org

A search for Momaday at this subscriber website finds a number of titles of his poems and printed sources in which the poems are published.

1675. Education Resources Information Center (ERIC). Washington, D.C.

http://eric.ed.gov

ERIC is a helpful resource for teachers, students, and others working in various fields, including American Indian literature and Native American studies. It provides information about a broad range of print and nonprint materials. A search at the ERIC home page will bring up a number of items related to Momaday's works.

1676. The Expanding Canon: Teaching Multicultural Literature in High School

www.learner.org

Eight one-hour video programs and teacher workshop guides are available at this website, which offers classroom approaches to teaching the literature. One of the programs, "Workshop 6," presents N. Scott Momaday and *The Way to Rainy Mountain*. It demonstrates how a class studies Kiowa culture and mythological themes. This and other programs may be viewed on the website or on the Annenberg Channel. ©Annenberg Media

1677. The Internet Public Library. "Native American Authors Project."

www.ipl.org

IPL Online Literary Criticism presents a brief background on Momaday and his books, a short list of his awards, and other online resources. This information can be accessed at:

www.ipl.org/div/natam/bin/browse.pl/A50

1678. The Literary Encyclopedia

www.litencyc.com

This literary reference source offers essays, ranging in length from fifteen hundred to four thousand words, on authors of international prominence. It provides free online access for only about the first six hundred words of an essay, requiring membership (month or annual) to access the entire item. Full essays about Momaday and eleven of his primary works are available for subscribers. ©The Literary Dictionary Co.

1679. Modern American Poetry (MAPS). An Online Journal and Multimedia Companion to *Anthology of Modern American Poetry*. Edited by Cary Nelson.

www.english.illinois.edu/maps/index.htm

This website offers an excellent presentation on Momaday and his poetry. Contents are compiled by Dr. Kenneth M. Roemer and includes his essay,

"N. Scott Momaday: Biographical, Literary, and Multicultural Contexts," with lists of major works and suggested reading. It also offers a selection of poetry by Momaday with comments by others, an online interview, excerpts from his published works, and art and illustrations in color. ©Department of English, University of Illinois, Urbana-Champaign. The web address directly to Momaday on this site is:

www.english.illinois.edu/maps/poets/m_r/momaday/momaday.htm

1680. National Museum of the American Indian (NMAI). Washington, D.C.

www.nmai.si.edu

The NMAI website offers a variety of information and learning resources for all ages. Information is available about Momaday, a founding trustee of NMAI. Archived webcasts are also available. ©Smithsonian Institution

1681. National Public Radio (NPR)

www.npr.org

A search of NPR's archives locates several conversations with Momaday about his books, readings by him, and book reviews that have been presented on the program *All Things Considered. Circle of Wonder: A Native American Christmas Story* was featured on some of these programs. Audio links are available.

1682. Native Networks

www.nativenetworks.si.edu

A wide variety of information can be found on this website, sponsored by the Smithsonian Institution and the National Museum of the American Indian. "A Momaday Interview," conducted by Joanna Hearne at the University of Arizona in March 2003, is featured. It focuses on *House Made of Dawn* and the filming of this novel. Interviews are also available with producer-director Richardson Morse and actor Larry Littlebird, who played the role of Abel. Links are provided to other information. ©Smithsonian Institution

1683. NativeWiki

www.nativewiki.org

NativeWiki, a project of NativeWeb and similar in structure to Wikipedia, is a free electronic database focusing its content on indigenous nations, peoples, and cultures of the world. Information ranges from biographical, geographical, and tribal to pictorial. NativeWeb is a nonprofit educational organization dedicated to using telecommunications, the Internet, and computer technology to disseminate information about and from indigenous peoples and organizations. ©NativeWeb, Inc.

1684. Oyate

www.oyate.org

This website provides reviews and articles about the Native experience in literature for children. Compiled by Doris Seale and Beverly Slapin, editors of *A Broken Flute* (AltaMira Press, 2005) and *Through Indian Eyes* (American Indian Studies Center, UCLA, ©1998), it includes *House Made of Dawn* and *The Way to Rainy Mountain*. This online reference tool for teachers, students, parents, and others is maintained by Slapin. ©Oyate

1685. Perspectives in American Literature (PAL): An Online Research and Reference Guide

www.csustan.edu/english/reuben/pal/chap10/momaday.html

PAL, compiled and edited by Dr. Paul R. Reuben, provides information about authors. Chapter 10, "Late Twentieth Century: 1945 to the Present," includes a list of Momaday's primary works and a short bibliography of works about him. ©Paul R. Rueben

1686. Poetics and Politics. Department of English, University of Arizona, Tucson

http://poeticsandpolitics.arizona.edu/main.html

Presents the first Poetics and Politics Reading Series, held in 1992. This series brought Momaday and twelve other acclaimed American Indian writers to the University of Arizona campus for presentations, discussions, and other events. His presentation, along with a graduate student essay about him and other information, can be accessed at http://poeticsandpolitics.arizona.edu/momaday/momaday_top.html

1687. Poetry Out Loud: National Recitation Contest. National Endowment for the Arts and The Poetry Foundation.

www.poetryoutloud.org

This site provides the complete anthology and program details of the National Recitation Contest in which high school students from across the nation participate. It is a poetry resource for teachers and students. Momaday is among the speakers and performers who participated in the making of *Poetry Out Loud: National Recitation Contest; The Anthology*. Available in print and compact disc forms. See also the sections "Anthologies—2005" and "Nonprint Media."

1688. Poets.org. From the Academy of American Poets.

www.poets.org

A biographical sketch of Momaday is available on this website, along with external links to other sites, including the Academy of Achievement. Although his poem, "The Bear," was awarded the Academy of American Poets Prize in 1962, it is not among the poems included on this site. ©The Academy of American Poets.

www.poets.org/poet.php/prmPID/1107

1689. Public Broadcasting System (PBS)

www.pbs.org

A search at the PBS homepage will retrieve several web pages pertaining to Momaday, particularly relating to his voice work and interviews that have aired on PBS channels across the nation. One of the most publicized series in which Momaday participated was *The West*, about the history of the American West. He has also lent his voice to other series and programs on *The American Experience*. He is featured in an essay, "N. Scott Momaday: Keeper of the Flame," at www.pbs.org/weta/thewest/program/producers/momaday.html.

1690. Storytellers: Native American Authors Online

www.hanksville.org

At the Welcome to Hanksville homepage, one finds two options: Storytellers: Native American Authors Online and the Index of Native American Resources. Although there is no web page specifically devoted to Momaday, a search of his last name produces listings with a number of article titles and page text matches leading to a variety of works by and about him. ©K. M. Strom.

1691. Wisdom of the Elders

www.wisdomoftheelders.org

Elder Wisdom, produced by Brian Bull (Nez Perce) and funded by several national organizations, features oral accounts of tribal elders and other information about them. Momaday is featured in "Program One: Elder Wisdom with Barbara Roberts." This multimedia program includes Momaday's address to the United Nations at the "Cry of the Earth" gathering in November 1993, a biography, readings, and images. Produced by Roberts, this program can be accessed at the following web address:

www.wisdomoftheelders.org/prog1/

Today, university, public, and other libraries subscribe to a wide variety of online or electronic databases specializing in general and specific subject areas or fields of learning. Through annual subscriptions or one-time perpetual rights, such libraries provide their users with access to these databases. Also, electronic books, or eBooks, in full text online, are increasing in number. *The Way to Rainy Mountain* is available in full text in electronic form through NetLibrary, Inc., an eContent provider for libraries and publishers that offers a growing collection of ebooks, ejournals, reference sources, and audiobooks. These materials can be accessed at libraries providing this service. Access from a home computer may also be available if a library provides free accounts to its patrons.

Several of the online databases that provide information about American Indian literature, history, culture, current events, and related subjects are American Indian History OnLine, Bibliography of Native North Americans (BNNA), Ethnic News Watch, North American Indian Thought and Culture, and North American Indian Drama. Online databases also provide full text and complete backfiles of hundreds of journals and periodicals. Using WorldCat, the world's largest comprehensive online catalog, will lead users to many types of materials by and about Momaday and other authors.

Teaching Momaday's Writings

This section of Part III presents a selection of books, essays, and articles by other authors that relate to teaching and learning about Momaday's books and poetry, in particular *House Made of Dawn* and *The Way to Rainy Mountain.* His writings have been used for instructional purposes in numerous textbooks, anthologies, and other resources for teachers and students. A number of the citations in this section refer to the following book: Roemer, Kenneth M., ed. *Approaches to Teaching Momaday's "The Way to Rainy Mountain."* Approaches to Teaching World Literature, no. 17, Joseph Gibaldi, ser. ed. New York: Modern Language Association of America, 1988. Following the first full citation to this book in entry no. 1694, shortened citations are used in subsequent entries as follows: In Roemer, ed., *Approaches to Teaching* (1988), page nos.

1692. Allen, Paula Gunn, ed. *Studies in American Indian Literature: Critical Essays and Course Designs.* New York: Modern Language Association of America, 1983. Allen was an expert in developing and teaching curriculum about American Indian literature. This book includes course designs and other resources for educators, primarily at the university level. In particular, see "Introductory Courses in American Indian Literature," 225–33; "Survey Courses," 234–39; and "Teaching the Indian in American Literature," 273–77.

1693. Allen, Rodney F. "Keepsakes: Using Family Stories in Elementary Classrooms." *The Social Studies* 89, no. 4 (July–August 1998): 189–90. Allen writes about Linda Winston's *Keepsakes: Using Family Stories in Elementary Classrooms,* published by Heinemann in 1997, in which the author tells about school children collecting and using family stories. Allen remarks on Momaday's use of "The Story of the Arrowmaker," which was introduced to him in his early childhood.

1694. Anderson, Lauri. "Gathering the Past: *The Way to Rainy Mountain* in Freshman Composition Courses." In Kenneth M. Roemer, ed., *Approaches to Teaching Momaday's "The Way to Rainy Mountain."* Approaches to Teaching World Literature, no. 17, Joseph Gibaldi, ser. ed. New York: Modern Language Association of America, 1988. 98–102.

1695. Bataille, Gretchen M. "Momaday and the Evocation of Identity." In Roemer, ed., *Approaches to Teaching* (1988), 78–84.

1696. Berner, Robert L. "*The Way to Rainy Mountain*: Structure and Language." In Roemer, ed., *Approaches to Teaching,* 54–60.

1697. Bloodworth, William. "Neihardt, Momaday, and the Art of Indian Autobiography." *Teaching English in the Two-Year College* 4, no. 2 (Winter 1978): 137–43.

1698. Brady, Margaret K. "Problematizing the Great Divide: Teaching Orality/ Literacy." *Journal of Folklore Research* 33, no. 1 (1996): 33–47. Brady, a folklorist teaching in a university English department teamed up with a colleague, a literary scholar, in organizing a graduate seminar to examine "the intersection of orality and literacy in contemporary American Indian literature." Transcribed oral and chirographic autobiographical works, including *The Way to Rainy Mountain*, were used. In summary, those who took part thought they had achieved a better understanding of the relationship between the oral and written word.

1699. Brumble, H. David, III. "*The Way to Rainy Mountain* and the Traditional Forms of American Indian Autobiography." In Roemer, ed., *Approaches to Teaching* (1988), 41–46.

1700. Caduto, Michael J. "Viewpoint: Ecological Education, A System Rooted in Diversity." *Journal of Environmental Education* 29, no. 4 (Summer 1998): 11–16. Caduto writes about developing children's interest in and knowledge of the environment.

1701. Caduto, Michael J., and Joseph Bruchac. *Keepers of the Earth: Native American Stories and Environmental Activities for Children*. Foreword by N. Scott Momaday. Golden, Colorado: Fulcrum, 1989, ©1988. This book is one of a series written by Caduto and Bruchac about subjects relating to animals, plants, and the environment. Joseph Bruchac has also published separately *Native American Stories* (2005), which contains stories from *Keepers of the Earth* and a foreword by Momaday.

1702. Carey, Gary, ed. *House Made of Dawn: Notes*. Lincoln, Nebraska: Cliffs Notes, 2000, ©1994. 82 pp. This Cliffs Notes is also available in electronic form.

1703. Cecil, Kathleen. "Walking a Maze of Views to the Center: Teaching Point of View." *English Journal* 93, no. 5 (May 2004): 54–59. The author discusses students' difficulties in comprehending literary themes and explains how the historical record aspect of *The Way to Rainy Mountain* may be used to help them discover themes.

1704. Charles, Jim. "Elders as Teachers of Youth in American Indian Children's Literature." *Studies in American Indian Literatures* 12, no. 1 (Summer 2000): 56–64.

1705. ———. "Finding a Way: Student Self-Discovery and N. Scott Momaday's *The Way to Rainy Mountain*." *English Journal* 86, no. 8, New Voices: The Canon of the Future (December 1997): 64–68.

1706. ———. *Reading, Learning, Teaching N. Scott Momaday*. Confronting the Text, Confronting the World, vol. 5. New York: Peter Lang, 2007. This is an informative guidebook, in particular for teachers and students at high school and college levels.

1707. Dillingham, Peter. "The Literature of the American Indian." *English Journal* 62, no. 1 (January 1973): 37–41. This is a brief critical survey of works to use in introducing the literature. It suggests the use of Momaday's poetry with children and *House Made of Dawn* and *The Way to Rainy Mountain* with older students.

1708. Dorris, Michael. "Native American Literature in an Ethnohistorical Context." *College English* 41, no. 2 (October 1979): 147–61. Momaday and *House Made of Dawn* are discussed among other writers carrying out a nontraditional creative role by writing in English and mostly for a non-Indian readership.

1709. Evers, Larry. "Native American Oral Literatures in the College English Classroom: An Omaha Example." *College English* 36 (1975): 649–62.

1710. Glazier, Jocelyn. "Multicultural Literature and Discussion as Mirror and Window." *Journal of Adolescent and Adult Literacy* 48, no. 8 (May 2005): 686–99. This article documents the experience of high school students as they read and responded to *The Way to Rainy Mountain*. The book was used as a "window" revealing another culture and a "mirror" reflecting their own.

1711. Grant, Agnes. "*The Way to Rainy Mountain* in a Community-based Oral Narratives Course for Cree and Ojibway Students." In Roemer, ed., *Approaches to Teaching* (1988), 138–44.

1712. Harvey, Karen D., and Lisa D. Harjo. *Indian Country: A History of Native People in America*. Golden, Colorado: North American Press, 1993, ©1994. Contains lesson plans and is accompanied by a teacher's guide written by the authors and published in 1994. An excerpt from *House Made of Dawn* (1968), 143, is presented at the beginning of chapter 13, "Tribal Restoration, Phase One Continued, 1944–1953," 189–90.

1713. Helbig, Alethea K., and Agnes Regan Perkins. *This Land Is Our Land: A Guide to Multicultural Literature for Children and Young Adults*. Westport, Connecticut: Greenwood Press, 1994. 240–41. This resource includes a brief sketch describing Momaday's novels and *The Way to Rainy Mountain.*

1714. Henley, Joan. "Exploring the Ways to Rainy Mountain." In Roemer, ed., *Approaches to Teaching* (1988), 47–53.

1715. Jaskoski, Helen. "Image and Silence." In Roemer, ed., *Approaches to Teaching* (1988), 69–77. Describes *The Way to Rainy Mountain* as a book that invites readers to take part in "a visionary experience beyond the reach of language" (77).

1716. ———. "Beauty Before Me: Notes on *House Made of Dawn* (N. Scott Momaday)." In *Teaching American Ethnic Literatures: Nineteen Essays,* edited by John R. Maitino and David R. Peck. Albuquerque: University of New Mexico Press, 1996. 37–54. Jaskoski provides an analysis of themes and structure of the book, and information about resources for teachers.

1717. Joyce, Audrey B. *American Contexts: Multicultural Readings for Composition.* New York: Longman, 2003. 345–51. Presents an excerpt from *The Names,* accompanied by questions for students.

1718. Kennedy, X. J., and Dana Gioia. *An Introduction to Poetry.* Tenth ed. New York: Longman, 2007. An excellent resource about poetry that includes poems by Momaday, with questions and activities.

1719. Kennedy, X. J., Dorothy M. Kennedy, and Dana Gioia. *Literature: An Introduction to Fiction, Poetry, Drama, and Writing.* 5th compact ed. New York: Pearson Longman, 2007. This anthology is accompanied by an instructor's manual and an interactive program, *MyLiteratureLab Resources.* Momaday's poem "Simile" is included in this edition.

1720. Lattin, Vernon E. "Momaday's Pastoral Vision in the Contexts of Modern Ethnic and Mainstream American Fiction." In Roemer, ed., *Approaches to Teaching* (1988), 124–31.

1721. Lee, A. Robert. *Multicultural American Literature: Comparative Black, Native, Latino/a, and Asian American Fictions.* Jackson: University Press of Mississippi, 2003. Three chapters include Momaday's works: chapter 1, "Landmarks: Ellison, Momaday, Anaya, Kingston," 20–21, 27–28, 36; chapter 2, "Selves: Autobiography, Autoethnicity, and Autofiction," 38–42; and chapter 4, "Fictions of the Indian, Native Fictions?" 90–91, 103–105.

1722. Lincoln, Kenneth. *Native American Renaissance.* Berkeley: University of California Press, 1983. This study of American Indian literatures focuses on literary history, tribal poetics, and translations from oral traditions. Writings by Momaday are discussed in chapter 5, "Word Senders: Black Elk and N. Scott Momaday," 82–121.

1723. Lucas, Kurt. "Navajo Students and 'Postcolonial' Literature." *English Journal* 79, no. 8 (December 1990): 54–58.

1724. Lundquist, Suzanne Evertsen. "College Composition: An Experience in Ethnographic Thinking." In Roemer, ed., *Approaches to Teaching* (1988), 110–15.

1725. ———. *Native American Literatures: An Introduction.* Continuum Studies in Literary Genre. New York: Continuum, 2004. 315 pp. Chapters cover a variety of topics: "What Are Native American Literatures?"; "How to Read Native American Literatures"; "The Best and the Best Known," with Momaday and his books on pp. 55–70; and "Themes in Native American Literatures."

1726. Macaruso, Victor. "Cowboys and Indians: The Image of the Indian in American Literature." "Special Teaching Literature Issue." *American Indian Culture and Research Journal* 8, no. 2 (1984): 13–21. This essay includes comments of a college instructor on teaching *House Made of Dawn* and *The Way to Rainy Mountain*, 16–17.

1727. Mattingly, Eileen M., and Lita Nicholson. "*The Way to Rainy Mountain*, by N. Scott Momaday/*The Whale Rider*, by Witi Ihimaera: A Curriculum Unit." Westlake, Ohio: The Center for Learning, ©2008. 1–24. This teaching guide contains five lesson plans with accompanying worksheets for use by teachers.

1728. *N. Scott Momaday's "House Made of Dawn": A Study Guide from Gale's "Novels for Students."* Vol. 10, chapter 6. Detroit, Michigan: Gale Group, 2002. Also available in electronic form.

1729. Oandasan, William. "*The Way to Rainy Mountain*: Internal and External Structures." In Roemer, ed., *Approaches to Teaching* (1988), 61–68.

1730. Papovich, J. Frank. "Journey into the Wilderness: American Literature and *The Way to Rainy Mountain*." In Roemer, ed., *Approaches to Teaching* (1988), 116–23.

1731. Rider, Janine. *The Writer's Book of Memory: An Interdisciplinary Study for Writing Teachers.* Mahwah, New Jersey: Lawrence Erlbaum Associates, 1995. New York: Peter Lang, 1998. Chapter 7, "Re/Membering Culture(s)," focuses on autobiographical writing and *The Way to Rainy Mountain*.

1732. Roemer, Kenneth M. "The Heuristic Powers of American Indian Literature:

What Native Authorship Does to Mainstream Texts." *Studies in American Indian Literatures* 2nd ser., 3, no. 2 (Summer 1991): 8–21. Roemer suggests the use of *The Way to Rainy Mountain* in discussions on the subject of authorship. It clearly demonstrates, in particular in relation to American Indian literature, that authorship can extend far beyond the individual author.

1733. ———. "Inventive Modeling: Rainy Mountain's Way to Composition." *College English* 46, no. 8 (December 1984): 767–82.

1734. ———. "Survey Courses, Indian Literature, and *The Way to Rainy Mountain*." *College English* 37, no. 6 (February 1976): 619–24.

1735. ———. "Teaching Indian Literature." In *Dictionary of Native American Literature*, edited by Andrew Wiget. Garland Reference Library of the Humanities, vol. 1815. New York: Garland, 1994. 347–52. Reprinted with new title: *Handbook of Native American Literature*, edited by Wiget. New York: Garland, 1996. 347–52. This essay discusses some of the common challenges faced by teachers when presenting the literature and includes references to *House Made of Dawn* and *The Way to Rainy Mountain*.

1736. ———, ed. *Approaches to Teaching Momaday's "The Way to Rainy Mountain."* Approaches to Teaching World Literature, no. 17, Joseph Gibaldi, ser. ed. New York: Modern Language Association of America, 1988. 172 pp.

1737. Roppolo, Kimberly, and Chelleye L. Crow. "Native American Education versus Indian Learning: Still Battling [Richard Henry] Pratt after All These Years." *Studies in American Indian Literatures* 19, no. 1 (2007): 3–31. This essay describes the experiences of the authors in teaching a one-week, three-credit-hour course in American Indian literature. *The Way to Rainy Mountain* was one of the books used.

1738. Ruoff, A. LaVonne Brown. *Literatures of the American Indian*. Indians of North America, Frank W. Porter III, gen. ed. New York: Chelsea House Publishers, 1991. This book provides an excellent introduction to American Indian oral and written literatures for students, teachers, and other readers. It introduces several of Momaday's books and includes a full-page photograph of Momaday and paintings by Al Momaday. In particular, see pp. 18, 20, 69–70, 88–89.

1739. Ruppert, James. "Theory, Discourse, and the Native American Literature Class." *Modern Language Studies* 26, no. 4 (Autumn 1996): 109–17.

1740. Scarberry-García, Susan. "Beneath the Stars: Images of the Sacred." In Roemer, ed., *Approaches to Teaching* (1988), 89–97.

1741. Schubnell, Matthias. "Tribal Identity and the Imagination." In Roemer, ed., *Approaches to Teaching* (1988), 24–31.

1742. Schulze, Patricia. "Teacher to Teacher: What Work of Literature Do You Recommend for Its Use of a Strong Oral Tradition?" *English Journal* 93, no. 1 (September 2003): 19–20. This teacher recommends *The Way to Rainy Mountain* and describes a teaching unit she has developed.

1743. Schweninger, Lee. *Literary Masters: N. Scott Momaday.* Gale Study Guide to Great Literature, vol. 12. Detroit, Michigan: Gale Group, 2001. 175 pp. An excellent resource in an inviting format for teachers and students.

1744. Smith, Marie. "Rainy Mountain, Legends, and Students." *Arizona English Bulletin* 13 (April 1971): 41–44.

1745. Smith, William F., Jr. "American Indian Literature." *English Journal* 63, no. 1 (January 1974): 68–72. This early overview of the literature includes books by both mother and son: Natachee Scott Momaday (*American Indian Authors*) and N. Scott Momaday (*The Way to Rainy Mountain*).

1746. Stensland, Anna Lee. "Integrity in Teaching Native American Literature." *English Journal* 72, no. 2 (February 1983): 46–48.

1747. Stott, Jon C. *Native Americans in Children's Literature.* Foreword by Joseph Bruchac. Phoenix, Arizona: Oryx Press, 1995. 146–48, 176. *House Made of Dawn* and *The Ancient Child* are briefly discussed in Stott's discussion about novels.

1748. Susag, Dorothea M. *Roots and Branches: A Resource of Native American Literature—Themes, Lessons, and Bibliographies.* Foreword by Joseph Bruchac. Urbana, Illinois: National Council of Teachers of English, 1998. A five-day lesson plan for use in teaching *The Way to Rainy Mountain* is in "Secondary Level Units, Lessons, and Activities," 78–80. See also annotated entries for *House Made of Dawn* and *The Way to Rainy Mountain*, 171–72.

1749. Trafzer, Clifford E. *As Long as the Grass Shall Grow: A History of Native Americans.* Belmont, California: Wadsworth/Thomson Learning, 2000. The preface provides a chapter-by-chapter outline of this book, which is designed to provide a general survey of cultural, social, and political history for students of Native American and other related studies. References to Momaday and his works are found in chapter 21, "Literature and Performing Arts," 471–500. See also "Native American Education," 405–10. (port.)

1750. ———. "'The Word Is Sacred to a Child': American Indians and Children's Literature." *American Indian Quarterly* 16, no. 3 (Summer 1992): 381–95. Trafzer critically reviews books for children that have translated in an exceptional manner stories from the oral tradition to the written word. He begins with a quote from *House Made of Dawn* (1968): "A child can listen and learn. The word is sacred to a child" (381).

1751. Trout, Lawana. "*The Way to Rainy Mountain*: Arrow of History, Spiral of Myth." In Roemer, ed., *Approaches to Teaching* (1988), 32–40. See also Trout's anthology in the section "Anthologies and Literary Collections Containing Momaday's Writings," entry no. 287.

1752. Vangen, Kathryn S. "The Indian as Purveyor of the Sacred Earth: Avoiding Nostalgic Readings of *The Way to Rainy Mountain*." In Roemer, ed., *Approaches to Teaching* (1988), 132–37.

1753. *"The Way to Rainy Mountain": With Related Readings.* The Glencoe Literature Library. New York: Glencoe/McGraw-Hill, 2001. The writings of other authors and poets are included in this book. Readings are designed for advanced middle school and high school students.

1754. White-Kaulaity, Marlina. "Reflections on Native American Reading: A Seed, a Tool, and a Weapon." *Journal of Adolescent & Adult Literacy* 50, no. 7 (April 2007): 560–69. The author presents her views for guiding students, from preschool through college, on their reading journeys. She quotes Momaday: "In the quest to make lifelong readers, we need not abandon the past to move into the future" (569).

1755. Wilson, Norma C. "Discovering Our Natural Resources in Language and Place." In Roemer, ed., *Approaches to Teaching* (1988), 85–88.

1756. Wormser, Baron, and David Cappella. *Teaching the Art of Poetry: The Moves.* Mahwah, New Jersey: Lawrence Erlbaum Associates, 2000. Momaday's poem "New World" is presented as an introduction to the world of chants in chapter 1, "Rhythm," p. 2.

1757. Yagelski, Robert P. *The Thomson Reader: Conversations in Context.* Boston: Thomson Higher Education, 2007. 70–75. The "Introduction" to *The Way to Rainy Mountain* is accompanied by questions to stimulate discussion and creative writing.

1758. Yancey, Kathleen Blake. "Dialogue, Interplay, and Discovery." Chapter 4 in *Writing Portfolios in the Classroom: Policy and Practice, Promise and Peril,* by Robert C. Calfee and Pamela Perfumo. Mahwah, New Jersey: Lawrence Erlbaum Associates, 1996. 83–102.

1759. York, Sherry. *Children's and Young Adult Literature by Native Americans: A Guide for Librarians, Teachers, Parents, and Students.* Worthington, Ohio: Linworth Publishing Inc., 2003. 124 pp. This book presents bibliographic and other information about Momaday's *Circle of Wonder* (book/audio cassette) on p. 10 and his mother's *Owl in the Cedar Tree* on p. 20.

1760. Zitzer-Comfort, Carol. "Teaching Native American Literature: Inviting Students to See the World through Indigenous Lenses." *Pedagogy* 8, no. 1 (Winter 2008): 160–70.

Dissertations and Theses

Dissertations

Most of the following dissertations are unpublished. When one has been published, the information is included.

1973

1761. Kousaleos, Peter G. "A Study of the Language, Structure, and Symbolism in Jean Toomer's *Cane* and N. Scott Momaday's *House Made of Dawn*." PhD diss., Ohio University, 1973. 215 pp.

1974

1762. DeFlyer, Joseph E. "Partition Theory: Patterns and Partitions of Consciousness in Selected Works of American and American Indian Authors." PhD diss., University of Nebraska, 1974. 394 pp. See chapter 5, "Indian and Christian: Momaday's Dual Structures of Consciousness in *House Made of Dawn*."

1975

1763. Smith, Rose Marie. "A Critical Study of the Literature of N. Scott Momaday as Intercultural Communication." PhD diss., University of Southern California, 1975. 174 pp.

1764. Strelke, Barbara A. "Images of Home and Place: Essays, Poems, Photographs." PhD diss., University of New Mexico, 1975. 246 pp. See chapter 6, "Place and the Remembered Earth: Land, Time, and Enduring Human Spirit: N. Scott Momaday, Racial Memory, and Individual Imagination," 176–95.

1765. Woodard, Charles Lowell. "The Concept of the Creative Word in the Writings of N. Scott Momaday." PhD diss., University of Oklahoma, 1975. 205 pp. Includes chapters about *House Made of Dawn*, *The Way to Rainy Mountain*, and Momaday's poetry.

1978

1766. Wilson, Norma Jean Clark. "The Spirit of Place in Contemporary American Indian Literature." PhD diss., University of Oklahoma, 1978. 219 pp.

1979

1767. Ludovici, Paula. "The Struggle for an Ending: Ritual and Plot in Recent American Indian Literature." PhD diss., American University, 1979.

1768. Nelson, Margaret Faye. "Ethnic Identity in the Prose Works of N. Scott Momaday." PhD diss., Oklahoma State University, 1979. 169 pp.

1982

1769. Solheim, David Ray. "Between the Sun and Earth: Poems." (Original writing) PhD diss., University of Denver, 1982. 117 pp.

1983

1770. Snider, John Michael. "The Treatment of American Indians in Selected American Literature: A Radical Critique." PhD diss., University of Illinois at Urbana-Champaign, 1983. 250 pp.

1984

1771. Papovich, John Guy. "I. Spin the Names of Earth and Sky: Native American Landscape Traditions and *The Way to Rainy Mountain*. II. Teaching the Homeric Poems in Translation: Seeing Homeric Values (Momaday)." PhD diss., University of Virginia, 1984. 220 pp.

1772. Sutherland, Janet Lynn. "Aufgehobene Welten: Orality and World View in the Fictional Works of N. Scott Momaday, Leslie Marmon Silko, and James Welch." PhD diss., University of Oregon, 1984. 263 pp.

1986

1773. King, Thomas Hunt. "Inventing the Indian: White Images, Native Oral Literature, and Contemporary Native Writers." PhD diss., University of Utah, 1986. 231 pp.

1774. Scarberry-García, Susan. "Sources of Healing in *House Made of Dawn*." PhD diss., University of Colorado at Boulder, 1986. 236 pp. This dissertation was printed by University Microfilms International, Ann Arbor, Michigan, 1989. 230 pp. Published in book form as *Landmarks of Healing: A Study of "House Made of Dawn."* Albuquerque: University of New Mexico Press, 1990. 208 pp.

1775. Wong, Hertha D. "Native American Autobiography: Oral, Artistic, and Dramatic Personal Narrative." PhD diss., University of Iowa, 1986. 249 pp.

1989

1776. Gonzalez, David Julian. "Because of the Blood in the Water: A Novel." PhD diss., University of Minnesota, 1989. 146 pp.

1777. Tu-Smith, Bonnie. "Alternative Visions: Perspectives on Community and Individualism in Multiethnic American Literature of the 1980s." PhD diss., Washington State University, 1989. 215 pp.

1990

1778. Blaeser, Kimberly Marie. "Gerald Vizenor: Writing—In the Oral Tradition." PhD diss., University of Notre Dame, 1990. 334 pp.

1991

1779. Arant, Tommy Joe. "*House Made of Dawn* and the Social Context of Contemporary Native American Literature." PhD diss., Duke University, 1991. 236 pp.

1992

1780. Bishop, Elizabeth. "Reshaping Ethnicity: The Half-blood as Shaman in Native American Literature." PhD diss., Bowling Green State University, 1992. 157 pp.

1781. Moser, Janette Irene. "Balancing the World: Spatial Design in Contemporary Native American Novels (Paula Gunn Allen, Louise Erdrich, N. Scott Momaday, Leslie Marmon Silko, James Welch)." PhD diss., University of North Carolina Press, 1992. 297 pp.

1993

1782. Moss, Maria, "We've Been Here Before: Women in Creation Myths." PhD diss., Universtat Hamburg, 1993. This dissertation has been published: *We've Been Here Before: Women in Creation Myths and Contemporary Literature of the Native American Southwest.* North American Studies, no. 1. Münster/Hamburg, Germany: Lit, 1993. 212 pp.

1783. Thompson, Craig Bunyard. "Speaking of Identities: The Presentation of American Indian Experience." PhD diss., University of California, San Diego, 1993. 214 pp.

1994

1784. Anderson, Eric Gary. "Southwestern Dispositions: American Literature on the Borderlands, 1880–1990." PhD diss., Rutgers University–New Brunswick, 1994. 263 pp.

1785. Brownlee, James Henry. "Limits, Risks, and Possibilities: Discourse and Religion in a Selection of Twentieth Century American Novels." PhD diss.,

University of Minnesota, 1994. 184 pp.

1786. Donovan, Kathleen M. "Coming to Voice: Native American Literature and Feminist Theory." PhD diss., University of Arizona, 1994. 252 pp. Published as: *Feminist Readings of Native American Literature: Coming to Voice.* Tucson: University of Arizona Press, 1998.

1787. Kim, Helen M. "Living the Fantasy: The Politics of Pleasure in Mass Culture." PhD diss., University of Michigan, 1994. 224 pp.

1788. Kosmider, Alexia M. "Tricky Tribal Discourse: The Poetry, Short Stories, and Fables of Creek Writer, Alex Posey." PhD diss., University of Rhode Island, 1994. 180 pp.

1789. Larson, Sidner John. "Issues of Identity in the Writing of N. Scott Momaday, James Welch, Leslie Silko, and Louise Erdrich." PhD diss., University of Arizona, 1994. 155 pp.

1790. Schein, Marie Madeleine. "The Evolution of Survival as Theme in Contemporary Native American Literature: From Alienation to Laughter." PhD diss., University of North Texas, 1994. 178 pp.

1791. Walter, Kelly Christine. "Native American Aesthetics in Twentieth-century Inter-American Literature." PhD diss., Pennsylvania State University, 1994. 148 pp.

1792. Weaver, Christopher Cannon. "Negotiating Personal and Communal Voices: Narrative and Identity in Composition Studies and the Fiction of Three Native American Authors (Momaday, Erdrich, Silko)." PhD diss., State University of New York at Stony Brook, 1994. 223 pp.

1995

1793. Burlingame, Lori Lynn. "Cultural Survival and the Oral Tradition in the Novels of D'Arcy McNickle and His Successors: Momaday, Silko, and Welch." PhD diss., University of Rochester, 1995. 361 pp.

1794. Liang, Iping Joy. "The Lure of the Land: Ethnicity and Gender in Imagining America." PhD diss., University of Massachusetts, Amherst, 1995. 209 pp.

1795. Shi, Jian. "Healing through Traditional Stories and Storytelling in Contemporary Native American Fiction." PhD diss., Lehigh University, 1995. 213 pp.

1796. Trusty-Murphy, Michelle Gay. "A Critical Model for Ethnic American Literature." PhD diss., Bowling Green State University, 1995. 154 pp.

1996

1797. Grant, Elizabeth Ann. "Hearing the Page: Teaching the Sound of Oral Traditions in North American Written Texts." PhD diss., St. John's University-New York, 1996. 297 pp.

1798. Kang, Yong-ki. "Poststructuralist Environmentalism and Beyond: Eco-consciousness in Snyder, Kingsolver, and Momaday." PhD diss., Indiana University of Pennsylvania, 1996. 276 pp.

1799. Lipnick, Catherine Jennifer. "The Ritual Function of Language: Re-membering the Mythic Vision in Native American Literature (N. Scott Momaday, Leslie Marmon Silko, Paula Gunn Allen)." PhD diss., State University of New York at Stony Brook, 1996. 606 pp.

1997

1800. Cutchins, Dennis Ray. "The Nativistic Trope in Contemporary Native American Novels." PhD diss., Florida State University, 1997. 244 pp.

1801. Erben, David Lawrence. "Textual Space and Ritual Transformation in Contemporary Native American Fiction (N. Scott Momaday, Louise Erdrich, Leslie Marmon Silko)." PhD diss., University of South Florida, 1997. 335 pp.

1802. Lumsden, Paul Lawrence. "The Bear in Selected American, Canadian, and Native Literature: A Pedagogical Symbol Linking Humanity and Nature." PhD diss., University of Alberta, Canada, 1997. 203 pp.

1998

1803. Budler, Laura J. "Storytelling and Hostility to the Novel in Four Contemporary Native American Novels (Louise Erdrich, James Welch, Leslie Marmon Silko, and N. Scott Momaday)." PhD diss., Northern Illinois University, 1998. 298 pp.

1804. LaChance, Leslie Marie. "What the Grandchildren Learned: The Relationship between English and Indigenous Languages in North American Indian Autobiography." PhD diss., University of Tennessee, 1998. 256 pp. See chapter 4, "What the Children Learned: English and Ancestral Languages in the Autobiographical Writings of Leslie Marmon Silko and N. Scott Momaday."

1805. Schauffler, Florence Marina. "Turning to Earth: Paths to an Ecological

Practice (Spiritual Values, Ethics)." PhD diss., University of New Hampshire, 1998. 208 pp.

1999

1806. Bissett, LaRell. "Indigenous Mexican and Native American Novelists: A Comparative Stylistic Study of Their Worldviews." PhD diss., University of Texas at Dallas, 1999. 385 pp.

1807. Orr, Delilah Gayle. "This Is About Healing: The Significance of the Feminine, Change, and Animal Lore (Native Americans, James Welch, Leslie Marmon Silko, N. Scott Momaday, Paula Gunn Allen, Medicine Women)." PhD diss., Arizona State University, 1999. 199 pp.

1808. Reid, Barbara Marie. "Re-wor(l)ding Indian Survival: Language and Sovereignty in Native American Literature." PhD diss., University of California, Berkeley, 1999. 178 pp.

1809. Su, John Joseph. "Post-modern Nostalgia: Narratives of Return and the Longing for Foundations (Ethics)." PhD diss., University of Michigan, 1999. 276 pp.

1810. Thompson, Alicia Rebecca. "The Frankenstein Paradigm: Marginalized Literatures as Monster and the Voice of Protest." PhD diss., Indiana University of Pennsylvania, 1999. 232 pp.

2000

1811. Hostetler, Phyllis Karen. "'Angles of Vision': N. Scott Momaday, the Native American Renaissance, and Effect on American Identity." PhD diss., University of California, Santa Barbara, 2000. 212 pp.

1812. James, Meredith K. "'Reservation of the Mind': The Literary Native Spaces in the Fiction of Sherman Alexie." PhD diss., University of Oklahoma, 2000. 165 pp. Includes references to Momaday.

1813. Katanski, Amelia Vittoria. "'No-one Can Dispute My Own Impressions and Bitterness': Representations of the Indian Boarding School Experience in Nineteenth- and Twentieth-century American Indian Literature." PhD diss., Tufts University, 2000. 282 pp. Book published based on doctoral dissertation: *Learning to Write "Indian": The Boarding-School Experience and American Indian Literature.* Norman: University of Oklahoma Press, 2005.

1814. Lamasney, Richard Andrew. "'Old-time Tunes': Irish Cultural Characteristics in Twentieth Century Irish American Prose." PhD diss., The Union Institute, 2000. 297 pp. In chapter 3, pp. 17–49, the author examines various texts, including Momaday's, to find common cultural themes in examples of ethnic American literature.

1815. McGurk, Celine. "From Trauma to Healing: The Metaphoric Role of the Veteran Figure in N. Scott Momaday's *House Made of Dawn* and Leslie Marmon Silko's *Ceremony*." PhD thesis, University of Ulster (Northern Ireland), 2000. National Library G06015164

1816. Todd, Diane M. "The American Dream in Literature: Women and Ethnics Need Not Apply." PhD diss., Indiana University of Pennsylvania, 2000. 287 pp.

1817. Tudor, Robert. "The Native American Postmodern-Mimetic Novel." PhD diss., University of Oklahoma, 2000. 178 pp.

2001

1818. Bomberry, Victoria Jean. "Indigenous Memory and Imagination: Thinking Beyond the Nation (Leslie Marmon Silko and N. Scott Momaday)." PhD diss., Stanford University, 2001. 210 pp.

1819. McCutchen, Calvin Kenneth. "Lifeweaving: Towards a Metaphysics of Cultural Identity (Leslie Marmon Silko, Gerald Vizenor, and N. Scott Momaday)." PhD diss., University of Texas at Arlington, 2001. 224 pp.

1820. Robins, Barbara Kimberly. "Acts of Empathic Imagination: Contemporary Native American Artists and Writers as Healers." PhD diss., University of Oklahoma, 2001. 297 pp.

1821. Roenneke, Almuth. "Die literarische Problematisierung des Einflusses der christlichen Religion auf das indianische Selbstbild im Romanwerk von D'Arcy McNickle, Paula Gunn Allen, N. Scott Momaday, and Louise Erdrich." PhD diss., Dresden Tech. Universität, 2001. 427 pp. (in German) Includes an analysis of the influence of Christian religion in *House Made of Dawn*.

1822. Sarve-Gorham, Kristan. "Answering the Western: The Frontier Myth in American Indian Fiction (Leslie Marmon Silko, N. Scott Momaday, Louise Erdrich, and Mourning Dove)." PhD diss., Emory University, 2001. 305 pp.

2002

1823. Hebebrand, Christina Marlis. "'We Are the People': Native American and

Chicano/a Literatures as Intersecting Indigenous Literature in the American Southwest." PhD diss., Case Western Reserve University, 2002. 248 pp.

1824. Mollard, Rhona Smyth. "Testaments of Colonialism: Six Native American Novels (John Joseph Matthews, D'Arcy McNickle, N. Scott Momaday, Leslie Marmon Silko, Linda Hogan)." PhD diss. (D.A.), St. John's University (New York), 2002. 162 pp.

1825. Myers, Jeffrey Scott. "Converging Stories: Race and Ecology in American Literature, 1785–1902." PhD diss., Tufts University, 2002. 207 pp. This ends with a chapter titled "Into the Present, Toward the Future: Thoughts on Willa Cather and N. Scott Momaday."

1826. Teuton, Sean Timothy. "Homelands: Politics, Identity, and Place in the American Indian Novel." PhD diss., Cornell University, 2002. 417 pp. See chapter 4, "'Where Are You Going?' The Social Motion of Place in N. Scott Momaday's *House Made of Dawn*." See also entry no. 1172.

2003

1827. Teuton, Christopher Barett. "Conceptualizing American Indian Literary Theory: Oral Theories and Written Traditions (N. Scott Momaday, Gerald Vizenor, Robert J. Conley)." PhD diss., University of Wisconsin–Madison, 2003. 240 pp.

2004

1828. Hearne, Joanna Megan. "'The Cross-Heart People': Indigenous Narratives, Cinema, and the Western." PhD diss., University of Arizona, 2004. 347 pp.

1829. Huddleston, Jason Todd. "The Dialectic of Self: An Existential Reading of Identity in Selected Contemporary American Indian Literatures." PhD diss., University of Texas at Arlington, 2004. 174 pp.

1830. Rice, David A. "Mediating Colonization: Urban Indians in the Native American Novel." PhD diss., University of Connecticut, 2004. 209 pp.

1831. Winston, Jay S. "'The Painful Task of Unifying': Fragmented Americas and 'The Indian' in the Novels of William Faulkner and N. Scott Momaday." PhD diss., University of Rochester, 2004. 352 pp.

2005

1832. Herman, Matthew Dale. "'Across Every Border': Nationalism, Cosmopolitanism,

Tribal Sovereignty, and Contemporary Native American Literature." PhD diss., State University of New York at Stony Brook, 2005. 228 pp.

1833. Schneider-Geest, Ev-Christin. "Von der single Metaphor zur tribal Metaphor: indianisches autobiographisches Schreiben bei Charles Alexander Eastman, N. Scott Momaday, and Leslie Marmon Silko." Doctoral diss., Christian-Albrechts-Universität zu Kiel, 2005. 275 pp. (in German)

2006

1834. Dadey, Bruce. "Rhetorics Rising: The Recovery of Rhetorical Traditions in Ralph Ellison's *Invisible Man* and N. Scott Momaday's *House Made of Dawn*. PhD diss., University of Waterloo (Canada), 2006. 365 pp.

1835. Singingeagle, V. Blanchard. "Coyote's Second Cousins." PhD diss., University of South Dakota, 2006. 399 pp.

2007

1836. Brigido Corachan, Anna Maria. "Nag mapu/la tierra que andamos/walking wor(l)ds: Native Cosmographies of the Americas." PhD diss., New York University, 2007. 316 pp.

2008

1837. Banga, Shellie Christine. "A Banquet of Silhouettes: William Least Heat-Moon's Travel Trilogy in Context." PhD diss. University of California, Davis, 2008. 204 pp. As a worldwide traveler and travel writer, Momaday plays a role in this study of Native American philosophy.

1838. Magagna, Anthony R. "Placing the West: Landscape, Literature, and Identity in the American West." PhD. Diss. University of California, Davis, 2008. 288 pp. Momaday's fiction is discussed in connection with landscape, place, and identity.

1839. Ruff, Mary M. "Tracking Whiteness: Portrayals of Whites in American Indian Literature." PhD diss., University of Texas at Arlington, 2008. 262 pp. Focuses on Leslie Marmon Silko, Louise Erdrich, and Linda Hogan. Chapter 3 presents some individual portrayals in other works, including *House Made of Dawn*.

2009

1840. Mazer, Benjamin A. "The Complete Poems of Frederick Goddard Tuckerman." PhD diss., Boston University, 2009. 371 pp.

Unpublished Master's Theses

1978

1841. Hudson, Jo Gayle. "The Contemporary Native American: A Group Interpretation Script Based upon Vine Deloria, Jr., *God Is Red*; N. Scott Momaday, *The Way to Rainy Mountain*; and Hyemeyosts [sic] Storm, *Seven Arrows*." Thesis (MS), North Texas State University, 1978. 92 pp.

1979

1842. Seekamp, Warren B. "Momaday's Pueblo Indian Triad: Heritage, the Word, and Imagination in *House Made of Dawn*." Thesis (MA), University of Louisville, 1979. 152 pp.

1843. Theoharris, Zoe. "The Problem of Cultural Integration in Momaday's *House Made of Dawn*." Thesis (MA), Emporia State University, 1979. n.p.

1982

1844. Greaves, Cristan Eveland. "To Regain the Sense of Place: A Study of the Prose of N. Scott Momaday." Thesis (MA), California State University, Fullerton, 1982. 88 pp.

1984

1845. Gruber, Barbara R. "Der Weg zum Regenberg: A Translation of N. Scott Momaday's *The Way to Rainy Mountain*." Thesis (MA), University of Wyoming, 1984. 122 pp. (in German)

1985

1846. Lorbiecki, Marybeth C. "The Mystical Presence of the Earth: Two Significant Novels of the Contemporary Southwest: *House Made of Dawn* and *Bless Me Ultima*." Thesis (MA), Mankato State University (Mankato, Minnesota), 1985. 121 pp.

1987

1847. Glenn, Norma Kerr. "Sit by the Fire—Listen to the Storyteller (James Welch, N. Scott Momaday, Leslie Marmon Silko)." Thesis (MA), California State University, Long Beach, 1987. 55 pp.

1990

1848. Leighton, Cecil Donald. "American Indian Veteran Post-combat Syndrome and Recovery in *House Made of Dawn* and *Ceremony*." Thesis (MA), University of California, Los Angeles, 1990. 68 pp.

1992

1849. Simpkins, Ann Marie Mann. "Inarticulateness and Regaining Voice (Ralph Ellison, N. Scott Momaday, Frantz Fanon, Martinique)." Thesis (MA), Eastern Michigan University, 1992. 58 pp.

1993

1850. Elsmore, Cheryl Laverne. "Contemporary American Indian Storyteller, N. Scott Momaday: Rhetorical Tradition and Renewal." Thesis (MA), California State University, San Bernardino, 1993. 79 pp.

1851. Marubbio, Miriam Elise. "The Edge of the Abyss: Metamorphosis as Reality in Contemporary Native American Literature (Leslie Silko, N. Scott Momaday, Gerald Vizenor, Louise Erdrich)." Thesis (MA), University of Arizona, 1993. 159 pp.

1994

1852. Wawrzyniak, Gail Moran. "Voices: Portraits of Women Revealed through Native American Literature." Thesis (MA), Hamlin University, 1994. 113 pp. Examines female characters in the books of Louise Erdrich, N. Scott Momaday, and Leslie Marmon Silko.

1995

1853. Marinella, Sandra J. "Healing Patterns in Three Ethnic American Novels" (Momaday's *House Made of Dawn*, Toni Cade Bamara's *The Salt Eaters*, and Rudolfo A. Anaya's *Bless Me Ultima*). Thesis (MA), Arizona State University, 1995. 117 pp.

1996

1854. Wallace, Karen Lynn. "Liminality and Myth in Native American Fiction: *Ceremony* and *The Ancient Child*." Thesis (MA), University of California, Los Angeles, 1996. 44 pp. An essay by Wallace with the same title appeared in *American Indian Culture and Research Journal* 20, no. 4 (Fall 1996): 91–119.

1997

1855. Potts, Henry M. "Native American Values and Traditions and the Novel: Ambivalence Shall Speak the Story (N. Scott Momaday, James Welch, Louise Erdrich)." Thesis (MA), McGill University (Canada), 1997. 76 pp.

1856. Ratt, Solomon. "Continuing Trickster Storytelling: The Trickster Protagonists of Three Contemporary Indian Narratives (N. Scott Momaday, James Welch, Gerald Vizenor)." Thesis (MA), University of Regina (Canada), 1997. 118 pp.

1857. Rowley, Leanne Summers. "Forging New Stories: The Intertextuality of Culture and Text." Thesis (MA), University of Alaska, Anchorage, 1997. 115 pp.

1998

1858. Coats, Mitzi J. "Antidote against Vanishing: Myth in *House Made of Dawn* and *Ceremony* (Silko)." Thesis (MA), Stetson University, 1998. 39 pp.

1859. Cruthirds, Rachel Brim. "The Creation of Self-Identity in Native American Autobiography (J. B. Patterson, John Neihardt, Black Elk, N. Scott Momaday)." Thesis (MA), University of Houston-Clear Lake, 1998. 82 pp.

1860. Reiland, Kathleen Ellen. "Emancipatory Discourse: The Rhetoric of Revolutionaries (N. Scott Momaday's *House Made of Dawn* and Rudolfo A. Anaya's *Bless Me, Ultima*)." Thesis (MA), California State University, San Marcos, 1998. 119 pp.

1999

1861. Benz, Charmaine Marjorie. "These Are Not the Stories." Thesis (MA), Michigan State University, 1999. 58 pp.

1862. Bowes, Tim A. "Culturally Distinctive Quests for Identity in N. Scott Momaday's *House Made of Dawn*, Leslie Marmon Silko's *Ceremony*, and Paula Gunn Allen's *The Women Who Owned the Shadows*." Thesis (MA), South Dakota State University, 1999. 106 pp.

1863. Dwyer, Margaret. "Hunting for an American Indian Environmental Ethic (N. Scott Momaday, Louis Owens, Leslie Marmon Silko)." Thesis (MA), University of Texas at Arlington, 1999. 60 pp.

1864. Murphy, Peter Gregory. "Romanticism and Naturalism in Native American Representation." Thesis (MA), University of Arkansas, Fayetteville, 1999. 64 pp.

2000

1865. Cervantes, Marlys Sheffield. "N. Scott Momaday's *House Made of Dawn*: The Crucial 'Silencing' in the Search for Identity." Thesis (MA), Oklahoma State University, 2000. 76 pp.

1866. Dudczak Gwyn, Betsy Lynn. "L'avenir est au mestissage: Christianity and Native American Traditional Spirituality in Momaday's *House Made of Dawn*,

Silko's *Ceremony* and *Gardens in the Dunes*, and Erdrich's *Tracks*." Thesis (MA), Oklahoma State University, 2000. 124 pp.

1867. Ryan, Terry. "Sacred Language, Sacred Land: Journeys in and around the Black Hills." Thesis (MA), University of Montana, 2000. 56 pp.

2001

1868. Kershner, Monica Nicole. "Stories from the Choir: An Exploration of Narrative Voice in N. Scott Momaday's *House Made of Dawn*." Thesis (MA), University of Nebraska at Omaha, 2001. 73 pp.

2002

1869. Walters, Mark Daniel. "The Return Journey as a Structure and Theme in Two Works by N. Scott Momaday (*The Way to Rainy Mountain* and *House Made of Dawn*)." Thesis (MA), Bemidji State University, 2002. 69 pp.

2003

1870. Murdock, Jennifer. "Myth Re-creation and Identity Reclamation in Selected Works of Silko and Momaday." Thesis (MA), Arizona State University, 2003. 68 pp.

2004

1871. Dayal, Rajesh. "A Difficult Path: Abel's Journey to Restoration in N. Scott Momaday's *House Made of Dawn*." Thesis (MA), Arizona State University, 2004. 77 pp.

2005

1872. Hoyt, Elizabeth M. "The Journey Motif in Contemporary Native American Fiction" (N. Scott Momaday, Leslie Marmon Silko, Louise Erdrich, Sherman Alexie, and James Welch). Thesis (MA), Indiana University, 2005. 96 pp.

2006

1873. Gaworecki, Michael Thomas. "Postindian Imagery in *House Made of Dawn*." Thesis (MA), San Jose State University, 2006. 83 pp.

1874. Handy, Amy Ashton. "Fortified Blood Memory: The Power of Everyday Places in N. Scott Momaday's *House Made of Dawn*." Thesis (MA), Southern Connecticut State University, 2006. 69 pp.

2007

1875. Harwood, C. Reed. "Performative Fiction: Articulating Religious Identities." Thesis (MA), University of Colorado at Boulder, 2007. 90 pp. *House Made of Dawn* is included in this study.

Other Theses

1876. Elliott, Peter J. "Questions of Identity and Orality Found along the Way to Rainy Mountain." Thesis (BA with honors), Amherst College, 1998. 45 pp.

1877. Gunness, Katherine S. "Literature and Culture: The Emergence and Implications of Native American Literature in the Late 1960s to 1970s" (N. Scott Momaday, Leslie Marmon Silko, Hyemeyohsts Storm). Thesis (BA), Princeton University, 1989. 114 pp.

1878. Temple, Susan Helen. "Healing by Convergences: Rethinking Identity Politics through Silko's *Ceremony* and Momaday's *House Made of Dawn*." Report (MA), University of Texas-Austin, 1997. 47 pp.

Index

For references to Part I, "Biography and Chronology," page numbers in italic type are used (e.g., *I: 10, 34, 72*). For references to the bibliographic citations in Part II, "The Works of N. Scott Momaday," and in Part III, "Works about N. Scott Momaday and His Works," entry numbers in roman (nonitalic) type are used (e.g., II: 36, 459; III: 848, 1380).

When a particular book or other work by Momaday is a subject or the focus of a critical or literary essay, an abbreviation of the Momaday title is shown following the entry number. The following abbreviations are used for this purpose:

AG	*Angle of Geese*
CW	*Circle of Wonder*
GD	*Gourd Dancer*
HMD	*House Made of Dawn*
IBH	*In the Bear's House*
IPS	*In the Presence of the Sun: Stories and Poems*
JT	*The Journey of Tai-me*
MMW	*The Man Made of Words*
"MMW"	address "The Man Made of Words"
NAM	*The Names*
TAC	*The Ancient Child*
WRM	*The Way to Rainy Mountain*

Titles of Momaday's works are shown within quotation marks or in italics and are followed by a description in parentheses (book, essay, poem, story, etc.). Books and other works by, or edited by, others are under the name of the specific author(s) or editor(s).